Revealing Male Bodies

Revealing Male Bodies

EDITED BY

NANCY TUANA

WILLIAM COWLING

MAURICE HAMINGTON

GREG JOHNSON

TERRANCE MACMULLAN

INDIANA University Press

Bloomington & Indianapolis

This book is a publication of

Indiana University Press
601 North Morton Street
Bloomington, IN 47404-3797 USA

http://iupress.indiana.edu

Telephone orders 800-842-6796
Fax orders 812-855-7931
Orders by e-mail iuporder@indiana.edu

© 2002 by Indiana University Press

The paper used in this publication meets the minimum
requirements of American National Standard for Information
Sciences—Permanence of Paper for Printed Library
Materials, ANSI Z39.48-1984.

Manufactured in the United States of America

Library of Congress Cataloging-in-Publication Data

Revealing male bodies / edited by Nancy Tuana . . . [et al.].
        p.   cm.
Includes bibliographical references (p.   ) and index.
ISBN 0-253-33991-X (cloth)—ISBN 0-253-21481-5 (paper)
1. Men—Identity. 2. Body, Human—Social aspects. 3. Body, Human
(Philosophy) 4. Masculinity. 5. Feminist theory. I. Tuana, Nancy.
        HQ1090 .R455 2002
        305.31—dc21   2001004647

1   2   3   4   5   07   06   05   04   03   02

To feminist men—past, present, and future.

CONTENTS

Preface: *What's a Nice Girl like You Doing in a Text like This?*
NANCY TUANA   ix

Introduction: *What Is Male Embodiment?*
TERRANCE MACMULLAN   1

Part 1. The Phallus and the Penis

1. Does Size Matter?
   SUSAN BORDO   19
2. Large Propagators: *Racism and the Domination of Women*
   RICHARD SCHMITT   38
3. The Future of the Phallus: *Time, Mastery, and the Male Body*
   JOHN ZUERN   55

Part 2. Masculine Myths and Male Bodies

4. Eating Muscle: *Material-Semiotics and a Manly Appetite*
   PATRICK MCGANN   83
5. The Disabled Male Body "Writes/Draws Back": *Graphic Fictions of
   Masculinity and the Body in the Autobiographical Comic* The Spiral Cage
   PAUL MCILVENNY   100
6. Dragging Out the Queen: *Male Femaling and Male Feminism*
   TERRY GOLDIE   125
7. A Man
   ALPHONSO LINGIS   146
8. Turnabout: *Gay Drag Queens and the Masculine Embodiment of the
   Feminine*
   STEVEN P. SCHACHT   155

Part 3. Constructing Male Space

9. The Body of White Space: *Beyond Stiff Voices, Flaccid Feelings, and Silent Cells*
   JIM PERKINSON   173
10. Brothers/*Others: Gonna Paint the White House Black . . .*
    CRAIG WILKINS   198

Part 4. Ethical Significance of Male Bodies

11. The Tall and the Short of It: *Male Sports Bodies*
    DON IHDE   231
12. Revealing the Non-Absent Male Body: *Confessions of an African Bishop and a Jewish Ghetto Policeman*
    BJÖRN KRONDORFER   247
13. A Father's Touch: *Caring Embodiment and a Moral Revolution*
    MAURICE HAMINGTON   269

Postscript: *The Phenomenological Challenge—The One and the Many*
    MAURICE HAMINGTON AND WILLIAM COWLING   287

FURTHER READING   291
CONTRIBUTORS   299
INDEX   303

PREFACE

What's a Nice Girl like You Doing in a Text like This?

NANCY TUANA

This text takes its origin from an absence and a presence. My research in feminist philosophies of the body had made me aware of the lack of attention to male bodies in the newly emerging feminist studies of the body and embodiment. Being a feminist who has always believed that our revolution will not be successful unless our concerns and methods address and are embraced by men as well as women, I saw this as a serious omission in the literature. At the same time that I became aware of this lack, I moved to the University of Oregon, where I quickly found myself in the unusual situation of working with a group of male graduate students who were specializing in feminist philosophy. This bodily presence presented me with the opportunity both to support their interest in feminist philosophy and to work with them on developing feminist readings of male embodiment. *Revealing Male Bodies* is the culmination of our five-year collaboration.

Our work on this anthology has been a model of collaboration in its richest sense. Before putting out our call for papers, we spent two years researching scholarship in the philosophy of the body. In that process, each of us found our own work and interests transformed. For example, when I sat down to write a paper on the sex/gender distinction, rather than my typical emphasis on female bodies and practices, I focused the lens of my analysis on male bodies; this shift in perspective helped me tend to the materiality of embodiment. In another case, our research into the phenomenology of Maurice Merleau-Ponty created opportunities for collaboration beyond the scope of this editorial project. When both Maurice Hamington and Greg Johnson framed their dissertations around Merleau-Ponty's philosophy of the body, they not only were influenced by work done in our editorial group, but turned to group members for philosophical advice and support.

The editorial work for this volume was also collaborative. We worked together at each step of the review process, making every effort to insure that all voices were heard and that each of us participated in all stages of the development of this volume. Nonetheless, there was an issue of hierarchy. Only one of us, and the female one at that, was a professor—and not just any professor. I was the dissertation advisor for all but one of the editorial board, and a senior member of the faculty. Yet I was, at the same time, the member with the least direct knowledge of male embodiment. Navigating the Scylla and Charybdis of this presence and absence, though sometimes difficult, enabled us to put our feminist politics into practice on more than one occasion.

My decision to work with a group of male graduate students was seen by some as being in tension with my commitment to feminism.[1] Why, I was asked, should I single out men? Why not include female graduate students? Although part of my answer to this question had to do with pragmatic concerns (even five is an unwieldy number of editors for a volume) there was a deeper philosophical commitment behind my decision. I believe that phenomenologies of male embodiment can best be undertaken by those who have moved through the world as men, and who thus have the requisite experiential base for such accounts. It does not follow from this that those of us who are not male cannot then use these accounts to add to the literature. Indeed, Susan Bordo's early "Reading the Male Body"[2] provides a perfect model: an excellent study of male embodiment by a female, feminist scholar, based on her careful reading of male accounts of male sexuality. Nor does it follow from this belief that male embodiment is somehow hegemonic or even very clearly delineated. As a scholar who has argued that the sex/gender and the male/female dichotomies are problematic, I believe that transgender experiences provide yet another important lens for accounts of embodiment.

It would be a mistake on our part or on the part of our readers to hope that one anthology could provide all the perspectives that should be included in an account of male embodiment. Still, we see this volume as an earnest first step toward developing a new area of scholarship. We are encouraged by the overwhelming response to our call for papers. Indeed, we received far more submissions than would fit into the pages of one book. This wellspring of interest reinforced our conviction concerning the importance of male embodiment and the need for more scholars to focus attention on this topic. Our work will have been successful if this volume encourages others to address the absence of attention to male embodiment in a way that extends the liberating impetus of feminism into the lives of boys and men. Although we do not deny the importance of the large body of scholarship on masculinity and male roles, we believe this literature is incomplete without the addition of perspectives on male embodiment.

NOTES

1. In fact, one of the original members of the editorial group, David Butle-Ritchie, raised this concern.

2. Susan Bordo, "Reading the Male Body," *Michigan Quarterly Review* 32, no. 4 (1993): 696–737.

INTRODUCTION

What Is Male Embodiment?

BACKGROUND AND MOTIVATION

The last decade has witnessed an astounding proliferation of literature on masculinity and male experience. From popular books pertaining to the emotions of adult males, to feminist eulogies for traditional manhood in the postmodern age, to scientific studies of the factors contributing to adolescent male violence, men have come under societal scrutiny to an extent previously unimaginable. However, while these texts examine the social, economic, sexual, psychological, and historical vagaries of manhood, fatherhood, boyhood, and masculinity, none pays serious attention to the role of the male body in shaping male lived experience. Therefore, despite the current vogue for critiquing, deconstructing, and diagnosing masculinity, there are few accounts of how men's lives are impacted by their embodied experiences and their perceptions of their own bodies. *Revealing Male Bodies* addresses this absence by initiating an interdisciplinary discussion of male embodiment.

The contributors to this anthology address the omission of accounts of embodied male experience from popular and academic discourses in three ways. First, they enliven the phenomenological investigations of embodiment pioneered by Continental European philosophers like Edmund Husserl, Maurice Merleau-Ponty, and Jean-Paul Sartre. Phenomenology, by developing a methodology that investigates human bodies as they are lived, freed Western philosophy from the constraints of Cartesian mind/body dualism, enabling it to explore the significance of the human body in experience. Where Descartes and other European thinkers framed the human body primarily as an obstacle that the mind must overcome or circumvent in its quest for truth, phenomenologists valorized it as "that very medium whereby our world comes into being."[1] However, an ironic lacuna inhabits the works of the original phenomenologists. The body that they examine is male; yet they do not see it as a male body *qua* male, but as a male body *qua* universal. Their investigations reside in the particularities of European, able-bodied, upper-class, male embodied experience, but they present their findings as generic. In so doing, they elide the extent to which the world discloses itself differently to differently embodied people. Instead of treating male embodied experience as universal or unqualified, the authors here reveal, and indeed revel in, the vicissitudes of male embodied experience in its racial, economic, and sexual variety.

Second, in addition to offering nuanced phenomenological explorations of male bodily experience, the authors in this volume enhance current analyses of the impact of social power on the body. The French philosopher Michel Foucault is generally credited with pioneering these analyses, called "inscriptive" because of their attention to how cultural ideals and norms are "scripted" onto bodies. Inscriptive accounts highlight the relationship between the body and power, as well as the myriad ways in which categories that seem natural at first blush (such as "male," "female," and "race") are in fact constructed over time through language and social practices. For example, essays in the first section of the anthology employ inscriptive accounts that reveal how male bodies are constructed to be culturally dominant (as illustrated by the symbolic prominence of the phallus), yet hidden (as evidenced by the absence of the penis from public view). A question we pose to our readers is whether inscriptive accounts are sufficient to flesh out the "bodies" of "male bodies" without the addition of phenomenological accounts. For this reason we have intentionally sought out authors who blend inscriptive and phenomenological approaches in order to provide accounts of lived male bodies sensitive to the interactions of flesh, culture, and sexuality.

Finally, the authors herein infuse the burgeoning dialogue on masculinity with the insights and critiques generated within feminist studies of embodiment. In so doing, these contributors make this anthology a bridge between feminist scholarly projects and investigations of male experience. The study of male embodiment benefits from the emergent literature on female embodiment crafted by thinkers such as Susan Bordo, Judith Butler, Elizabeth Grosz, and Iris Marion Young. These writers reveal the ways women have been (and are still) denied full personhood and autonomy in Western society by being identified with their bodies, while transcending these constraining, patriarchal ideals by formulating liberatory models of female embodiment. Scholars of male embodiment gain from these feminist authors an understanding of the ways that gendered concepts and practices constitute all human embodiment, as well as clues on how to rework constricting gender constructs. Further, investigations into the particularities of male embodiment resolve a conundrum for feminists studying embodiment. While feminist scholars saw the need to analyze all aspects of human embodiment, many were not in a position to conduct adequate analyses of male embodiment because they did not have the relevant life experience. Therefore, this anthology takes up the gauntlet thrown down (sometimes implicitly, sometimes explicitly) by feminist philosophers who called out for men to direct a feminist gaze at male embodiment.

Now some readers might be asking themselves, How can male authors direct a *feminist* gaze at male embodiment? In order to answer this question and understand the impetus behind this project, it is necessary to quickly clarify a few myths and misconceptions regarding feminism (while apologizing to the readers for whom this is old hat). First and foremost, the apparent contradiction (between a *feminist* analysis and *male* embodied experience) stems from the myth that feminism is either a field dedicated solely to the study of women and constructions of femininity, or worse, an antagonistic political movement whose goal is to obtain power and status for women over and against men. These varieties of feminism would be worth refuting were it not for the fact that they exist only as bugbears in the imaginations of anti-feminist detractors. As feminism is an evolving and heterogeneous tradition, it resists a single, unifying definition. While in its early historical stages, feminism did concern itself primarily with the liberation of women from arbitrary and often violent male domination, it has since expanded its purview to become an advocate on behalf of all people suffering socially imposed domination due to categories of class, race, caste, sexuality, ability, age, and gender. The analyses herein are feminist in that they examine the ways in which dominant, male-defined ideals of gender, power, and sexuality oppress women and men alike, and inhibit our ability to live more meaningful lives. Therefore, turning a feminist gaze upon the ways that boys and men are both privileged and constrained by ideals of masculinity, manhood, and fatherhood is merely another step in feminism's task to "unweave the web of oppression and reweave the web of life."[2]

THEORISTS AND METHODS

This anthology contains an eclectic group of contributors who provide a wealth of (often divergent) perspectives on male embodiment. It is useful, therefore, to provide a brief overview of some of the theorists and methodologies that readers will encounter in this volume. To this end I will look at the works of Michel Foucault, Maurice Merleau-Ponty, and Jacques Lacan, as well as offer a description of liberatory theories.

Michel Foucault is perhaps the most prominent influence on the various contributors to this volume. As inheritors of his intellectual legacy, these authors are certainly not alone; all fields of the humanities bear the incontrovertible mark of this Gallic philosopher and critic nearly two decades after his premature death from HIV/AIDS in 1984. Dozens of books are published every year in philosophy, cultural studies, geography, sociology, and gender studies that would have been impossible without his visionary work on the inscription of the human body by history, power, and knowledge. However, few authors that use his work, as either a foundation or a foil, fully agree about its ramifications or usefulness. That said, I will highlight aspects of his theory that surface in the present volume.

Simply put, Foucault was the philosopher who, more than any other, forced us to examine the centrality of power dynamics within human existence. He put forth the still-challenging thesis that power is inseparable from knowledge, and vice versa. As he said in his 1977 work *Discipline and Punish:* "We should admit . . . that power produces knowledge . . . ; that power and knowledge directly imply one another; that there is no power relation without the correlative constitution of a field of knowledge, nor any knowledge that does not presuppose and constitute at the same time power relations."[3] By tying knowledge to the struggle for power and domination, Foucault struck at the very root of philosophy's ancient quest for truth and science's modern quest for certainty. Beyond rendering previously innocuous practices into struggles for social domination, Foucault's analysis demonstrated that the belief in human progress that has been at the heart of the Western tradition since the Enlightenment is an unwarranted gambit, as our progress is only illusory. Even changes that at first glance seem unambiguously positive, such as the substitution of medieval torture with Enlightenment-era "panopticism" as a means of punishment, merely indicate an insidious deepening of social control.[4] In fact, his unflinching examination of Enlightenment-era prisons best demonstrated society's ability to control the individual by fostering habits of self-monitoring in lieu of control through threat of physical castigation. Foucault termed a society's manipulative procedures "biopolitical techniques," because they impacted the body for political ends.[5] Where the medieval victim of brutal, bodily torture endured horrific physical agony, the Enlightenment prisoner, though largely free of physical pain, was caused to internalize the corrective and omniscient gaze of the prison warden. Where earlier prisoners had their bodies broken, Foucault claimed, later ones lost their very souls.

Foucault tracked power struggles in human history using a genealogical method adopted from the work of Friedrich Nietzsche.[6] In Foucault's hands, genealogy functions as a sort of rival to the history presented by dominant social institutions. Where history in the traditional sense attempts to reveal the origins of certain ideas, communities, or practices, genealogy strives to fragment seemingly unified entities. The most significant aspect of Foucault's genealogy is his inscriptive analysis of the role of the human body in history (an analysis that continues in the present volume). Of genealogy he stated, "Its task is to expose a body totally im-

printed by history."[7] From this we see that each individual only understands her or his body according to the social and historical context in
which she or he lives. For example, a female body that might be seen as
the apex of health and robustness in the 1920s would be seen as a problematic body in need of dieting or worse in the 1980s. This method both critiques the normativity of contemporary mores regarding bodies and calls
into question the ahistoricity of foundational categories (such as "body,"
"self," and "individual").

Foucault executed a crucial shift in his treatment of the body between
1976 (when he published the first volume of *The History of Sexuality*) and
1984 (when the last two volumes were published). His analyses of the body
before 1976 focused on the ways in which sociohistorically specific disciplines, institutions, and practices of power controlled individuals by altering their relation to the body (for example, the way the Catholic practice
of confession caused the believer to loathe her or his body because of its
sinful, sexual urges). Here bodies function as passive fulcrums upon which
society exerts its manipulative power over individuals. However, the later
volumes offer a more nuanced account of the relationship between bodies
and power. Perhaps reflecting a new optimism, his later works cast the body
as the field in which the individual could cultivate a "care of the self" or
ethics of self-love and creation.[8] An example of this new attitude towards
the body is his analysis of the ancient Greek emphasis on restraint in sexuality. By casting sex as something that must be moderated for the sake of
the individual's well-being (rather than avoided as inherently sinful activity), sex becomes a facet of life through which a man might define himself
by setting his own limits and striving to meet them.[9]

As the contributions here attest, Foucault's work remains a germane
exploration of power and the body. However, he has been criticized for the
broad brushstrokes he used to represent power as all-encompassing and
monolithic. For example, feminists claim that by overlooking differences
regarding gender, class, sexuality, and so on, his theories of autonomy and
self-stylization only apply to subjects that are relatively free of external repression.[10] Yet feminists have also found great promise in Foucault's ability
to concretize and thematize the human body without sexualizing or biolog-
izing its essence. Similarly, proponents of the Frankfurt School (particularly Jürgen Habermas and Thomas McCarthy) agree with his general
critique of reason as a sociohistorically determined phenomenon, but disagree with his wholesale critique of power. Instead, critical theorists insist
on a crucial distinction between power that becomes pernicious without
careful critique (as in Stalinist Russia or Senator Joseph McCarthy's Red-
hunts), and the necessary exercise of power directed by reason (e.g., the
power granted to an educator in order to foster a fruitful learning environment).

We find the second most prevalent influence on the authors in this anthology in the post-war writing of the French philosopher Maurice Merleau-Ponty. Employing and extending Edmund Husserl's project of phenomenology, which is the quest for understanding the essential nature of things, Merleau-Ponty radically refigured conversations about the body, lived experience, and the manner in which bodies interact with the world. In his major theoretical work *Phenomenology of Perception,* published in 1945, Merleau-Ponty argued that the body is the true subject of experience, for it is through the body that we form relationships to the objects of the world.[11] The experiencing self is not an immaterial mind or soul, but the bodily organism. Accordingly for Merleau-Ponty the body is not merely a passive vessel receiving stimuli, but a meaning-producing entity in itself. Bodies make our experiences of the world meaningful by organizing the various objects of cognition and forming these sensed experiences into coherent patterns. The body does not stand apart from these experiences but is intimately entwined with them. Moreover, bodies are interconnected in such a way as to form a complex set of embodied relations that renders any sort of Cartesian dualism incoherent. Merleau-Ponty reveals that we find the sentient and sensuous life of the body at the heart of even our most abstract cognitions.

Merleau-Ponty emphasizes the reciprocal relationship between the body and the world. That is, since the body is an active subject, it is the point from which we take in and relate to the objects in the world. However, the body is also another object within the world. He notes that "my body is made of the same flesh as the world . . . the world *reflects* it, encroaches upon it and it encroaches upon the world (the felt *[senti]* at the same time the culmination of subjectivity and the culmination of materiality), they are in a relation of transgression or of overlapping."[12] Just as we touch the world, the world touches us; it is through this reversibility that meaning arises. For Merleau-Ponty this radical interdependence suggests that the body is not, nor could it be, an enclosed set of possibilities separate from the world it inhabits. Rather, the relationship of body to world is fluid and continuously refined according to the unique contours of each embodied experience.

In one way or another, all the articles in this anthology elucidate Merleau-Ponty's basic insight regarding the body. Bodies, male bodies in this case, are constructed of flesh and world. The authors whose work is presented here have delineated cartographies of male embodiment that detail Merleau-Ponty's phenomenological account of embodied experience. Moreover, these lived bodies—flesh and blood entities whose relationship to the social/political realities of daily life constitutes one of the most basic ways in which bodies and world are entwined—participate in the structure of meaning, as well as the systems of racism, sexism, and ableism that influence our cognitions of and comportments within the world. As a result, the movement of actual bodies through the world is either constrained or enriched by these constructions, which variously enhance or present seemingly insurmountable obstacles to our full presence in the world.

In addition to Foucault's inscriptive accounts of the socialized body and Merleau-Ponty's phenomenological investigations of embodied experience, authors herein make use of the theory of the noted French poststructuralist thinker and psychoanalyst Jacques Lacan. Indeed, a number of the works that comprise the first section of the anthology occupy an intellectual terrain first cleared by Lacan's inimitable interpretation of Sigmund Freud's theories on the roles of the penis and the phallus in identity formation and language. In 1966, his almost impenetrably dense lectures were made available to the world in the two-volume *Écrits*, which was translated into English in 1977.[13] While *Écrits* addresses a wide range of issues concerning human cognition, gender, and identity formation, I will limit my brief sketch to those parts of his theories used by this volume's contributors, especially his distinction between the penis and the phallus, as well as his claims about the relationship between the phallus and language.

Lacan, like Freud, distinguishes between the penis and the phallus. The penis is simply the male sexual organ; it is a real, fleshed part of a human body. The phallus is a cultural construct that, in a variety of complex representations, stands as a symbolic double for the penis. In Lacanian terms, the phallus comes to mark sites of power, authority, and, perhaps most importantly, desire. It represents a distinctly masculine superiority that extends beyond the body into realms of intellectual authority, political power, and cultural preeminence. However, despite its ancient and persistent association with masculine power, Lacan argues, somewhat counterintuitively, that "in a more primordial sense, the mother is considered, by both sexes, as possessing the phallus, as the phallic mother."[14]

For Lacan, the phallic mother is a fantasy created in the mind of the child. The fantasy stems from the infant's perception of the mother as an omnipotent being who is free to fulfill or deny all the child's wishes. As the child grows and enters the realm of language, the symbolic mother's status is relocated to the symbolic father. Though this displacement of power from the mother to the father results in the association of maleness with power and of femaleness with powerlessness, it is crucial to remember that, for Lacan, the symbolic mother remains the original source of power.

From this it is apparent that what is often called the phallic economy, which includes but transcends language, affects the development of subjectivity in both women and men. Within the phallic economy, men achieve dominance because of their possession of the penis, which marks them as the legitimate bearers of phallic power. At the same time, the phallic economy exerts its control over the lives of men in the form of castration anxiety: a fear, latent in the unconscious since childhood, that any transgression of the order dictated by the father will result in sexual mutilation.

Conversely, women negotiate what Freud called "penisneid" or penis envy: the sense of incompleteness that arises from lacking a "big, visible penis."[15] Thus, the phallus represents a vision of completeness for both sexes.

The phallus conditions more than the development of subjectivity in men and women: it is for Lacan the foundation upon which language, our system of symbolic meaning, rests. As he said in his 1958 lecture "The Signification of the Phallus": "For the phallus is a signifier, a signifier whose function, in the intrasubjective economy of the analysis, lifts the veil perhaps from the function performed in the mysteries. For it is the signifier intended to designate as a whole the effects of the signified, in that the signifier conditions them by its presence as a signifier."[16] Like any symbol within language, the phallus points to or stands in for a thing in the world. However, unlike other signifiers, it is a symbol that stands in for the totality of desired things. It is the signifier *par excellence* (or the "unparalleled signifier" in Lacan's words) that stands in for the object of the original desire that we experienced as prelinguistic infants.[17] While we eventually learn to use particular signifiers to demand objects in the world ("bottle," "food," "toy," etc.), there remains a primordial desire beneath all these demands that cannot be satisfied by these material things. As Mikkel Borch-Jacobsen says in his *Lacan: The Absolute Master,* "[the child] will always demand something else—namely, the exact thing that [the mother] does not give (and cannot give, since it is no object): her pure love."[18] The phallus is the privileged signifier that stands in for this occluded object of desire, which all other acts of signification vainly strive to name.

There is, however, a further complexity to Lacan's theory. While the symbolic order constructs woman's body as a lack and man's body as phallic, remember that the phallic mother remains the source of phallic power. It is *her* love, which sloughs off all conventional signification, that the child desires. Thus, there remains a sense in which the *man* stands in the symbolic position of lack, while the *woman* serves as the model of desire. According to Lacan, both men and women have a relationship to the phallus, but the terms under which the power dynamics manifest themselves within this relationship are, of course, heavily weighted in favor of the male. Male bodies, the sites from which patriarchal authority is deployed, are still valorized by Lacan as bearers of the true signifier of authority.

The fourth and final set of methodologies applied in this volume we will call liberatory theories. Liberatory theories are not a distinct field of study like psychoanalysis or phenomenology. Instead, this term demarcates theorists and theories that are concerned with the elimination of systems of domination. Liberatory theories provide a lens through which we can study the ways in which human beings are oppressed because of race, gender, sexuality, age, caste, class, religion, nationality, or physical ability. This approach is made up of various methods of analysis including Marxism, feminism, disability studies, pragmatism, queer theory, critical theory, postcolonialism, and race theory. While these fields have different foci, they also converge because the various systems of oppression intertwine and support each other in complex ways. While we might be able to provisionally speak of gender oppression by itself (say in a discussion of women's political disenfranchisement), this isolation is only temporary, because it is not possible to fully understand gender oppression without also exploring the ways class, race, and religion impact the political situations of women.

While it would be impossible to adequately discuss all the different liberatory theorists referenced by the contributors to this volume, it is worthwhile to mention some of the themes common to their work. Perhaps the most prevalent is the revelation of identities that previously seemed homogeneous as disparate and heterogeneous. For example, virtually all the essays in the volume disrupt the idea of a uniform notion of manhood. Another central theme is that social power and hierarchies are organized along various axes. That is, a person who might be granted certain privileges based on gender might also experience marginalization in terms of race or class. Related to this analysis of the multiple axes of power is the recognition that identities are formed in the confluence of different, sometimes competing cultural formations (such as gender, race, sexuality, ethnicity, class, ability, and so forth). Liberatory theorists remind us that far from having one simple identity (like "woman," "Asian," or "middle-class"), we all partake of different cultural categories that often present us with conflicting or divergent scripts of behavior.

THEMES AND INTERCONNECTIONS

Having discussed their theoretical background, we can now turn to the essays that comprise this anthology. Contributors to part one, "The Phallus and the Penis," navigate the relationship between the symbolic power of the phallus and the particularity of the penis. The Western cultural ideal of the phallus represents the attributes of traditionally defined masculinity: hardness, invulnerability, physical mastery, and dominance.[19] These authors explore the tension between these cultural ideals of manhood and the real, embodied experiences of men (as represented by the penis). They show that once we direct our attention toward the multiplicity of men's embodied experiences, we see that the phallic ideal is less a goal for which men should strive than a myth that needs to be replaced. In the words of our first contributor, Susan Bordo, "The phallus is haunted by the penis."[20]

Bordo sets the tone for this section with her essay "Does Size Matter?", whose title asks if the size of a man's penis has a significant bearing on his partner's sexual pleasure. Using her characteristic mix of wit and insight, Bordo leads her reader across a sprawling range of discourses (including evolutionary biology, postcolonialism, advertisements for phalloplasty, and the Clarence Thomas/Anita Hill hearings) in pursuit of an answer. Her investigation reveals an unusually uniform dogmatism regarding this question: though there is evidence to the contrary, we cleave to the commitment that the answer must be, "No, size does not matter."[21] She concludes that this question, and many others pertaining to our embodiment, will remain indecipherable until we break down the conceptual walls that separate our study of nature and biology from our understanding of culture and imagination.

Richard Schmitt's "Large Propagators: Racism and the Domination of Women" also addresses the rift between the cultural phallus and the biological penis, but he trains his attention on the structures of patriarchy and White supremacism that have been inseparable from Western civilization for the last five centuries. Specifically, Schmitt interrogates White society's long-standing obsession with the penises of Black men. Drawing from a series of historical and existential resources, he excavates the root of White patriarchy's stereotype of the lustful, insatiable Black man. He argues that this stereotype ferments White supremacist violence against Black men and women of all races. Further, the construct of the out-of-control Black rapist is a projection of the violence perpetrated by White men in the maintenance of racial and gendered privilege.

"The Future of the Phallus: Time, Mastery, and the Male Body" by John Zuern starts with a phenomenological examination of a group of stunt-cyclists. Where the other theorists in this section work on a large, cultural scale, Zuern focuses on these particular youths and their attempts to master their own bodies. In so doing, he casts new light on the relationship between time, subjectivity, and Lacan's idea of the phallus. Zuern reveals that their exhaustively performed stunts (or "dicking around" in their own vernacular) serve as their entrance into manhood. These cyclists must master their techniques in the abyss of time—the brief eternity between the moment they propel themselves into the air and the instant they return to earth. Thus, Zuern argues that the future is a proving ground in which youths on the threshold of manhood risk bodily injury in pursuit of the phallic ideal through mastery of the body.

The essays in the second section, "Masculine Myths and Male Bodies," continue to look at men whose embodied experiences are out of sorts with ideals of masculinity and manhood. These works suggest new models of masculinity based on the particularities of male embodied experience. Patrick McGann's "Eating Muscle: Material-Semiotic and a Manly Appetite," harnesses the tension between the ideals of manhood he was raised to accept and the realities of living with Type II diabetes. As a man raised in Texas, his conception of masculinity was built upon a pair of unshakable assumptions: real men watched football and ate huge portions of red meat whenever they pleased. Lamentably, his body's condition rendered this "comfortable" script of manhood a recipe for suicide. This tension yields precious fruit in McGann's hands; he uses it to interrogate the value of traditional Western definitions of masculinity and prod his reader toward a richer understanding of what makes a man. Using autobiography (both his own and those of pro-football players) and feminist theory, McGann reveals the subversive potential of the male body that does not conform to society's ideals of masculinity.

Paul McIlvenny's "The Disabled Male Body 'Writes/Draws Back': Graphic Fictions of Masculinity and the Body in the Autobiographical Comic *The Spiral Cage*" addresses the conflict between the myth that men must be autonomous and impenetrable, and the experiences of men living with physical impairments. He offers an exegesis of the autobiographical comics of Al Davison, a White Englishman who writes and draws about his life with spina bifida. In his analysis, McIlvenny not only debunks myths about dis/ability but, more rewardingly, reverses them: he shows that it is ableist society, not people with physical impairments, who need to change, learn, and adapt. Like McGann, he uses Davison's autobiography and Judith Butler's theory of performativity to work a kind of alchemy; distilling the base metal of adversity into a refined ideal of manhood.

"Dragging Out the Queen: Male Femaling and Male Feminism" by Terry Goldie also adroitly develops Butler's theory in the context of male lived experience. While McIlvenny uses Butler's theories to reinterpret disability, Goldie applies her theory of performativity to the elaborate world of drag. Although Goldie's work does not share the overtly emancipatory tenor of the previous articles, he nevertheless reveals the ephemeral and unstable nature of our conceptions of gender, masculinity in particular. He does not merely study the phenomenon of the drag queen; he uses his own experience in drag to problematize the ways it has been theorized. In particular, he rejects the common idea of drag as a fetish in favor of a more nuanced treatment in which drag is an attempt to imagine a diffuse, less constrained sexuality through its positioning of the male body as a sexualized body, in opposition to the phallic economy. His analysis raises the possibility that men might learn to experience their bodies as sexualized objects without feeling shame, thus breaking the association of masculinity with sexual dominance.

Alphonso Lingis's "A Man" does not seek to transform traditional masculinity. Instead, his work awakens the dormant, transgressive power at the heart of manhood: virility. With great cunning, Lingis argues that virility manifests itself as the courage to trespass all boundaries. Thus, while gender theorists have long argued that masculinity is a construct that maintains unjust and abstract boundaries, Lingis contends that masculinity rests on the transgression of limits, not their enforcement. His revitalized sense of virility clears the way for a transformed model of manhood in which passion for justice replaces the desire for material wealth, and a man is measured according to his willingness to take risks and not his social status. He concludes by presenting the uncompromising life of Che Guevara as a model of virility.

Steven P. Schacht's essay "Turnabout: Gay Drag Queens and the Masculine Embodiment of the Feminine" also addresses the subject of men in drag. Schacht offers a detailed phenomenological analysis of the intricate process of going into drag that provides an illustrative counterpoint to Goldie's critique of dominant theories of drag and transgender. While Schacht's account of his lived experience of drag is valuable in itself, he also uses it to develop theoretical insights. In particular, Schacht's reading of drag highlights the tenacity of patriarchal models of status. He shows that the drag community—a community where the subversion of traditional gender roles is *de rigeur*—maintains the structure of the larger straight community, in that both grant men social prestige according to their ability to embody certain corporeal ideals. Where men in non-drag communities garner status according to their ability to reproduce their culture's ideal of a manly physique (such as a well-muscled body and wedge-shaped torso), drag queens attempt to achieve a stylized, feminine form (with elaborate coiffures and voluptuous curves) for the same end. Schacht shows that the male performance of femininity is merely another skill whose mastery affords social dominance and reinforces the ideal, critiqued by Lingis, that social status is the measure of a man.

Essays in part three, "Constructing Male Space," take up the topic of space and its relation to male bodies. For these authors "space" is not merely an unmarked absence of objects or the emptiness between bodies. Instead, these articles deal with humanly constructed spaces that involve histories and invite certain behaviors while eschewing others. They explore how different sorts of male bodies interact with different spaces, according to the purpose of the space as well as the racial and physical makeup of the particular body. They reveal that, far from being neutral or empty (as one might first imagine), space is laden with political, social, racial, and cultural significance. This fact that different spaces are marked for different purposes means that certain bodies are able to inhabit certain spaces without a second thought, where other bodies (such as Black, male bodies in this country) find their movements hampered and their actions monitored.

The first essay in this section, Jim Perkinson's "The Body of White Space: Beyond Stiff Voices, Flaccid Feelings, and Silent Cells," reveals the unwarranted privileges attached to White, middle-class, male embodiment. Perkinson carefully elucidates these largely unnoticed privileges and raises the question of their ethical ramifications. He accomplishes this by juxtaposing the blithe naiveté with which White, middle-class men pass through various spaces (like shopping malls or suburban enclaves) with the hassles and wary glances (and worse) that greet Black men attempting to negotiate these same spaces. Using the theories and methods of Foucault and

W. E. B. Du Bois, he shows how the increased monitoring of our urban and suburban spaces by sophisticated technologies have led to both an increased racialization of space (where suburbs and upscale urban neighborhoods are marked as White, and less desirable urban areas are marked as Black and Latino) and the divergence of White, male experience from the experiences of non-White men. He challenges White men to recognize and resist the structures that grant them privileges while visiting violence on non-Whites.

Craig Wilkins continues to explore the confluence of Black male bodies and spaces marked by anti-Black racism in his essay "Brothers/*Others:* Gonna Paint the White House Black . . ." In it he lovingly explores the singular importance of the Million Man March for Black men, the African American community, and all Americans. He argues that the March should be understood as more than an act of fraternity by Black men: it was a singular, revolutionary event that challenged American conceptions of property, space, and race. Black men redefined the historical understanding of the proper place for Blacks and their marginalization within American society. The occupation of the Mall in the nation's capital by the bodies and voices of Black men was a uniquely empowering act precisely because Americans have always used the organization of physical spaces to indicate authority and power. Wilkins argues that the March redefined the Mall from a conspicuously White space of relaxation and passivity into one of contestation and activity. Black men used their physical presence in the heart of the nation to challenge our society's historical insistence on warehousing Black men in prisons or urban slums.

If indeed the gender of the body we inhabit affects how we come to know and interact with the world, then male embodiment should play a role in what we construct as moral. The final section of *Revealing Male Bodies* focuses upon the ethical implications of male embodiment. The articles in this section share a strong experiential dimension. The authors balance reflections upon their own experiences with the implications of these experiences for larger issues surrounding male embodiment. Clearly the three articles in this section do not provide an exhaustive account of the ethical significance of male embodiment, but they do explore the depths of three sites of analysis: athletic bodies, spiritual self-reflection, and fatherhood. Ethics is broadly construed in this section not as simply rules or consequences, as is the tradition in philosophy, but as part of the intersubjective space of human interaction where the gender of the body is confronted. The authors in this section reveal that the epistemological significance of meeting the world in and through a male body has moral consequences as well.

In a fitting return to the beginning of the anthology, "The Tall and the Short of It: Male Sports Bodies" by Don Ihde responds to Bordo's claim that the phallus is haunted by the penis. Ihde believes it is actually the penis that is haunted by the phallus, and it is this impossible icon of masculinity that impacts male development and understanding of the body. Ihde draws upon personal experience and, in particular, how his experiences compare with those of his teenage son, to question notions of monolithic phallic power. Ihde calls for further exploration of the multiple manifestations of phallic power rather than stereotyping the male experience of this cultural construct. Ihde finds what he argues are superficial characterizations of phallic power, such as those found in the notions of the male gaze, to be reinforcing misplaced and cursory understandings of male and female experience. Ihde problematizes essentialist and inscriptive accounts of embodied experience by exploring the continuities of experiences between himself and his son. Further, his work offers an interesting point of tension with the essay by Perkinson regarding the issue of policing. Ihde examines how he and his son experienced a kind of social policing, where adolescent males are channeled into distinct peer groups according to socially relevant bodily features (such as height, muscle build, and athletic ability). This is analogous (but only to a point) with the kind of policing of suburban space described by Perkinson. Both address the ways that male bodies are always already encoded with socially relevant meaning. However, while Ihde describes the impact of informal body policing within the setting of a largely homogeneous secondary school community, Perkinson examines how "neutral" spaces become racialized according to White supremacist attitudes through the *literal* policing of those Black male bodies that venture into "White" space.

Björn Krondorfer's "Revealing the Non-Absent Male Body: Confessions of an African Bishop and a Jewish Ghetto Policeman" finds a resource for exploring male embodiment in an unlikely activity: confessional writing. The historical significance of confessional writing was not lost upon Foucault, who identified it as central to ordering religious and civil power in Western civilization since the Middle Ages. While autobiographical writing is more expansive and may get its impulse from a variety of sources, including political motivations, the more personal confessional writing, which is the act of laying bare one's vulnerabilities and foibles on paper, has direct implications for a man's spirituality and morality. Krondorfer finds the body ironically central to confessional writing through what he terms the "non-absent body." The body and its actions and desires are pervasive in these texts, although they appear to be acts of pure mental discipline and self-reflection. Krondorfer integrates the reflections found in Augustine's *Confessions* with the recently discovered *Am I a Murderer? Testament of a Jewish Ghetto Policeman* by Calel Perechodnik and his own emotive reactions to the texts. The result of this integration is a unique juxtaposition of the writer's experience of his body and the reader's visceral response which brings to the fore the forgotten role of the body in literary analysis. One of the intriguing ethical questions integrated into Krondorfer's analysis is whether the soul-searching that men undertake in confessional writings ultimately facilitates resistance or reinforcement of existing social norms.

Continuing this section's emphasis upon the experiential dimension of morality, Maurice Hamington's "A Father's Touch: Caring Embodiment and a Moral Revolution" applies feminist care ethics to male embodiment in a phenomenological analysis of washing his daughter's hair. Care ethics is a relational approach to morality that is less concerned with rules or consequences than with promoting healthy connections between individuals that allow each party to grow, thrive, and flourish. Hamington argues that in simple acts of touching a great deal is communicated, much of which is preconscious and with moral implications. Tactile interactions between bodies are more than functional; they provide a basis for expressing what it means to care. Such interactions are so mundane that they have been largely lost to canonized moral theories. Nonetheless, these embodied exchanges largely constitute what it means to care as the necessary conditions for human flourishing and community. Given the inconsistent history of fatherhood in this country, Hamington believes a revolution in the morality expressed through men's bodies is possible if acts of care are attended to, thematized, and encouraged in fathers to the same extent that caring activities have been associated with motherhood.

This anthology is intended as a contribution to an ongoing, dynamic conversation, and not as the final word on male embodiment. For it to be useful and illuminating, this conversation must continue to include a wide range of voices from all realms of human experience and endeavor. In our opinion, the fruitful study of male embodied experience must draw on interdisciplinary work, be informed by feminist and other liberatory scholarship, and be enriched by phenomenological attention to the body, as well as place the biologist in communication with the Bard. While, out of necessity, we might temporarily flee the din of rollicking discussion for the comfort of our chosen professional arenas, we must return to the conversation to make our work relevant, informed, and complete. It is on this faith in community and dialogue that this anthology rests.

NOTES

1. Drew Leder, *The Absent Body* (Chicago: University of Chicago Press, 1990), 5.

2. Linda Alcoff and Elizabeth Potter, "Introduction: When Feminisms Intersect Epistemology," in *Feminist Epistemologies,* ed. L. Alcoff and E. Potter (New York: Routledge, 1993), 4.

3. Michel Foucault, *Discipline and Punish: The Birth of the Prison,* trans. Alan Sheridan (New York: Vintage, 1978), 27.

4. Ibid., 195. See also "Nietzsche, Genealogy, History," in *Language, Counter-Memory, Practice,* ed. Donald Bouchard, trans. D. Bouchard and Sherry Simon (Ith-

aca: Cornell University Press, 1977), 139–164. The panopticon was a revolutionary prison model where prisoners were regulated not by physical bonds or threat of punishment, but by an architectural design that enabled the wardens to observe any prisoner at any moment.

5. Foucault, *Discipline and Punish*, 158.

6. See Nietzsche's *The Genealogy of Morals,* trans. Walter Kaufmann and R. J. Hollingdale (New York: Vintage Books, 1966), and *The Gay Science,* trans. Walter Kaufmann (New York: Vintage Books, 1974).

7. Foucault, "Nietzsche, Genealogy, History," 148.

8. Foucault, *The Use of Pleasure,* vol. 2 of *The History of Sexuality,* trans. Robert Hurley (New York: Vintage Books, 1985), 6.

9. The gender-specific language here reflects the fact that this concept of sexuality applied in ancient Greece only to males.

10. For more feminist perspectives on Foucault see Susan Hekman, ed., *Feminist Interpretations of Michel Foucault* (University Park: Pennsylvania State University Press, 1996), and Lois McNay, *Foucault and Feminism: Power, Gender and the Self* (Cambridge, Mass.: Northeastern University Press, 1993).

11. Maurice Merleau-Ponty, *Phenomenology of Perception,* trans. Colin Smith (New York: Routledge, 1995).

12. Maurice Merleau-Ponty, *The Visible and the Invisible,* ed. Claude Lefort, trans. Alphonso Lingis (Evanston: Northwestern University Press, 1968), 248.

13. Jacques Lacan, *Écrits: A Selection,* trans. A. Sheridan (New York: Norton, 1977).

14. Ibid., 282.

15. Sigmund Freud, *Introductory Lectures on Psycho-Analysis,* trans. J. Strachey (New York: Norton, 1966), 394.

16. Lacan, *Écrits,* 285.

17. Ibid., 277.

18. Mikkel Borch-Jacobsen, *Lacan: The Absolute Master* (Stanford: Stanford University Press, 1991), 208.

19. For an excellent study of an important source of the evolution of the phallus and its impact on ancient Greek society see Eva C. Keuls, *The Reign of the Phallus: Sexual Politics in Ancient Athens* (New York: Harper & Row, 1985).

20. Susan Bordo, "Reading Male Bodies," *Michigan Quarterly Review* 32, no. 4 (1993): 696–737.

21. Even medical experts (with the exception of phalloplasty surgeons) reassuringly chorus a negative reply to the question. This would doubtlessly amuse Foucault to no end. While in virtually every other aspect of our lives medical doctors encourage self-monitoring and concern (over our diet, our exposure to the sun, the ergonomics of our working environment), on the issue of penis size doctors issue only palliative encouragement that no matter what their size, men are large enough to satisfy their mates.

Part 1. The Phallus and the Penis

Chapter 1
Does Size Matter?

S U S A N   B O R D O

CULTURAL PERSPECTIVES ON THE MATTER OF SIZE

The young girl stands in front of the mirror. Never fat to begin with, she's been on a no-fat diet for a couple of weeks and has reached her goal weight, 115 lb., at 5′4″—exactly what she should weigh, according to her doctor's chart. But goddammit, she still looks dumpy. In her mind is this Special K commercial that she's seen a few times on television: a really pretty woman admiring herself in a slinky, short, black dress, long athletic legs, every curve perfect, lean-sexy, nothing to spare. Self-hatred and shame start to burn in the girl, and other things too. When the commercial comes on, the woman's sleek body is like a magnet for her eyes; she almost feels in love with her. But envy tears at her stomach, and is enough to make her sick. She'll never look like that, no matter how much weight she loses, no matter how many hours she spends on the Stairmaster. Look at that stomach of hers, see how it sticks out? Those thighs—they actually jiggle. Her butt is monstrous. She's fat, gross, a dough girl.

It's a depressingly well-documented fact that when girls and women are asked to draw their bodies or indicate their body size with their hands, they almost always overestimate how much space they take up, and tend to see themselves as too fat no matter how thin they are. This once was thought to be a "body image distortion" unique to those with anorexia nervosa. We now know that seeing ourselves as "too fat" is a norm of female perception. Average weight statistics and medical charts are irrelevant. What matters is the gap between the self and the cultural images. We measure ourselves not against an ideal of health, not even usually (although sometimes) against each other, but against created icons, fantasies-made-flesh. Flesh *designed* to arouse admiration, envy, desire.

I've been writing and lecturing on these female body issues for years. At almost every talk I've given, someone in the audience (mistakenly concluding that because I had talked about women, I believed they had the

---

This is a slightly altered and expanded version of a chapter by the same name in *The Male Body: A New Look at Men in Public and in Private* (New York: Farrar, Straus and Giroux, 1999).

exclusive franchise on body-insecurity) has challenged me: What about men? What about baldness? Height? Muscles? All these examples are well taken. But no one has ever brought up the best analogy: men's insecurities about penis size. I myself did not realize exactly how perfect the analogy was until I read a 1996 study in which pediatrician Peter Lee found that college men, no matter what their actual dimensions, tend to underestimate their penis size. In a mirror image of women's perception of themselves as too big (even when they are at or below average weight), men tend to see themselves as too small—even with "average"-size penises (currently defined by doctors as four inches non-erect and six inches erect).

Where do men get their ideas about how big their penises "ought" to be? Some, like comedian Tim Allen, first get them from a child's-eye view of their fathers' penises:

My father would take me and my brothers to pee, and you're just dick tall, and your dad's is out. This whale of a penis would fly out, and you have a mushroom cap that two hands could barely pull out from your body. And your dad's penis would—thrummm! And you'd scream at this huge, hairy beast of an ugly—"Goddamn! Aw, God!" And we'd leave the bathroom and all go, "Shit! Did you see that?" (quoted by Nancy Friday in *The Power of Beauty*)

Some men get their ideas about penis size from other guys in the locker room. Some become convinced they are too small because a partner has told them they don't measure up; Scott Fitzgerald, as Hemingway recounts in *A Moveable Feast,* developed anxieties after Zelda told him (Hemingway quotes) "that the way I was built I could never make a woman happy. . . . She said it was a matter of measurements." (Hemingway takes Fitzgerald off to the restroom to inspect him and declares him "perfectly fine," but he remains unconvinced.) But many men, like women, get their ideas about how big they should be from the bodies of cultural icons: the Jeff Strykers and Harry Reemses of video porn and sex magazines, hired specifically for their endowments. (In the late 1990s, I'm sure the guys in the underwear ads are doing their part, too.)

These guys are as off-the-charts vis-à-vis average penis size as the runway model is vis-à-vis the average female body. In the August 1997 issue of *Playgirl*, with non-stop penises from cover to cover, the only man who appears to have an "average" member is Brad Pitt, who is featured in a set of paparazzi photos. I was glad to see Pitt in there—proof that a man can be incredibly sexy without being incredibly well hung. *Playgirl*, although officially edited with a female reader in mind, is sold alongside *Torso, Jock,* and *Hustler;* I'm sure it has a male readership among both straights and gays. In any case, I've heard (from a friend who knows some vendors) that because of Pitt, one of those men who appeal to virtually every sexual and gender orientation, this particular issue sold out as soon as it hit the stands.

Unfortunately, the beauty of diversity is not exactly the message conveyed by the penis stats and descriptions listed in the magazine's "Sex International Network" want ads: "Very hard 7" cock. Big balls." "7½" thick penis—dark meat." "8" penis, very long lasting. I stay hard after I come." "Love masturbating 2–3 times a day with my 8" cock." "9½" hard penis, very wide and ready to please any woman." "8½", cut, rock hard cock." "11" cock looking for a beautiful blonde female." "7" hard, thick cock. I stay hard all night and I know I can take care of you." And so on.

The humongous penis, like the idealized female body, is a cultural fantasy. It exists in the flesh; some men—like those featured in the photos and want ads of *Playgirl*—do have very large penises. But let's put it this way: if a Martian were planning a trip to Earth and was given a *Vogue* and a *Playgirl* to enlighten him on what to expect from human women and men, he'd get a very misleading impression. So does the average male reader or viewer of porn. And even if he knows, on some level (from his experience in locker rooms and the like) that the Harry Reemses and Jeff Strykers of the world are not the norm, that knowledge may pale beside the power of the iconography: the meanings attached to having an impressively large member. The woman in the Special K commercial is a "real" woman too (although these images are, increasingly, digitally manipulated); it's the fact that she so perfectly, precisely embodies current notions about femininity and beauty that makes her a fantasy, and an oppressive standard for the ordinary woman to aspire to.

Think, to begin with, about that adjective "impressive," which came spontaneously to my mind as I wrote the phrase "impressively large member," and all that it conveys. We wouldn't usually describe large breasts as "impressive," would we? (That sense of "bodacious" isn't in the dictionary and I'm not sure that I know exactly what it's supposed to mean, but it sure doesn't seem to suggest a body part demanding respect.) In contrast, the penis so large as to take a lover's breath away is a majestic penis, a commanding penis. From romance novels ("His strength was conspicuous beneath her hands, his muscles prominent, steel hard. He was strikingly large . . . so *very* large . . .") to the erotic fantasies in the back pages of *Playgirl* ("I watched in curiosity and amazement as he unzipped his pants, revealing a magnificent cock. . . . As his manhood sprung out at me, hard and thick, I gasped and stared . . .") to gay male erotica ("Lew's breath was stolen by Jeff's cock. Sure, the mountain man had seen a few in his time. Many. Some were as nicely shaped. A few were as tasty-looking. But none were as gigantic.") the encounter with the male stud's member is typically one of gasping astonishment at his "magnificent" size. Perusing this literature, I couldn't help but think (with a mental chuckle) about Freud's description of the origins of penis envy; little girls, he wrote, "notice the penis of a brother or playmate, strikingly visible and of large proportions." Sounds quite a bit like the rhetoric of erotica to me, with its fantasy of a penis so impressive it simply dazzles the onlooker, takes his or her breath away.

Recently, the magnificent male member has even found a place on prime-time television, when the wildly popular comedy series *Ally McBeal* devoted two episodes to Ally's affair with an artist's model who is so fabulously endowed that Ally's foxy roommate Renee, doing a clay sculpture of him in class, has to ask for more clay. *We* don't get to see the original—but we are treated to many shots of Ally and Renee's bulging eyes and open mouths. After class, at a restaurant, Ally and Renee wave rubbery sausages about, as they discuss whether the model's member was an implant or natural (*"super*natural," suggests Renee). When Ally accepts a date with the guy, her female colleagues—who have spent hours standing around discussing the size of this guy's penis—snigger, "Don't get hurt!" They don't mean emotionally.

The bedazzlement of the magnificent member need not be sexual, however. The warlords of the Ottoman Empire publicly posted their genital measurements for conquered tribes to admire. Appearing a "big man" to other men is an important aspect of men's preoccupation with size. I've personally heard three different variations on the following joke, most recently the garbled version told in the movie *Slingblade*. Three men are urinating off a bridge together. "River sure is cold," says the first man. "It's deep, too," says the second. "Sandy bottom," says the third. The joke is our contemporary version of the fresco at the Roman ruins at Pompeii (circa A.D. 79), which depicts a wealthy man using his enormous penis to counterbalance several bags of money on a scale. The big penis is worth its weight in gold, the winner in contests among men. One young man, who had his penis pierced to endow his "little dick with a lot of fucking attitude," suggests, "the big size thing develops in the school locker room when you're a kid. The big-dicked guys send out signals that say, 'We're better,' 'We're more masculine than you,' or 'We deserve to be here, look at the size of our dicks.' "

Penile augmentation is an increasingly booming business in this culture, and many men who have their penises enlarged do it for "display purposes." "I'd always been happy in an erect state," says one man; "I never had any complaints from my wife—but I had a lot of retraction when flaccid. It's not that I want to flaunt myself at the gym, but I didn't want to feel that self-conscious." Others do want to "flaunt"; according to surgeon Melvyn Rosenstein, the typical phalloplasty patient "wants to get big so he can show himself off to other men, to say 'Mine is bigger than yours,' like a buck deer displaying its antler." Most phalloplasty patients, doctors add, do not have especially small penises. "The overwhelming majority of men I do are unquestionably normal," says Rosenstein, "I had a guy in the office yesterday who was concerned that he was small. I assured him that he was normal, but he said 'Let's go ahead and do it.' "

Most phalloplasty patients, then, are haunted by a humiliation that is likely only imagined. The cultural backdrop of their anxieties, however, is not imagined, any more than women's anxieties about the size of their breasts are of their own making. "He's the nicest guy I ever dated. But he's just too small." So reads the bold print of an ad from Dr. Gary Rheinschild, who specializes in penile augmentation and who in 1995 claimed to have performed more than thirty-five hundred such operations. Rheinschild also uses phrases like "shower syndrome" and "locker room phobia" (to describe what the man I've quoted above suffers from) and hopes to make penis enlargement "as common as breast implants." But even before cosmetic surgeons began their campaigns, ads hawking miracle products for increasing penis size both exploited and exacerbated already-existing male insecurities by drawing on the equation "penis size = manliness." "Dramatic Increase in Penis Size!" boast the makers of "NSP-270," marketed in the eighties:

> Boys who couldn't measure up to the Navy's proud standards of manhood . . . who would never be able to satisfy a "woman in every port" . . . who would disgrace the uniform if they were ever allowed to wear it . . . were given massive dosages of this amazing sex nutrient . . . [and] suddenly and dramatically experienced—*Proud Erections! Dramatic New Ability in Intercourse! Supercharged Sperm That Now Can "Do The Job!"* . . . And, most amazing of all, fantastic growth in penis size!

Cultural practices aimed at enhancing penis size are not exclusively Western, either. Penile augmentations—making use of pins and inserts— are performed in many cultures. Groups ranging from the Caramoja tribe of northern Uganda to the sadhus of India have practiced the technique of tying weights to the penis in order to make it longer. The sadhus, who believe that God dwells in the penis, stretch themselves to lengths of twelve to eighteen inches. By contrast, John Bobbitt's boast to Jenny Jones that his penis is "stronger and bigger than ever" with a fraction of an inch added on by the surgery that re-attached it seems pretty flaccid. (Bobbitt went on to have an augmentation that, he claims, added three inches in length and one inch in girth, and made his penis "like a beer can.")

Most of the transformations wrought by penile augmentation in this culture—usually gains of a couple of inches at most—lack the clear, ritualistic drama of organs that have been augmented—like the sadhus'—into hyperbole. But symbolically, the change can be just as potent, a fact that surgeons exploit. "I get [my clients] to see this as an incredible change in their lives," Dr. Jamie Corvalaan explained to *Esquire* reporter John Taylor. "I tell them, 'This is going to change your self-image, change the way you walk, sit, look, do business, pursue women. You will now act like a man with a big penis.' " How does a man with a big penis act? Well, we know that he can exhibit himself with pride in the locker room. The surgeons, addressing the concerns and fantasies of men who perceive themselves as small, promote the large penis as the route to self-confidence, assertiveness, social authority. But men who are born with large penises, as I've discovered from talking to several, may experience their size as embarrassing excess rather than a cause for pride. When one of these men described his large penis to me as "a problem," my immediate reaction (thankfully, not outwardly expressed) was similar to that which I've had when very slim women complain that they just can't keep the weight on: "That's a *problem?*" But further conversation revealed that this man had indeed had problems, not only in being too large for many partners but also with an abiding sense of shame.

The fact is that many human cultures have been somewhat ambivalent about very large penises. Yes, they advertise male potency, and have often functioned as symbols of reproductive fertility. But at the same time, like very large breasts, they may be viewed as gross and a sign that there is nothing much "upstairs" (the body's endowments being seen as hydraulically regulated, I guess: what accumulates at one end has been forced out the other). Also, body-part size and excessive sexuality have often been joined in the Western cultural imagination, and thus don't fit well with the heroic, civilized ideals that men are supposed to uphold. Ancient Greece, a highly masculinist culture but also one that placed great emphasis on male self-control in matters of sexuality, favored "small and taut" genitals. "Large sex organs," as Eva Keuls points out, "were considered coarse and ugly, and were banished to the domains of abstraction, of caricature, of satyrs, and of barbarians." In those domains, the penis was often represented as grotesquely huge, as though absorbing all the sexual excess that the "civilized" Greek would not permit in his own self-conception. There are some interesting depictions of Christ with a large penis, possibly an erection. But typically, in classical Western art, the convention has been to represent the heroic body as muscular, but the actual penis as rather small.

Since the beginning of the African slave trade, White Europeans have projected *their* anxieties about excess sexuality onto stereotypes of the sexually voracious, overendowed Black beast,[1] stereotypes that got brought right onto the floor of the United States Senate during the Clarence Thomas/Anita Hill sexual harassment hearings. Since 1991, we've nationally televised so many grotesque absurdist moments involving sexual body parts—including news conferences on Bill Clinton's "distinctive" penile features—that it may take some straining to remember how startling it was to hear the words "Long Dong Silver" actually coming out of Orrin Hatch's prune mouth. He led up to it laboriously, strategically. "And she said 'He described pornography with people engaging in oral sex.' Is *that* a black stereotype?" "No," replied Thomas. Hatch: "People engaging in acts of sex with animals?" Thomas: "No." Hatch: " 'Long Dong Silver'—Is *that* a black stereotype? Something like 'Long Dong Silver'?" When Thomas said yes, Hatch performed the outraged innocent with gusto. "Well! I'm concerned! This really bothers me!"

Hatch's shock was feigned for effect, of course. He knew very well that Long Dong Silver is racialized pornography. Long Dong is of a piece with the brown dildoes that feminist writer Heather Findlay encountered in a sex-toy shop: "I turned and looked. They were not Dildoes; they were *monstrosities*. Twenty-four inches and thick as my arm. 'Big Black Dick' said the wrapper. . . . I looked around for some 'Big White Dick' or even 'Big Flesh Colored Dick.' No luck." Race, she concludes, "permeates American culture."

Yes, and not just American culture, but the Western psyche. James Gould and Carol Grant Gould quote Frantz Fanon on the racial fantasies and dreams of his White psychiatric patients: "One is no longer aware of the Negro, but only of a penis: The Negro is eclipsed. He is turned into a penis." White boys like Norman Mailer have envied this instinctual status (in "The White Negro," he admires the Negro's "art of the primitive" and calls jazz "the music of orgasm"), and some Black rappers and athletes may capitalize on it. (Jack Johnson, the first African American world heavyweight boxing champion, wrapped his penis in gauze to emphasize its size as he paraded around the ring during his public matches.) But primitive manhood has no place under the robes of a Supreme Court justice. There were moments when I felt deep pain for Thomas. To be on the brink of *real* respectability—perhaps the most respectable position this country can offer—and to be tailgated by Long Dong Silver! "This dirt, this sleaze," Thomas told the committee, "is destroying what it has taken me forty-three years to build." The White senators could empathize, even identify with the pain of facing charges of sexual misconduct that threaten to destroy one's career. But they could not bond with the racial dimension of Thomas's predicament, only look on it with horror.

Anita Hill was the first to mention Long Dong Silver. But once he had been let loose in the Senate, Thomas knew he would be dogged by him, whatever he did, so he made a bold and cunning move. Rather than allow the equation "Negro = Penis" to remain unspoken, doing unconscious damage to his hopes of confirmation, Thomas drew attention to Long Dong Silver's racial overtones, thus suggesting that Thomas *himself* was the real victim—of ugly, racial stereotyping. The strategy was exploitative and outrageously misplaced. Hill was a Black woman, as people seemed to forget, with little to gain by resorting to racial smears; even if she had been lying, she could easily have come up with a different, equally offensive but racially neutral, image. Thomas's strategy, however, proved triumphant. The senators, going out of their way to prove to the world that *they* (unlike Fanon's patients) did *not* see the Black man as penis, made him a Supreme Court justice.

Still, it cost Thomas. "Yes," he had replied through clenched teeth in response to Hatch's deliberately leading question, "the size of sexual organs would be something. . . ." It was an awful moment, no matter whose side one was on. Thomas could barely get the words out, groping to make the stereotype clear while at the same time distancing himself from it; his use of the subjunctive mood (as though he were describing a possible universe) and the vague phrase "the size" were unconscious protection against his own contamination by the image he was exploiting. He knew that racist imagery, once released from the collective unconscious, is apt to run amok. And so it did. Thomas won the day, but a sympathetic *People* magazine story which appeared later that week, showing Thomas piously reading the Bible on the couch with his wife Virginia, made his crotch the visual focus of every photograph.

YES, BUT DOES SIZE *REALLY* MATTER?

The magnificently large penis, as we've seen, is an icon of cross-cultural potency. So it's not surprising that size matters very much to men. When a *Glamour* magazine survey asked men whether they would rather be (a) five feet two inches tall with a seven-inch penis or (b) six feet two inches tall with a three-inch penis, 63 percent of the respondents picked (a) and only 36 percent picked (b).

Yet there is an extensive medical, scientific, and cultural literature designed to counteract the notion that penis size "matters" to a partner's sexual pleasure, a reassurance that—although by no means scientifically rigorous or convincing—has become virtually official dogma today. I have no comparative statistics, but I suspect that because of this reactive "counterculture," far fewer contemporary men are as obsessed with and tormented by insecurities about penis size as women are about weight. "Penis size has never been shown to affect sexual pleasure for men or women"— I've read some version of this claim over and over, everywhere from popular magazine articles to sophisticated scholarly books on the construction of gender to medical guides. An example of the latter is Abraham Morgentaler, who says (in *The Male Body: A Physician's Guide to What Every Man Should Know about His Sexual Health*), that he offers the following story in an attempt to calm his patients' anxieties about size: "President Lincoln was extremely tall for his time and was once asked his opinion on the proper length of a man's legs. His commonsense answer was that a man's legs should be long enough to reach from his hips to the ground. In similar fashion, a man's penis should be long enough to reach inside his partner."

Hmmm. . . . Sounds a bit like the old sexist joke about breasts, that more than a mouthful is wasted. But many female doctors seem to agree with Morgentaler. Lenore Tiefer, associate professor of urology and psychiatry at the Albert Einstein College of Medicine, when challenged to explain why the partners of phalloplasty patients had more climaxes after the operation, offers the following: "Whatever increases a man's sexual confidence will probably make his wife happier." Without even considering it, Tiefer discounts the possibility that her husband's larger penis might be what's giving her those orgasms.

On the issue of penis size, then, men are continually getting mixed messages. Phalloplasty surgeons continually stoke male anxieties with advertising campaigns at the back of fitness magazines that proclaim "SIZE DOES MATTER," and humor abounds with jokes about the little member's sexual inadequacy (Q: Why are women such bad mathematicians? A: Because for years they've been told that this [thumb and forefinger a few inches apart] is eight inches. Q: What are the three most ego-deflating words a man can hear? A: Is it in?). In the HBO comedy series *Sex and the City,* four girlfriends lament and giggle over the "gherkins" and "miniature pencils" of past lovers. (It's not just "men behaving badly" on television nowadays.) But when a man seeks advice from his family doctor, he's told that size is irrelevant to a partner's pleasure.

Doctors routinely dispense reassuring bromides, sometimes drawing on biology. That's how Morgentaler goes on to justify his leg/penis analogy: "For this is the essential biological function of a penis in the first place, to enter the vagina so that semen is deposited near the opening of the uterus, called the cervix. A larger penis does not necessarily perform this task better than a smaller penis." Well, perhaps—if all a woman's wanting is to get pregnant. But even in that case, looking to biology—unless one does so in a highly selective way—will not necessarily yield reassurance for males. Sexual selection among many species is based on the principle of sexual dimorphism—females go for those males whose distinctively male traits (traits that the females lack) are bigger or more colorful than those of other males. Darwin was the first to notice this, and to speculate that it was a kind of conspicuous "advertising" (he didn't use that word, of course) for prospective mates. Gould and Gould quote him: "It cannot be supposed that male birds of paradise or peacocks, for instance, should take so much pain in erecting, spreading and vibrating their beautiful plumes before the female for no purpose."

Sometimes, although not always, the sexual organs will be involved. Male chimps display their erect penises to females as sexual enticement. The penises of high-ranking baboons are more turgid, and thus hang farther out, than those of their subordinates. Both reptile and mammalian penises exhibit an amazing range of decorative enhancements to make them appear more substantial. Such displays among animals do not serve only to attract potential mates of the opposite sex; they're also meant to assert dominance over potential rivals of the same sex, and thus gain an evolutionary advantage. Interesting, isn't it, that this is just what those phalloplasty doctors promise the augmented male; he can "increase sexual confidence" with women and "act like a man with a big penis" with other men.

Equally interesting is the seeming aversion in the literature on evolution to acknowledging the biological importance and variety of penile display. James Gould and Carol Grant Gould have written a fascinating book called *Sexual Selection: Mate Choice and Courtship in Nature.* Although we learn a great deal about long tailfeathers, big antlers, and enlarged claws in this book, there isn't a single entry in the index for "penis." Male primate "flashing" is simply ignored. And when it comes time for the biologists to produce examples of *human* sexual enticements and advertisements, the missing penis is even more striking for its absence. Darwin alludes vaguely to "handsomeness" and "appearance." Popular science writer Deborah Blum produces the rather ethnocentric illustration of height. "Tall men," she writes, "are routinely rated most attractive by women, and in fact are more appreciated by all of society." (Does this hold true among Asians, I wonder? Or Eskimos?)

Could it be that evolutionary science is uncomfortable with the idea of the penis on display for sexual "selection" (or rejection)? If so, science and popular culture have been entirely in synch. It wasn't until the mid-seventies, remember, that *Cosmopolitan* published that daring centerfold of Burt Reynolds, his penis hidden demurely behind his hands. ("Equality at last!" Helen Gurley Brown declared.) It took two more decades before Hollywood allowed viewers their first brief glimpse of a naked penis—Tom Berenger, playing a man in retreat from "civilization" in *At Play in the Fields of the Lord.* After that, we occasionally got frontal nudity, but "full" hardly describes it. "Flashing" is more accurate, as some man streaked across the screen, en route and with great dispatch: into the lake, scurrying to the bathroom. As male body-watchers strained to catch these little tidbits, so fleeting you could miss them if you blinked, more and more movies seemed *constructed* in order to get some entirely naked female in full frontal view. Interesting, isn't it, how many more plots seem to "demand" that actresses take all their clothes off than that actors do?

Of course, over the course of the twentieth century, gay artists and photographers had created a rich, sensuous, and dramatic tradition which—unlike classical art—was unabashed in emphasizing, sometimes fetishizing, the penis. When such representations began to go mainstream—through, for example, Bruce Weber's fashion photography for Calvin Klein—the old taboos began, at last, to break down. But even as recently as 1997, the Academy Award–nominated British film *The Full Monty* could present a full-nudity male strip show as a daring departure from the conventions of (heterosexual) male stripping. Much about that film was a (very likeable) fantasy, but this premise was not. Groups such as the Chippendales may flaunt their bulging bundles, but they never strip naked. In contrast, even in Hollywood entertainment that's not oriented toward the after-hours viewer, it's become almost obligatory for a crime movie or thriller to set a scene in a bar, where the men discuss their business while some fully naked female stripper slides up and down a pole, legs apart, thrusting her butt at them (and us), almost inviting entry.

For reasons that I detail in *The Male Body* but do not have the space to go into here, removing that bottom piece of clothing from the male body has clearly been a struggle for this culture. Consider, as a humorous but revealing example, the furor that was caused in 1961 at Mattel Toys when a female executive argued that Barbie's new partner Ken ought to have a "bulge" in his groin. Barbie's own breasts, if translated into human proportions, would have made her Jayne Mansfield. But the designers had to try out three different versions of Ken's crotch in an effort to appease nervous male executives. Charlotte Johnson, Barbie's clothing designer, recalls: "One was—you couldn't even see it. The next one was a little bit rounded, and the next one really *was*. So the men—especially one of the vice presidents—were terribly embarrassed. . . . So, Mrs. Handler and I picked the middle one as being the one that was nice-looking. And he said he would never have it in the toy line unless we painted Jockey shorts over it."

Some might argue that the furor over Ken's bump was to protect innocent children from an overly sexually explicit plaything. After all, these dolls weren't designed as a course in sex instruction. But we're not talking here about testicles, shaft, head—just a little plastic mound. And if keeping sexual messages muted was the issue, then how did Barbie get away with being a bosomy vamp (modeled after a German sex toy, by the way), while even an anatomically vague allusion to Ken's sexuality was so problematic? Significantly, the plan to give Ken a "permanent swimsuit" was abandoned only when Charlotte Johnson, Barbie's clothing designer, pointed out that little girls would undoubtedly scrabble at that painted swimsuit and scratch if off, anyway—an invasion of Ken's privacy that seemed even more loathsome to the male execs. Better that Ken be undressed to begin with than have little girls strip him of his dignity.

Evolutionary biologists, no less than the Mattel management, have been affected by ideologies of gender, particularly when they address questions of human sexuality. So have social scientists. Commenting on the use of penis pins among the Dyaks of Borneo, anthropologist D. E. Brown dismisses the notion that such pins (called "palangs") could bring pleasure to women. "The neurology, physiology, and anatomy of the female genitalia provide little or no clear evidence [of this]," he states decisively, adding that according to Kinsey and his associates, "the inner walls of the vagina are generally insensitive." Versions of this finding continually recur in the medical literature on phalloplasty. Even Thomas Laqueur, a proponent of the social constructionist view that the way we interpret sexual data is always mediated by ideas about gender, is remarkably confident that he's describing objective "fact" when he writes that the vagina is a "far duller organ" than the clitoris. Elsewhere, he describes the vagina as "impoverished."

Oh really? Reading these "scientific" findings, I was reminded of the arguments of some early second-wave feminists, who insisted that vaginal orgasm is a myth concocted by Freud and other male scientists intent on yoking female sexuality to intercourse and reproduction. I liked the critique of ideology, but I didn't like the fact that I was asked to pay for it by denying my own experience. Like those feminists who claimed that only something called a "clitoral orgasm" was real, Brown and his colleagues' construction of reality ignores the testimony of many actual women. "Before Paul got his palang, I thought I had a good sex life," says one Dyak woman, "Now I tell him if he ever takes it out, it constitutes grounds for divorce." "Much more exciting than just a regular penis," says another.

Are these women having tactile hallucinations? More to the point, does it matter? Perhaps the physiology of the vagina is different than had been supposed (as some now argue, pointing to the tremendous amount of clasping and other vaginal activity that takes place during orgasm). But perhaps *ideas* have something to do with the pleasure the palang gives, too. The rhinoceros, revered by the Borneans for its vitality, virility, and fertility, has a "natural" palang. In altering his body to be more like that of a virile animal, does the Bornean man enhance the fantasy power of his penis, and thus his ability to stimulate and excite his partner?

We don't have to choose between physiology and fantasy. In fact, we do so at peril of radically misunderstanding the *kind* of physiology we have—one that is tremendously suggestible to the cultural "superstructure" of ideas, associations, images. Whatever our nerve endings, sexual excitement and orgasm are never simply a matter of touching the right buttons. Or perhaps better put, not all our buttons are so clearly marked and located as the clitoris. Some of them can't bear to be touched at all, and thrive on distance and denial. Some of them are so diffuse that only the merger of two bodies will satisfy them. Some of them are in our metaphors: throbbing members, hot honeypots—or, on the nastier end of the spectrum, drills and slits. "Huge, throbbing members" may send some people into ecstasy, while "big dicks" repulse them (or vice versa). A lot may depend on just *what* you imagine you have inside you. We could thus poll a hundred people, gay or straight, and probably get a pretty wide range of answers to the question of whether or not size matters to pleasure. Some preferences would undoubtedly reflect differences in anatomy and physiology. None of them, however, would be describing some "purely" physiological or anatomical set of facts.

Arguably—although I admit my claim is controversial—even non-human animals attract (and intimidate) each other through the excitations of fantasy. Think, for example, of those bodily hyperboles that "advertise" sexual superiority by exaggerating particular body parts—horns, tails, etc. George Hersey has called these animal hyperboles "biofantasies"—aptly, I think, for these enhancements are generally not *functionally* of all that much use. Big, heavy tails—like the enormous antlers of many species of deer and elk—are not just useless, but a downright impediment to defense against predators. They make moving through vegetation more difficult, and flight more cumbersome. Big, colorful crests can attract a predator just as easily as a prospective mate. With the exception of those features (antlers, for example) used in ritual, rarely harmful, contests with other males, the sole value of these sexual dimorphisms is to advertise the overall genetic superiority of the animal who displays them.[2] Bigger means better—but symbolically. In 1982, Swedish geneticist Malte Andersson did an experiment that proves this point. Male widowbirds drag around enormous tails of six feet or more in length. Andersson glued extra feathers on some, snipped some short, and left others as they were. The augmented tails won out (tails over head, as it were) with the females, attracting more mates than even the "showiest natural tail" and making it virtually impossible for the snipped birds to find mates.

The body of the human male, no less than that of other species, has been a continual arena for metaphorical display and advertisement—not necessarily truthful—of sexual and social potency. Our symbolic augmentations range from the most concrete—penile lengthening (the guy who is intimidated by the large penis of the cocksman with the locker next to his isn't afraid of what that burly penis could do to him in a fight, but he probably *does* tend to imagine that the guy who flaunts it so brazenly has the "balls" to clobber him)—to the power-symbolism of muscles (unless one is a manual laborer, muscles have little use-value in our management- and service-oriented culture; the potency of muscles resides largely in their cultural meanings[3]) to pumped-up literary metaphors ("throbbing manhood," "proud member," etc.) to the most abstract augmentation of all: the phallus. The phallus—the penis's symbolic "double," signifying generic male superiority—began its career as a symbol of reproductive potency (in the worship of Osiris and Dionysus) but ultimately came to stand for an authority that is not biological at all, but rather advertises manly capacity to transcend the power, needs, desires—and even the biological sex—of the body.[4]

Like the decorative flourishes of the penises of other animals, all of these human augmentations enhance the male body with a promise of sexual satisfaction or power. But like everything else that is human, they are a product of both biology and culture, and transcend purely reproductive function. Proud members are as much—actually, more—a fetish of male homosexual as heterosexual imagery, and have a place (although a controversial one) within lesbian culture, too, in dildoes that are designed to look like actual penises. Women nowadays work out as rigorously as men, as ads for women's exercise equipment capitalize on the equation of muscles and toughness. "A man who wants something soft and cuddly to hold should buy a teddy bear," declares a Reebok ad, its kickboxing, grimacing model looking like she will take no prisoners. (Strikingly, as women have started to pump up too, the ideal male body—as depicted in underwear ads and the like—has become more ostentatiously muscular. Clearly some of us, at least, want to retain those dimorphisms!) Some women stand as though they have phalluses; claiming space with their legs and groins in a challenging and confident way. In *GI Jane,* after being beaten and bloodied by her training officer, Jordan O'Neill (played by Demi Moore, who shaved her head and did everything she could to make her neck-muscles compete with her breast implants)—who has defiantly gone through men's training and testing to prove her equal mettle—is told by him to "seek life elsewhere." The comment takes her over the edge. "Suck my dick!" she replies. That woman thinks she has a phallus—and who would deny it?

Recognizing the body's symbolic dimension addresses (and perhaps solves) a mystery that has challenged evolutionary biologists: the unusual evolution of the human penis to fourfold its size over the last seven to nine million years. The increase serves no obvious physiological purpose in reproduction. Gorillas measure 1.25 inches on an average erection, and (as Deborah Blum drolly puts it) "still manage to get a female gorilla pregnant. So why, exactly, does a human male need five inches or greater?" Evolutionary anthropologist Jared Diamond briefly considers, then basically discards, the notion that the size of the human penis has evolved to advertise potency to prospective mates. Women, he argues, "tend" to report that "the sight of a penis is, if anything, unattractive. The ones really fascinated by the penis and its dimensions are men. In the showers in men's locker rooms, men routinely size up each other's endowment."

Diamond is right, as we've seen, about men's interest in comparative size. But what he misses, whether in connection with men's interest *or* women's, is the fact that finding a large penis (or any penis) visually attractive is not required to revere its potency or virility. (Among the Borneans, we should note, the well-hung rhinoceros is not renowned for its beauty.) When I was a preteen, I shuddered at the thought that someday I would "have" to look at a penis; yet I was well aware that the penis was an organ of formidable power, and I was drawn to it as such. At a slightly younger age, I had cringed, too, over the pictures of the beast in my illustrated book of fairy tales. But when he put his huge paw on Beauty, I was thrilled (an erotic subtext that Disney's recent cartoon exploits to the hilt with its highly sexualized beast). Beauty is *not* an essential feature of the beast, but of the girl who liberates the prince in him. While movies may poke fun at the homely, nebbishy nerd, unhandsome but "virile" male actors like Telly Savalas and Dennis Franz have frequently become sex symbols in our culture.

My point is not so much about beauty, though, as about ideas. It may turn out, as some scientists claim, that we are drawn to each other simply through smell. If so, we have constructed an elaborate edifice of ideas to obscure that fact. It is ideas that endow the body with beauty and ugliness, ideas—if one subscribes to an evolutionary view—which advertise our dominance or reproductive fitness (or lack of it) to each other. Full lips, sociobiologists like to point out, are favored in women because they signify a high estrogen endowment. Perhaps. But the preference—as seems not to be the case for the male dog who will run blindly across several fields in hot pursuit of an odor—is one which culture can invalidate, too. Consider the aesthetic racism that prevailed in the West until very recently against Black and Jewish features; was that not perverse, evolutionarily speaking? Equally perverse (from an evolutionary point of view) seems the current cultural preference for skinny or muscled female bodies; if such bodies advertise anything, it's reproductive inadequacy, since female bodies require a certain level of body fat in order to produce the estrogen required to sustain reproductive cycling. Is aesthetic preference for such bodies a mode of "natural" population control? If so, it would be a strangely selective one, affecting those portions of the world's population—relatively affluent groups in advanced, industrialized countries—most likely to use birth control anyway.

We are creatures of biology *and* creatures of the imagination. Indeed, our tremendous imaginative capacity is a feature of our distinctive evolution. That's why the opposition between nature and culture is a red herring. Human diversity—cultural, sexual, and otherwise—far from providing proof that biology has no purchase on us, can be seen as a consequence of our evolutionary development. That is, for good biological reasons, it's not in our "nature" to have one script, sexual or otherwise, given the tremendous environmental diversity and challenges that human primates, dispersed all over the globe, have had to deal with. Our physiology itself allows for this flexibility. In the first two years of life, the brain increases enormously in size and develops countless synapses that it did not have at birth. During this period, as psychologist William Pollack points out, the brain is "pliable and plastic" and tremendously open to learning from experience. It's "wired to accommodate developmental interactions that further shape the nervous system after birth." That makes good evolutionary sense. "Complex animals," as Richard Wrangham notes, "have complex mental and emotional systems underlying their behavior." That complexity, not surprisingly, manifests itself culturally.

We clearly have a lot to gain by bringing biologists and theorists from the humanities together in collaborative exploration of the human body. So far, however, such an understanding has been impeded by an artificial academic division, with characteristic blind spots on each side. The way this division has evolved in the twentieth century, it often seems like the work of some perverse Cartesian administrator who decided to put certain people in charge of pure bodies and other people in charge of disembodied minds, and then sat back to see which group would knock the other out of the ring. Did you know that most texts on evolution do not even have "consciousness" in their indexes? I checked out quite a few and found no entries on any of the following: "thinking," "consciousness," "mind," or "experience." There were, of course, many entries listed under "brain." There were also a few under "intelligence," described as analogous to a simple, inheritable physical trait, listed side by side with visual acuity, manual dexterity, and so on. Humanists, on their part, have typically gone in exactly the opposite direction, treating reason, consciousness, thought—or more recently, language, discourse, and representations—as the *only* items in their dictionary.

This Cartesian division has created an academy with a radically split personality, each aspect of which is the mirror-image of the other, virtually shaped, like the Cartesian division between mind and body itself, in radical, mutual opposition. On one side of town, those who reduce human beings to the study of what Descartes called *res extensa*—mindless bodies—have made "the new science of the brain" (as *Newsweek* calls it) all the rage; for many of these folks, hard-wiring is the key to most human behavior. On the other side of town, among humanists and social scientists too exclusively influenced by poststructuralist theory, with its emphasis on how language and representations shape the "matter" of experience—indeed, according to some, create the very notion of "materiality" itself—it is being declared just as unequivocally that (as Donna Stanton has put it) "bodies are not born. They are in fact made by culture."

So philosophers and literary theorists, while currently hot for "the body," often forget that the body is made of flesh and blood, and has an evolutionary history. Thomas Laqueur, for example, arguing that the notion of "two sexes" is entirely a cultural, historical creation, ignores the larger evolutionary picture and potentially instructive comparisons with other animals, including our own ancestors. "Anything one says about the biology of sex," he writes, "even among the brute beasts, is already informed by a theory of difference and sameness. Indeed, if structuralism has taught us anything it is that humans impose their sense of opposition onto a world of continuous shadings of difference and similarity." Everything informed by theory—*true*. Therefore the evolutionary literature on sexual dimorphism among animals is mere ideology, and utterly uninstructive? *False*—unless we're willing to dismiss Laqueur's argument for the same reasons. For please note that Laqueur's argument, too, is informed by a theory of difference and sameness—one that has decided that the world is composed of "continuous shadings of difference and similarity" rather than oppositions. In this connection, it is striking that he *does* mention some animals. They are those—like the hare, the hyena, and the cassowary bird—that scientists have viewed as sexually ambiguous, androgynous, or bisexual. Laqueur *does* use evidence from the animal world to buttress his point, but very selectively.

Scientists, on their part, commit the mirror-image error and ignore how extensively symbolic constructs feed into human history, influencing the evolution of flesh and blood. In considering the issue of whether or not size matters to a partner's pleasure, for example, many evolutionary biologists—even sophisticated thinkers like Jared Diamond, as we've seen—seem to forget that no one who has grown up in a human society ever has purely physical sex. And while humanists may be over-entranced with Lacan at the expense of Darwin, biologists seem not to have *heard* of the phallus, or indeed even pondered how ideologies of masculinity—not only nerve endings—set bodies alive with desire or aversion. In this connection I was struck by *Psychology Today*'s finding that women who rate themselves as highly attractive were much more concerned about penis size than other women. "Of women describing themselves as 'much more attractive than average,'" psychiatrist Michael Pertschuk reports, "64 per cent cared strongly or moderately about penis width and 54 per cent cared about penis length. Women who rated their own looks as average were about 20 per cent lower." The large penis, then, may be as much a status symbol, proof of entitlement to the best that nature has to offer, as it is a pleasure wand. Which isn't to say that large penises (relative, of course, to their partner's size) don't have a potential for contact and stimulation that smaller penises may lack, and this potential may indeed explain why the human penis has evolved to its present size. But it's also true that such stimulation, unavoidably, needs to be interpreted as pleasurable or unpleasurable by the person who is feeling it, and as human cultures have developed, they have provided a great many associations, images, and ideas to assist the body in this task.

Just as no one ever has purely physical sex with another body, no one ever achieves an objective view of one's own. Young men, you will recall, have trouble seeing their penises realistically and consistently judge them to be smaller than they actually are. In part, that's because it's not really flesh-and-blood penises that shape a young man's perception of what his penis should be, but a majestic imaginary member—a phallic penis, one might say—against which no man's penis can ever measure up. As psychologist Anthony Quaglieri insightfully notes, thinking that one's penis is smaller than it should be is not really about inches but "about how men are trained by the world to see ourselves as not enough."

Does size matter? Absolutely, yes. But the matter of size is as "mental" as it is "material"—never just a question of nerve endings but always a collaboration with the imagination, and therefore with culture.

NOTES

1. Robert Mapplethorpe's controversial photograph *Man in a Polyester Suit* satirically illustrates this racist opposition between the White man's "civilization" and the Black man's primitive endowments, by showing a gigantic organ spilling out from the unzipped fly of a Black man in a tidy business suit, whose polyester material jokingly represents the tacky, K-Mart artifice of "civilization."

2. Evolutionary theorists are mixed when it comes to the question of whether that advertising is "truthful" or not; some argue that since the dimorphisms may hinder flight or fight, the animal is "lying"—he's actually less equipped for survival. Others claim that the huge energy investment in useless features could only be borne by an animal of superior endowments in other respects.

3. Have you ever seen an advertisement that displays a muscled torso *and* a smiling, warm face? The broad grinning faces of the competitors in bodybuilding shows seem misplaced, stuck on the wrong physique. On television, that BowFlex guy just won't crack a smile, even standing in front of the silliest-looking exercise machine I've ever seen: "Yes, our equipment may look a little different. That's because we've designed it to *function correctly.*" The hard body is a "take no shit" body.

4. There is unfortunately not the space in this essay to explain the concept of the phallus and its evolution. For more, see "What Is a Phallus?" in Susan Bordo, *The Male Body: A New Look at Men in Public and in Private* (New York: Farrar, Straus, and Giroux, 1999).

BIBLIOGRAPHY

Blum, Deborah. *Sex on the Brain: The Biological Differences between Men and Women.* New York: Viking Penguin, 1997.
Cook, Kevin. "Is Bigger Better?" *Vogue,* April 1995, 266–268.
Dervin, Daniel. "The Bobbitt Case and the Quest for a Good-Enough Penis." *Psychoanalytic Review* 82, no. 2 (1995): 249–256.
Diamond, Jared. *Why Is Sex Fun? The Evolution of Human Sexuality.* New York: Basic Books, 1997.
Findlay, Heather. "Freud's 'Fetishism' and the Lesbian Dildo Debates." *Feminist Studies* 18, no. 3 (1992): 563–579.
Ford, Michael. *Best Gay Erotica 1996.* Pittsburgh: Cleiss Press, 1996.
Friday, Nancy. *The Power of Beauty.* New York: Harper Collins, 1996.
Gould, James and Carol Grant Gould. *Sexual Selection: Mate Choice and Courtship in Nature.* New York: Scientific American Library, 1989.
Hemingway, Ernest. *A Moveable Feast.* New York: Scribner, 1964.
Hersey, George L. *The Evolution of Allure: Sexual Selection from the Medici Venus to the Incredible Hulk.* Cambridge, Mass.: MIT Press, 1996.
Keuls, Eva C. *The Reign of the Phallus: Sexual Politics in Ancient Athens.* Berkeley: University of California Press, 1985.
Laqueur, Thomas. *Making Sex: Body and Gender from the Greeks to Freud.* Cambridge, Mass.: Harvard University Press, 1990.
Lee, Peter. "Survey Report: Concept of Penis Size." *Journal of Sex and Marital Therapy* 22, no. 2 (1996): 131–135.
Lehman, Peter. "Penis Size Jokes and Their Relation to Hollywood's Unconscious."

In *Comedy/Cinema/Theory,* edited by Andrew Horton, 43–59. Berkeley: University of California Press, 1991.

Lord, M. G. *Forever Barbie: The Unauthorized Biography of a Real Doll.* New York: Avon, 1994.

Mailer, Norman. "The White Negro: Superficial Reflections on the Hipster." *The Time of Our Time.* New York: Random House, 1998.

Morgentaler, Abraham. *The Male Body: A Physician's Guide to What Every Man Should Know about His Sexual Health.* New York: Fireside Books, 1993.

Playgirl. August 1997.

Pollack, William. *Real Boys.* New York: Random House, 1998.

Pronger, Brian. *The Arena of Masculinity: Sports, Homosexuality and the Meaning of Sex.* New York: St. Martin's Press, 1990.

Rowanchilde, Raven. "Male Genital Modification: A Sexual Selection Interpretation." *Human Nature* 7, no. 2 (1996): 189–215.

Taylor, John. "The Long Hard Days of Dr. Dick." *Esquire,* September 1995, 120–130.

Tiefer, Lenore. "The Medicalization of Impotence." *Gender and Society* 8, no. 3 (1994): 363–377.

Wrangham, Richard, and Dale Peterson. *Demonic Males: Apes and the Origin of Human Violence.* New York: Houghton Mifflin, 1996.

Chapter 2

Large Propagators

Racism and the Domination of Women

RICHARD SCHMITT

W. E. B. Du Bois wrote, "To the ordinary American or Englishman, the race question at bottom is simply a matter of ownership of women; white men want the right to use all women, colored and white, and they resent the intrusion of colored men in this domain."[1]

At first blush that seems off the mark: racism is about slavery and its economic advantages; it is about the exploitation of nominally free labor; it is about so-called European civilization and the European belief in their superiority that gave them license to visit extreme barbarity on other peoples; it is about colonialism and imperialist expansion. But while all of this is true, it is as incomplete as Du Bois's pronouncement: none of the ways in which Whites have taken advantage of persons of color by drawing racist distinctions prepares us for racism being as visceral as it is. Racism is not just the belief that Whites have about their superiority; it is a deep feeling of disgust and attraction, of revulsion, fear, and desire. In order to understand racism at its most bodily and inarticulate we need to think about racism as sexual, because "racial hatred is carnal hatred."[2]

There are many explanations of this carnal hatred; but it also has an interesting and—to many—surprising history. After examining both, we will be able to see that Du Bois was making an important and central point about this sexual racism: it is not fully intelligible except as part of the attempt by White men to control women—both Black and White. What is more, the narrowly genital focus of sexual racism reveals very clearly White men's conceptions about their own sexuality.

THE MOST FAMILIAR STORY

White men have long whispered about the penises of Black men being bigger than their own. Travelers to Africa early on reported that African men have "large propagators."[3] They have joked uneasily about the potency of Black men being greater than theirs. They have worried that "their" White women preferred Black men and that Black men wanted nothing more than to sleep with White women. They have excused their own sexual licentiousness by tales about the lustfulness of Black women. Today Whites, especially men, still believe that Black men, in the words of Michelle Wallace, are "hung like an ape and fuck like an animal."[4]

James Baldwin articulates the most familiar explanation of this myth. "The white man's unadmitted—and apparently to him unspeakable—private fears and longings are projected onto the Negro."[5] The fears and fantasies of monstrous Black penises reveal White men's fears about their own sexual inadequacy, as they project onto Black men their own anxieties about their limited sexual powers. Fanon asks: "Still, on a genital level, when a white man hates a black man is he not yielding to a fantasy of impotence?"[6] Fanon too interprets White preoccupation with Black men and their sexual potency as a projection on Blacks of the White man's fears about his own small penis, his lack of staying power, or what he fears is his stunted sexuality. The same view is echoed by Calvin Hernton and Ronald Hyam.[7] But is it perhaps true that, on the average, Black genitals tend to be larger than those of Whites? On this, there is considerable disagreement. Many authors, Fanon among them, regard this as pure myth.[8] Others incline to the opinion that there is some factual foundation to these stories.[9] I have been unable to find any scientific evidence for or against these claims. But obviously the facts are of relatively minor importance, for what Baldwin, Fanon, and others tell us is that *regardless of the facts* Whites believe that Black men have larger genitals, keep their erections longer, are more easily aroused sexually, are more passionate in their lovemaking, and are better able to satisfy women sexually. What is more, White men hold these beliefs *because* they fear that their own sexual equipment, powers, feelings, and performances are less than they should be. It is not clear *why* large penises are thought to be so important; the common wisdom these days is that penis size does not affect the sexual satisfaction of one's partners. But in this case too it is not clear whether that widely shared opinion is based on a careful study of facts or results from wishful thinking. Obviously, the issue is not the physical size of anyone's actual body parts but a set of complex feelings, sexual and otherwise, that the image of the large penis symbolizes.

What are the feelings that attach to this image of the large penis? Whites say: "*They* have enormous penises, they are always off in the bushes with someone, they are insatiable. My penis is just fine. Women love it. Not a gross thing like *theirs*. Sometimes I worry that mine might be just a little small. But that's silly. I wonder what it would be like to have a really large penis." Whites don't just notice in passing that Black penises are bigger. Whites are and have been for a long time obsessed by them: obsessed by size in general, obsessed by issues of their own size in comparison to that of others. But the whole comparison is, in the end, reassuring. Blacks are clearly inferior—an inferiority that is spelled out in different ways: they are heathens, they are slaves, they are Black, they are a threat to the pure White women in our homes, they are poor and have a deficient family structure. But if the penises of the inferiors are bigger than mine, then big penises must be one more mark of belonging to a lesser breed, and mine, though it be smaller by comparison, is just right. The fear of our own inadequacy projected onto Black men can also be turned around into a kind of assurance that Whites are sexually adequate because we civilized men have civilized penises. Whatever we have is just right.

That reassurance is, however, never complete, because there is, of course, another thought in the background: Whites are superior in every respect to Blacks, but if Black men have bigger penises and their sexual performance outshines that of White men, what does greater power, intelligence, wealth, and even beauty matter? After all, in some primitive corner of his soul a man thinks that what matters most in his life is his sexual performance, and size, he thinks, is part of that. (I will come back to this at the end of this paper.) There is always room for the wedge of doubt that I am less of a man because my penis is insignificant. The reassurance of superiority does not last.

THE MOST FAMILIAR STORY IS NOT
THE COMPLETE STORY

Sexual feelings are full of ambiguities and ambivalences. It is unlikely that what Whites imagine or whisper about is unequivocally due to an obsession with White penis size—many more and more complex feelings are involved. The story about Black sexuality that has been circulating for five hundred years or more has other psychological roots. I will mention a number of other meanings one can easily find in the myth of the huge black penis.

As Gilman understands it, Whites do not project a sexuality on the Black man which they themselves would like to have, but rather project onto others the faults they fear in themselves and thereby purge themselves of those evils. Fears of an excessive and uncontrolled (perhaps uncontrollable) sexuality are stilled by ascribing this unmanaged sexuality to Black men and to other groups that are in disfavor. Thus, Whites can rest assured that they are good, because the evil which they secretly fear in their own nature is manifest in other groups who are for that reason despised and scapegoated.[10] White fantasies of Black sexuality arise from fears about their own barely suppressed desire and aggressions.[11] What Whites project on Blacks is not their fear of sexual inadequacy but a more general sense of being "bad" for having proscribed desires or feeling aggression against authority figures. The Black man is a creature of the "lower" desires, "bad," savage, undisciplined, untrustworthy therefore, and perhaps outright dangerous. But I am good because I am not that way. I react to the painful and therefore barely conscious fears about my own desires and aggressions by elaborating on how bad others are. It is a peculiar sort of finger-pointing. The shoplifter pursued into the street by the store employees points down the street shouting, "He went that way!" hoping to distract attention from himself. Similarly, the legends about Black sexual prowess point the finger away from my own desires and aggressions, which are too frightening to confront directly.

But the talk about Black genitals is not merely an attempt to purge hidden fears of White desires and aggressions. It responds to more general ambivalence about sexuality. For most persons sexuality itself evokes desire and fear. Sex attracts and repels. The degree of sexual repression has varied over the almost four centuries since the first Black men and women appeared in North America. It also varied in different parts of the country—it was severe in the New England and much less so in the early Southern colonies. In the nineteenth century, repression became more intense (and more unforgiving by far for White women than for White men). During most of this period sexuality was not a topic for public conversation. It was always a private matter, to be transacted in the dark, often a bit furtively. Shameful for White women, it was a challenge and an arena of possible failure for men. The fantasies of enormous genitals and sexuality triumphant may well have carried overtones of this complex ambivalence over sexuality itself. The fantasies express both attraction and repulsion—desire for an overpowering sexuality and fear of its irresistible force, which threatens self-control. When personal sexuality is secret and shameful, fantasies must concern a sexuality that belongs to others and that, in fact, is little known. But, at the same time, we can exorcise fear to some extent by talking about what frightens us and by mentally rehearsing fearful events so as to make them less disturbing. Thus, people talk about frightening events after they occur in order to stop the tremors, and also steel themselves for future fear by anticipating what will happen, preparing themselves through storytelling. Rehearsing sexuality in words can lessen fear of sexual acts.

Much sexual feeling and activity is accompanied by guilt—witness the nineteenth-century hysteria about masturbation.[12] For so long sexuality was sinful and sexual desire stood in need of control. Sexual feelings and actions were always dangerous in some unspecified way, and "giving in" to them bore the punishment of guilt. Black sexuality was imagined as unrestrained, uncontrolled, "savage," and primitive. In comparison then, White male sexuality was contained and thus, if not free of guilt, less blameworthy. White men could lessen their guilt over their own sexual desires and acts if they considered that their sexual self-control was admirable and heroic compared to the wantonness of Blacks. In addition, White men may have—they certainly should have—felt guilt over their treatment of Black women.[13] They may have transferred that guilt onto Black men in the giant penis fantasy.[14]

To the extent that the Black genitals are seen as huge and grotesque, these fantasies may reverberate with fears not only of sexual inadequacy or secretly desired transgressions but more vaguely of the monstrous unknown that lurks in parts of the world far away (or perhaps just around the corner). At the edge of consciousness dwell fears of a world distorted, unpredictable, and therefore unmanageable. This dread of a world gone mad and out of control surfaces in fears about deformed and misshapen human bodies, as well as the uneasiness produced by creatures that do not fit clearly into familiar categories: persons of unexpected size, with missing limbs, with extraordinary disabilities, with unaccustomed sexual habits. These aberrations in nature are signs of a world that is unpredictable, in which the unexpected may happen at any moment, leaving us uncertain about how to act, what to do, and what to expect. Encounters with such persons are frightening to children, and in adults the childish panic still leaves its traces. Images of distorted bodies, especially of distorted genitals, occasion a complex feeling of fear and pleasurable attraction. In the early nineteenth century, a Black woman remarkable for her enormous buttocks was on public display in Paris and London and crowds came to marvel at this anomaly, as they marveled at many others.[15] Gaping at the grotesque body of a human of a different type fills us with dread about the inconceivable possibilities that exist in the world at the same time as it reassures us that *our* world is ordinary, normal, predictable, and intelligible. The stories about oversized genitals of despised groups resonate with many of these fears and with our anxious attraction to what is unexpected, unknown, grotesque, and distorted about human bodies. The stories foreshadow a possible cosmic disorder that may be threatening us.

There may well have existed other motivations for talking about a rampant and dangerous Black sexuality. A White man cannot say that his penis is too small; he needs to talk about the enormous members of Black men. Similarly, a gallant White Southern gentleman could not confess that he was afraid of slave insurrections, of slaves fighting back, being insubordinate. Yet that was an ever-present fear in a society that was militarized to keep down slaves, where every man needed to take his turn patrolling the roads at night to catch slaves absent from their plantations without proper permission.[16] Perhaps the talk about the unruly sexuality of Black men and women was an oblique way of giving vent to the unease of living closely with a hostile subject population that was known sometimes to revolt and seemed always evasive and alien.[17] The constant threat felt by men could only be mentioned obliquely by expressing fear that White women were in danger.

Fantasies about Black genitalia and sexuality do not all spring from White fears. They have their origins also in Whites' *pleasure* at their superiority, and in pleasurable sexual fantasies. The fantasies about enormous penises and inexhaustible sexual energy, of a sexuality not inhibited by guilt or concealed behind the grave facade of the man of affairs or the statesman, are a source of delight that civilized men can fully savor because they *are* safely civilized, securely in control of their sexual urges. Rationality, clear thinking, and self-control are important traits that the European has always ascribed to himself and that have made him feel especially or perhaps exclusively civilized. Deeply embedded in this conception of civilization is a sharp distinction between mind and body, between rationality and passion, between self-control and sexuality. The European conception of reason constantly and insistently denies that it is the reason of a sexual being.[18] While he experiences the delicious shudders of imagining a feared and grotesque sexuality, the White man can also by implication congratulate himself on representing the highest stage human beings have reached and on his superiority to the animalistic sexuality of Blacks. The myth of Black sexuality allows him another avenue for bragging about European, White civilization.

At the same time the civilized European (as well as his American descendant) is afraid of his sexuality and ashamed of it. Sexuality cannot be enjoyed outright but only in a roundabout way. Back room talk and snickering about Black sexuality is a form of pornography—sexually exciting fantasies about the sexual lives of others. It is a way of experiencing vicarious sexual pleasure when actual sexual pleasure is forbidden or fraught with prohibitions and guilt. It is, moreover, sexual pleasure which is guilt-free because it is not his; he can freely succumb to its attraction and enjoy in the person of a slave what in his own person he could not enjoy without fear and guilt. While he enjoys his own superiority, he can also taste the pleasures of unbridled sexuality vicariously in his fantasies about others.

In conclusion, we need to realize that what Whites have been saying about Black men, they have also been saying about Scotsmen,[19] about Gypsies,[20] and about Jews.[21] In each case, the group that thinks itself superior suspects their inferiors of having abnormally large sexual organs. In each case, the same profusion of fears may well come into play: of sexual inadequacy; more generally, of being bad; of sexuality, with consequent guilt about sexual feelings and desires; and finally, of grotesque natural phenomena as reminders that the order of the universe is precarious and may break down at any moment. But there are also pleasures: the pleasure of lurid sexual fantasies; the pleasure of being—as the master thinks—more civilized.

A SCHEMATIC HISTORY

No doubt, there are other psychological themes that make fantasies of Black sexuality compelling and fascinating to Whites, but missing in the preceding reflections is the *history* of these White Europeans and the Blacks, Jews, Gypsies, or Scotsmen about whom they fantasize. Purely psychological explanations tend to be timeless: they discuss the feelings, anxieties, and yearnings of all human beings and pass by the complex changes that both racism and more specifically sexual racism underwent in the course of the history of Black men and women in North America. The stories about the "large propagators" of African men, about the unabashed sexuality of Africans—men and women—have a history. These images and stereotypes have altered over time, and it is not too difficult to see that some of the change originated in response to the changing conditions of White men and of their relations to Black men and to women, White and Black.

From the very beginning of slavery in North America, it was clear that racism was constructed by persons in power in order to encourage discord among the servants and slaves. In the seventeenth century, Englishmen made a very precarious living in Virginia, depending heavily on the Indians for food, until they began growing tobacco in the 1620s. In 1619, the first Black slaves were imported from the West Indies, but the bulk of the work was done by White indentured servants from England. These servants were bound to service for a limited number of years; the Blacks were servants for life. But otherwise White and Black servants seem to have worked together amicably, partied and slept together, and occasionally married.[22]

By 1650, there were about five hundred Blacks in Virginia, most but not all of them slaves.

> And all, servant, slave, or free, enjoyed rights that were later denied all
> Negroes. There is no evidence in the period before 1660 that they were
> subjected to a more severe discipline than other servants. Some slaves were
> allowed to earn money of their own and to buy their freedom with it. They
> bought and sold and raised cattle of their own. . . . While racial feeling
> undoubtedly affected the position of the Negroes, there is more than a little
> evidence that Virginians during these years were ready to think of Negroes
> as members or potential members of the community on the same terms as
> other men and to demand of them the same standards of behavior. Black
> men and white serving the same master worked, ate, slept together and
> together shared the same escapades, escapes and punishments.[23]

But after 1676 that relatively idyllic situation changed. That year, John Bacon, a young man of the upper class, led a very bloody rebellion of the poor. The ostensible issues were complex and had a lot to do with Bacon's personal ambition, but what the rulers of the colony perceived was a mob of poor people—*both White and Black*—who demanded more power for themselves. The powerful men of Virginia responded to popular discontent by introducing racial legislation, specifically laws against interracial marriages. They tried to separate Whites from Blacks, and tie the poor Whites to them through their racial identity. They drew the line between White and Black in sexual terms.

But Virginians had always felt threatened by the danger of servile insurrection and their fears increased as the labor force grew larger and the proportion of blacks in it rose . . . to keep a threat of another Bacon in everyone's mind. If freemen with disappointed hopes should make common cause with slaves of desperate hope, the results might be worse than anything Bacon had done. The answer to the problem, obvious if unspoken and only gradually recognized, was racism to separate dangerous free whites from dangerous slave blacks by a screen of racial contempt.[24]

The new attention to racial differences focused on interracial sexuality, a focus deliberately fostered by the new laws forbidding interracial marriage. Whatever racist feelings already existed between Whites and Blacks had not previously seemed to interfere with their shared lives and common cause against the rich leaders of the colony. But such racist feelings were now deliberately strengthened by the rules that made interracial sexuality illegal. Racism was fostered by insinuating that there was something amiss with Black bodies.

Nevertheless, sexual relations between White and Black did not end. It is a familiar fact that White men were free in their sexual relations with slave women, who had little to say about this. It is less well known that there also always were sexual relations between White women and Black men.[25] Some Black men accused of attacking White women were let off by the courts and not molested by anyone else.[26] In at least two cases, White men got a divorce from their wives because they gave birth to mulatto babies, but nothing happened to the Black fathers. Another White man was not granted a divorce from his White wife, who had had sex with a Black man, when she argued that her husband's violence had induced her to find a Black lover.[27] Until the Civil War, White women had sexual relations with Black men, and while it was frowned upon, it was also accepted as one of the things that will happen. Violence to the Black men involved was by no means the inescapable consequence of these relationships.

Slaveowners faced new problems in the early years of the American republic. Under the influence of the rhetoric of freedom and universal human rights of the American Revolution, abolitionist sentiment ran high even in the South. In 1830, the Virginia legislature came within a few votes of abolishing slavery.[28] At the same time, when the number of freedmen increased, breaking down the automatic equation of being Black with being a slave, measures to control the slaves became more difficult. "People who had always been absolutely subjected were now in many instances outside the range of the White man's unfettered power."[29] In response, segregation between Whites and Blacks became more stringent, including legal restrictions on where Blacks could go, where they could sit, etc. Here we see once more that racism did not well up spontaneously from the soul of the ordinary White Southerner but was encouraged through legislative mandate by the people in power. Whatever inclination Whites may have possessed toward racist fear and hatred, it was carefully nurtured by legislators.

It was not until the end of the Civil War, when Black men voted and many got elected to political office, that White hysteria over Black sexuality reached a fever pitch. What is more, there was no longer the generalized fear about interracial sex—a fear that so far had coexisted with knowledge about and a certain acceptance of sexual relations between White women and Black men. Now the fear of Black male sexuality became more and more explicitly fixated on male genitals and on the violence threatened by the Black male penis. The psychological origins of the fears and fantasies discussed in the preceding sections account for the power that such propaganda campaigns could wield. The myth of Black sexuality connects with enough unconscious and barely conscious feelings in Whites to make such lies appealing and, if repeated often enough, persuasive. The myths may have arisen spontaneously from the White unconscious; after all, they originated rather early in the contacts between Black men and Whites. (Although whatever White men thought about the sexuality of Black men, slave and free, these beliefs rarely if ever gave rise to the sort of violence and brutality that was the daily bread of Blacks in the United States from the end of Reconstruction until well into the 1960s.) The myth of the large Black penis and all it implies is nourished on the fertile soil of Whites' many conflicting and ambivalent feelings about their own sexuality and their place in the world. However, the belief that the large (compared to that of Whites) Black penis constituted a *danger* directly to White women— and therefore to the men whose women they were thought to be—was planted there by unscrupulous leaders. Only the actions of specific groups in the post-Reconstruction South turned those beliefs and images into a justification for a reign of terror that lasted a hundred years.

This was a period of profound change in the United States. With the end of the plantation economy, entrepreneurial capitalism came to the South. For a number of years, political power was no longer in the hands of the large plantation owners, but of the financiers, railroad tycoons, and bankers.[30] Industrialization proceeded apace and people moved from the country into the city. Among Blacks, there was a certain amount of prosperity. Some received a classical education—then the prerequisite for positions of leadership.[31] Well-educated Blacks made money.[32] They lived in big houses and drove around in elegant carriages. Many Whites, by contrast, were impoverished in the years after the war. Women, White *and* Black, went out to work in larger numbers. As the South industrialized and built a flourishing textile industry, lower-class White women went to work, earned money, and became more independent. Upper-class women joined clubs and did volunteer work and thus left the home, to an extent, and played roles in the public world.[33] Black women got educations as good as those of men. They too studied the classics, were trained to be teachers and leaders, and quickly assumed those roles.

Southern White men saw their traditional world slipping away from them as industrial capitalism replaced plantation agriculture, women became less dependent on men, and Blacks used their new freedom to become educated and acquire economic and political power. The old alliance between rich and poor Whites was seriously threatened in the 1880s by the Populists, who—for a while—built a powerful *multiracial* movement of small farmers. Whites responded hysterically to this range of changes with well-orchestrated efforts to return Blacks and White women to their subordinate position and reestablish the old alliance against them. They mounted a concerted campaign to persuade Whites that Black men were a constant and serious threat to the honor and safety of White women, because Black men had huge genitals and an insatiable sexual appetite, particularly for White women. Because Blacks were dangerous to White women—rich and poor—White men needed to stick together to defend their women. The picture of the sexually savage Black man "hung like an ape" became a commonplace.

"When white men created and exaggerated the danger of black rapists they underscored white women's dependency on white men, a tactic that put both black men and white women in their places."[34] The supposed threat against White women rendered them more dependent by putting them more firmly under the protection of White men. Nobody suggested that White women should learn to defend themselves or construct mutual aid and protection networks among women. The centerpiece of the campaign placed the burden for preserving White womanhood, and European civilization in general, squarely on the broad and capable shoulders of White Southern men. Thus just when White women began to have more of a presence outside the home, the patriarchal power relations were reestablished.

You can give substantiality to a lie by repeating it over and over, and that is what newspaper reporters, Harvard professors, ministers, and politicians did. It became fashionable to worry publicly about the Blacks' propensity to rape, just as today public figures commonly worry about the illegitimate children of Black teenagers.[35] But you can also add substantiality to a myth by *enacting* it, which Southerners did in an orgy of lynching and castration. The myth of the Black threat to White purity was enacted by a campaign of violence against Black men that did not abate until the 1960s.[36]

Lynching was an established practice in the United States. But until the terror of the post–Civil War period, the majority of lynching victims were White. It was only after Whites "discovered"—or manufactured—the rapist hiding in every Black man that lynching victims in the South were all

Black.[37] Castration likewise had been practiced before the Civil War, but a Black slave was castrated not primarily as a defense against his ungoverned sexuality but because it was cheaper than executing him. If the state executed a slave, who was after all someone's property, it had to reimburse the owner. Many other types of mutilation would impair a slave's ability to work. But castration did not cost the state nor affect the slave's labor; therefore the meaning of castration was not primarily sexual.[38]

In the 1880s and 1890s, a reign of terror began against Black people in the American South that centered on unrelenting propaganda about Black rapists. *Harper's* and many scholarly magazines took up this cry and even Blacks like Frederick Douglass had come to believe it. Ida B. Wells was a Black writer and editor in Memphis who became the foremost anti-lynching activist in the country. She checked out the widespread allegations of rape of White women by Black men, investigating 728 lynchings. It turned out that in only a third of the cases were the victims even accused of rape. Moreover, not only men but also women and even children were lynched. She published her findings in her own paper and in a Black-owned paper in New York, reporting numerous consensual unions of White women and Black men, six in Memphis alone, and denouncing "the old threadbare lie" of rape to justify lynchings. The Memphis presses, of which she was part owner, were burned down by a White mob. She never returned to the city after that, but continued her crusade while working for the New York paper.[39]

It is clear that the myth of the large Black penis has many different sources, aside from a possible basis in fact. It draws its persuasive power from many diverse feelings, sexual and otherwise, of Whites—feelings that are only circuitously and often accidentally connected to Black men. They might have been attached to Native Americans, had Europeans found their way to the Americas before they traveled into Africa. But the myth would never have become so powerful and pervasive and such a threat to the very lives of Black men without the concerted efforts of political leaders from the seventeenth century on, especially at the end of the nineteenth century. To a considerable extent, the myth of the huge Black penis is (White) manmade. The psychological mechanisms discussed in the first section of this paper suggest some reasons that political leaders were able to persuade White men of the great sexual powers of Black men. But those mechanisms alone do not account for the campaign of lynching that was justified by whispering about giant Black genitals.

PENIS POWER

It is time we returned to W. E. B. Du Bois. The domination of all women—Black and White—was central to racism in two ways.

We have already encountered the first one: The myth of the large Black penis that threatened all White women was a fiendish invention. It was as successful as it was because it served to solidify White male control over Black men. That brought with it increased control over Black women because their husbands, lovers, sons, and nephews were always at risk (besides, some women were also victims of lynching). They had to be terribly careful not to enrage the Whites, who on the slightest pretense would go on a murderous rampage. In a society which prided itself on its chivalrous treatment of women, Black women were not protected. At the same time, the myth of the large Black penis asserted that the safety of White women could only be protected by White men. The more they were in peril, the more they were beholden to White men for safety. All White women were at risk and thus all White men were called to protect women. The myth's appeal to male images of strength—providing for the family and keeping it safe—closed the ranks of White men across class lines and turned poor farmers against their Black former allies in the struggle against the wealthy. Thus the myth reestablished the power of White ruling circles by reattaching to itself the poorer Whites with an unshakable loyalty rooted in racism and patriarchy.

In one move, the campaign to broadcast the myth of the large Black penis that wants to possess White women, if necessary by violence, rebuilt the power of wealthy White men, which had been seriously eroded by the destruction wreaked by the Civil War, and by Emancipation and Black people's accession to power and greater economic possibilities. The myth built a strong bulwark against the growing restiveness of women against patriarchal control—a restiveness due to the participation of women, White and Black, in Reconstruction; their growing economic independence; their agitation for women's suffrage and their active participation in labor organizing; their increased access to education and early moves into professional careers; and the development of birth control and the attendant greater biological freedom of women. The myth breathed new life into the cross-class alliance of White men against women and Black men that had been threatened by interracial union organizing and the interracial populist movement of the 1880s.

But the myth was of course just that—a myth. It was a lie made plausible by endless repetition and by the dramatic enaction of Black rapist fantasies in lynchings. Not all lies can be spread by repetition: they must in some way ring true; they must strike the listener as eminently plausible. Whites were prepared to believe that Blacks were in some ways less "civilized" than they. They believed Blacks to be more sensual, perhaps more emotional, and in some ways more joyful. But in order to be less civilized they had to be comparable to Whites; they needed to be like them. If Black penises could be seen as weapons, threats, instruments of power and violence, it is because Whites already understood that all penises had that possibility. That conception of the penis must have resonated with White men and women. The myth of the Black penis raised the alarm over the growing power of Black men and women in the society, but in order for the transliteration of the threat to White power into the myth of the Black penis to occur to anyone and then to prove so persuasive, the penis must have already been familiar as an instrument of power. Otherwise the notion of Black power being a sexual threat to White women would have appeared a desperate and far-fetched fabrication on the part of people who could not adjust to the change brought by the Civil War and by Emancipation.

Here one form of racism—sexual racism—is closely connected to patriarchy. Sexual domination has been one way in which men have dominated women. Men have regarded and still regard the penis as an instrument for controlling women, and they compete with other men in stories, rarely truthful, of their sexual performances. Men contend with each other to be the better sexual performer. Lucy Candib and I, reflecting on the ubiquitous fear of impotence among men, developed this male conception in great detail.[40] Men, in some often deeply hidden corner of their souls, think of themselves as sexual performers. Their manhood is always in question because it wields power over women, either to grant or withhold sexual satisfaction, or more brutally to do violence to them. To be a man is to be powerful in this very specific way—powerful in relation to women. The penis is a weapon, an instrument of control. Their standing as men therefore depends on their potency compared to other men. The man *is* his penis. Real men have functioning, potent, ever-ready penises. The man whose penis is not functioning properly—is not performing properly whenever the opportunity presents itself—is not really a man. The essence of manhood is owning a penis that functions—a penis that becomes erect easily and frequently, that is able to penetrate, that is, like a good weapon, always at the ready. "To the man, his ability to have and keep erections is one of the main foundations of his masculinity."[41] Men who have erectile problems are completely devastated. Zilbergeld quotes some of his patients as saying, "I feel like an absolute nothing. . . . the center has been taken out of me. . . . I just don't feel like a man."[42]

Potency is so important because it allows the man control over sexuality and with it an important form of control over the relationship and the woman. Men exploit women; they get more than they put into the relationship by way of expressions of affection, personal and intimate attention, and day-to-day services in the forms of meals, homes, and children and their upbringing. But to the extent that women provide for them, men are also dependent on them and thus male control is easily undermined. But sexual relations, defined by stereotypical men as male penetration, are under male control; as long as the penis is powerful so is the man attached to it. This is sufficiently important to men to be endlessly joked and bragged about. (When has there been a day lately without a story or a joke about Viagra?) Owning a functioning penis is a measure of control, of power.

This assumption that manhood is lodged in the penis is ubiquitous. It is by no means held only by Southern racists or Victorian middle-class patriarchs. Here is what Gerda Lerner says: "When black men are prevented from defending their women and children, they are symbolically castrated and assaulted in their essential dignity."[43] The inability to protect those you love is a serious injury to a person. If that person is a man, we can say that it is a serious injury to his manhood—his life as a man. Then comes a jump: an injury to one's manhood is said to be a sexual and genital injury, as if the penis were the essence and epitome of the man. But that is not obvious, even though it seems so to most persons. A man's penis may be in fine working order, but he may be shiftless, passive, irresponsible, unprincipled, and brutal. Shall we say that his manhood is intact nevertheless because his manhood is in fact identical with his sexual functioning?

Ida B. Wells provides us with a much more humane conception of manhood. She writes about the struggle of Black men after Reconstruction to resist the efforts to take away their vote—efforts for which many risked and some lost their lives: "Scourged from his home; hunted through the swamps; hung by midnight raiders and openly murdered in the light of day, the Negro clung to his right of franchise with a heroism that would have wrung admiration from the hearts of savages. He believed that in the small white ballot there was a subtle something that stood for manhood as well as citizenship, and thousands of brave black men went to their graves, exemplifying the one by dying for the other."[44] Here manhood is not thought of as the ownership of a competent penis but as being brave, principled, and prepared to fight for one's rights and those of one's group.

Not only White men hold this misogynist view of the male body and the penis. bell hooks observes that a similar view of manhood is current among Black men: "The discourse of black resistance has almost always equated freedom with manhood, the economic and material domination of black men with castration, emasculation. Accepting these sexual metaphors forged a bond between oppressed black men and their white male oppressors. They shared the patriarchal belief that revolutionary struggle was really about the erect phallus."[45]

The myth of the giant Black penis is more intelligible in a setting where all men, White and Black, think of themselves as embodied in their sexual organ and, ultimately, estimate their own worth by the functioning of that organ. Manhood consists centrally in the domination of women through male sexuality, now narrowly defined as the erect penis. Here the domination of women comes to lie very close to the domination of Black men by Whites. In many situations, the struggle for the liberation of women appears to be in conflict with the fight to liberate people of color. But when it comes to sexual racism, the interests of Black men and women of all colors are very close together. The myth of the giant Black penis that is hostile and a threat to White women is closely linked to the conception of the White penis that is an instrument of domination of women, both Black and White.

The Black penis became so important in the racist hysteria of the end of the previous century because penises are instruments of power. This is the second way in which Du Bois was right about the intimate connection between White male control over women and racism. As Black men *and* women were threatening the established social, political, and economic arrangements and thus to deprive the traditional White leadership of their power, that threat was translated into genital terms because men—then and now—see the penis first of all as an instrument of power. It gives them power over women, and in their comparisons of sexual performance and penile size it gives them power over other men.[46] That Black men were—for a while—more powerful than they were during slavery is beyond question. No one saw any oddity in transposing this power into genital terms because the penis was accepted as the epitome of male power.

While the myth of the Black superpenis may have some basis in fact, and certainly has psychological roots, it is also the deliberate product of wealthy White men who wanted to drive a wedge between poor Whites and Blacks. It is also, we see now, the product of a prevailing conception of masculinity that identifies manhood with having a functioning penis, and defines a functioning penis as an instrument of domination of women. The canard of the super-potent Black male is closely connected with the domination of women. Patriarchy and racism are, in this instance, inextricably linked.

NOTES

1. Quoted in Paula Giddings, *When and Where I Enter: The Impact of Black Women on Race and Sex in America* (New York: Bantam Books, 1984), 61.

2. Calvin C. Hernton, *Sex and Racism in America* (New York: Anchor Books, 1965), xii.

3. Winthrop Jordan, *White over Black: American Attitudes toward the Negro, 1550–1812* (Chapel Hill: University of North Carolina Press, 1968), 34; Ronald Hyam, *Empire and Sexuality: The British Experience* (Manchester: University of Manchester Press, 1992), 204.

4. Michelle Wallace, *Black Macho and the Myth of the Superwoman* (London: Verso, 1990), 71.

5. James Baldwin, *The Fire Next Time* (New York: Dial, 1963), 96.

6. Frantz Fanon, *Black Skin, White Masks,* trans. Charles Lam Markmann (New York: Grove Press, 1967), 159.

7. Hernton, *Sex and Racism in America,* 114–115; Hyam, *Empire and Sexuality,* 204.

8. Fanon, *Black Skin, White Masks,* 170.

9. Jordan, *White over Black,* 159; Hyam, *Empire and Sexuality,* 205.

10. Sander Gilman, *Difference and Pathology: Stereotypes of Sexuality, Race and Madness* (Ithaca: Cornell University Press, 1985).

11. Joel Kovel, *White Racism: A Psychohistory* (New York: Vintage Books, 1970).

12. Gilman, *Difference and Pathology,* 192.

13. Michael Banton, *Race Relations* (New York: Basic Books, 1967), 156; Michael Dyson, *Race Rules: Navigating the Color Line* (Reading, Mass.: Addison-Wesley, 1996), 84–85.

14. Hernton, *Sex and Racism in America,* 14.

15. Gilman, *Difference and Pathology,* 85.

16. Joel Williamson, *The Crucible of Race: Black-White Relations in the American South Since Emancipation* (New York: Oxford University Press, 1984).

17. Jordan, *White over Black,* 153.

18. Thomas C. Patterson, *Inventing the West* (New York: Monthly Review Press, 1997).

19. Banton, *Race Relations,* 157.

20. Martin Bernal, *Black Athena: The Afroasiatic Roots of Classical Civilization,* vol. 1 (New Brunswick: Rutgers University Press, 1987), 201.

21. George Mosse, *Nationalism and Sexuality: Respectability and Abnormal Sexuality in Modern Europe* (New York: Howard Fertig, 1985), 142.

22. Thomas F. Gossett, *Race: The History of an Idea in America* (Dallas: Southern Methodist University Press, 1963), 29.

23. Edward S. Morgan, *American Slavery, American Freedom: The Ordeal of Colonial Virginia* (New York: Norton, 1975), 154–155.

24. Ibid., 328.

25. Eugene D. Genovese, *The World the Slaveholders Made* (New York: Vintage Books, 1971), 422.

26. Dinae Miller Somerville, "Rape, Race and Castration in Slave Law in the Colonial and Early South," in *The Devil's Lane: Sex and Race in the Early South,* ed. Catherine Clinton and Michelle Gillespie (New York: Oxford University Press, 1997), 74–89.

27. Martha Hodes, *White Women, Black Men: Illicit Sex in the 19th Century South* (New Haven: Yale University Press, 1997), 73.

28. Banton, *Race Relations,* 120.

29. Jordan, *White over Black,* 410.

30. C. Vann Woodward, *Tom Watson: Agrarian Rebel* (London: Oxford University Press, 1938), 53.

31. Glenda Elizabeth Gilmore, *Gender and Jim Crow: Women and the Politics of White Supremacy in North Carolina, 1896–1920* (Chapel Hill: University of North Carolina Press, 1996), 37.

32. Giddings, *When and Where,* 26.

33. Gilmore, *Gender and Jim Crow,* 95.

34. Ibid., 96.

35. Giddings, *When and Where,* 28.

36. Martha Hodes, "The Sexualization of Reconstruction Politics: White Women and Black Men after the Civil War," *Journal of the History of Sexuality* 3 (1993): 402–417.

37. Williamson, *The Crucible of Race,* 183ff.

38. Somerville, "Rape, Race and Castration."

39. Giddings, *When and Where*, 28.

40. Lucy Candib and Richard Schmitt, "Fear of Losing It: The Fear of Impotence" in *Rethinking Masculinities: Philosophical Explorations in Light of Feminism*, ed. Larry May, Robert Strikwereda and Patrick Hopkins (Lanham: Rowman and Littlefield, 1996).

41. Bernie Zilbergeld, "The Man behind the Broken Penis: Social and Psychological Determinants of Erectile Failure," in *Erectile Disorders*, ed. R. C. Rosen and S. R. Leiblum (New York: Guilford, 1992), 27–51.

42. Ibid.

43. Gerda Lerner, ed., *Black Women in White America: A Documentary History* (New York: Vintage Books, 1992), 170.

44. Ibid., 201.

45. bell hooks, *Yearning: Race, Gender and Cultural Politics* (Boston: South End Press, 1990), 57–58.

46. Candib and Schmitt, "About Losing It."

Chapter 3

The Future of the Phallus

Time, Mastery, and the Male Body

JOHN ZUERN

> It is as much of my essence to have a body as it is the future's to
> be the future of a certain present.
> —Maurice Merleau-Ponty, *Phenomenology of Perception*

In the courtyard just below the window of my office at the University of
Hawai'i at Mānoa, a group of young men has gathered to practice stunts
with bikes. One by one, they speed up a ramp of plywood and vault into
the air, straining to force the bike through a specific, painstakingly choreo-
graphed configuration of twists and whirls before returning—sometimes
crashing—to the ground. The others wait their turns and watch critically.
From time to time, they offer advice, less often praise. When one of them
loses control of his landing, careens into a recycling bin, and lies prone in
the midst of scattered soda cans, they drop their bikes and rush to hunker
down around their comrade, not touching him but conveying through
their proximity a restrained concern that approaches, perhaps only in contrast to their usual bravado, a kind of tenderness. The fallen one rises shak-
ily and attends to a scraped elbow while his companions right the bin and
gather up the cans. They are on alert now; their eyes scan the spaces between the buildings. But it is a hot Sunday afternoon and the chances that
campus security will arrive to drive them away, as frequently happens, are
slim. The space is theirs. They have commandeered it, for a couple of
hours at least, repurposing not only the physical architecture of the university through their defiant means of occupying and moving through its
structures, but also the university's function as an institution of learning.
They are engaged in a physical education, a physics, a social studies, a
political science, a psychology, and an aesthetics—a set of courses that does
not so much resist the curriculum sanctioned by the educational state apparatus (and protected by a substratum of the repressive state apparatus[1])
as it reveals, from an oblique, airborne angle, the fundamental aims of
official education: to steer students in the "right direction," to consolidate
"communities" by reproducing the relations that ensure the continuance

of society's functions, to legitimate the differential positioning of embodied subjects (laboring bodies marked by sex, by race, by an array of "abilities" or "capacities") within social space and social time.

To confer upon the scene I have described an exemplary status within a discussion of a distinctively male experience of corporeality and socialization is to confront a number of theoretical difficulties, only some of which may ultimately be resolved. The bikers share the courtyard, although almost never at the same time, with a group of skateboarders. Both groups are exclusively male; I have been paying attention to them for more than a year now, and while young women are sometimes present as spectators, I have never seen a woman take part in their activities. This exclusivity is the most obvious marker of the "maleness" of this form of socialization through physical display and resistance to authority, but it is at the same time an unstable phenomenon: there are, of course, women bikers and skateboarders, and the masculine hegemony of these sports is not uncontested by all male participants. A recent letter from a male eighth-grader to the editors of *Thrasher* magazine represents an attempt to intervene in the sexist discourse of skateboard culture: in school, this letter-writer has been "learning about gender-fair and gender-biased and how to recognize it in articles and stories," and his letter decries *Thrasher's* failure to recognize the participation of women in the sport and its tendency to represent women as "sex objects rather than skater objects."[2] The glib response of the editors, who give this letter the heading "Gimme Girls," provides in turn an illustration of the imaginary masculine privilege and empowerment that many theorists of gender designate as "phallic": "Is it our fault that girls always take their clothes off whenever we're around?"[3]

This confrontation goes only so far toward showing that the sexism of cultural formations as aggressively masculinist as the target audience of *Thrasher* is not monolithic. At best, it can be characterized as a skirmish in a still inchoate struggle, among and within apparatuses (here, an eighth-grade curriculum which has put a critique of sexism on the agenda versus those divisions of the publishing and recreation industries for whom sexism *is* the agenda as long as it serves their marketing interests), and among and within individual men and women: the struggle to imagine, preliminary to realizing in historical time, what feminist philosopher Elizabeth Grosz calls "a non-patriarchal future."[4] The young letter-writer is situated at the intersection of phallic power (imagined, perhaps, but backed up by a garrison of real social structures) and an imagined future (now marshaling its forces). This suggests to me that thinking of the phallus in relation to futurity, imagining, that is, what can be isolated and designated by the expression "the future of the phallus," offers a way of thinking about male bodies as such and, with a series of qualifications, may suggest how the male body might be construed as an agent in the struggle against masculine hegemony.

This essay examines the male body's position—and potentiality—within the structures of society from a perspective that emphasizes temporality, in particular futurity, as a crucial dimension of what phenomenologist Maurice Merleau-Ponty calls the "explosion or thrust which is subjectivity itself"[5] and as an important consideration in understanding how subjects come into being as, and experience being, gendered subjects. The phenomenological category of temporality is implicit in many accounts of embodied, gendered subjectivity but is frequently overshadowed by other theoretical concerns. The first section of the essay reviews two concepts that have become key to many discussions of gender difference: the phallus as a privileged signifier, a concept drawn from Jacques Lacan's reformulation of Freud's thought on sexual difference; and "interpellation," a model of the constitutive link between ideology and the human subject elaborated by Marxist philosopher Louis Althusser. I argue that both concepts are founded upon models of temporality and that both imply an orientation of the subject toward the future. The following section turns to Louis Althusser's posthumous memoir, *The Future Lasts Forever,* a compelling supplement to his model of interpellation and a powerful reflection on the experience of male corporeality in terms of phallic power, anxiety, and futurity. Taking a number of approaches to the question of whether the phallus has a future, the concluding section discusses the difficulty of moving from theoretical models of the gendered body to bodily practices that can intervene in the history of sexism, but also anticipates—for futurity, like the phallus, is experienced as anticipation, as hope and anxiety—a place for the male body in a more hopeful and less terrifying world.

PROJECTIONS: THE PHALLUS, IDEOLOGY, AND TEMPORALITY

In her essay "The Constructed Body," sociologist Colette Guillaumin turns to her observations of male skateboarders in Montreal and Paris to elaborate a nuanced social-constructivist argument about society's "direct and indirect interventions in the fabrication of the sexed body."[6] Guillaumin notes that in most societies, men's gestures and body postures demonstrate a greater sense of the mastery of space than do those of women, and she ties these spatial habits to the greater license afforded to male children. The young skateboarders

> met with constant and repeated failure but attempted the task again and again without any sign of discouragement. Sometimes their effort achieved some success, causing me to think that the time devoted to this activity— obviously unlimited, obviously habitually renewed—would permit them finally to master this feat satisfactorily. . . . They kept practicing—with more failures than successes, since this action required difficult techniques—but

freedom of space and time was the *sine qua non* of their exercise, and corporal ease the result."[7]

Guillaumin contrasts such activities with those typical of girls, who are given less freedom to associate with peers and whose activities are more often restricted to and oriented toward maintaining the space of the home. "The availability of time and space, tools for building corporal mastery, is specific to male children and adolescents and will continue to be their property in later life."[8] While Guillaumin's study draws upon neither Lacanian psychoanalysis nor the work of Althusser, her conclusions offer a productive point of departure for assessing the concepts of the phallus and interpellation as means for understanding the differential embodiments of men and women in society. "Societies," Guillaumin writes, "are based on preventing potentialities and on channeling the energy of an individual female into a specific body, but they are also based on the repression of this energy and, as a final resort, on the censuring of the self."[9] How might psychoanalysis, and Althusser's selective adaptation of psychoanalysis, take up the implications of this description of an imposed hierarchy of sexual difference—an imposition which sustains the relative expansion of male capacities and the incapacitation of women—to illuminate that imposition as an ongoing event, in the lives of individual men and women, of internalization and incarnation?

LACAN'S MODEL OF THE PHALLUS

Beginning in the early 1950s, Parisian psychoanalyst Jacques Lacan's seminars quickly became a focal point for exchanges among a wide variety of thinkers in the humanities and social sciences. Lacan's effort to reformulate the theories of Sigmund Freud in light of more recent developments in linguistics and structuralism made him a highly influential and controversial figure on the French intellectual scene, and the dissemination of his work abroad has had a significant impact on many disciplines outside of psychoanalysis itself, including feminism and theories of gender and sexuality, literary criticism, cinema studies, and cultural studies.[10]

The concept of the phallus as a privileged signifier is one of the most notorious outcomes of Lacan's theoretical project. The opening statements of his essay on "The Signification of the Phallus" follow Freud in situating the castration complex at the foundation of the sexed subject's ability "to identify with the ideal type of his sex"[11] and to eventually assume the roles of lover and parent in heteronormative society. Lacan argues that, even for Freud, the penis or phallic object that is so central to the Oedipus complex and castration anxiety can never be fully ascribed to male anatomy, but rather functions as a sign of plenitude which the child initially associates with the mother and her body, what Freud terms the "phallic mother."[12] The phallus takes on its dynamic role in the sexual identifications and sexual relations of subjects of both genders when the child recognizes that the mother does not have the phallus and construes this perceived lack as the mother's desire for the phallus, which the child wishes to satisfy. Lacan recasts the father's prohibition of incest in the classic Oedipal model as the father's "law," which controls access to the phallus as the central object of the libidinal economy: the (heterosexual) boy will seek to confirm his possession of the phallus in his future relations with women, and the (heterosexual) girl will go on to "receive" the phallus from the bodies of men.[13]

Lacan's own understanding of the phallus owes much to Ferdinand de Saussure's description of the linguistic sign as a combination of a signifier and a signified—a combination that is essentially arbitrary, gaining its meaning only within the differential system of other signs.[14] For Lacan, the phallus operates in the psychic life of the subject as a signifier, but does not signify the penis; on the basis of "clinical facts," Lacan asserts that the subject's relationship to the phallus is established "without regard to the anatomical difference of the sexes."[15] Lacan assigns to the phallus the place of the privileged, enabling element within the system of differentials that is language, and also in the entire field of signification through which human culture is maintained. The phallus is not connected with any particular signified because it "stands for" signification itself, occupying the place of the "bar" that separates signifier from signified and splits the human subject, "the slave of language,"[16] whose desires are alienated in the system of signification. "The phallus is the privileged signifier of that mark in which the role of the *logos* is joined with the advent of desire."[17] Lacan elevates the phallus from a mark of sexual difference to the very condition of possibility of any significatory marking whatsoever, thus bringing signification as such under the aegis of the phallus in a gesture that is arguably descriptive of matters as they stand in heteronormative and patriarchal society, but that many of Lacan's critics understand as a confirmation of patriarchy and heteronormativity.[18]

Lacan's justification of his insistence on the term "phallus" clarifies his theoretical aims without exonerating them of the charge of phallocentrism and heterosexism: "It can be said that this signifier is chosen because it is the most tangible element in the real of sexual copulation, and also the most symbolic in the literal (typographical) sense of the term, since it is equivalent there to the (logical) copula. It might also be said that, by virtue of its turgidity, it is the image of the vital flow as it is transmitted in generation."[19] Lacan's rhetoric appears to attribute such literal interpretations of the phallic function to hypothetical others ("on peut dire"); he goes on to trump these simplifications (which he has nonetheless put into play) in stating that the phallus functions only insofar as it is veiled, "as itself a sign of the latency with which any signifiable is struck, when it is raised (*aufgehoben*) to the function of signifier."[20]

For Lacan, human desire is always for the "desire of the Other," a desire that is further alienated because it relies on systems of signification for its expression. The phallus, as privileged signifier, conditions the terms of exchange in this vexed rendition of "I Want You to Want Me." "Here," Lacan writes, "is signed the conjunction of desire, in that the phallic signifier is its mark, with the threat or nostalgia of lacking it."[21] In his next sentence, "Of course, its future depends on the law introduced by the father into this sequence," Lacan underscores the decisive role of the signifying systems that preexist the subject—the symbolic order, in which the function of the father in the Oedipal drama is assumed by the father's Name, which designates and positions the subject as a social being—in setting and directing the course of the phallus's function in the life of the subject.

Lacan's account of the phallus presents a desire that is at once aroused and undercut by an anxiety occasioned by the possibility of a lack, and Lacan ascribes to this desire a futurity determined within the field of socially defined signs. His model does not emphasize this orientation to the future; it stresses rather the law on which the subject's psychic and social future depends.[22] If we move the emphasis here onto futurity to examine the implications of the model for the subject's experience of time, it is important not to confuse the phallus with a "goal"[23] but to recognize it as providing the conditions of possibility for a *want* that incorporates—literally—into the body of the subject the subject's orientation toward a coming time as a tension, an apprehension. Insofar as they must be articulated within existing systems of meaning, such tensions and apprehensions acquire a social definition, not only in strictly sexual terms but in terms of the myriad experiences of a body that is "timed." Grosz argues that the phallus "if interpreted socio-politically," can "be seen to represent some of the ways in which subjects are positioned in different locations within a hierarchized social geography."[24] If we recognize (as distinct from accepting) Lacan's model of the function of the phallus as a signifier, an analysis concerned with the social and political fates of men and women must recognize that the phallus also operates to situate subjects within differentials of temporality.

Grosz has herself argued that "in order to reconceive bodies, and to understand the kinds of active interrelations possible between (lived) representations of the body and (theoretical) representations of space and time, the bodies of each sex need to be accorded the possibility of a different space-time framework."[25] As signification links the body that produces material vocal and gestural signs to social discourse, temporality draws the material body into the routines, schedules, and agendas of our existence as social beings. Both women and men experience futurity as a kind of strain on the body: the internal sense of forward orientation and anticipation in the face of what social historian Reinhart Koselleck has described as the "horizon of expectation," where the future is felt in the present as an anticipation that "directs itself to the not-yet, to the nonexperienced, to that which is to be revealed. Hope and fear, wishes and desires, cares and rational analysis, receptive display and curiosity: all enter into expectation and constitute it."[26]

Phenomenology can and does offer an account of the quotidian experience of the passage of time in relation to the body's tensions and anticipations. In an early essay, Lacan acknowledges the importance of Merleau-Ponty's focus on the subject's lived experience in *Phenomenology of Perception,* but Lacan conjoins the phenomenological consideration of experience with an account of the unconscious, which structures experiences from behind the scenes—from outside the pale of the methods of phenomenology.[27] Furthermore, Lacan's rereading of Freud in terms of structural linguistics leads him to associate the operations of the unconscious with those of language, and to situate all the dimensions of the classical Freudian psychodynamics that shape the experience of the subject within the systems of signification—language, kinship structures, cultural norms, etc.—that preexist any individual subject. For all its limitations, Lacanian psychoanalysis opens up the phenomenological account in two important directions: toward the subject's unconscious and toward the codes that order the subject's social world.

If we remain—temporarily, at least—within Lacan's model in order to isolate an experience of the body and futurity which can be called "male," we must first acknowledge that when it comes to the phallus, being a man is never enough. "Even in Lacan's terms," Grosz writes, "the penis can only ever approximate the function of the phallus. 'Having' a penis, i.e. being a man, is no guarantee of warding off lack. On the contrary, rendering them equivalent has problems of its own, manifested in anxieties about sexual performance (impotence fears) as well as a sometimes desperate search for the other through whom the man can have his position as the possessor of the valued/desired organ confirmed."[28] Both men and women occupy their bodies, in the sense of inhabiting their imagined, projected spaces as well as of the range of activities they perform, in accordance with fundamental experiences of lack and differentiation which are channeled through our culture's organization of gender difference. That differential organization shapes the experience of the body as "wanting" in different ways for men and women.

Men have, of course, particular expectations regarding the future of the body itself: some of us (and we can't always know in advance who we are) can look forward to the loss of hair, a decline in our libido, the diminution of our potency, "prostate trouble" or prostate cancer, and a higher likelihood of other cancers. Men in industrialized societies have the statistical probability of dying earlier than women. Recent pharmacological developments to address these conditions have received wide coverage in the U.S. media. It is striking that drugs purporting to remediate impotence and halt or reverse hair loss have been celebrated far more than those that promise to prolong life.[29] What, exactly, are we men seeking to preserve and restore? It can be said that men seek in medicine and in our general "care of the self" to preserve our youth, virility, potency, etc., but what is at stake is differentiation: our difference from losers (old, weak, impotent men), and also the whole set of differentiating attributes which stabilize our privileged positions as men within our society insofar as these attributes can be displayed via our bodies.[30] What we seek to master is the control of the cultural meaning of the body itself, our offering of our bodies to the world as *meaningful*.

In the game of pass-the-phallus, men are poor losers. But like the tokens put into play in other games, the phallus gains its meaning and value only in passing from possession to loss within a structured—and temporally bounded—system. The football in itself is less important than having it, wanting it, knowing where it is at all times. The phallus is less a thing than a condition of difference and, in its temporal dimension, of nostalgia (for its loss) and anticipation (of its recovery and possession). In the body's long haul, during which many men propel themselves into bodily practices aimed at the warding off or recovery of loss, we find a way of thinking of the phallus in relation to men's moment-to-moment experience of futurity. For an understanding of the role of the phallus in the subjectivization of men and the incarnation of male subjectivity through the conditioning—spurred and fueled by tensions, anticipations, apprehensions, and hopes—of male bodies, it is important to make a distinction between not having and not having *yet*.

As a condition of difference that, for men, defines their potentiality and privilege within the social field, the phallus is inserted, as it were, into the very futurity of the male subject. But at the same time, the phallus serves as the vestibule of the future, a horizon of masculine expectation. We see in Lacan's (perhaps disavowed) preliminary arguments for the choice of the term "phallus" that the penis is figured culturally and for the most part biologically as a penetrative and excretory implement and not as a receptive orifice, although the urethra is entered in a variety of sexual practices and medical procedures (when a man is tested, for example, for certain venereal infections).[31] The penis is a vestibule, a passageway to and from the interior of the body. Metaphors used to describe the phallus—as a bar, for example, or a threshold—participate in the same spatial paradox of the metaphor of "horizon," which is both limit and opening, restriction and possibility. If we consider the function of what Lacan calls the phallus to be "vestibular," we retain the concept's link to corporeality and the experience of the body; the metaphor of the vestibule, drawn from both anatomy and architecture, suggests the interpenetration and intercanalization of spatiality, temporality, and corporeality. A notion of a "vestibular phallus" might also deprivilege the male body, not only by emphasizing passages and openings but also by situating the phallus's function in the "vestibular apparatus" through which our bodies maintain their balance, orientation, and equilibrium in the physical and social world.[32]

The anatomical vestibular apparatus consists of sensory receptors that register vibration, gravity, and acceleration. It mediates, through a configuration of neuromotor checks and balances, the sensory exchange between the body and the external world. If, for example, I am on a bike flying off the end of a ramp, my vestibular system correlates a rush of information about my body's precarious position in space. It tries to correct the imbalance of my body, signaling my brain, which in turn triggers automatic responses in my muscles, which I am also consciously trying to control. "Restricting one's body or extending it and amplifying it," Guillaumin writes, "are acts of rapport with the world, a felt vision of things."[33] What both Guillaumin and I have noted in the young bikers and skateboarders, in their determined rehearsal of a prowess they rarely achieve, is emblematic of a balancing act that is at once corporeal and ideological. In the freedom of time and space that society affords young men—although perhaps not so readily as Guillaumin suggests—these guys are "dicking around," and in dicking around they are perpetually confronting horizons of masculine expectation. They expect something of themselves, of course, but this expectation is inextricable from the expectations and desires of others—of their present companions and of a symbolic order with its "views" of them, its constructions and agendas not only of gender but of an array of values and attributes. They are, in part, learning to be men *for men,* to compete with and care for other men. The vertiginous flight of their stunts is only one manifestation of a perpetual vertigo at the brink of their gendered futures in society. Their actions unfold in a mode of experiment, inquiry, and apprehension. What if, as my bike shoots off the ramp, I turn the handlebars *this* way? What if, as I kneel beside my injured friend, I venture to touch him? How will the mark of difference shift onto me and my body? Will it bring me adulation, ridicule, suspicion? What will it—what will I—mean *then,* in that soon-to-arrive future I cannot see but am working, body and soul, to foresee and to navigate? Such questions are, of course, not necessarily conscious even in the form of a perceptible anxiety about one's appearance or demeanor. Men who "act like men" are not "deciding" moment to moment to act as they do; their masculinity is in general automatic, but it is articulated in the anticipatory questing and questioning of embodied subjectivity.

ALTHUSSER'S MODEL OF INTERPELLATION

In Louis Althusser's terms, these young men—and all of us—are being interpellated, transformed by ideology into subjects "inserted into practices governed by the rituals of the ISAs [ideological state apparatuses]."[34] Althusser's intellectual project bears a striking similarity to Lacan's in that Althusser, too, undertakes to reread a classic body of work—the founding texts of Marxism—from a perspective informed by later theoretical developments, in particular structuralism.[35] Althusser and Lacan associated with one another throughout the 1960s and 1970s, and Althusser's conception of how social institutions such as the school, the church, and the family imbue individual subjects with dominant ideologies draws heavily, though selectively, from Lacan's psychoanalytic account of the development and structure of human subjectivity.

In his tremendously influential essay "Ideology and Ideological State Apparatuses," first published in 1969, Althusser's presentation of the mutually constitutive relations between ideology and subjectivity, as well as his insistence on the material existence of ideology, turn on notions of internalization and embodiment that are never fully articulated, but that inhere in the ambiguities of terms such as "recognition," "behavior," and especially "attitude." His well-known illustration of interpellation as a "hailing" of a person on the street, the shout of "hey, you there!" that causes the person to turn around, demonstrates that ideology functions by way of its own "obviousness" and naturalness. The subject's recognition that he or she is the one being addressed is meant to show that the apparent self-evidence of our very sense of "who we are" is imbricated in ideology's positioning of us as subjects. Ideology takes on its material existence in the practices of subjects. As an interpellated subject, the "individual in question behaves in such and such a way, adopts such and such a practical attitude, and, what is more, participates in certain regular practices which are those of the ideological apparatus on which 'depend' the ideas which he has in all consciousness freely chosen as a subject."[36] Ideology is inside us; its material existence is grounded in the concrete practices of subjects who behave as they do because they have been interpellated by ideology and recognize themselves in ideology, a recognition that entails—is in fact dependent upon—the misrecognition of their "real conditions of existence."[37]

I want to explore here the implications of what strikes me as a curious inconsistency in regard to temporality in Althusser's model of interpellation. When, in his essay on "Freud and Lacan," Althusser undertakes to isolate the object of psychoanalytic knowledge, the unconscious, he engages in an impassioned description of a struggle in time, a "war without memoirs or memorials," waged throughout "the long forced march which makes mammiferous larvae into human children, masculine or feminine subjects."[38] In a description of the process of interpellation he offers in "Ideology and Ideological State Apparatuses," using as his example the ideology of Christianity, he notes that this ideology "obtains from [subjects] the recognition of a destination (eternal life or damnation) according to the respect or contempt they show to 'God's Commandments.' "[39] Yet earlier in the same essay, when he presents the scene of the subject "hailed" in the street, he expressly comments on the problem of admitting temporality into his model:

> Naturally for the convenience and clarity of my little theoretical theatre I have had to present things in the form of a sequence, with a before and an after, and thus in the form of a temporal succession. There are individuals walking along. Somewhere (usually behind them) the hail rings out: "Hey, you there!" One individual (nine times out of ten it is the right one) turns around, believing/suspecting/knowing that it is him, i.e. recognizing that "it really is he" who is meant by the hailing. But in reality these things happen without any succession. The existence of ideology and the hailing or interpellation of individuals as subjects are one and the same thing.[40]

Althusser's commitment to a view of ideology as "eternal" is consonant with his commitment to a materialist view of history as "a process without a subject,"[41] but it is nonetheless difficult to understand how the operation of interpellation can take place outside of time, even if we concede that the "human time" of anticipation and futurity is itself an ideological production. For Althusser, recognition is the vehicle for the ideological conditioning of the subject, for the installation of the subject into the social relations that ensure and reproduce relations of production. If, however, we adhere to Lacan's model of the mirror stage, on which Althusser draws, we must also take into account the role of *anticipation* in identification and account for the projection of an imagined selfhood into a projected, imagined future. Lacan describes the mirror stage as "a developmental event that decisively projects the formation of the individual into history,"[42]

> a drama whose internal thrust is precipitated from insufficiency to anticipation—and which manufactures for the subject, caught up in the lure of spatial identification, the succession of phantasies that extends from a fragmented body-image to a form of its totality that I shall call orthopaedic—and lastly, to the assumption of the armor of an alienating identity, which will mark with its rigid structure the subject's entire mental development.[43]

Even if we acknowledge the schematic nature of Althusser's street drama, we can observe that the subject's act of turning around in response to the hail incorporates the idea of a temporal orientation as well as a spatial movement: the subject anticipates something, wonders "what's going to happen now?" Althusser's own use of the term "attitude," modified by "material" and "practical,"[44] suggests not only beliefs articulated through bodily positioning and comportment, but also an outlook, an orientation within temporality.

What does the interpellated subject anticipate? In a gesture reminiscent of Lacan's offering and then dismissing crude anatomical metaphors to justify the use of the term "phallus," Althusser remarks that the appeal of the ideology's "hailing" "cannot be explained solely by 'guilt feelings,' despite the large numbers who 'have something on their consciences.' "[45] It would seem, however, that conscious "guilt," implying the apprehension of a specific punishment, is less likely the operative factor here than an apprehension in the face of differentiation, of being singled out: "How will the mark of difference pass to me now?" For subjects and ideological apparatuses to orient themselves and maintain their equilibrium, they must maintain the systems of difference that operate orthopedically to sustain their obviousness, to keep them from moving "out of true." My suggestion that the phallus has a vestibular function in the orientation of the gendered subject in the social world is based in part on Lacan's description of how the comprehensive experience of a whole body *and* a coherent identity emerges and is maintained through an orthopedic projection marked by anticipation.

If the phallus has a function in the interpellation of men as men and the installation of men as privileged subjects in the apparatuses of our society, it achieves these effects because, for men, the phallus is always coming. This crude formulation points to the confluence of male social and corporeal pleasures (especially those pleasures that signal our masculinity to ourselves and to the world) and the particular directions taken by the anticipatory, vertiginous pulse of male subjectivity in the face of incapacity and absence, a pulse which is registered in the body and which serves as at least one of the wavelengths for the transmission of ideologies of masculinity.

Ideologies reproduce themselves within and through our desire for psychic equilibrium—our desire to recognize ourselves as coherent selves— but they also trade on our sense of destiny, operating upon the phenomenal *orientation toward* that steers men's ideological and, to a great extent, corporeal becoming. Ideology, which Althusser describes as an expression of "a will, a hope, or a nostalgia,"[46] appeals perhaps most efficiently to our sense of not measuring up, of not being there yet, of moral and physical inadequacy, but generally it captures our attention because it apprehends our apprehension. Men *expect* phallic power and privilege; hardly anything in the current organization of culture discourages this sense of entitlement. But, as Jacqueline Rose observes, "the phallus can only take up its place by indicating the precariousness of any identity assumed by the subject on the basis of its token."[47] Kaja Silverman likewise describes the "masculine sexual organ as the signifier of a fictive wholeness" which "frees the male subject from the necessity to confront his own 'nothingness.' "[48]

From the psychoanalytic viewpoint, castration subtends all mastery. The phallus's promise of absolute substantiality is always giving way to its radical unattainability. In its relation to the phenomenological experience of futurity, as in its function in the imagined (but no less lived and effective) experience of a present and potent male corporeality, the phallus reveals itself as a hole atop a pole, a tunnel at the end of the light. The expectations of men, their demands and illusions predicated on the rights of men, arise out of an anxiety from which emerge, in turn, not only their achievements but also their disappointment, their rage, their multiform acts of violence and self-destruction.

MASTERING CASTRATION

Violence and self-destruction are the hallmarks of Althusser's *The Future Lasts Forever*, published in France in 1992, two years after Althusser's death. In this account of his experiences from his childhood in Algeria, where he was born in 1918, through the late 1980s, Althusser sets out to lay bare the conditions of possibility for his achievement of mastery in his career as a philosopher as well as for his cataclysmic loss of control in his personal life, and he does so by taking into account, to a degree unprecedented in his other works, the human body. The writer's own body, celebrated and reviled, figures in Althusser's narrative in ways that both extend and put into question the above discussion of the phallus, ideology, and futurity, offering significant insights into the configuration of history, mastery, and the experience of masculine corporeality.

Taking its place in the long history of narratives that foreground male potential and male anxieties at the often drastic expense of women's bodies, empowerment, and becoming, *The Future Lasts Forever* tells a story of masculine *Bildung* that turns upon the destruction of a woman: Hélène Legotien, whom Althusser strangled in November 1980. Declared unfit to plead, he was hospitalized for three years and spent the remainder of his life in relative seclusion in a Paris apartment. While it is of paramount importance not to overlook the role of mental illness in Althusser's life and in the murder of his wife, it is difficult to exclude the category of gender difference from our view of the violent course his illness takes. Althusser's description of his own fears following the murder reinforce such a perspective: at the sanitarium, he tells us, "I had looked in terror at the base of a woman friend's neck and asked myself in a state of anguish: what if I were to do it all over again (strangle a woman)?"[49] What can his story tell us about the potentialities of the male body that we don't already know all too well?

Althusser's long experience as an analyst and his acquaintance with psychoanalytic theory—Lacanian and otherwise—introduce an obvious hermeneutic problem into a reading of *The Future Lasts Forever* that seeks to uncover and problematize the concept of the phallus. Despite his assertion that he has no "intention of engaging in 'self-analysis' " (47), Althusser, having mastered the interpretive frameworks of psychoanalysis, delivers a life story in which the shaping force of those frameworks is almost always evident. Amidst all the accumulated and carefully constructed "evidence" confirming the validity of psychoanalytic models, however, it is possible to find in *The Future Lasts Forever* a perspective on the body that, while it is only tentatively articulated, counters the phallus and suggests the limitations of the psychoanalytic version of the body's story.

The characters of Althusser's Oedipal drama are perfectly cast. His distant and brutal father, Charles Althusser, "never once intervened in my life to steer me in any particular direction, nor did he reveal anything of his own life which might have given me some idea about self-defense, schoolboy fights, and, later on, about virility" (49). His mother, Lucienne, is depicted as a sexually repressed, intensely phobic hypochondriac whose fear led her to excessively supervise her children's activities. The writer's early memory of bathing with his sister Georgette binds sexual hierarchies to genitality and reinforces the image of an obsessive, controlling, intrusive mother: "I can still hear my mother saying, 'Do you see, your sister is a delicate creature and much more exposed to germs than a boy'—and showing me to make her point she went on: 'You've got only *two holes,* but *she has got three*' " (50).

An added dimension to this cast of characters, one which would seem to highlight the phallus's role in setting the terms of the exchange of desire, is the fact that Lucienne had initially been engaged to Louis, Charles's younger brother, a pilot killed when his plane was shot down over Verdun. That Althusser was named after this dead uncle and prospective father is the source of particular anguish for him. Bearing a dead man's name, the signifier of his mother's frustrated hopes, he projects and realizes his future in terms of the fulfillment of another's desire: "I sought to win my mother's affection," Althusser writes, "in order that I might become the person she loved, who was for ever beyond me and sanctified by death. I *would seduce her by fulfilling her desire*" (56). He explains, "I strove for goodness, purity, virtue, a pure intellect, a disembodied state, academic success, and to crown it all a 'literary' career" (57). His success, he argues relentlessly, is born of seduction and fraud; he attributes his mastery in the world of academics to his capacity to conceive of himself as "the father's father" in relation to other accomplished men—including Marx, "mastering his own thought better than he had done" (222). All these maneuvers seek to shore up his sense of coherency and selfhood by fulfilling the other's desire, "making myself loved in order to exist" (89).

One of the text's most classic formulations of phallic anxiety in relation to selfhood and manhood occurs in Althusser's description of his fantasy identification with the image of a victim of the Crusades, killed by a stake that penetrates his anus. He speculates that it is the "dead Louis who was always *behind* me" who is penetrating and destroying him (46). Equally classic, and even more revealing of the function of the phallus as a privileged signifier, is his rendition of a scene of "castration." Althusser describes how at thirteen he began experiencing nocturnal emissions: "with considerable satisfaction, I had registered an acute, burning sensation of pleasure at night in my sexual organs, followed by an agreeable feeling of relief" (51). One morning, his mother calls him into his bedroom, pulls back the sheets to reveal the stains, and declares, "Now you are a man, my son!" (51). Althusser is enraged at what he views as an assault on his privacy, "just as if she had looked into my pants or grabbed hold of my penis to show it off (as if it belonged to her)" (51).

We might easily view this scene as an example of interpellation, one which takes into account Althusser's own notion that the subject is "always already" interpellated: Althusser reports being aware that he was having wet dreams, and that these were connected to his maleness and his genitals (see 51); his mother's proclamation inserts this awareness into another register, into the rituals of gender identification that structure and reproduce the family as an ideological state apparatus and that propel the subject into the future as a gendered subject. Lucienne indeed confers upon the pleasures and functions of her son's body a social meaning, but Althusser, casting the scene solely as an invasion, ignores the possibility that his mother might be trying to reassure him. "It was truly a form of rape and castration. I had been raped and castrated by my mother, who felt she had been raped by my father (but that was her affair, not mine.) *Family fate* was indeed inescapable" (51).

Althusser's interpretation of this invasion-by-signification as not only castration but also rape compels us to recognize how Althusser reaps the benefits conferred upon him by the phallus and to view "castration" as itself an ideological formation that produces particular—and, for men, particularly functional—representations of gender difference. Elsewhere *The Future Lasts Forever* is not inattentive to Lucienne's brutalization at the hands of her husband, her extreme isolation and loneliness, or the anxieties that undermine her health, but here Althusser's metaphor of rape does not compare his experience to his mother's own vulnerability so much as it co-opts her suffering, making Lucienne's own fears into a weapon in the defense of male integrity and male rights. Lucienne's pain is rendered hypothetical—she "feels" she has been raped—whereas the rape of the son is presented paradoxically as both metaphorical and *more* real—he knows he has been raped. The phallus, the privileging differential that enables metaphor, permits a reversal that obliterates the position from which Lucienne speaks and experiences her world as a woman in French-controlled Algeria: her fears about her body and her children's bodies, her frustration at maintaining a household, the anxieties brought on by the concatenation of privilege and threat in her life as a colonial subject. As in Althusser's first rape fantasy based on the Crusaders' victim, all historical background, all associations with political and social domination and violence are occluded by the family drama. By the same token, the castration narrative masters even physiology in Althusser's story. In his youth, Althusser suffered from phimosis, the contraction of the opening of the foreskin. While the condition is understandably disturbing to a young man, Althusser views it in terms of his mother's violation, recalling his fear that he did not have "a proper man's penis, and never would; or perhaps something had been removed (by whom)? My mother, of course" (137).

Parallel to such grimly predictable narratives runs another representation of masculine embodiment. As a young adolescent, Althusser discovers in the bodily coordination required by physical exercise—in his case tennis, swimming, and cycling—a way to "distinguish my own techniques visibly and effectively from those of the family, and if not yet to 'have my own thoughts in my own body' at least to take charge of my own body for myself according to my own desires. In this way I began to break free of the rules and norms of the family" (77). Emphasizing distinction and prowess, this is certainly the language of mastery, but does it also include the idea of an alternative course, one that unfolds in a future that is not fully subsumed by "the destiny of the family," by patriarchal hegemony?

My interest here, as throughout this essay, is not to seek in male physical activity some kind of liberatory potential which would be unavailable not only to women but also to men who do not or cannot perform such activities. I do, however, want to explore the implications of what Althusser means by "thinking for himself in his body," a formula that resonates throughout *The Future Lasts Forever*. Althusser appears to find in his memories of bodily activity another means of grounding his commitment to materialism: "The discovery that a person could take control of his body and in the process think freely and powerfully, in other words with and in that body; that is to say, the discovery that *the body was capable of thinking* as it realized its full potential really excited me, as it confirmed what I had truly experienced for myself" (219). Ideas are valuable "so long as they break through the stifling layer of ideology and bring me face to face with stark reality, as if I were making actual physical contact with it (yet another modality of the body)" (224).[50] Although Althusser's emphasis on thought discovered in and articulated through the body's contact with the physical world is not free of the Oedipal signature—physical labor, he writes, "determined the course of my life and enabled me to discover my own true desire rather than that of my mother" (214)—at least two moments in the text provide indicators of a kind of corporeal knowledge and practice that might counter phallic privilege and other ideologies of castration.

The first is a memory of adolescence. During a camping trip in the Alps with his scout troop, Althusser experiences his first bout of depression following an argument with a member of his patrol. He and his close friend Paul de Gaudemar, who has a stomachache, are taken to a nearby barn in which they spend the night, "tenderly entwined in our mutual anguish and crying over our fate. I remember very clearly having an erection as we hugged each other; that was all that happened but the unexpected erection was a most pleasurable experience" (84). In a later episode, Althusser and this same friend set off on a cross-country hiking expedition on which these intimacies occur twice more. In these clearly idyllic scenes of mutual solace and pleasure between men, does Althusser present the image of a male body with an erection but without the phallus? Do these scenes counter the "phallic masculinity" Lawrence R. Schehr views as "a perversion of maleness" which "dismisses a model of pleasure that does not find its anchor in a model of power; it artificially separates sexualities, grosso modo, homo- and hetero-, of the male variety, with no valid reason other than an ideological stricture."[51] They do, I think, but for a very short time, representing an interval within the ongoing interpellation of the boys as masculine subjects, a circumscribed moment of promise in which phallus and futurity are not interlocked. Phallic distinctions return quickly: "One might have thought," Althusser writes, "that I was destined to become a homosexual without my suspecting it, but that was certainly not the case" (85). Intent to assert the heterosexuality of himself and his friend, Althusser almost immediately has Paul fall in love with a girl—a girl the real Paul de Gaudemar would not meet until two years later.[52]

A second example offers a different encounter of the body and the world, one that may also not escape a certain kind of romanticism, but that nonetheless puts forward another kind of promise. At what Althusser characterizes as the moment his readers have been waiting for, he seems to promise an explanation of his provocative and often repeated formulation of the thinking body:

> If, even in the most dramatic dreams and emotional states, the "subject" is concerned essentially with itself, in other words with internal, unconscious objects which analysts refer to as subjective (in contrast with external objects that are objectively real), the legitimate question everyone asks is the following: how could the projections of and investments in these phantasies issue in action and in a body of work (books of philosophy as well as philosophical and political interventions) which were totally objective and had some impact on the real world? (227)

What directly follows in answer to this question is a detailed critical history of the student revolts of May and June 1968 in relation to the labor movement in Paris, the efforts of students to recruit workers to their cause, and the failure of the French Communist Party to seize the moment for revolutionary change. Althusser then offers an extended defense of his decision to remain in the Party, criticizing those who left for sacrificing their chance "of acting *politically,* in other words having some effect on the course of history, which again at the same time meant being involved in struggle within the Party," and upholding his role within the Party as a critical voice and as a representative of those who "wanted, and still want, to think about the day, as yet unknown, when society will be rid of relationships based on the market" (240).[53] It is in collective political activity, Althusser insists, that the body comes to know and to articulate its thought. As Althusser's life history clearly reveals, political action does not necessarily have beneficial, "therapeutic" effects on its individual participants, but that is not its purpose. Insofar as ideological apparatuses produce and condition individual subjects and their destinies, however, it is only by transforming those apparatuses that we make way for new articulations of subjectivity and ameliorate relations among embodied subjects.

"It would be too easy," Althusser writes, "simply to fall back on the things I have expounded at length about the impressive 'roots' and 'structure' of my unconscious 'subjectivity' . . . ." (228). It may well be equally too simplistic to uphold engagement in "progressive politics" as a way out of the (phallic?) divisions that structure our society, enabling some at the expense of others. It is worth noting in this regard that Hélène Legotien is one of the only women Althusser ever mentions as a politically active figure. For all of its limitations, however, Althusser's tentative portrayal of a body that thinks through contact with the social world reconditions the notion of "futurity" I have been elaborating in terms of a resolutely social and collective vision of agency.

THE PRODUCTION OF PROMISE

Early in *The Future Lasts Forever,* Althusser describes a photograph of himself taken in an Algiers park when he was ten years old: "a thin, indolent creature with narrow shoulders which would never be very manly. I had a pallid face, dominated by an over-large forehead, and looked lost as I stood alone on the white path of some huge, empty park. I wasn't a boy at all, but a feeble little girl" (56).[54] Men have a hard time not thinking with the phallus; it is hard for us not to perceive our strength as men in correlation with a weakness we mark as feminine, in ourselves and other men as much as in women. I cannot speak for how women think of the phallus, but it seems to be the case for both sexes, as Butler has observed, that "the boundaries of the body are the lived experience of differentiation, where that differentiation is never neutral to the question of gender difference or the heterosexual matrix."[55] Likewise Grosz insists that "the sex assigned to the body (and bodies are always assigned a single sex, however inappropriate this may be) makes a great deal of difference to the kind of social subject, and indeed the mode of corporeality assigned to the subject."[56] What is striking about Althusser's assessment of his ten-year-old body is that he sees not only its past deficiencies but also its lack of *promise:* those sloped shoulders "would never be very manly." For Althusser, as for many men on the horizon of masculine expectation, "promise" is the legible union of the phallus and futurity in the system of social signs.

If we adhere to the ideal that all human beings have promise or "potential," we must also admit that the promise of any particular individual comes into view only within those social institutions and activities to which individual attributes and capacities are relevant and in which they will (or will not) be realized. Just as a body is visible to us only as a certain *kind* of body—even a body stripped of clothing and displayed against a blank background is defined by the ideological negative space of our constructions of gender, race, age, fitness, health, beauty—so too a "future" is unthinkable outside the historical trajectory and the multiple, overlapping time-frames of a particular social world. Apart from our shared mortality, there is no one future for all of us (unless of course we engage in the many available planetary doomsday scenarios). Nor are futures "unique" to individuals; futurity is stratified by factors that are congruent but not identical with the same factors that render bodies visible as certain kinds of bodies: gender, race, age, health. Significations and real structures founded on gender distinctions, conditioned and held in place by a function I have been calling the "phallus," are certainly among the most powerful of these determining factors in the lives of individuals.

Throughout this essay, the formulation "the future of the phallus" has had at least three valences: (1) the phallus itself is a temporal construction insofar as it is the object of an anticipatory orientation of the subject; (2) the phallus is a function or condition of privileged difference reinforcing the differential positioning of men and women in social space and social time; and (3) the phallus is a theoretical concept with a certain degree of explanatory power that may or may not serve a forward-looking project of cultural reorientation and transformation. Addressing this last consideration, it seems clear that if the phallus really is, as Lacan claims, the condition of possibility for difference that drives signification (and, in turn, gives our libidinal "drives" their cultural meaning), then its domain includes all difference that accrues cultural meaning and psychic investment. For Lacan, the concept of the phallus as a privileged signifier allows for an account of sexuality and relations between the sexes, but to what extent can it account for other differences that shape the experiences of embodied, gendered subjects? What can the concept of the phallus reveal, for example, about the differences among the spaces and times society "gives" to a young man in Paris, in Montreal, in Algiers, or in Honolulu?

When I watch the bikers practicing below my window, I must acknowledge, with Guillaumin, that they are taking advantage of a set of privileges that are, if not denied to young women outright, generally less available to them. I am equally aware, however, that these young men are themselves by no means a homogenous group. Some of them are *haole*—a Hawaiian term that means "foreign" but generally denotes "White" (I know that a few of these are sons of faculty members at the university). The majority of them are "local"—another term with a set of resonances particular to Hawai'i, designating, according to Hawai'i-born literary critic Stephen Sumida, "a racially mixed and charged, class-conscious polyethnicity."[57] Whatever privilege "the phallus" confers upon each of these young men is bound up with a host of considerations: Hawai'i, like the Algeria of Althusser's youth, is a colony of a world power; the courtyard on which the bikers and skateboarders practice their stunts rests on ceded land, the rights to which are contested by a number of Native Hawaiian groups. An energetic movement for Native Hawaiian sovereignty is receiving wide support (as well as hostile opposition) here and abroad. Hawai'i, unlike the mainland United States, did not experience an economic resurgence in the 1990s and continues to languish in a slow economy exacerbated by a downturn in tourism, the decline of the sugar industry, and spectacular mismanagement by state government. The state has an inordinately high rate of unemployment, drug abuse, and suicide among men. Hawai'i's public schools are among the lowest-rated in the country. Many young job-seekers are compelled to leave the islands, a choice that many find painful. In November 1998, over 70 percent of Hawai'i voters passed an amendment to the state constitution that restricts marriage to opposite-sex couples, ending, for the moment, the flexibility of a constitution that had drawn hopeful attention to Hawai'i as a state in which same-sex marriage might receive legal recognition. What it might mean for any of the young men outside my window to "be a man" cannot be fully isolated from the welter of these and other factors. Gendered identity and gendered bodies come into being within spaces and structures that do not always, at first glance, have much to do with gender, but provide the conditions of possibility for the production of gender difference and the future trajectories of differently gendered subjects.

Lacan's theoretical aims led him to abstract the phallus from the male body (but not from male privilege, which, as both his and Althusser's projects amply demonstrate, can also rule in abstraction) and to suggest that it functions as the privileged signifier and the signifier of privilege which shapes the future of the gendered subject. "If the phallus is a privileged signifier," Butler argues, "it gains that privilege through being reiterated. And if the cultural construction of sexuality compels a repetition of that signifier, there is nevertheless in the very force of repetition, understood as a resignification or recirculation, the possibility of depriveleging that signifier."[58] In isolating the dimension of futurity in the presumed function of the phallus in the embodiment of male subjectivity, I have tried to suggest one of the dimensions in which such a reiteration occurs. I can imagine that this particular form of futurity, the anxiety or anticipation of individual men, might serve as a locus for the depriviliging of the phallus, or for what Butler calls an "aggressive reterritorialization"[59] that denaturalizes its connection to the male body and transfers its power to other bodily and cultural positions. However, I believe that the emphasis needs to be shifted further in both directions: back to the body and its practices and ahead to a collective future.

How can men, within and against the regime of the phallus, imagine an alternative future for themselves, an alternative disposition of their bodies within the body of society, an alternative orientation, on the one hand to their own power and privilege as male, and on the other hand to those features of the social terrain that impede or tyrannize the unfolding of personal and collective futures, including the phallus itself as an obstacle within culture to a man's own becoming? Not by indulging in a mysticism of the body as a "vital" component in social transformation, nor by reducing the problem to "getting in touch" with our vulnerabilities or "feminine sides," but by engaging in a struggle against the violence of male privilege. Such an engagement must include an acknowledgment of the mutually constitutive relationship between the pleasures of our male bodies (including the "enjoyment" of rights) and the suffering of other bodies, male and female, within present social formations, including the particular kind of suffering incurred by the foreclosure of the future.

I will conclude with one example of how the intervention of phallic power has impinged upon individual futures. The 1998 amendment to the constitution of the state of Hawai'i closed a loophole in the law that may have allowed for the legal recognition of same-sex marriages in the state. What had been an opening, a horizon of possibility in the codification of social relations, was converted through language into a barricade. I am not simply dicking around with spatial metaphors. The overwhelming victory of the amendment defining marriage exclusively as a union between a man and a woman can be seen as a large-scale version of "Gimme Girls," the dismissive response of the *Thrasher* editors to their eighth-grade reader's appeal for more gender equity. The referendum was a triumph of patriarchal violence, which took the form, in this case, of homophobia. For those whose rights have been restricted by this legislation, the violence is real. The futures of bodies were at stake in the struggle between the Protect Our Constitution coalition (the group opposing the amendment) and Save Traditional Marriage (advocates of the amendment), not only through the official sanctioning of bodies united in love, but through the official protections afforded to those bodies. For example, in the wake of the amendment, the Hawai'i Public Employees Health Fund has ceased to provide health coverage for unmarried partners of public employees.[60] That those who most enjoy the privileges of patriarchy—"family men," a key constituency relentlessly targeted by both campaigns—failed in this instance to exercise their capacity to extend their rights to others, to facilitate the potential joy of others rather than perpetuate their exclusion and suffering, constitutes a (typical) conjunction of the politics of the phallus and collective ethical impotence.[61]

If men cannot simply do away with the phallus—or, since the phallus has always already been done away with, if we cannot completely divest ourselves of the myth of castration and our inexorable wanting—how can that wanting be turned from reaction and violence into a productive practice, or, as Althusser put it, into a manner "of acting *politically*, in other words having some effect on the course of history?" How can it inform a practical attitude? For it is certainly a matter of "attitude," if we take attitude in all its possible dimensions: a mental outlook, a disposition, an orientation, and a commitment of the mind and the body to the future. Another way to pose the question of the future of the phallus is, How, under what social conditions of possibility, can a man make good the promise of his body and ensure, at the same time, that the future of the phallus does not last forever?

NOTES

I wish to thank my colleagues Cynthia Franklin, Michael Hayes, Laura Lyons, Joseph Tobin, and Christine Yano for their helpful comments throughout the development of this essay.

1. My description here of the university and campus security as "state apparatuses" draws, of course, upon Louis Althusser's influential article "Ideology and Ideological State Apparatuses (Notes towards an Investigation)," in *Lenin and Philosophy*, trans. Ben Brewster (New York: Monthly Review Press, 1971). The utility of Althusser's model of the interpellation of subjects, which is also developed in his essay on the "ISAs," for an understanding of the relationships among futurity, mastery, and male corporeality will be central to the discussion that follows.

2. Seth Hahn, letter to the editor, *Thrasher* 211 (August 1998): 10.

3. Editorial response to Seth Hahn, *Thrasher* 211 (August 1998): 10.

4. Elizabeth Grosz, *Jacques Lacan: A Feminist Introduction* (New York: Routledge, 1990), 124.

5. "We are saying that time *is* someone, or that temporal dimensions, in so far as they perpetually overlap, bear each other out and ever confine themselves to making explicit what was implied in each, being collectively expressive of that one single explosion or thrust which is subjectivity itself. We must understand time as the subject and the subject as time." Maurice Merleau-Ponty, *Phenomenology of Perception*, trans. Colin Smith (New York: Routledge & Kegan Paul, 1974), 422.

6. Colette Guillaumin, "The Constructed Body," in *Reading the Social Body*, ed. Catherine B. Burroughs and Jeffrey David Ehrenreich (Iowa City: University of Iowa Press, 1993), 41.

7. Ibid., 47.

8. Ibid., 48.

9. Ibid., 57.

10. Elisabeth Roudinesco's critical biography *Jacques Lacan*, trans. Barbara Bray

(New York: Columbia University, 1997), provides an excellent introduction to La-can's work and the controversies surrounding it. Roudinesco's more general history of psychoanalysis in France, *Jacques Lacan & Co.: A History of Psychoanalysis in France, 1925–1985,* trans. Jeffrey Mehlman (Chicago: University of Chicago, 1990), is orga-nized around Lacan's activities. David Macey's study *Lacan in Contexts* (London: Verso, 1988) situates Lacan within the intellectual developments of his time. An exceptionally clear and critically engaged analysis of Lacan's contribution can be found in Grosz's *Jacques Lacan: A Feminist Introduction.*

11. Lacan, *Écrits: A Selection,* trans. Alan Sheridan (New York: Norton, 1977), 281.

12. See Sigmund Freud, "New Introductory Lectures on Psychoanalysis," in *The Complete Works of Sigmund Freud,* vol. 22, trans. and ed. James Strachey (London: Hogarth Press, 1933), 126, 130.

13. See Lacan, *Écrits,* 289–291. The concluding paragraphs of "The Significa-tion of the Phallus" suggest how this model plays itself out in actual social relations among men and women.

14. Ferdinand de Saussure, *Course in General Linguistics,* ed. Charles Bally and Albert Sechehaye, trans. Wade Baskin (New York: McGraw-Hill, 1966), 65–70.

15. Lacan, *Écrits,* 282.

16. Ibid., 148.

17. Ibid., 287.

18. Luce Irigaray's work, for example, represents an effort to produce an ac-count of women's sexuality that is not predicated upon the phallus; see *This Sex Which Is Not One,* trans. Catherine Porter (Ithaca: Cornell University Press, 1985), and *Speculum of the Other Woman,* trans. Gillian C. Gill (Ithaca: Cornell University Press, 1985). In *Lacan in Contexts,* Macey offers both a genealogy and a critique of the concept of the phallus in Lacan's thought (183–192). Grosz, in *Jacques Lacan: A Feminist Introduction,* assesses the viability of Lacanian psychoanalysis for projects seeking to transform prevailing cultural formations and organizations of sexuality, sexual relations, and gender. While she recognizes that Lacan's transposition of Freud's biological categories into the domain of signification opens up the possibil-ity of historical analyses and, potentially, transformative rereadings and reposition-ing, Grosz also views Lacan's thought as "committed to an a priori privilege of the masculine that is difficult, if not impossible, to dislodge" (123). Likewise Jane Gal-lop, in *Reading Lacan* (Ithaca: Cornell University Press, 1985) remarks that "the phallic signifier serves well as an emblem of the confusion between phallus and male which inheres in language, in our symbolic order" (140). Several contribu-tions to *Differences* 4, no. 1 (1992) advance insightful challenges to the concept of the phallus, in particular Kaja Silverman's "The Lacanian Phallus" (84–115) and Charles Bernheimer's "Penile Reference in Phallic Theory" (116–132), in which Bernheimer diagnoses the concept as "a dream of perpetual erection and symbolic potency" (130).

19. Lacan, *Écrits,* 287.

20. Ibid.

21. Ibid., 289.

22. The temporal dimensions of subjectivity are by no means ignored in Lacan-ian psychoanalysis. As I note in my discussion of interpellation in the next section, Lacan describes the formation of the child's sense of an "I" in the "mirror stage" as a process founded on anticipation. In *Bodies That Matter: On the Discursive Limits of "Sex"* (New York: Routledge, 1993), Judith Butler gives an account of the ego in Lacanian theory that takes up its temporality and, in particular, its orientation to the future: "The ego is formed around the specular image of the body itself, but this specular image is itself an anticipation, a subjunctive delineation. The ego is

first and foremost an object which cannot coincide temporally with the subject, a temporal *ek-stasis;* the ego's temporal futurity, and its exteriority as a *percipi,* establish its alterity to the subject" (75).

23. "As a signifier," Grosz explains, "the phallus is not an object to be acquired or an identity to be achieved. It is only through the desire of the other that one's position—as either being or having—the phallus is possible" (*Jacques Lacan,* 125).

24. Ibid., 121.

25. Grosz, "Space, Time, and Bodies," in *Space, Time and Perversion: Essays on the Politics of Bodies* (New York: Routledge, 1995), 100. I will not be addressing large-scale temporal frameworks such as those Julia Kristeva discusses in "Women's Time," in *Feminist Theory: A Critique of Ideology,* ed. Nannerl O. Keohane (Chicago: University of Chicago Press, 1981), where she argues that "female subjectivity" participates in a temporality of a form different from "time as project, teleology, linear and prospective unfolding: time as departure, progression, and arrival—in other words, the time of history" (35). My concern here is with how the body feels time and how men "feel the phallus" in relation to time.

26. Reinhart Koselleck, *Futures Past: On the Semantics of Historical Time,* trans. Keith Tribe (Cambridge, Mass.: MIT Press, 1985), 272.

27. "Propos sur la causalité psychique," in Jacques Lacan, *Écrits* (Paris: Éditions du Seuil, 1966), 179.

28. Grosz, *Jacques Lacan,* 118.

29. In this context, one should note the irony that one of the possible side effects of Propecia, a drug used to treat hair loss, is decreased sex drive. Physical exercise also has its ironies in relation to futurity and gender identification. I used to lift weights with a man who was disdainful of the efforts of serious bodybuilders to develop large pectoral muscles, because, as he said, "when they get old they'll have to wear a bra."

30. Kenneth R. Dutton argues, "Any man who looks in a mirror and concludes that he looks too skinny or out of condition, not to mention the man who undertakes an occasional light work-out just to 'firm up', is acknowledging—even if subconsciously—the possibility of a more highly developed appearance with which his present appearance is compared" (*The Perfectible Body: The Western Ideal of Male Physical Development* [New York: Continuum, 1995], 196).

31. In *Mourning Sex: Performing Public Memories* (New York: Routledge, 1997), Peggy Phelan discusses the "inverted penetration" depicted in Robert Mapplethorpe's photograph *Lou,* in which the nude male model inserts a finger into his urethra (37–39).

32. Grosz's useful schematic list of the features of the phallus in Lacanian discourse points in several instances to an orienting function: it is, for example, "a mark or badge of social position" and "represents the name of the father, through which the subject is positioned in culture" (*Jacques Lacan,* 125–126).

33. Guillaumin, "The Constructed Body," 47.

34. Althusser, *Lenin and Philosophy,* 181.

35. The major texts in Althusser's oeuvre are *For Marx,* trans. Ben Brewster (New York: Pantheon, 1969), and *Reading Capital,* which he co-authored with Etienne Balibar, trans. Ben Brewster (London: Verso, 1969). Gregory Elliott undertakes a critical analysis of Althusser's contribution in *Althusser: The Detour of Theory* (London: Verso, 1987). Yann Moulier Boutang's biography, *Louis Althusser: Une biographie,* vol. 1 (Paris: Grasset, 1992) offers many insights into Althusser's life and work.

36. Althusser, *Lenin and Philosophy,* 167.

37. The circularity of Althusser's formulation has drawn sharp criticism not only because it leaves little space for resistant agency on the part of the subject, but also

because it cannot fully account for the entry of the human subject into its system. Michèle Barrett addresses the utility of Althusser's theory for a gender-based analysis of society in "Althusser's Marx, Althusser's Lacan," in *The Althusserian Legacy,* ed. E. Ann Kaplan and Michael Sprinker (London: Verso, 1993), 169–182.

38. Althusser, *Lenin and Philosophy,* 206.

39. Ibid., 178

40. Ibid., 174–175.

41. See ibid., 122.

42. Lacan, *Écrits,* 4.

43. Ibid. Lacan describes the mirror stage as an event in which "the child anticipates on the mental plane the conquest of the functional unity of his own body, which, at that stage, is still incomplete on the plane of voluntary motility" (*Écrits,* 18). See also *The Seminar of Jacques Lacan: Book I—Freud's Papers on Technique,* trans. John Forrester (New York: Norton, 1988), in which Lacan describes the mirror stage as the occurrence, "for the first time, [of] the anticipated seizure of mastery" (146). For Lacan, anticipation remains a principal orientation of the subject in temporality; see, for example, "Le temps logique et l'assertion de certitude anticipée," *Écrits,* French edition, 209–211.

44. Althusser, *Lenin and Philosophy,* 167.

45. Ibid., 174.

46. Althusser, *For Marx,* 234.

47. Jacqueline Rose, "Introduction—II," in *Feminine Sexuality: Jacques Lacan and the École freudienne,* ed. Juliet Mitchell and Jacqueline Rose, trans. Jacqueline Rose (New York: Norton, 1982), 40.

48. Silverman, "The Lacanian Phallus," 113.

49. Louis Althusser, *The Future Lasts Forever: A Memoir,* ed. Olivier Corpet and Yann Moulier Boutang, trans. Richard Veasey (New York: New Press), 271. Hereafter citations from this volume will be indicated in the text by page number. Unless otherwise noted, all emphases in the quoted passages are in the original.

50. One of Althusser's principal sources for the idea of the inextricability of thought and body is Spinoza's *Ethics,* in which he discovers "the body as *potentia,* both as a force *(fortitudo)* and as an opening on to the world *(generositas),* a disinterested gift" (*The Future Lasts Forever,* 218). Warren Montag discusses the importance of Spinoza for Althusser's thought in "Spinoza and Althusser against Hermeneutics: Interpretation or Intervention?" in *The Althusserian Legacy,* ed. E. Ann Kaplan and Michael Sprinker (London: Verso, 1993), 51–58. A description of Spinoza's concept of "conatus" that is useful for an understanding of Spinoza's influence on Althusser can be found in Sylvain Zac, "The Relation between Life, Conatus, and Virtue in Spinoza's Philosophy," *Graduate Faculty Philosophy Journal* 19, no. 1 (1996): 151–173.

51. Lawrence R. Schehr, *Parts of an Andrology: On Representations of Men's Bodies* (Stanford: Stanford University Press, 1997), 27.

52. See Boutang, *Louis Althusser,* 81.

53. Gregory Elliott presents a cogent history of Althusser's involvement in the PCF in *Althusser: The Detour of Theory,* 187–244.

54. The photograph is reproduced on page I of the illustrations in Boutang, *Louis Althusser.*

55. Butler, *Bodies That Matter,* 65.

56. Elizabeth Grosz, "Space, Time, and Bodies," 84.

57. Stephen Sumida, "Sense of Place, History, and the Concept of the 'Local' in Hawai'i's Asian/Pacific Literatures," in *Reading the Literature of Asian America,* ed. Shirley Lum and Amy Ling (Philadelphia: Temple University Press, 1992), 216.

58. Butler, *Bodies That Matter,* 89.

59. Ibid., 86.

60. See Kevin Dayton, "Unwed Partners Losing Benefits," *The Honolulu Advertiser,* 20 June 1999, A1.

61. I am indebted to Alison Regan and Amy Sawyer, key organizers of the Protect Our Constitution coalition, for many enlightening discussions throughout the campaign.

Part 2. Masculine Myths and Male Bodies

Chapter 4

Eating Muscle

Material-Semiotics and a Manly Appetite

PATRICK MCGANN

> And now
> I taste it again.
> The meat of memory.
> The meat of no change.
> I raise my fork in praise,
> and I eat.
> —from Mark Strand's "Pot Roast"

Meat, football, and Texas still live somewhere inside my body, conjoined, impossible to render entirely separate from one another, or from me, even though I have eaten vegetarian for nine years, lived elsewhere for twelve. Residues of Texas ethos—Cowboys, Longhorns, pickups, country music, leather, smoked ribs, barbecue, chili, big appetites—call up the meat of memory.

Downtown Lubbock, Texas, was mostly an empty shell of its former self in the early 1980s, the economic life of the city having shifted from the center to the southwest side and the South Plains Mall. The only reason I traveled downtown was Chandlers and chicken-fried steak, an often misunderstood meat. Billy Clyde Puckett, a fictional former Texas Christian University (TCU) football legend and retired all-pro New York Giant immortal, explains in *Life Its Ownself* why chicken and steak are joined in one name:

> A chicken-fried steak was a cheap piece of beef that had been tenderized— had the shit beat out of it. Then it was cooked in a batter like fried chicken. . . . The chicken-fried steak was invented in 1911 in Lamesa, Texas by a man named Jimmy Don Perkins. He was cooking in a café and got his orders mixed up. They can talk about Davy Crockett all they want to. Jimmy Don Perkins is my hero.[1]

Although I have never claimed Perkins as a personal hero, I did take personal delight in lunch at Chandlers, a long rectangular room with worn booths of dull maroon vinyl lined up along one wall. I always went with my partner, who introduced me to the restaurant, the two of us the youngest patrons. For a little over three dollars, a lunch order of chicken-fried steak consisted of one-and-a-half pieces of meat, a pile of french fries, a Texas-size roll, and an iceberg lettuce salad, all of it slathered with cream gravy—even the lettuce. I loved the low price, the large portions, the sheer West Texas bounty of it all, and saved the roll to sop up every smear of gravy, leaving me satisfied, glutted, happy.

At forty-three, fifteen years after developing Type II diabetes,[2] I still struggle with this residual holdover of meat, football, and Texas, and still desire to eat, if not meat, then as much as I damn well please. But to do so can make me ill: stomach pains, lightheadedness, blurred vision, fatigue, and muscle aches. Diabetes has done more than create symptoms of ill health; it has shaken the foundations of my masculine world, disorienting my perceptions of myself, as is apparent in this journal entry written on June 13, 1984, two days after I had been administered a glucose tolerance test:

> Dr. Smith talked to Mom on Monday, and he suspects I am a borderline diabetic, because my blood sugar shot up to 190 the first blood test, but began to lower after that. . . . It's odd how finding out something like this changes your whole perception of yourself. It makes me seem weak, more vulnerable. I've never really had any major health problems, especially not one that was going to continue for the rest of my life. That's what's odd about it I suppose: it's something that will never correct itself, something that won't heal. 25 yrs. from now I'll still have to make sure my body doesn't take in too much sugar.

I began educating myself about diabetes, and learned that managing it involved more than simply avoiding sugary foods. If I were to listen to my body, I would have to transform my eating habits more completely, make larger life changes, and possibly give up chicken-fried steak.

I want to situate this conflicted bodily experience—my customary eating habits affiliated with masculine norms and the chronic illness that demands different norms—within a theory of material-semiotic that opens into profeminist male perspectives and bodies. In such a theory, both the actual and the figurative are "constitutive of lived material-semiotic worlds."[3] In other words, material life, consisting of natural and manufactured objects, and semiotics, consisting of cultural signs and meanings grounded in histories, cultures, and ideologies, are inextricably tangled. I am arguing against a particular view of the postmodern: a theoretical position that asserts we can *only* know the world through "a network of socially established meaning systems, the discourses of our culture,"[4] that assumes language, discourse, semiotics are all-encompassing, and that selves and cultures are formed solely through the powers of textuality. I *am* arguing for a "version of the world as active subject."[5] By this, I mean that both the material and the semiotic participate in the creation of worlds, and I insist that corporeality share in the power of semiotics.

I want to make a further and even stronger claim: agency potentially resides in the interactions between material and semiotic worlds. Because of the easy assumption within the postmodern that we can only know the world through meaning systems, it is also easy to assume a limited directional pattern: semiotics always determining the meanings of bodies, and never bodies determining the meanings of semiotics. As I suggest, however, in the earlier part of this introduction, my body both subsumes hegemonic meanings of masculinity and appetite, and defies those meanings. This corporeal transgression disorients because it disrupts a familiar text. But it also serves as an opportunity for new textual and embodied positionings that exist counter to hegemonic meanings. In other words, the body's disruption allows for the possibility of choice: one can choose to resist meanings that ignore or disregard aspects of bodily experience that transgress and exist outside the normative, and pursue instead different, more accountable, meanings. It is in the choosing that agency resides. As Donna Haraway argues, "The split and contradictory self is the one who can interrogate positionings and be accountable, the one who can construct and join rational conversation and fantastic imaginings that change history."[6] A theory of material-semiotic where conflicted bodies/selves are not only recognized but valued enhances the possibility for continual critical investigation of familiar, hegemonic texts.

This possibility is especially important for men's movements into profeminism. Michael Kaufman proclaims that men's contradictory experiences of power can be the basis for their embrace of feminism.[7] Recognizing masculine contradictions means attending to what might be construed as moments of failure—times when men find themselves incapable of modeling normative masculinity—and recasting these moments by ascribing positive value to them. Developing diabetes, then, became a way for me to open up space for examination and critique of gendered eating habits, as well as an opportunity to explore new textual and embodied positionings.

In what follows I first interrogate representations of male appetite, distinguishing them from female hunger, locating the rhetorical male body, among other places, within the textual world of United States football narratives. I include my own lived experience as it relates to these representations. The latter part of the paper will further develop how my contestatory struggles with diabetes challenged complacent acceptance of male eating habits, allowing me to investigate familiar and new positionings, and ultimately moving me in the direction of feminism.

A MANLY APPETITE

Men's affinity for large portions of food that are male-identified is amply documented in popular culture. If we turn to the newspaper comics, there is Sarge's compulsive junk-food eating in "Beetle Bailey." In a 1997 "Hi and Lois" comic strip by Walker and Browne, the mother, at the sink washing dishes, asks her young daughter if she liked the meal. The daughter answers that everyone did, especially her father because his "button's undone." The last frame of the strip, juxtaposed with the first frame, signifies male-differentiated space: While the mother works at the kitchen sink, the father, having finished his work—consuming the meal—occupies the living or family room. He is shown leaning back in what is most likely a favorite armchair, grinning, eyes closed, his belt undone and pants unsnapped to free his bulging belly. The male body is marked by its pleasure in fullness, and clearly this is normative.

Reversing the positions—the mother in the chair, stomach bulging, pants undone—results in a mis-marking, a transgression of female norms. Denial and restriction are marks of feminine food practices in contemporary United States culture, the ultimate goal being the "slender" body. If "appetite" describes masculine desire and fulfillment, then "hunger" characterizes the opposing feminine condition: appetite fulfills the desire for weight, bulk, substance; hunger the desire for lightness, loss, smoothness. While appetite can be indulged, hunger must be controlled and overcome. Compulsive eating, according to Susan Bordo, is represented as "natural"—even lovable—for the male figure: "Men are *supposed* to have hearty, even voracious appetites. It is a mark of the manly to eat spontaneously and expansively, and manliness is a frequent commercial code for amply portioned products: 'Manwich,' 'Hungry Man Dinners,' 'Manhandlers.' "[8]

Certainly voracious appetites characterize football players in the United States. Gary Shaw writes of his years as a University of Texas Longhorn linebacker during the early to mid-sixties, describing team dinners as "controlled bedlam." He learned that the usual practice was to "stack food high on [a] plate—always more than any two could handle." The Texas Longhorn players ate "aggressively": "It was almost as if you had to show how voracious you could be—as if this was some verification of virility."[9] Voracious appetites apply in pro football as well. Tim Green, defensive end for the Atlanta Falcons for eight years during the 1980s and '90s, admits that "most NFL players eat a lot."[10] He attributes this to the need to maintain or increase body size and strength—an example of the intermingling of the material and semiotic. Because the text of football is in part physical domination, bodies capable of dominating physically must be manufactured. In other words, while we might assume football bodies are simply and irreducibly biological, in fact Green suggests there are also important ways in which they are intentionally constructed through food consumption. "Appetite," in the sense I have been discussing, is learned as a means of forming the dominating male body in U.S. culture. And the way in which the football body is constructed is normative within a material-semiotic:

hegemonic cultural meaning molds the body to serve the interests of masculinity, rather than the body challenging the interests of hegemonic, masculine meaning.

Even though my body in no way fits the physical prototype for football, my restaurant preferences still fall in line with "appetite" needs. I desire food that appeals to me and is served abundantly; if I have to choose between the two, large portions win. In other words, I can eat at the finest restaurant and passionately love the colors and tastes on my plate, but if the portions feel small to me, if when I finish eating a trace of hunger still lingers in the pit of my stomach, I walk away feeling cheated, dissatisfied. Chances are I will eat more once I am home.

"Fullness," in my experience and in late-twentieth-century U.S. hegemonic forms of masculinity, I am proposing, is a major component of male appetite. Such a claim, is, of course, culturally bound, and very much tied to the privilege of U.S. consumerist culture; food consumption in poorer cultures obviously might contrast with consumption in ours, and "appetite" in the poorer segments of our own society might be constructed differently than in middle- and upper-class segments. This caveat applies to the second claim I want to make about men consuming food: another significant component of normative male appetite in late-twentieth-century U.S. culture is male-identified foods. Certain food items are designated as more "filling" than others, and therefore more appropriate for male consumption, although as I have suggested these items vary depending on cultural location. A parody of a middle-class male diet is represented in the "Real Man Food Groups" in Bruce Feirstein's *Real Men Don't Eat Quiche*.[11] Although intended as humor, the list nevertheless captures in exaggerated form male-identified food preferences[12]—especially of a man who can afford to eat fast food frequently. Under the group "Protein," various forms of the hamburger predominate: "Hamburger, Cheeseburger, Bacon-cheeseburger, California burger, Pizza burger, Chili burger, Big Mac, Whopper." Of the five groups—"Protein," "Liquids," "Carbohydrates," "Nourishment," and "Fruit and Vegetables"—the "Protein" group lists the most examples—eleven—while the "Fruit and Vegetables" category has the fewest—two. All the listings under "Protein" involve meat, steak being at the top of the list. Of the two listings under "Fruit and Vegetables," only one is an actual vegetable: corn on the cob; the other is orange soda.

Since, Carol Adams points out, fruits and vegetables, as second-class foods in a patriarchal culture, are more likely to be consumed by women and affiliated with the feminine, the masculine act of denigrating this group is a sexist act.[13] Meat and vegetables function as signifiers which clarify this hegemonic difference: meat, according to the *American Heritage Dictionary*, represents "the essence or principal part of something," while vegetable is defined as "suggesting or like a vegetable, as in passivity or dullness of existence, monotonous, inactive."[14] Thus "meat" has positive associations in such catchphrases as "the meat of the matter," while "vegetable" is used to describe mindless activity, such as "vegging out in front of the tube," or is used to identify a person who is "brain dead" but kept alive through modern technology. The word "fruit" also has hegemonic significations as a derogatory term for gay men, also indirectly denigrating women since it is gay men's identification with the feminine that is a negative marking.

The signifying category of "male-identified foods" is strongly reinforced by the male body's seemingly natural desire for fullness, although as I have made clear, the need for a feeling of fullness is a result of material-semiotics and not solely biological functioning. The fullness seems biological because of its immediacy and felt sense in the body. But culturally sanctioned ways of achieving and understanding fullness are gender coded. If the "social control of female hunger operates as a practical 'discipline' . . . that trains female bodies in the knowledge of their limits and restraints,"[15] then the social affirmation of male appetite operates as a signifying practice that educates male bodies in the knowledge of their freedoms and privileges. Fullness is a sign of male entitlement.

No other food represents this entitlement more than meat, *the* signifier of all male-identified food signifiers. The belief that a meat-free diet results in a weak and ineffective body is still deeply embedded in U.S. culture. My youth in Texas was perpetually meat-centered. The most renowned genre of restaurant was the steak house, some of which presented an ongoing challenge to patrons (implicitly understood to be directed to men): eat a sixty-four-ounce steak in less than half an hour and receive your meal free. An upright freezer, always filled with a side of beef, stood in a corner of our garage, the individual pieces wrapped in white paper, stamped words identifying the different cuts. I grew up eating steaks, hamburgers, pork chops, pot roast, meatloaf, shit-on-a-shingle, hot dogs, bologna, sausage, with never a meatless meal unless it was breakfast, which I rarely ate. As a young man I drove to Pinkies, a liquor store outside the city limits, to buy their barbecue sandwiches; stood around the grill in my father's back yard, drinking beer and watching over the meat; attended goat roasts where the meat had been buried and roasting for days, the pieces so tender they simply fell away from the bones. Sometimes I amazed my family by eating over half a package of hot dogs. One or two bologna sandwiches and chips were the staples of my sack lunches from seventh grade though twelfth.

The centrality of meat and its gendered meanings become readily apparent in an examination of the world of football, one of the United States' most male-identified blood sports. In football narratives steak often functions not only as the principal course of any meal—even breakfast—but also as a gift and award. Gary Shaw found that he had to be quick to get any meat since the platters with three different meat selections were always the first to empty at Longhorn team meals.[16] At Syracuse University in the early 1960s, Dave Meggyesy, a defensive tackle, writes that the pre-game breakfast tradition consisted of "orange juice, steak, scrambled eggs, tea and toast." He speculates that the coaches insisted "on a high protein meal capped off with a semi-raw steak" because of the assumption "that tearing into a piece of bloody meat gets a player in the right frame of mind for hitting."[17] Tim Green claims that eating steaks before game time was an NFL practice in the 1950s and '60s, before knowledge of nutrition challenged such eating habits; but he acknowledges that "that old notion of an athlete getting strength from meat has died hard. The only way a team won't have some guys eating steaks before a game is not to have them available."[18]

Green also provides an example of steak being used to reward players for wreaking brutal carnage in a game. The coach for the Atlanta Falcons' special teams during the 1980s and '90s was Keith Rowan, who, during a punt team meeting, showed a video clip of Rambo launching an explosive arrow that kills a North Vietnamese officer. He then yelled that they were "going to blow them [the opposing team] up! . . . We'll throw our bodies around and blow people up!" One of Rowan's standard practices was to reward the special teams athlete who played most savagely with the "Big Meat" award—dinner at a steak house.[19] Billy Clyde Puckett, the protagonist of the novel *Life Its Ownself*, cites numerous examples of high school football players being wooed by colleges, including the story of Dump McKinney, who every week during his senior year would "find a parcel of twelve prime New York strips on his doorstep. They were the gift of an anonymous University of Florida fan who hoped Dump would transport his gifted arm to Gainesville."[20]

The power and appeal of steak extends to football supporters as well as players. In Odessa, Texas, at Permian High School, where up to twenty thousand fans might attend a football game, coaches and the booster club board attended the annual steak feed, where they "sat at long tables inside a warehouse and ate delicious slabs of rib eye as thick as the Bible."[21] Meat dominates a recent *Washington Post* article by Roxanne Roberts on tailgate parties before the debut of the Washington Redskins at the new Jack Kent Cooke Stadium. The article names a plethora of grilled meats: New York strip steaks, marinated chicken, gourmet jerk chicken, gourmet beef half-smoke, hamburgers, hot dogs, Italian sausages. When Roberts, following the lead of a French chef in Louisville, suggests that the tailgaters fix healthier food—a portobello mushroom sandwich and tomato salsa, for instance—the idea was met with "polite guffaws." The dictum is: "Anything goes, as long as it's grilled meat."[22] Grilling, the single form of home food preparation which is male-identified, maintains contemporary men's sense of connection with the domination over the animal, and distances them from the kitchen, a female domain.

Football is linked to the patriarchal values Carol Adams claims are expressed through the killing of animals and eating of meat: "ferociousness, territorial imperative, armed hunting, aggressive behavior, . . . vitality and virility."[23] All of these values—with the exception of armed hunting—can readily describe football imperatives. Steak, the bloodiest of meats, holds special status in football because it "most strikingly represents the brute power of nature, undiminished by acculturation."[24] Consuming it represents no less than the equation of meat with power: men eating muscle to become muscular.

DIABETES AND UNRULINESS

The regulatory masculine practices affiliated with meat and meals are hegemonic but not foundational. As Judith Butler argues, "the possibility of multiple identifications (which are not finally reducible to primary or founding identifications that are fixed within masculine and feminine positions) suggests that the law is not deterministic and that the law may not even be singular."[25] In other words, hegemony is always contested by unruliness: feelings, theories, and experiences that exist in contradistinction to the law. If the law is to persist, the unruliness must be subdued by reducing it to "otherness" or by somehow incorporating it within the boundaries of hegemonic discourse to control the disorder and maintain regulatory fictions.

All I have written about in the previous section is subject to contestation. While the dominant image of a football player, for instance, is one of overwhelming physical, animal-like power, the image can, on occasion, turn unruly. The cover of the paperback edition of Shaw's *Meat on the Hoof* is a photograph of a football player from one shoulder to the waist, his arm cradling a dirt-stained helmet, a stamp on the muscle just below the shoulder pad saying, "Inspected by *NCAA*," like the inspection stamp on a side of beef. Green, when he writes about the combines—an opportunity for NFL coaches and scouts to have the physical status and capabilities of potential draftees carefully examined—uses meat imagery pejoratively. He compares the weighing and measuring of athletes to "the cold efficiency of a slaughterhouse," the men recording your statistics "handling you like a quartered slab on a hook."[26] After a morning of agility drills, you "are mercifully loaded up with the other players onto a bus instead of a cattle truck and transported to a local hospital that has the necessary gizmos to further scrutinize what you once thought was your own body."[27] These examples represent a shift in positioning, from the male body *incorporating* meat, which signifies power and strength, to the male body *as* meat, signifying an object to be used and consumed. In the first position, the male is the controller, in the second he is the controlled. He becomes distanced from his body. There is no better illustration of this than the experience of playing injured; the stories are legion of college and pro football athletes staying in games with broken ribs, fingers, sprained ankles and knees, concussions, and back injuries, and when they are ill. They do so for numerous reasons: because they are fierce competitors, or because the coaches expect it, or because they are constantly uncertain about their position on the team. According to Green, "In order to have any kind of lasting career [in the NFL] by taking a job from one of the older guys and fending off the younger guys behind you, you have to play hurt." Someone will take your job if "you prove to the team that 'you cannot be relied on week after week.' (That's code for playing with pain.)"[28]

This contestatory representation—football player as a "quartered slab on a hook"—potentially moves the male body closer to one of the positions occupied by the female body. Fiddes claims that "women are meat in the sense that it [meat] is consumed as a statement of power."[29] Adams makes a connection between women being raped and the slaughterhouse: "Just as the slaughterhouse treats animals and its workers as inert, unthinking, unfeeling objects, so too in rape are women treated as inert objects, with no attention paid to their feelings or needs. Consequently, they feel like pieces of meat."[30] While I am in some sense equating the male body in football with the female body in rape, there are of course significant and important differences: rape yields no sense of power for women, and in fact is intended to do just the opposite, while football clearly privileges men. The economic rewards, the adulation, the special treatment, all serve to subdue bodily disruptions, making pain "just a part of football." The ability to endure pain becomes a badge of privilege.

Again, I by no means want to suggest that the two experiences—football and rape—are equivalent; but I do want to suggest that there are possible contestatory connections, that the imagery of the football player as a slab of meat might help men to begin to understand why a person who is raped might feel like a slab of meat. The same applies to issues of weight in the NFL. While the normative cultural perception of a football player's appetite is the consumption of large amounts of food, this proves not to be the case for those considered overweight. Green explains that there is a "bounty on bellies" in the NFL; weight limits are set by coaches and players are fined fifty to a hundred dollars weekly for every pound of excess. Strategies for dealing with the extra weight include dieting "like middle-aged housewives, counting calories and using diuretics," as well as wearing a rubber suit during practice, riding an exercise bike, sitting in the sauna, and spitting into little paper cups to eliminate water weight the day before they have to step on the scale.[31]

My experience with diabetes is in some ways similar to that of overweight football players. Although I only played organized (flag) football in seventh grade, and have always been slim (presently 5'10" and 150 lb.), after I developed diabetes at the age of twenty-eight, I went from eating whatever and however much I wanted to a much more restricted diet. Once diagnosed by the doctor, I was told to stay away from sugary foods; but after a few weeks of doing so, I was still caught in blood sugar swings, though not as severe. During this time my journal indicates that for reasons I am unable to recall, I was increasing my intake of protein: "I've been avoiding sugar, and loading up on protein: peanuts, beans, meat, but I don't know whether it's doing any good since I still don't feel quite right. I feel better than I did, but I still don't have much energy, or at least not enough energy." In several entries I complain about exhaustion, sluggishness, my head feeling fucked-up.

Three weeks later, after reading a number of books about controlling diabetes, my eating habits had begun to change more dramatically. As is clear from another journal excerpt, foods that I had initially "loaded up on"—peanuts, for example—I now found problematic:

> Some foods that I think up my blood sugar:
> white bread
> noodles
> milk? (yes, there's sugar in whole milk)
> fruit juice
> things with honey instead of sugar (cookies, ice cream)
> any fatty foods: cheese, peanuts, etc.

The most recent scientific thinking, I learned, about Type II diabetes (and to some extent Type I), prescribed both a diet rich in complex carbohydrates (vegetables, fruit, legumes, grains) because they break down into sugar more slowly and evenly than simple carbohydrates (sugar); and a diet low in fatty foods, since high caloric content can overwhelm the Type II body's capabilities of converting and using blood sugar.

As a hot dog, french fry, and bologna man, I was dismayed. Initially overwhelmed by the prospect of losing all my familiar foods, I wandered around the kitchen in a state of dazed confusion, until I was gently guided in the direction of cookbooks by my partner (we had been together a year). Her collection was wide and eclectic, consisting of the conventional (*The Fanny Farmer Cookbook*), and also the unconventional, such as *Recipes for a Small Planet*, written during the movement in the late 1960s and early '70s to link the global politics of hunger with issues of diet and food availability.[32]

I began to embrace a new food practice, based more on whole foods and less on tossing hot dogs into boiling water, as is once again expressed in my journal:

> August 14, 1984, Saturday
> A year ago if anyone had told me I'd be writing down recipes I would have
> told them they were crazy. Now I think about cooking constantly, because I

love to eat good food; it makes me feel good about myself, amazingly good; and the surprising thing is that it all tastes good.

Not only had my tastes in food begun to change, but also my tastes of food. I noticed for the first time that slight edge of sugar sweetness added to lunch meats and barbecue potato chips, and I started to appreciate more fully the tangs and subtle savor of fruits and vegetables.

These changes in diet and taste were made at the urgings of my body, suggesting a material-semiotic not bound by iron-clad determinism, yet never free of discourse. Judith Butler explains how this is so: "Always already a cultural sign, the body sets limits to the imaginary meanings that it occasions, but is never free of an imaginary construction."[33] Diabetes became for me both a challenge to hegemonic forms of masculine eating—a contestatory site allowing for new movement, new understandings and connections—and a continual battle to maintain the familiar.

Either way—clinging to old meanings and practices or moving toward new—contestation is initiated by the threat of lost meaning. The chronic part of diabetes meant there was no end to it; I would never be the same as I was pre-diabetes. My body became a threat to my sense of masculine self:

> July 8, 1984, Sunday
> I feel like I'm floundering; I've lost some measure of confidence along the way, and I can't figure out why. Maybe it's because I've finally found myself in situations that I'm not sure I can entirely handle, because I've seen myself as much more fragile than I ever previously imagined, because things around me are changing so quickly that I feel I can't get a grasp on them. I'm not as strong as I thought I was, which certainly puts a huge dent in my self-image. I feel like I need to be taken care of for a while, but that's just not feasible.

Although diabetes and my sense of masculinity in the above passage are invisible referents, they occupy the interstices between the words, and are undeniable hidden presences. If physical strength, competence, and endurance qualify as hegemonic masculine qualities in U.S. culture, then my diabetes and newfound physical vulnerability rendered me inadequate as a male. If control over surroundings and emotions are typical male characteristics, then my confusion and inability to master either my feelings or my circumstances meant I was failing in the masculine arena. For me, the usual meanings of manhood had been turned upside-down.

Loss of meaning, although disorienting and distressing, is important in the creation of new imaginary and embodied spaces. And these spaces become both cultural and personal; newness is neither natural nor constructed in isolation. Agency resides not in the individual's power to create and impose new meaning on cultures, but in the power to choose among already existing or possible cultures and add to them.

Developing diabetes moved me closer to the hegemonic feminine: I had to start watching what I ate and how much I ate, hunger became more familiar, and vulnerability became a chronic part of my life. Hegemonic cultures of masculinity disallow any such movement, and if I was to continue with the familiar masculine regulatory texts, I would have to escape or deny my body. But the insistence of material experience—the sluggishness, feeling fucked-up—inclined me toward a more positive semiotic.

Initially, I derived new bodily meaning and practices from diabetic and alternative medicine cultures. While they helped me develop new eating habits that benefited my physical well-being, they helped less in positively re-imagining the issue of vulnerability—perhaps the greatest challenge to my conventional sense of masculinity. I was unable to deny the limitations of my body while struggling with the symptoms of diabetes, yet had no means of constructively understanding and using my physical limitations. Caught in the old meanings of vulnerability—weakness, inadequacy, fragility—as defined by regulatory masculine texts that had themselves become inadequate, I sought out more favorable interpretations. I found them in feminist and men's profeminist cultures, which also became linked with vegetarian cultures. bell hooks captures the essence of my changing attitude: "I believe true resistance begins with people confronting pain, whether it's theirs or somebody else's, and wanting to do something to change it. And it's this pain that so much makes its mark in daily life. Pain as a catalyst for change, for working to change."[34] Whereas vulnerability inscribed within the gendered fields of masculinity connotes weakness and the feminine, within the gendered fields of feminism it intimates a potential for strength and solidarity.

A recognition of hook's perspective from a profeminist male subject position might read something like this: men's denial of and removal from their own emotional and bodily pain results in the denigration of the pain of the other; within the logic of the masculine field, this justifies the other's oppression. Men's awareness and acceptance of their pain, then, can potentially serve as a means to disassemble the hierarchical differential between those who are supposedly "pain-less" and strong, and those who are "pain-full" and weak. Such a perspective recognizes the value of contestatory experience. As Michael Kaufman puts it: "Our awareness of men's contradictory experiences of power gives us the tools to simultaneously challenge men's power and speak to men's pain. It is the basis for a politics of compassion and for enlisting men's support for a revolution [feminism] that is challenging the most basic and long-lasting structures of human civilization."[35] Men's recognition of their pain can lead to the recognition of others' pain, and a desire to change both the individual behavior and the social structures and discourse that result in oppressive suffering. In this movement toward recognition and change exist the strengths of connection and solidarity.

The pain of diabetes became a way into vegetarianism and feminism.[36] Initially I ate more healthily simply to relieve my suffering, but over time a growing awareness and acceptance of my vulnerability resulted in a sense of connection to others' suffering that I had previously overlooked or dismissed. Vegetarianism had seemed a practice of people on the fringes, the counterculture who dressed in sandals, ate tofu, and lived in communes, representing the anti-masculine. I was hardly the type. But in discussions with my partner and with friends, I began to consider the suffering of animals who were raised to be killed and eaten. Although often the talks were philosophically framed (my partner is a feminist philosopher), what influenced me most was not rational argument. Instead, I was swayed by bodily imagining, by shadow experience: the feeling of an imaginary electric jolt to my forehead, like a cow about to be slaughtered.[37] I had gone on a high school field trip to a slaughterhouse, and even though I saw carcasses hanging from hooks, dripping blood, I did not imagine the animal's experience. Now that I was closer to vulnerability, the dividing lines between what Carol Adams calls the "absent referent" and the animal were less resolute: "Through butchering, animals become absent referents. Animals in name and body are made absent *as animals* for meat to exist. Animals' lives precede and enable the existence of meat. If animals are alive they cannot be meat. Thus a dead body replaces the live animal."[38] Meat, through the removal of the head and other body parts, through packaging in Styrofoam and cellophane, loses its connection with the animal it once was and becomes self-contained, free from its relationship with a living being capable of suffering. The transformation of animal into meat began to seem like an act of domination rather than the fulfillment of a biological need, and a growing politics of compassion spurred me to convert to vegetarianism. When I grocery shop now, I move quickly through the meat section or avoid it altogether, because the sight of animal flesh too easily conjures up the animal.

The concept of the "absent referent" eventually transgressed the boundaries of meat and animals, spilling over into feminism and the issue of rape. Earlier in the paper I explained how Adams links the slaughterhouse with sexual violence: in each instance animals and women are objectified, a means to an end, their suffering irrelevant. Comprehension of these parallel trajectories led me in the direction of anti-rape work. I became the Director of Outreach and a speaker for Men Can Stop Rape, a D.C.-based, profeminist, non-profit organization that speaks to high school and college students, challenging them to think of rape as an issue for both women and men. The organization assumes that sexual violence is a choice men make to exert power over others, and that therefore men should play a role in stopping it. We focus on helping young people—especially males—become aware of rape-supporting attitudes and behaviors and develop non-violent strategies for speaking out against them.

I am suggesting that my commitment to feminism and my vegetarianism are woven together. Adams asserts that "men who choose not to eat meat repudiate one of their masculine privileges," and thereby "challenge an essential part of the masculine role."[39] We choose a politics of compassion over domination—a repudiation that moves us closer to feminism. We join female vegetarians in contesting the familiar masculine texts of meat and physical strength, replacing them with the strengths of connection and solidarity. Our bodies and food practices become our unruly ethics.

FOOD, FEMINISM, AND MATERIAL-SEMIOTIC

I would not claim that my change in diet was the singular factor that led me to embrace profeminism. In fact, within the confines of a material-semiotic it is difficult for me to distinguish which led to which—diabetes to vegetarianism and profeminism, or vice versa. Without diabetes as motivation to alter my eating habits, my understanding of feminist issues might have been seriously diminished; on the other hand, without feminism, it seems likely my diet would have been defined solely by the issue of health. It would also be just as accurate to reverse the sequencing: feminism and vegetarianism were a way into diabetes. They offered me positive ways to construct my diabetes that hegemonic forms of masculinity did not.

Nor would I claim that I am done struggling with masculine eating habits. While I have managed to reject the signifying order related to men and meat, I still struggle with the issue of fullness. As a diabetic, it is better for me to eat a light dinner, because a large evening meal will often keep me awake at night. Yet I have been socialized to think of the last meal of the day as the most indulgent. Work is over and I can relax while partaking of the pleasure of food, eating my fill. Much of the time I still desire that heaviness in my belly, and have not yet learned to live gracefully with what feels like hunger. When I do manage to eat a light dinner, frequently I go to bed dreaming of breakfast.

Finally, I would not claim that any man who develops diabetes will become a profeminist vegetarian. Such a declaration would be absurd. While I extended my growing comprehension of the "absent referent" to activist work in Men Can Stop Rape, such work is not a foregone conclusion. A contestatory possibility means nothing in and of itself, as Judith Butler explains: "The task . . . is not to celebrate each and every new possibility *qua* possibility, but to redescribe those possibilities that *already* exist, but which exist within cultural domains designated as culturally unintelligible and impossible."[40] The possibility only becomes meaningful when it is redescribed, its unruliness made newly intelligible. Diabetes, for instance, becomes an opportunity to redescribe the male body and masculine eating habits. And these new descriptions only become intelligible through re-peated exegesis. Even though diabetes served to facilitate my support for feminism, this support would not have developed without repeated exposure to feminist culture and theory through my partner and her friends.

A necessary part of redescribing the unruliness is finding areas of overlap with those who occupy positions outside the hegemonic masculine. Overlap does not suggest, though, that men's experience is in the end the same as women's, or other men's. Difference is an important part of ideological critique, addressing power relations not only between men and women but also among women and among men. There are masculinities, rather than the singular masculinity, as is noted by several men's studies scholars.[41] But if difference is the sole defining factor of critique, then opportunities for cross-linking become obsolete and men's advocacy for feminism increasingly unlikely. Trapped inside hegemonic positions of masculinity, men need ways out. If we assume that all males "experience a range of needs and feelings that are deemed inconsistent with manhood,"[42] then I am claiming that those needs and feelings—those moments of unruliness—can serve as a means of moving men in the direction of non-hegemonic positions. Further, if those inconsistent needs and feelings are often attributed to others, their recognition not only helps to create potential sites of overlap and connection, but also to instigate critique of the inconsistencies.

For example, how do I explain this? I now find the prospect of eating chicken-fried steak at Chandlers, with cream gravy slathered all over the meat, the french fries, and the iceberg lettuce salad, downright unappetizing. Rather than leaving me satisfied, glutted, and happy, I have no doubt that such a meal would make me sick. I can hardly tolerate the thought of it. And yet once upon a time, wild horses couldn't have kept me from eating at Chandlers. I am suggesting this kind of bodily inconsistency represents the possibility for generating change. Such an assumption requires that we think of the male body as much more malleable than we might normally, and think that the masculine penchants for fullness and meat are neither biological nor everlasting regulatory scripts for male appetite. The conflicted body can, if not determine the semiotic, then at least compel the search for different semiotics that potentially challenge normative masculine texts. This potential represents a different kind of bodily power, a different kind of strength from physical domination, and the chance for a non-hegemonic world, a different future.

NOTES

1. Dan Jenkins, *Life Its Ownself* (New York: Signet, 1984), 277–278.
2. Type I diabetes requires insulin shots and usually develops when a person is

a child or teenager. Type II usually develops when a person is older and overweight, and often can be controlled by diet, exercise, and oral medication if needed. I do not fit the prototype for Type II diabetes; I am thin and it developed when I was in my late twenties. Recently I was told I probably have glucose intolerance instead. I am writing as though I have Type II diabetes, however, because that is what I assumed I had for many years; and because the symptoms—if not the cause—of Type II and glucose intolerance are the same.

3. Donna J. Haraway, *Modest_Witness@Second_Millennium.FemaleMan©_Meets OncoMouse™* (New York: Routledge, 1997), 2.

4. Charles Russell, "The Context of the Concept," in *Romanticism, Modernism, Postmodernism,* ed. Harry Garvin (Lewisberg, Pa.: Bucknell University Press, 1980), 183.

5. Donna J. Haraway, *Simians, Cyborgs, and Women: The Reinvention of Nature* (New York: Routledge, 1991), 199.

6. Ibid., 193.

7. Michael Kaufman, "Men, Feminism, and Men's Contradictory Experiences of Power," in *Theorizing Masculinities,* ed. Harry Brod and Michael Kaufman (Thousand Oaks, Calif.: Sage, 1994), 142–163.

8. Susan Bordo, *Unbearable Weight: Feminism, Western Culture, and the Body* (Berkeley: University of California Press, 1993), 108.

9. Gary Shaw, *Meat on the Hoof* (New York: Dell, 1972), 36–37.

10. Tim Green, *The Dark Side of the Game: My Life in the NFL* (New York: Warner, 1996), 194.

11. Bruce Feirstein, *Real Men Don't Eat Quiche* (New York: Pocket Books, 1982), 76–77.

12. See Kim M. Mooney and Erica Lorenz's "The Effects of Food and Gender on Interpersonal Perceptions," *Sex Roles* 36, nos. 9/10 (1997): 639–653, for an example of a sociological study verifying female- and male-identified foods.

13. Carol J. Adams, *The Sexual Politics of Meat: A Feminist-Vegetarian Critical Theory* (New York: Continuum, 1990), 26, 36.

14. Ibid., 36.

15. Bordo, *Unbearable Weight,* 130.

16. Shaw, *Meat on the Hoof,* 36.

17. Dave Meggyesy, *Out of Their League* (New York: Paperback Library, 1971), 53.

18. Green, *Dark Side of the Game,* 196.

19. Ibid., 298.

20. Jenkins, *Life Its Ownself,* 115.

21. H. G. Bissinger, *Friday Night Lights* (New York: Harper Collins, 1990), 180.

22. Roxanne Roberts, "In the Parking Lots, the Grill of It All," *Washington Post,* 15 September 1997, B1+.

23. Adams, *Sexual Politics of Meat,* 189.

24. Nick Fiddes, *Meat: A Natural Symbol* (New York: Routledge, 1991), 90.

25. Judith Butler, *Gender Trouble: Feminism and the Subversion of Identity* (New York: Routledge, 1990), 67.

26. Green, *Dark Side of the Game,* 5, 6.

27. Ibid., 7.

28. Ibid., 95.

29. Fiddes, *Meat,* 154.

30. Adams, *Sexual Politics of Meat,* 54.

31. Green, *Dark Side of the Game,* 41.

32. Fanny Farmer, *The Fanny Farmer Cookbook,* 12th ed., revised by Marion Cunningham and Jeri Laber (New York: Alfred A. Knopf, 1980); Ellen Buchman Ewald, *Recipes for a Small Planet* (New York: Ballantine, 1975).

33. Butler, *Gender Trouble*, 71.

34. bell hooks, *Yearning* (Boston: South End Press, 1990), 215.

35. Kaufman, "Men, Feminism," 160.

36. Diabetes was not my only way into feminism, though. My relationship with my partner has been more influential in terms of my involvement with feminism and the profeminist men's movement.

37. Cows are stunned before they are killed, so that they supposedly die painlessly.

38. Adams, *Sexual Politics of Meat*, 38.

39. Ibid., 193.

40. Butler, *Gender Trouble*, 148.

41. See for example Jeff Hearn and David L. Collinson's "Theorizing Unities and Differences between Men and between Masculinities," in *Theorizing Masculinities*, ed. Harry Brod and Michael Kaufman (Thousand Oaks, Calif.: Sage, 1994), 97–118.

42. Kaufman, "Men, Feminism," 148.

Chapter 5

The Disabled Male Body "Writes/Draws Back"

Graphic Fictions of Masculinity and the Body in the Autobiographical Comic The Spiral Cage

PAUL MCILVENNY

For the purposes of this essay it is assumed that comics are a mature and sophisticated medium, a set of cultural signifying practices in which masculinity, ability, embodiment, and sexual difference can be interrogated by their creators and readers.[1] I focus on the graphic life narratives of Al Davison, in which he writes and draws in the comics medium his disabled male body, both as a topic and a performance. Some readers may never have encountered autobiographical comics, so different from the superhero or "funny animal" genres that they may have read as a child. Since the 1960s, adult comics have slowly but surely developed into quite a feast of genres and styles, and autobiographical comics especially are a distinctive and rewarding domain for gender analysis, particularly when men tell the stories of their lives through their conceptions of their bodies.[2]

We urgently need to investigate how a hegemonic notion of masculinity informs and interacts with men's experiences of embodiment, but Lennard Davis pointedly reminds us that "while many progressive intellectuals have stepped forward to decry racism, sexism, and class bias, it has not occurred to most of them that the very foundations of which their information systems are built, their very practices of reading and writing, seeing and thinking, and moving are themselves laden with assumptions about hearing, deafness, blindness, normalcy, paraplegia, and ability and disability in general."[3] I shall heed Davis's summons and attend to certain normative assumptions about the disabled male body in order to explore masculine subjectivity, identity, embodiment, and self-representation from a different perspective.[4]

Recent theory has attempted to grapple with the materialization of gendered and sexualized bodies. In her celebrated performative theory of gender, Judith Butler draws on the many senses of "perform" to extend the application of performativity from acts and their doings to normative acts and their effects. It is the ritualized repetition of norms that constitutes the "temporalized scene of gender."[5] Butler contends that "sex" is part of a regulatory practice that produces the bodies it governs. Arguing against radical constructivism and linguistic monism, she navigates a path that calls for a return to "the notion of matter, not as a site or surface, but as *a process of materialization that stabilizes over time to produce the effect of boundary, fixity, and surface we call matter.*"[6] Certain bodies are constitutively excluded, erased, foreclosed, yet they return to haunt the very terms of discursive legitimacy.

Attending to the performance and materialization of the gendered body is imperative, but how is the disabled male body to be conceived in such a performative theory?[7] What happens to the theory when the cultural inscription of disability is one of failure or the inability to act or perform—does the theory omit the disabled body from its purview? What of the fragmented body of a man with an impairment or a debilitating disease? For disabled men it may be more a question of how to do things, how to get *others* to do things, or even how to be *undone* or *not done unto,* as well as how to do things with words or signs. Unfortunately, Butler's token examples are rarely illustrative of the bodily experiences of these "other Others." This I hope to correct by focusing the analytical weight of performativity theory on one example of a body that is always already marked as not a "proper object" and yet is desperate to perform a semblance of masculinity. Of course, in autobiographical comics by disabled men it is not just the material body that should interest us; we must also look for tensions in any notion of "manhood" between the graphic fictions of the masculine body, the body of the text, the body of the male narrator, the graphic body of the character "I," the cultural body, and the body politic.

AL DAVISON'S *THE SPIRAL CAGE*

Al Davison, a White Englishman born with spina bifida (a congenital defect in which one or more vertebrae fail to unite during the embryo stage, resulting in exposure of part of the spinal cord and often permanent paralysis), has published a black and white autobiographical comic called *The Spiral Cage,* which recounts in a rich comic style the trials and joys of growing up a "disabled" man in English society. In an interview, Davison has said that he began his autobiographical project in 1984.[8] The work was first published in the United States in 1988, and that version comprises a chronological narrative of forty pages, interspersed with dream sequences, childhood memories, and a fairy tale embedded in an appended story.[9] For the comic's 1990 publication in the United Kingdom, Davison substantially revised it, added many new pages (a new total of 105), and organized it into five thematic sections.[10] In this paper I focus on the second version, but also use as a comparative resource the shorter, chronological, first version.[11]

In reference to the second version, Davison has claimed that "organizing the material thematically gives a clearer understanding of my life. Each section shows the improvement in different aspects of my life."[12] The differences between the two versions are marked and noteworthy: not only do many fresh dimensions emerge with the addition of new pages and the organization of the autobiography into thematic narratives of transformation, but the whole tone of the autobiography is altered by his growing spiritual self-confidence and his post-1988 heterosexual relationship with Maggie Lawrence. Prompted by criticisms, and reengaged from the perspective of a harmonious relationship (he is reincorporated into the social body), he rewrites, reorders, and adds to the earlier version.[13]

The copy text on the jacket of the 1990 edition reads, "Doctors considered him a hopeless case, condemned for life to the inescapable 'spiral cage' of his own DNA. But they reckoned without the fighting spirit of Al and his parents, and this book movingly portrays in Al's own words and pictures his struggles to overcome his 'disability' and the prejudice that surrounds it. A true story of one man's coming to terms with his physical, artistic and spiritual potential, that will move you to laughter and tears." I argue that Davison's gendered life narrative allows us to trace the cultural intelligibility of the disabled male body and the discourses of masculinity[14] that constrain and work against men with impairments. We have a chance to observe the self-representation and visualization of the male body as fragmented and abject in relation to significant "others" and a disabling society and body politics. In order to tackle Davison's autobiography we need to reconsider first the relations between autobiography, masculinity, dis/ability, and the body.

DISABILITY AND MASCULINITY

"Invalid," "handicapped," "spastic," "cripple," and "spacka" are terms used in good and bad faith to describe and label a person with a bodily impairment. One only has to look in a dictionary or a thesaurus to get a sense of the moral evaluation of the term "able" and its antonyms. If one is "able" and male, then one is capable, apt, fit, efficient, proper, skilful, and clever. The opposite is to be incompetent, incapable, silly, weak, feeble, and inept. Indeed, people with impairments have often been considered grotesque creatures of disorder.

Following Butler, Sidonie Smith contends that "while there are unlimited material differences from one body to another, only certain body parts make up the 'meaningful' cultural and social differences. The body is thus parceled out and policed through discursive systems that establish identities through differences, that normalize certain bodies and render other bodies culturally abnormal, even grotesque."[15] Smith argues that various discourses of identity work to fragment the body, to recognize its parts in order to give it a gendered, sexual, or racial identity. Thus, the nominative identification of material bodies as "male" or "female," "able" or "disabled" is based on the alignment of certain body parts and specific functions. Consequently, only certain bodies are normalized while other bodies are rendered culturally abnormal or grotesque. In their list of the discursive norms of the grotesque, Stallybrass and White include the following: impurity, heterogeneity, disproportion, decentered, and eccentric arrangements, a focus on gaps, orifices, and symbolic filth, and materiality. They argue that "the grotesque physical body is invoked both defensively and offensively because it is not simply a powerful image but fundamentally constitutive of the categorical sets through which we live and make sense of the world."[16] That is why we must take more than a passing interest in incompleteness and the chaotic or "grotesque body" in contemporary culture.

What happens to men when their bodies are seen as fragmented, or they fail or malfunction? How does a boy grow up to be a man when he has a physical impairment? What happens to my sense of identity when my able and healthy body becomes ill and is dis-eased? In order to address these questions we should take note of historical changes in Western cultural notions of the male body in the discourse of hegemonic masculinity. Lynne Segal notes that in tandem with the bourgeois ideals of "Christian manliness" in the nineteenth century, we find a stress on "spiritual, cerebral and moral precepts" and "the dignity of labour and the importance of manly independence and autonomy."[17] By the close of the nineteenth century, a competing "muscular masculinity" emphasized sport and physical labor, as well as celebrating a spartan athleticism and conformism. In comparison, contemporary hegemonic masculinity in relation to the male body often emphasizes ability, superhuman strength and stamina, physical violence, unemotionality, hardness, autonomy, potency, assertiveness, authority, the abjection of other bodies (the feminine, the homosexual, the grotesque), and the shame of failure.[18] We can see these qualities in the proliferation of contemporary media discourses (in English) on and about the male body: in magazines such as *Men's Health* or *Arena Homme Plus,* in commercial advertising, and in popular films such as *Born on the Fourth of July.*[19] In contrast to the oppressive cultural discourses circulating in many of these media, Davison's graphic autobiography is an important contemporary intervention into the pervasive alignment of normative notions of ability and masculinity.[20]

MEN'S LIFE NARRATIVES AND DISABILITY: AGAINST ABLEIST CULTURE

In the Western tradition of men's written autobiography, narratives most often concern the growth of the autobiographer's mind—for example, first influences, the realization of a capacity for self-determination, and an emergent sexual awareness. In his insightful critical autobiography, David Jackson finds that most traditional male autobiographies search for a true self, present a chronological, linear, and ejaculatory narrative structure, support the myth of unified identity, split the personal from the social, and are falsely universal.[21] It is clear from the first pages of Davison's graphic autobiography that it will qualify as a masculine *Bildungsroman*, a "tale of progressive travelling of a life from troubled or stifled beginnings; in which obstacles are overcome and true self actualized or revealed; and then the tale may, prototypically, end, or it may go on to document yet further troubles turned to triumphs."[22] Nevertheless, the tension between his sense of masculine identity and society's ableist understanding of hegemonic masculinity leads to some significant anomalies. For example, in her analysis of the absence of the body in male autobiographies, Shirley Neuman notes that men's autobiographical preludes most often represent the adolescent boy's relation to his body as an "unresolved oscillation between carnal longing and romantic yearnings, which are confused and commingled with artistic aspirations."[23] This relation poses a problem for Davison since his disabled body is one that, unusually for males in Western societies, is often excused or excluded from carnal knowledge.[24]

The social model of disability has emerged recently as disabled people have begun to challenge the institutions that control their lives. The model rejects medical and constructionist perspectives because "it is not disabled people who have defined the experience, neither have they had control over either medical treatment or the social consequences of impairment. Thus if disability is to be made sense of, it is non-disabled society and its institutions which should be the subject of study."[25] From this empowering perspective, able society is the disabler, and we need to reconceive the terms "impairment" and "disabled." Several disability rights organizations have officially proposed the following revised definitions: "*Impairment* is the lack of part or all of a limb, or having a defective limb, organ or mechanism of the body. *Disability* is the loss or limitation of opportunities that prevents people who have impairments from taking part in the normal life of that community on an equal level with others due to physical and social barriers."[26]

Irving Zola has pointed out that people with life-long impairments are mostly born into "normal" families. Hence, they are socialized into an *ableist* culture and have to adopt a disabled identity: "We think of ourselves in the shadow of the external world. The very vocabulary we use to describe ourselves is borrowed from that society. We are *de*-formed, *dis*-eased, *dis*-abled, *dis*-ordered, *ab*-normal, and most telling of all *in*-valid."[27] Davison was born to apparently "able," working-class parents, and has an older sister with cerebral palsy; however, when Davison brings us up-to-date with background details about his family in "Some Family Sketches," we discover that his parents have grown old and are now infirm or "impaired" themselves.[28] His father, Frank "Mad Max" Davison, has had several heart attacks, and his right leg has been amputated. He now rides an electric tricycle. His mother, Nellie "Evil [sic] Knievil" Davison, has had a stroke and several heart attacks. She now drives an electric wheelchair. These vicissitudes of aging suggest that the notion of being "differently abled" or "temporarily abled" may be more appropriate than the portentous epithet "disabled." It is undeniable that many "normal" bodies will become aged bodies with disabilities, but Featherstone and Turner argue that additionally the "threat of bodily betrayals (the risk of disabling illness, the erosion of the surface of the body, the impairment of communicative skills)" often stigmatizes the elderly, and can produce a deep disjunction between the body and the self.[29]

Davison has said that he wanted to "challenge people's assumptions about disablement. One of my original ideas was for the book to be used in colleges and schools."[30] Its usefulness as an educational tool is undoubted, but when we compare the two published versions we can also see more in his autobiography than simply its value to the disability movement. Importantly, in recreating the newer version, Davison was engaged in reconstituting a sense of masculine identity. For example, the tone of melancholy and self-pity that characterizes his reflections in chapter 3, before he dramatically smashes the mobility "aids," is in the second version turned outward into anger at the disabling, alienating, "destructive," "hateful" comments of "normal" society. Susan Friedman suggests that "alienation is not the result of creating a self in language, as it is for Lacanian and Barthesian critics of autobiography. Instead, alienation from the historically imposed image of the self is what motivates the writing, the creation of an alternative self in the autobiographical act."[31] This is precisely what Davison realizes through the graphic creation and bodily representation of his life narrative.

GRAPHIC FICTIONS: CHARACTERIZATION AND IDENTIFICATION

In relation to the gendered body, Shirley Neuman argues that the histories of autobiography construe the self as individuated and coherent rather than as "the product of social construction and as a subject-in-process and work consistently toward repression of the representation of bodies in autobiography."[32] Neuman and other critics interpret this in terms of the impact of traditional male autobiography on women's self-representation: women either do not write at all, or they seek "to invent a self that is female and noncorporeal, a self outside Western cultures' inscriptions of femininity."[33] This is an important insight, but we should not forget that some men too have suffered from the binary equations of masculinity with the spiritual/intellectual and femininity with the natural body. Indeed, in an earlier paper, Neuman notes that although most autobiography discursively effaces the corporeal, some autobiographies do represent the body, and so the question becomes, What is the extent to which that representation reiterates and reinforces the social codes constructing male bodies or the extent to which it reconfigures them?[34] She attends to "anomalous moments" in which a masculine body ruptures and exceeds the discursive effacement of the corporeal. In a similar fashion, Davison draws upon fabulous and genre-specific male characters (for example, Batman and the scarecrow) to locate a sense of self outside of the dominant culture's inscriptions of disability as confining, dependent, and irremediably corporeal. He is (re)generating graphic fictions of masculinity to recover the abject body, to make it culturally intelligible in positive ways.

Feminist critics point to the absent male body in traditional autobiographical writings, yet in autobiographical comics the body of the "self" is unavoidably present in the sense that it is represented graphically. It is commonplace to draw the "I" as an embodied character,[35] in addition to narrating the "I" in the text. The body of the autobiographer is repeatedly presented to the spectator as a surface, a set of lines, shapes, textures, and body parts. Indeed, the disabled body can present a particular challenge to the viewer: the visual and tactile qualities can easily promote both desire and disgust—the latter is especially prominent in men's self-reflections on their own failing or injured bodies.

Dorothy Dinnerstein claims that myth-images of half-human beasts like the mermaid and the Minotaur express an old, fundamental communal insight: that our species' nature is internally inconsistent; that our continuities with, and our differences from, the earth's other animals are mysterious and profound.[36] For her, the female mermaid and the male Minotaur are metaphors for the psychological trauma of current (hetero)sexual arrangements. Notwithstanding her insights, Dinnerstein's noting that the semi-human are monstrous in cultural terms merely confirms the hegemony of ableism. Transgressive human-creatures represent all that is bestial, monstrous, grotesque, and unnatural, so that "normal" humans can be otherwise. She is correct to point to the typical gendered differences between female and male mythical human-creatures; Davison, however, plays with them in his autobiography and subverts them in his semi-fictional version of the mythological tale of the Minotaur.[37]

In the first chapter of Davison's autobiography, for example, he visualizes himself as half-boy, half-fish, a fabulous creature who leaps from the dreams of the newly born Davison, whom we see sleeping in a hospital cot under the shadow-casting bars of the moonlit windows of the institution. After leaping into the air from the water, the mermaid boy's acrobatics in the sky continue over a series of panels, until, like Icarus who flew too close to the sun, he suddenly begins to fall helplessly back into the water. A few pages later, in a composite matrix[38] of panels and sounds headed "Night-shades," the mermaid boy reappears in three panels, replaying the moment of alienation and frustration as he plunges back into the water. Clearly, the cross-species imagery is used here because Davison was born paralyzed from the waist down, a condition/impairment which renders him "legless," born for a different medium than bipeds. Davison is also suggesting that a body with an impairment transgresses boundaries, yet may be wholly at ease: it is not inherent that an infant be "dis-abled" from birth as if it was a natural category or judgment. In the remainder of the thematic chapters, Davison goes on to investigate why it is that the water-born are anathema to the gravity-struck air of society's understanding of disability.

One explicit literary influence on the child Davison was Mary Shelley's *Frankenstein, or the Modern Prometheus,* which he is shown reading in the hospital in chapter 2 (see Figure 1). He quotes passages from the novel and illustrates the male creature's anguished thought processes in a three-by-three matrix of parallel cross-cutting panels:[39] Davison, who is reading in the hospital bed, is juxtaposed with depictions of the creature. It is unfortunate that popular twentieth-century representations of Frankenstein have turned the creature into the monosyllabic monster who runs amok, terrorizing the neighborhood. In contrast, across the second, fourth, and sixth panels, Davison focuses on the creature's contemplation of his dissimilarity to the "normal" local people. The creature first admires the bodies of the "normal" cottagers, but in looking at his reflection, his monstrosity is made visible, and he sees what they see, namely the hideous body, the repressed fragmentary body of the disabled. The very last panel shows the reader the boy's torso and legs as he asks the nurse, "What duz despond-inse and mortificatshun mean?" Clearly, Davison is not horrified by the creature's abjection. Instead, he identifies empathetically with the creature's feelings and sensations of being different, the "monster that I am," and with the possibility of humiliation and shame, of despair and dejection.[40]

The scarecrow makes an appearance in chapter 4, as well as on the front cover's middle panel. It is clear that Davison identified with the scarecrow as a child, and a recollection returns at a moment of desolation. He is wandering home lonely in a storm, feeling emotionally rejected by the empty house of a female friend he had hoped to find at home—a common theme in the earlier version of his autobiography. On the way back he notices a scarecrow in a field. As we are drawn in to a close-up of mutual gaze between Davison and the scarecrow, the panel cross-fades analeptically back to his childhood. He remembers his encounter with a scarecrow when he was a young boy in his wheelchair, enamored by a scarecrow dancing in the winds of a storm. The scarecrow's uncoordinated and comic dance is visualized across the remainder of the black, panel-less page.

FIGURE 1.
Davison's encounter with Shelley's *Frankenstein*.

Courtesy of Al Davison

FIGURE 2.
In a Batman costume, Davison
makes his first steps.

If, as Sidonie Smith suggests, "the bodily home can be an illusive terrain, perhaps the home of a stranger," we may find that we are not "at
home" in our bodies.[41] In his critical review of *The Wizard of Oz*, Salman
Rushdie suggests we view the film from the perspective of the exile making
a "home."[42] In *Oz*, the male scarecrow without a brain, given to comic
pratfalls and general bodily clumsiness, is a "hollow man" (T. S. Eliot's
term)—without Great Qualities—who searches for "home" and a brain,
but not an attentive and demanding body. With the help of Dorothy and
her companions he finds intelligence within. The scarecrow, therefore, reinforces the lay-belief that disabled people are somehow less intelligent
than "normal," that physical disability means mental incompetence. Continuing with this interpretation, *Oz* represents a social constructionist theory of disability with liberal individualistic tones—one's disability is the
result of social norms and pressures, yet one can escape (go west on the
Yellow Brick Road) and overcome stigma and oppression through a journey of self-discovery (within a temporary alliance of difference).

As a child, Davison regularly appears in male costume or active in masculine role play; for instance, he appears as Gene Kelly in *Singin' in the Rain* (with his sister supplying the legs), or he imagines himself as a pirate or adventurer scaling the bookshelf-ship to rescue (or steal) a book from the crew. On several occasions, Davison appears in a Batman or Superman costume. The most ironic and playful moment occurs near the end of the first chapter (see Figure 2) when he takes his first public steps toward the viewer in his Batman-logo shirt and cape, beaming to those present at the clinic: "Look. Mam! I can walk!" Equally poignant is the short reflection about the time he enters a telephone box, transformed from the mild-mannered Clark Kent into Superman, only to find the wheelchair is stuck. He calls the police station and reports that he, "supaman," is trapped in a telephone box and needs help.[43]

Peter Middleton urges that men turn their gaze inward to examine and name male subjectivity in modern culture, including popular culture.[44] He wishes to produce an emancipatory men's discourse that challenges men's idealized representations of their subjectivity and power as men. One way to begin to find out about the formation of modern masculine subjectivities is to ask the question, How does a boy become a man? Hypermasculine action comics are one of a range of symbolic armatures for boys to identify with largely absent adult men, with their actions and their bodies, giving them what manhood most desires, namely unlimited strength, unrestricted movement, and unbounded space. Rather than following the conventional path and dismissing superhero comics, shoving the genre into the superficial psychological mire of preadolescent boy's power fantasy, Middleton argues that superhero comic books are a substitute world, a fantasy that is a symptom of the social structures of desire and emotion produced by the general absence of continuity between men and boys. In short, boys read superhero comics because they do not have close relationships with their fathers or access to their fathers' work environments. Other critics argue that superhero comics are less about unlimited and unbridled power than about powerlessness. In his essay "The Myth of Superman," Umberto Eco suggests that in spite of all his powers, Superman is "a creature immersed in everyday life, in the present, apparently tied to our own conditions of life and death."[45] As a child, Davison had little access to the environment of a "normal" boy and lacked continuity between his cared-for world and the worlds of the active boys and working men—he was powerless, or more to the point, disempowered. Moreover, he had an abusive and paranoid father. Middleton's interpretation of the role of comics in boys' lives suggests that superhero comics, role-playing, and dressing the body in fiction provided Davison with the means to perform a substitute fantasy world in which the ironic structure of much of the best of the genre matched his own sense of powerlessness.

THE VISUAL AND THE TACTILE

Disability, according to Davis, presents itself to "normal" people through two main modalities—function and appearance.[46] The person with an impairment is visualized, brought into a regulating field of vision, and thus comes to be seen as disabled by "normal" persons. Disability is a specular moment, in which the power of the gaze to control, limit, and police the body of the disabled person is brought to the fore. From the perspective of media production, David Hevey suggests that images of disabled people, particularly those used by charity advertising, have constructed disabled people as "the refuse of the social body."[47] He sets down a contrasting agenda for "disability" photography that can be applied also to "disability" comics: "A truly empowering 'school' of positive disability imagery must contain the signs of the pain, the sign of the reclamation of the body, the revisualizing of the 'flaw' of the impairment, the marks of struggle and overcoming, and signs for a future. Access and representation are the goals but fantasy and reality, subjectivity and objectivity must all play their part in the naming of a disability image identity."[48] Given the strength of disgust or repulsion that "normal" people feel at the sight of an impairment when it is manifestly visible, Davison confronts the "able" gaze by representing himself graphically in myriad ways, for example, by putting his adult body in full view, often naked and in some pain or anguish. Although this depiction is uncharacteristic of images of men in most advertising campaigns, it does occur in recent charity images. This sort of charity advertising encourages the "normal" viewer to feel pity and compassion for a pathetic and vulnerable disabled man. Davison, however, anesthetizes the controlling gaze through his use of mirror imagery.

Mirror-like surfaces and their reflections recur throughout Davison's autobiography, and the mirror is an important spiritual symbol. In the first version of his autobiography, it is not clear until near the end that there is a spiritual moral to the mirror symbolism and imagery. In the second, he makes clear the importance of spirituality to his life narrative by invoking the Zen Buddhist writings of Nichiren Daishonin on the head page of every thematic chapter. The first chapter opens not with his birth but with a depressing view of a naked, prostrate adult Davison suffering bouts of M.E. (myalgic encephalomyelitis), more commonly known as post-viral fatigue syndrome. To cope with the debilitating effects of M.E., Davison remembers how his study of martial arts brought him inner strength and confidence. The following page shows him kneeling on the floor; he is reading "On Attaining Buddhahood" from the writings of Nichiren. The last panel on this page contains a superimposition of six heads in a fan-shape, which represent stages in the development of Davison's life and self-knowledge to the present. The text (quoted from Nichiren's *Major Writings*) reads:

If you wish to free yourself from the sufferings of birth and death you have endured through eternity and attain supreme enlightenment in this lifetime, you must awaken to the mystic truth which has always been within your life. [next panel] While deluded, one is called a common mortal, but once enlightened, he is called a Buddha. Even a tarnished mirror will shine like a jewel if it is polished. A mind which presently is clouded by illusions originating from the innate darkness of life is like a tarnished mirror, but once polished, it will become clear, reflecting the enlightenment of immutable truth. Arouse deep faith and polish your mirror . . .

Thus begins Davison's spiritual journey and the framing narrative.

In Zen Buddhist philosophy, the mirror is the instrument of enlightenment, a symbol of wisdom and knowledge. A tarnished mirror is the symbol of the spirit darkened by ignorance. Davison incorporates this idea into his autobiography. For example, chapter 5 is entitled "Mirror without a Reflection" and refers to his self-perception before he met his lover Maggie Lawrence. At one point, while he is travelling to visit Maggie, he reflects on the changes in his life. Before his relationship with Maggie, he was "like a mirror without a reflection, desperate for love." A mirror appears again when Davison creates a short parable illustrating his rejuvenated philosophy of life, based on the Buddhist aphorism, "Even a tarnished mirror will shine like a jewel if it is polished. Arouse deep faith and polish your mirror night and day." We can presume he has learned to attend and care for his "mirror," and his life has thus become complete, full of "the treasures of the body" and "the treasures of the heart"; as a result, the autobiographical narrative comes to a happy standstill.

But Davison's use of the mirror symbolism is not confined to Buddhist references. For instance, while looking into a pool of gutter water the boy Davison demonstrates a child's (or a Buddhist's) logic when he claims that the sun must be small because it appears small in the reflecting surface of the pool. Moreover, he believes that his splashing in the puddle ought to cause the sun to splash because if in the mirror his reflected face smiles, then he does too. We can interpret this not only as a decentering of the ego, but also as a playful deconstruction of reality and appearance. Through the child's narrative he is indicating that appearances can have more "life" or more "cause" than the real, and that reality is duplicitous. This fits with Butler's claim that the representational status of language, which claims that signs follow bodies as their necessary mirrors, is not mimetic at all.[49] The signifying act contours the body that it then claims to find prior to any and all signification.

On the same page his final comment is directed to his mother while he sits on the bed contorting himself in front of the mirror: "Where duz me reflection go . . . a mean when am not looking at the mirra?" We can think through the child's reasoning with the help of Lacan and the concept of the "mirror phase." For Lacan, the earliest infant experience is that of the fragmented body—the body is an assemblage of arms, legs, and surfaces. These representations of fragmented body parts are called *imagos*. Symbolically, when the child points to an image in the mirror the child (mis)recognizes that unified image as his or her self. But what does the phase comprise for the child with a visible impairment—a direct *imago* of the repressed fragmented body—when he or she points in the mirror? Does the child fail to recognize unity or does the child assume the "disabled body" and identify with it?

In fiction, mirrors often work as boundaries between one world and another. On another page of his autobiography, Davison sits by his window while the viewer observes from outside. In one panel we see him through the window as well as the reflection of the street scene in the window pane. In the next panel in close-up we see the inside of his room and a picture of a woman on the wall, but with the fragments of the street reflected in the relative darkness of the reflection of his head. This is suggestive of the permeability and fragmentation of the boundaries between "inside" and "outside." Neither is independent of the other. Davison inhabits a transient border zone in which he is struggling to define an identity not wholly socially inscribed (outside), but which will permit him to be a creative artist and to enter that social world through the window of his "interior" autobiography.

The next occasion that the reader views a reflection, it is of a fatigued Davison in the bathroom chancing upon himself in the mirror[50] (see Figure 3). This event triggers a complex sequence of conflicting voices across a matrix of associative, aspectual panels: his named disabled friends, his childhood fear and anger, and the taunting and disparaging, as well as the loving, voices of "normal" people. Thus, he shows us that the disabled body is a fiction forced on him by a disabling society.

Robert Connell notes that "true masculinity is almost always thought to proceed from men's bodies—to be inherent in a male body or to express something about a male body." Either the body drives and directs action, or the body sets limits to action. However, he argues that neither social determinism nor biological determinism, nor a combination of both, is a sufficient basis for an account of gender. Connell suggests that bodies in their own right do matter. He argues that "there is an irreducible bodily dimension in experience and practice; the sweat cannot be excluded." The physical sense of maleness is central to our cultural interpretations of masculinity. Masculine gender is (among other things) a "certain feel to the skin, certain muscular shapes, postures and ways of moving."[51]

Davison explores not only the cultural politics of the gaze, but also of touch—an often forgotten or rejected sense and sensory experience for many men—which Connell brings to the fore. In some psychoanalytic thinking (such as that of Didier Anzieu), the skin is a metaphor for wholeness, completeness, the intact ego.[52] Davison was born with an open wound

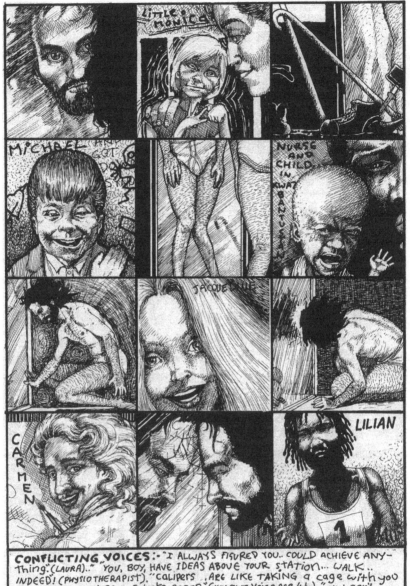

FIGURE 3.
Conflicting voices that support and oppress.

at the base of his spine, a rupture of the skin, and a paralysis of the lower body. Near the end of the second version of his autobiography, he is given a massage for the first time by his new lover, Maggie. She touches and caresses his thin lower legs and scarred back, the two zones of stigma that he has trouble acknowledging. One zone is publicly visible and marks him as a weak man, the other is invisible yet marks the rupture of the impervious and impenetrable exterior of his masculine body. He recalls the emotion he felt when she first kissed his scar, and still cannot quite believe that a woman could find him attractive. As well as the declarations of love, it is the kiss and the tender touch by another to the ruptured skin that return a transformed ego, now intact—and a new pleasurable acceptance by Davison of his own passivity.

OVERCOMING THE "CAGE"

Davison states that the title of his autobiography "came from a feeling of being trapped in a cage that continually changed its perspective, from hospital rooms and walking sticks [canes], callipers [braces], various restrictions that are put on you by society."[53] In his introduction to the autobiography, Alan Moore, a famous comics writer, interprets it as referring to the inflexible spiral of DNA, a biological genetic code by which Davison's body is defined and from which he wishes to escape. For scientists, however, the spiral of DNA is a double helix, and so a better reading, which avoids a simple essentialist "your body is your destiny" argument, would use DNA as a metaphor for the dual interlinking and binding of both the social and the biological, an invalid binding or "cage" that Davison seeks in some way to challenge and subvert in his graphic autobiography.

In the second version of *The Spiral Cage*, Davison explicitly and more emphatically charts his gradual rejection of the "cage" of Christian charitable views of disability, and his gradual conversion to Zen Buddhism—he is a Nichiren Shoshu Buddhist. As an adult, Davison draws upon a Buddhist philosophy and sense of self to counteract the Judeo-Christian attitude to the disabled body that he encounters in English society and in his father, and thus he reconfigures his conception of self, body, and environment. Not only does he look to the East for a philosophy for meditation, he also trains bodily in the complementary discipline (Karate-Do, Shoto-Kai) of martial arts, which enables him to defend himself physically when he is picked on by male bullies. Despite the media portrayal of disabled men as vulnerable and needy, some men see him as a legitimate target of their aggression, and they wish to compound what they perceive as his "failed" masculinity.[54]

Davison also confronts the "cage" of asexuality imposed on the "disabled": sex and procreation with or among the disabled is culturally proscribed, to the extent that state institutions have in some cases performed compulsory sterilization. Davison notes that "people get shocked that the disabled have sexual urges. Treat them like children, that makes them easier to deal with."[55] Quite often in his autobiography, Davison draws himself naked, exposed to the voyeuristic gaze of the reader. For instance, a four-by-six matrix of parallel cross-cutting panels shows an associative set of naked self-representations—of Davison in pain, terror, delusion, anger, bewilderment, sexual desire—along with three erotic drawings of naked women.[56] Clearly, Davison is a disabled man with heterosexual desires and fantasies.

Jenny Morris notes that for a disabled women there is a partial congruity between normative roles of being a woman and being disabled—e.g., passivity and dependency—yet a disabled woman may be unable to fulfil her "role" as homemaker, wife, and mother, and as a physically attractive woman. In contrast, a disabled man fails to measure up to the dominant culture's definition of masculinity—strength and autonomy—which means that the disabled man is often seen as dependent and emasculated. In this context the wheelchair is the ultimate symbol of dependency and lack of autonomy.[57] We must admit that Davison is not exempt from the impulse to perform masculinity by denying his emasculation. In Davison's autobiography we only see his infant self in a wheelchair on two occasions: once in a telephone box when "Superman" gets stuck; and a second time in a nightmare dream sequence. Otherwise, from an early age Davison is shown repeatedly rejecting such mobility "aids." He is torn between a wish to be a "normal" boy and a desire to resist the social pressure that he conform to the dominant ideas of his disability. On various occasions we do see Davison with canes, crutches, braces, and a makeshift trolley, but the link between the regulating gaze of "normal" society and the identity-defining "aids," which are "like taking a cage with you wherever you go," is made and dramatically broken in a five-page sequence in chapter 3. With focused, brooding violence, using his martial arts expertise, Davison smashes the canes and leg braces. They end up in the dustbin, and visibly transformed he borrows his sister's "normal" shoes to walk out into the sunshine, the beginning of a new identity that refuses to be intelligible as the "other Other."

PERFORMING THE "DISABLED" MALE BODY

In regard to autobiographical narratives as performative occasions through which "selves" are culturally produced, Smith reasons that every day, in many locations, in response to sundry occasions, people assemble, if only temporarily, a "life" to which they assign narrative coherence and meaning. Whatever the occasion, the autobiographical speaker becomes a performative subject.[58] She argues that "the specificities of flesh determined the degree and kind of interiority assigned the self-regulating subject. Interiority became an effect, and not a cause, of the cultural regulation of always already identified bodies, bodies that were sexed and gendered, . . . bodies that were deemed unruly or grotesque."[59] From this perspective, we can see that the textualization and figuration of the exteriority of Davison's male body produces his interiority as a masculine subject. In addition, he is both performing the masquerade of masculinity and resisting the inscription of a "failed" masculinity on his "damaged" body, as we shall see again in the next example.

Davison has said that one of the things he is fighting against is "the labelling of people as disabled. It makes our situation worse. Society should be geared towards helping everyone's individual problems, not just putting people into categories."[60] Consequently, Davison takes a skeptical view of medical and institutional discourses. When he learns to walk at the end of the first chapter, it is in marked contrast to the pronouncements of medical "fact" by the doctors who advise his parents. In his observations (at age twenty-one) at the beginning of the autobiography, he notes with irony, "I was born with severe spina bifida, a condition which leaves you paralyzed from the waist down, and can also leave you with brain damage. First 'they' said I wouldn't live . . . then they said I shouldn't live. . . . my parents disagreed." Clearly, impairment is being socially inscribed with moral and ethical implications, an inability to act, function, and take responsibility as a subject in "normal" society. A few pages later in chapter 1, Davison checkerboards a whole page with text and picture panels, a composite recognizable as a doctor's (typed) medical report on his "hopeless" condition, combined with "X-ray" drawings of the focalized parts of his body. The last panel makes it clear that the doctor has been referring to the X-rays in his evaluation. This page contrasts with the prefacing pages, in which it is clear that Davison did resist and overcome the sociopsychological hurdles implicit in the medical report.

On a later page (see Figure 4), immediately after Davison depicts himself as a boy in a Batman costume who manages to stand and walk on his own—a "gwait twick"—despite received medical opinion (see Figure 2), he uses a parallel cross-cutting panel matrix in which an identical panel of his male doctor expressing disbelief ("I don't believe it") at the "miracle" of his autonomous achievement, iterates in every other position. The juxtaposed panels are filled with images of his delighted mother, approving parents, and the little Black girl whom he aims to impress at the clinic. The reiteration focuses on the medical voice of authority which is repeatedly shattered by the hope and faith of patients and their witnessing parents who refuse to live within the confines of the "spiral cage" of medical case studies. The performative sense of "He will not walk," which inscribes an authoritative subject, the expert (who knows best) within the discourse of

FIGURE 4.
Reactions to Davison's unexpected first steps as a child.

the medical institution, is demonstrated by one brief performance from Davison to be an attempt to produce materiality as an effect, an attempt to frame the limits of the normative masculine body by exclusion.

CONCLUSION

It is clear from his autobiography that Davison was born into a society and culture that was intent on regulating his "damaged" male body, its performance and his masculine identity. In citing himself in relation to his impairment and normative notions of the masculine body, Davison often resists the cultural inscription of his body as the masculine "feminine." He refuses to be still, to be inactive, to lack mobility, to be confined by so-called aids to mobility, and so he may be accused too easily of conforming to hegemonic norms of masculine conduct. I argue that the disabled male body in comics can still pose a double threat to hegemonic masculinity: as well as being shown to be vulnerable, and so providing an echo of failure, it can actively refuse to remain invisible, negatively defined by the regulating gaze of other men, the medical establishment, and a patriarchal society that disables those men whose bodies do not fit gender norms.

Davison's graphic autobiography is created from the perspective of a male artist with an impairment. Through the medium of comics he can challenge in some fashion the ableist and masculinist cultural and social norms. Davison "writes/draws back" his own developing vision of masculinity through conflict, a successful though traumatic transition from boy to man. Moreover, his autobiography is pedagogic in its thematic structure: we can learn from his struggles over his right to walk, his spiritual journey, his channeling of creativity into an artistic vocation, and his learning to "polish his mirror" to know himself and to accept the love of a woman. As Tom Shakespeare notes, "non-disabled men have things to learn from disabled men, and could profitably share insights into gender relations, sexuality and, in particular, issues of physicality and the body."[61] However, we must remember that his respect for bodily control and narrative closure, his rejection of dependency, his consummation of a heterosexual relationship, are all accomplished painfully. Davison struggles to perform, and yet ironize, the masquerade of hegemonic masculinity that "normal" men with unearned privilege and power often accomplish, to their distinct advantage, all too easily.

NOTES

1. It is unfortunate that Art Spiegelman, one of the "stars" of the (re)emergence of serious adult comics in the Anglo-American world, begins his idiosyncratic

historical and aesthetic overview of "commix" in the following shock tone: "Throughout most of its 150-year-old history, the comic strip has been the hunch-backed, half-witted, bastard dwarf step-child of the graphic arts" (Spiegelman, "Commix: An Idiosyncratic Historical and Aesthetic Overview," *Print* 42, no. 6 [1988], 61).

2. The term "adult comics" can have an unfortunately narrow association with pornographic literature in the popular imagination. For a discussion of the use of the term to include all comics for older readers—political satire, autobiography, underground comics, as well as erotic fantasy—see Roger Sabin, *Adult Comics: An Introduction* (London: Routledge, 1993). To my knowledge there are at least fifty male comics creators who have written (and drawn) their autobiographies in the comics medium, of whom twenty or so have devoted a substantial proportion of their creative output to autobiography. Two stand out for their honest exploration of masculinity, impairment, and embodiment: Al Davison's *The Spiral Cage* (London: Titan Books, 1990) and Harvey Pekar and Joyce Brabner's *Our Cancer Year* (New York: Four Walls Eight Windows, 1994). Autobiographical storytelling in a diverse range of oral and visual media is examined in Sidonie Smith and Julia Watson, ed., *Getting a Life: Everyday Uses of Autobiography* (Minneapolis: University of Minnesota Press, 1996).

3. Lennard J. Davis, *Enforcing Normalcy: Disability, Deafness and the Body* (London: Verso, 1995), 4–5. Even in Judith Halberstam's otherwise challenging critique of the protected status of male masculinity through her analysis of the diversity of female masculinities, we find a lengthy discussion of the gender politics of public bathrooms for men and women, but without a consideration of the "third sex" bathroom for the disabled (see Halberstam, *Female Masculinity* [Durham, N.C.: Duke University Press, 1998], 20–29).

4. Unfortunately, there has been very little research on the experiences of disabled men. In a recent article, Tom Shakespeare complains that "in years of researching disability I have only ever read one article concerning disabled men" (Shakespeare, "When Is a Man Not a Man? When He's Disabled," in *Working with Men for Change*, ed. Jim Wild [London: UCL Press, 1999], 47).

5. Judith Butler, "Critically Queer," *Gay and Lesbian Quarterly* 1 (1993): 21.

6. Judith Butler, *Bodies That Matter: On the Discursive Limits of "Sex"* (London: Routledge, 1993), 9 (Butler's emphasis).

7. Although Butler's main concern is with the materialization of "sex," she cautions, "Clearly, sex is not the only norm by which bodies become materialized, and it is unclear whether 'sex' can operate as a norm apart from other normative requirements on bodies" (ibid., 243, n. 1).

8. Dave Thorpe, "Al Davison: Breaking Free," *Speakeasy* 108 (1990): 35–39.

9. Al Davison, *The Spiral Cage: Diary of an Astral Gypsy* (Long Beach, Cal.: Renegade Press, 1988).

10. Davison, *The Spiral Cage* (1990). Much of the material for the thematic sections is drawn from Davison's daily comics diary, a graphic record of his life. Other pages are clearly memories of his childhood. Pages and panels are often dated and located geographically. Unless otherwise noted, references in this chapter to Davison's *The Spiral Cage* are to the second version (ibid.; it has no page numbers).

11. *The Minotaur's Tale*, a third graphic novel published in 1992, is not explicitly autobiographical but it does rewrite ("write back") the Greek myth from the contemporary point of view of a disabled man whose life story bears some resemblance to Davison's (see Davison, *The Minotaur's Tale* [London: VG Graphics/Dark Horse Comics, 1992]).

12. Quoted in Thorpe, "Al Davison," 37.

13. From personal correspondence with Davison it appears that he is planning a third version that will narrate a very different perspective on his relationship to his father than was minimally suggested in the first two versions.

14. The concept of "masculinity" is problematic for a number of reasons, but I use it here as a useful rubric. For recent critiques see Jeff Hearn, "Is Masculinity Dead? A Critique of the Concept of Masculinity/Masculinities," in *Understanding Masculinities: Social Relations and Cultural Arenas,* ed. Mairtin MacanGhaill (Buckingham: Open University Press, 1996), 202–217; John MacInnes, *The End of Masculinity: The Confusion of Sexual Genesis and Sexual Difference in Modern Society* (Buckingham: Open University Press, 1998); and Alan Petersen, *Unmasking the Masculine: "Men" and "Identity" in a Sceptical Age* (London: Sage, 1998).

15. Sidonie Smith, "Identity's Body," in *Autobiography and Postmodernism,* ed. Kathleen Ashley, Leigh Gilmore, and Gerald Peters (Amherst: University of Massachusetts Press, 1994), 268.

16. Peter Stallybrass and Allon White, *The Politics and Poetics of Transgression* (London: Methuen, 1986), 23. Stallybrass and White reflect on "an unnoticed slide between two quite distinct kinds of 'grotesque,' the grotesque as the 'Other' of the defining group or self, and the grotesque as a boundary phenomenon of hybridization or inmixing, in which the self and other become enmeshed in an inclusive, heterogeneous, dangerously unstable zone" (193). If we separate the two, it becomes possible "to see that a fundamental mechanism of identity formation *produces* the second, hybrid grotesque at the level of the political unconscious *by the very struggle to exclude the first grotesque*" (193, emphasis in original)—a double articulation.

17. Lynne Segal, *Slow Motion: Changing Masculinities, Changing Men* (London: Virago, 1990), 105.

18. According to Julia Kristeva, the abject is that which "disturbs identity, system, order. What does not respect borders, positions, rules" (Kristeva, *Powers of Horror: Essays on Abjection* [New York: Columbia University Press, 1982], 4). The abject represents what human life and culture exclude in order to sustain themselves. Following Judith Butler, I suggest that the repudiation of bodies for their impairment is an "expulsion" followed by a "repulsion" that founds and consolidates culturally hegemonic identities (Butler, *Bodies That Matter,* 13).

In the life of the all-male North American writer Ernest Hemingway, Lynne Segal finds a revealing feature of the ideal of "normal" tough-guy masculinity: "a 'pure' masculinity cannot be asserted *except* in relation to what is defined as its opposite. It depends on the perpetual renunciation of 'femininity.' No one can be 'that male' without constantly doing violence to many of the most basic human attributes: the capacity for sensitivity to oneself and others, for tenderness and empathy, the reality of fear and weakness, the pleasures of passivity" (Segal, *Slow Motion,* 114). The "masculine feminine" will always return to haunt the "real man," encouraging the fear and paranoia of failure. See Kaja Silverman, *Male Subjectivity at the Margins* (New York: Routledge, 1992); David Jackson, *Unmasking Masculinity: A Critical Autobiography* (London: Unwin Hyman, 1990); R. W. Connell, *Masculinities* (Cambridge: Polity Press, 1995); and Thomas J. Gerschick and Adam S. Miller, "Coming to Terms: Masculinity and Physical Disability," in *Men's Health & Illness: Gender, Power, and the Body,* ed. David Sabo and Davis Frederick Gordon (London: Sage, 1995), 183–204.

19. See Colin Barnes, *Disabling Imagery and the Media: An Exploration of the Principles for Media Representations of Disabled People* (Halifax: The British Council of Organisations of Disabled People/Ryburn Publishing, 1992); Steve Craig, ed., *Men, Masculinity and the Media* (London: Sage, 1992); Davis, *Enforcing Normalcy;* Ann

Pointon and Chris Davies, ed., *Framed: Interrogating Disability in the Media* (London: BFI, 1997); and Mark Simpson, *Male Impersonators* (London: Cassell, 1994).

20. Life narratives and the storytelling of men (and women) who have become (not been born) impaired through illness or accident have been examined by Arthur W. Frank, *The Wounded Storyteller: Body, Illness, and Ethics* (Chicago: University of Chicago Press, 1995); Thomas J. Gerschick, "Sisyphus in a Wheelchair: Men with Physical Disabilities Confront Gender Domination," in *Everyday Inequalities: Critical Inquiries*, ed. Jodi O'Brien and Judith A. Howard (Oxford: Blackwell, 1998); Gerschick and Miller, "Coming to Terms"; and Madonne Miner, " 'Making up the Stories As We Go Along: Men, Women, and Narratives of Disability," in *The Body and Physical Difference: Discourses of Disability*, ed. David T. Mitchell and Sharon L. Schneider (Ann Arbor: University of Michigan Press, 1997).

21. Jackson, *Unmasking Masculinity*.

22. Liz Stanley, *The Auto/biographical I: The Theory and Practice of Feminist Auto/biography* (Manchester: Manchester University Press, 1992), 11.

23. Shirley Neuman, " 'An Appearance Walking in a Forest the Sexes Burn': Autobiography and the Construction of the Feminine Body," in *Autobiography and Postmodernism*, ed. Kathleen Ashley, Leigh Gilmore, and Gerald Peters (Amherst: University of Massachusetts Press, 1994), 296.

24. See Tom Shakespeare, Kath Gillespie-Sells, and Dominic Davies, *The Sexual Politics of Disability: Untold Desires* (London: Cassell, 1996).

25. Jenny Morris, "Gender and Disability," in *Disabling Barriers—Enabling Environments*, ed. John Swain, Vic Finkelstein, Sally French, and Mike Oliver (London: Sage/Open University Press, 1993), 85–92.

26. Vic Finkelstein and Sally French, "Towards a Psychology of Disability," in *Disabling Barriers—Enabling Environments*, ed. John Swain, Vic Finkelstein, Sally French, and Mike Oliver (London: Sage/Open University Press, 1993), 28. For a discussion of the politics of defining impairment, disability and handicap see Susan Wendell, *The Rejected Body: Feminist Philosophical Reflections on Disability* (London: Routledge, 1996), 11–33.

27. Irving Kenneth Zola, "Communication Barriers Between 'the Able-Bodied' and 'the Handicapped,' " in *Psychological and Social Impact of Physical Disability*, ed. Robert P. Marinelli and Arthur E. Dell Orto (New York: Springer, 1984), 144.

28. Readers of both published versions of Davison's autobiography may have the impression that Davison's parents were supportive of his sister and him as they grew up, coping with their impairments. From personal correspondence with the creator, it is clear that this is not completely true. Davison's relationship with his father was "anything but okay." He says that his father was shamed by his mother for being a failure as a "man"—both for his own inabilities and for producing two disabled children—which may be one of the reasons his father believed the double-bind that while disabled men inevitably are failures, they must appear as "normal" as possible. In his eyes, Davison and his sister were "the Devil's children." As a result, Davison's father abused both children.

29. Mike Featherstone and Bryan S. Turner, "Body & Society: An Introduction," *Body & Society* 1, no. 1 (1995): 7.

30. Quoted in Thorpe, "Al Davison," 35.

31. Susan Stanford Friedman, "Women's Autobiographical Selves: Theory and Practice," in *The Private Self: Theory and Practice of Women's Autobiographical Writings*, ed. Shari Benstock (Chapel Hill: University of North Carolina Press, 1988), 41.

32. Neuman, " 'An Appearance Walking,' " 293. Neuman points out that the representation of the body, when present at all, "is to be found almost entirely in narratives of childhood, where supposedly untempered bodies are (mis)repre-

sented with Rousseauistic rather than Hollywood idealism, as uninscribed with culture" (ibid.).

33. Ibid., 294.

34. Shirley Neuman, "Autobiography, Bodies, Manhood," in *Autobiography and Questions of Gender*, ed. Shirley Neuman (London: Frank Cass, 1991), 137–165.

35. One distinctive feature of autobiographical comics is the interminable visual self-representation of the author as character. For instance, in one panel in the autobiographical narrative "Our Lovely Home," Robert Crumb notes that "it's a weird experience to keep drawing *yourself* over and over again . . ." (Aline Kominsky-Crumb, Robert Crumb, and Sophie Crumb, *The Complete Dirty Laundry Comics* [San Francisco: Last Gasp, 1993]). Because of the graphic realization of the author-character—a citational signature that attempts to visually reproduce the integrity of the self—readers can easily objectify the author and create distance. We cannot inhabit the author's persona as easily as we can in many written autobiographies (see also Elizabeth W. Bruss, "Eye for I: Making and Unmaking Autobiography in Film," in *Autobiography: Essays Theoretical and Critical*, ed. James Olney [Princeton, N.J.: Princeton University Press, 1980], 296–320; and Catherine Portuges, "Seeing Subjects: Women Directors and Cinematic Autobiography," in *Life/Lines: Theorizing Women's Autobiography*, ed. Bella Brodski and Celeste Schenck [Ithaca: Cornell University Press, 1988], 338–350).

36. Dorothy Dinnerstein, *The Mermaid and the Minotaur: Sexual Arrangements and Human Malaise* (New York: Harper Collins, 1977), 2.

37. Davison, *Minotaur's Tale*.

38. I use the word "matrix" in the sense suggested by Judith Butler, to point to "an originating and formative principle which inaugurates and informs a development of some organism or object" (Butler, *Bodies That Matter*, 31). Its etymology suggests the association of femininity with materiality.

39. In terms of the conventional reading of Western comics, panels relate directly to immediately prior panels; that is, a viewer interprets a panel in relation to the panel conventionally just prior to the current one, and the interpretation process is called closure. Transitions between panels can be roughly categorized in terms of their function in the narrative (McCloud, *Understanding Comics* [Northampton, Mass.: Kitchen Sink Press, 1993]). Davison often uses delayed or deferred closure. Coherent sequences are juxtaposed in alternate panels within the matrix layout of the page, so the closure of one panel does not occur in the next adjacent panel. A comics reader can then "read" other meanings into the juxtaposition of two or more sequences. This technique is similar to parallel editing or cross-cutting in the cinema, but with a crucial distinction. Because of Davison's extensive use of parallel cross-cutting, panels often create a checkerboard design on the page as a whole, an effect not possible in the single-screen cinematic medium. See Figures 1, 3, and 4 for examples.

40. In the later semi-fictional comic book, *The Minotaur's Tale*, Davison invokes another male monster from classical literature. Davison reinterprets the mythology in a contemporary setting and tells the story from the perspective of the Minotaur, no longer the grotesque symbol of a psychic state of perverted domination.

41. Smith, "Identity's Body," 267.

42. Salman Rushdie, *The Wizard of Oz* (London: BFI Publishing, 1992).

43. An unforeseeable double irony is that Christopher Reeve, the archetypal star of the wholesome film adaptations in the 1970s and 1980s of the comic book *Superman*, became a tetraplegic after a horse riding fall in 1995. In his autobiography, Reeve confesses that he was a long time in denial over his disability. He could not admit that his body would no longer be mastered, that he would no longer

perform and compete against other men, judging himself by society's standards of masculine independence and autonomy (Reeve, *Still Me* [New York: Random House, 1998]).

44. Peter Middleton, *The Inward Gaze: Masculinity and Male Subjectivity in Modern Culture* (London: Routledge, 1992).

45. Umberto Eco, "The Myth of Superman," in *The Role of the Reader* (London: Hutchinson, 1981), 107–143.

46. Davis, *Enforcing Normalcy*, 11.

47. David Hevey, *The Creatures Time Forgot: Photography and Disability Imagery* (London: Routledge, 1992), 123.

48. Ibid., 119.

49. Butler, *Bodies That Matter*, 30.

50. Robert Crumb, an autobiographical comics creator who often collaborates with his wife, Aline Kominsky-Crumb, faces a mirror on one of the front covers of *Self-Loathing Comics,* their recent appropriately named collaboration. Crumb's front cover is poignant—he draws himself shocked at his loathsome image in the mirror. Yet he who looks in the mirror is graphically represented for the viewer as identical to the mirror image. We do not see a depiction of Crumb as Crumb imagines himself, his self-image, but only a representation of how Crumb sees himself with disgust in the reflected image. He exclaims, "IS THAT ME?! MY GOD! IT IS!!" Crumb shows us the anxiety that occurs when we rediscover the fragmentation of the subject in the duplicity of memory, self-image, and visual perception (Kominsky-Crumb and Crumb, *Self-Loathing Comics* 2 [Seattle: Fantagraphics Books, 1997]).

51. Connell, *Masculinities,* 45, 51, 52.

52. Cited in Davis, *Enforcing Normalcy*, 147.

53. Quoted in Thorpe, "Al Davison," 37.

54. For an analysis of this odious dimension of Davison's experiences with other men see Paul McIlvenny, "Disabling Men: Masculinity and Disability in Al Davison's Graphic Autobiography, *The Spiral Cage,*" in *Bending Bodies: Moulding Masculinities,* vol. 2, ed. Søren Ervø and Thomas Johansson (Aldershot, U.K.: Ashgate, 2000).

55. Quoted in Thorpe, "Al Davison," 39.

56. In comparison with an earlier page filled with loose self-portraits drawn while temporarily blind (the result of M.E.), we could say that alternate panels in the matrix here were also drawn while he was in the same state, a liminal period in which expression or novelty reigns and the constraints of social convention are temporarily suspended. For an analysis of the relations between blindness and art, see Jacques Derrida, *Memoirs of the Blind* (Chicago: University of Chicago Press, 1993).

57. Morris, "Gender and Disability," 85–92. Morris gives a timely warning that we should not generalize from the experience of disabled men to a universal experience of disabled people. It is equally true that we should not generalize from the experience of particular disabled men to the experience of disabled men in general, as if there were a unitary experience of subordinated/marginalized masculinity for all men with impairments. With regard to popular cinema, Morris notes that "the association of disability with dependency and lack of autonomy has in fact been used by film-makers in recent years to explore an experience of vulnerability for men" (187).

58. Sidonie Smith, "Performativity, Autobiographical Practice, Resistance," *A/B: Auto/Biography Studies* 10, no. 1 (1995): 17.

59. Ibid., 19.

60. Quoted in Thorpe, "Al Davison," 37.

61. Shakespeare, "When Is a Man Not a Man?" 53.

Chapter 6

Dragging Out the Queen

Male Femaling and Male Feminism

TERRY GOLDIE

The term "drag queen" apparently is a development from the combination of "draggle-tail" and "queen." If a fox has a wet tail, it drags it and presents a "draggle-tail" look, depressed and somehow deficient. Similarly the woman who does not look after the train of her dress or who has a dirty or hand-me-down gown looks draggle-tailed and becomes a drag queen. The journey from this to the man dressed as a woman is not a long one. Thus the drag queen is a draggle-tail woman. Still, "drag queen" remains one of those terms which everyone understands but no one uses with precision. The performer imitating Joan Rivers in a gay bar is a drag queen, but is it the right term for that strange Margaret Thatcher lookalike in the drug store? In both cases, there is a man behind the clothing, but what is behind the man? Why would he transpose his body to make it such a sight/site?

The photographs I include here, all of me, provide a counterpoint to this.[1] The first is a rather stereotypical shot, or at least stereotypical of some aspects of drag (Figure 5). The stance is rather demure while the dress is tight, short, and red. I offer it here because as far as I can tell it is a reasonable representation of what I have been told is my success at drag and this photograph is the one I usually use as my "calling card" in this context. I sent it to one friend who showed it to her husband. According to her he said, "Nice-looking girl, although the outfit's a bit tarty isn't it?" I have never met the man so I can't vouch for his eyesight, but this seems a reasonable statement of what I want to see in the image.

Richard Ekins' *Male Femaling: A Grounded Theory Approach to Cross-Dressing and Sex-Changing*[2] is an excursion through various males who pursue overtly cross-gendered self-presentation. Ekins uses terms such as transvestite and transsexual but not as definitions. Instead he refers to "body femaling," in which the emphasis is on body modification such as genital surgery and breast enlargement, "erotic femaling," the manifestation of elements of a female appearance for sexual satisfaction, and "gender femaling," in which the emphasis is on replicating the "real girl," in style or appearance. It is impossible to find comfortable and accurate demarcations of these terms as they are invested too much in the subjectivity of the person using them. Ekins is searching for a sociological approach that

Courtesy of Beatrix Thomasi

FIGURE 5.

encompasses all relevant behaviors without implying anything inferior or superior about any of them. However, the result is dry and descriptive, and demonstrates little awareness of the variety of forces compelling male femaling or the variety of contexts in which it is understood.

An extreme contrast to Ekins' distant tone is found in Janice Raymond's *Transsexual Empire,* which treats all male femaling as attempts to infiltrate and usurp womanhood. As Judith Butler states in *Bodies That Matter,* Raymond "places drag on a continuum with cross-dressing and transsexualism, ignoring the important differences between them."[3] More important, however, she foregrounds female and feminist opposition. Drag has often been criticized as a false representation of femaleness or as a misogynist burlesque, but there seems to be more to Raymond's attack than this. It is as if for her drag is the ultimate domination, in which men not only control but also become the female body. To Raymond, distinctions between such patriarchal ventures are meaningless.

Butler erases her own distinction when she, without justification, uses drag as a category for Venus Xtravaganza. In the film *Paris Is Burning* Venus is a particularly pathetic figure: a Latina street hustler whose aspirations to be a White suburban housewife are cut short by what seems like her inevitable murder by a bad trick. Although she has elements of the drag queen or "gender femaler," she is more a stereotypical transsexual, or "body femaler." Jay Prosser's excellent book *Second Skins: The Body Narratives of Transsexuality* details Butler's misdiagnosis of Venus.[4] But there is another possible error in using the term "drag" to designate Venus: "drag queen" emphasizes the creation of an image, rather than the expression of the person within, as is the case for the transsexual. The root of "drag queen," the draggle-tail queen, is a designation based on appearance. Thus it is highly appropriate that the primary use of the term "drag queen" is for performers, such as female impersonators in nightclubs. It represents not the internal female, the goal of Venus Xtravaganza, but rather the female as display. Venus wished to go far beyond representation, but for the drag queen my wordplay on sight/site is quite appropriate: a male subject caught within a place of femaleness.

This distinction between the transsexual and the drag queen can be extended. Butler states that Venus seeks "a certain transubstantiation of gender."[5] Prosser's lengthy critique explores the "Eucharistic sense"[6] of transubstantiation, but he ignores the reality of transubstantiation in the Catholic liturgy: the bread and wine *really* become the body and blood of Christ. Regardless of how one perceives transsexuality, such a transubstantiation, a *real* change, seems to be the goal. In a surprisingly doctrinaire comment in the otherwise nuanced arguments of *Volatile Bodies*, Elizabeth Grosz denies this possibility: "Men, contrary to the fantasy of the transsexual, can never, even with surgical intervention, feel or experience what it is like to be, to live, as women."[7] This statement is similar to scientific dismissals of the claim of transubstantiation. One of the major distinctions between the Catholic and Protestant cosmologies is the latter sees the Eucharist as not transubstantiation but metaphor. So here, to follow this very loose analogy, the drag queen might seem more like the Protestant. The goal is not transubstantiation but fantasy and metaphor.

Prosser analyzes the many instances in transsexual autobiographies in which a mirror provides a key moment of identity. While most transsexuals claim that they have essential genders that come from within, they are concerned, at times obsessed, with seeing glimpses of that gender in the apparently wrong-gendered image in the mirror and in cross-dressing so that the inner self can see a physical reflection of that psychological truth. Prosser notes that many transsexuals exert great effort to take photographic self-portraits that provide a permanent view of this body of the identity. This seems to follow Althusser's concept of interpellation, although perhaps in reverse. The process is not the way in which the hegemony calls or names you, but rather the way you can manipulate that calling to be interpellated as you would wish to be.

In my own life I have found photographs have an importance which cannot be met by mirrors. The fluidity of the mirror, in which my subjectivity and myself as object are both very much in motion, creates a situation that is too dynamic for me to judge. Although the essence of the process is that I am within the object, I need to be able to judge the object, which requires separation. As in the transsexual autobiographies, my reading of myself in these images is obviously subjective. The captions give the credits for the photographs but I would like to emphasize here that the photographers are both "real girls" and heterosexual women. The clothing was my choice, but the style and presentation were primarily under the control of the photographers (who chose the spaces). There is a dimension in which these images are defined by someone other than myself, far more than if I were just looking in the mirror. In yet one more twist of subjectivity, however, I have selected these shots to suit the article.

In the present context the drag queen is homosexual. Prosser provides a series of distinctions that help to explain this specificity: "In contradistinction to the transsexual, the transgenderist crossed the lines of gender but not those of sex; in contradistinction to the drag queen, the transgenderist's feminine gender expression was not intrinsically bound up with a homosexual identity nor could its livedness be made sense of through drag's performativity."[8] The term "livedness" would be easy to pass over, but it seems to encapsulate questions of experience which are germane here. Because if the drag queen is only observed, then there is no experience within. Instead, part of my exercise here is not just to make the personal, my personal, a focus for intellectual discussion: it is also to analyze the inside of that experience, and to try to recognize the process of living the experience. If experience is always of the subject, how is the subject controlled by this explicit movement into object? The exterior is displaced so that the subject is placed in a new site. For me, the "livedness" is defined by exactly the parts Prosser mentions, the "intrinsic" homosexuality and the performative.

Not that intrinsic homosexuality has an intrinsic relationship with female representation. Drag has been attacked by gay men as contributing to demeaning stereotypes which are part of heterosexist misunderstandings of homosexuality, such as the essential effeminacy of the homosexual male. In contrast, many gay men view homosexuality as an excess of masculinity rather than a lack. This is a cliché of gay pornography, but it is also a philosophical claim by figures such as André Gide.[9] Another pejorative interpretation is that the drag queen is a representation of the female which allows the homosexual to avoid having anything to do with biological women. As Butler notes, compulsory heterosexuality views drag as a necessary pathology for homosexuality: "the only place love is to be found is *for* the ostensibly repudiated object where love is understood to be strictly produced through a logic of repudiation; hence, drag is nothing but the effect of a love embittered by disappointment or rejection, the incorpora-

Courtesy of Pamela Lewis

FIGURE 6.

tion of the Other whom one originally desired, but now hates."[10] It is not difficult to reject this, one more illness theory for our behavior. It could belong in the same category as the usual ridicule of the pathetic drag queen, from the cross-dressed hula dancer in Walt Disney's *The Lion King* to schoolyard taunts such as "Your father wears a dress."

But drag could be a sexual object without constituting embitterment or repudiation. In *To Wong Foo with Love, Julie Newmar,* a film almost universally derided by the drag community, there is one moment worth considering as a positive insight. In this, the Wesley Snipes character claims that drag is a manifestation of a homosexual excess, of too much sexual energy to be contained in male clothing. The second photograph here is particularly suited to this argument (Figure 6). The attire and the posture present the drag queen body as, in Butler's terms, "a place" of "love"—a feminized sexual object. It re-places the male body (and the male mind). Still, the pose shows the lack of breasts, and so at the same time underscores that though the male body may be re-placed it is still in place.

When I first gave a version of this article as a conference presentation, I thought of dressing in drag, but I decided against it. This is not simply because a man in drag would seem ridiculous at an academic conference. Drag is always to some degree ridiculous. More importantly, drag is defined by its situation. If it is first and foremost appearance, it must be seen in a context, can be understood only in a context. Thus it is very much a site, with all the geographical continuities. And a sight or a display is never only what it claims to be by the person producing the display. This is one element of the performativity of drag. Butler maintains elsewhere that "performance as bounded 'act' is distinguished from performativity insofar as the latter consists in a reiteration of norms which precede, constrain, and exceed the performer and in that sense cannot be taken as fabrication of the performer's 'will' or 'choice.' "[11] As Butler notes, "in speech-act theory, a performative is that discursive practice that enacts or produces that which it names."[12] The classic example is the marriage ceremony and its "I do's."

This returns to context. The drag queen in performance could be, as so many female impersonators over the years have claimed, a "normal" man in women's clothing, putting on a show. The representation is contained, or if not contained is tricking the performer himself. Drag as performative, in a non-performance space, is intended excess. What does it mean? Can any such drag queen understand him- (her-?) self? This presumably is one reason why I like the photographs, which give me a controlled context, if only as an historical moment. They are quite unlike a video, with all the flux of motion. Instead, they are an emplacement, in which I can study the site, perhaps a site of love, but most definitely a site of sex.

It is almost a cliché of commentary on cross-dressing that the best drag queens were Mae West and Marilyn Monroe. The essence of the drag queen on stage is a performance of femaleness, and who could do this better than a woman who had devoted her life to such a performance? In *Gender Trouble,* Butler states, "In imitating gender, drag implicitly reveals the imitative structure of gender itself—as well as its contingency."[13] While West and Monroe seemed to highlight this contingency, they were not so much performing gender in general but performing a particular aspect of gender, female sexuality, and specifically the sexuality of the seductress: West the manipulative and Monroe the innocent. This is quite different from someone like Sharon Stone, who might radiate sexuality but does not make a similar coherent performance of it.

And yet perhaps for the drag queen I am presenting, in the emphasis on performativity, the Sharon Stone of the late eighties is a better example: someone whose sexuality seemed to exceed her own contained performance. But once again it is sexuality that provides the mark. The professional drag performers who concentrate on stars that do not perform a similar sexuality, such as Carol Channing and Barbra Streisand, still emphasize the more sexualized elements of the originals. This is the focus for many attacks on drag queens by feminists. They claim, accurately, that they are just

Courtesy of Pamela Lewis

FIGURE 7.

one more example of men objectifying women, although in this case the male inhabits the object.

I do not quibble with the argument that drag queens operate in some way with a fetishized sexuality. I also do not question that the aspects of female sexuality which are highlighted are often those which many progressive women reject. The third photograph represents availability, accessibility, and probably a desire for a dominant sexual partner (Figure 7). Identity is denied and is replaced by feminine clothing, a rather abandoned pose, and long legs. The presentation highlights elements of the body that are usually deemed most sexual and in ways that emphasize contrast with maleness, whether by shaving legs or adding types of jewelry seldom seen on men. The specific sexuality of these things can be seen in heterosexual pornography, where the men are often nude but the women usually have some articles of clothing. These are often specifically fetishistic, such as stiletto heels, but they include such apparently absurd elements as very feminine hats. The sexuality is from the feminine as well as from the female.

Something that crosses between the body and the dress for both women and drag queens is makeup, again something foregrounded in heterosexual pornography. Makeup is a way of writing on the body, particularly for the drag queen, who stays within the limitations of what has been called "glamour makeup." This is the makeup that is always recognized as makeup by even the most myopic, straight male but is described as "highlighting" or "enhancing," rather than crossing that barrier to categories such as "theatrical," which is regarded as transformative. This might be compared to one of Grosz's comments on the way the body is offered to the world:

> The notion of corporeal inscription of the body-as-surface rejects the phenomenological framework of intentionality and the psychoanalytic postulate of psychical depth; the body is not a mode of expression of a psychical interior or a mode of communication or mediation of what is essentially private and incommunicable. Rather, it can be understood as a series of surfaces, energies, and forces, a mode of linkage, a discontinuous series of processes, organs, flows, and matter.[14]

So makeup is of the body, of the mind, of the performative.

This is true not only of the drag queen, but perhaps in the present argument the context should be limited to conscious, even self-conscious, makeup. The woman who habitually puts on a trace of lipstick each morning is doing little more than "getting dressed." But glamour makeup has many parts, many of which could be examined philosophically. Comments by cosmeticians that "enhancing the eyes is most important" could be met by the aphorism that "the eyes are the window of the soul." In the case of the drag queen, the male eyes look out at the world looking at the female eyeshadow. The eyes are placed, the alluring eyes of so many advertisements, as the look of love? As looking for love? I feel a need for the constant assertion that the man always remains within the "drag queen" as I am depicting "her" here. There are very few cross-dressers who are truly not readable by anyone, but this is a complicated issue, for which I have been able to discover only anecdotal evidence. It is much like the comments many of us make about "always being able to tell" ethnicity, race, occupation, age, hairpieces, etc.: the only way of assessing our accuracy would be to check the object of each comment ("Excuse me, sir, are you wearing a toupee?"). In my experience heterosexual women make the strongest claim that all male femalers are readable. I have no idea why this is true, except perhaps that they, as a group, have more of a tendency to believe in a quintessential femaleness. Again to refer only to my own experience, gay men, lesbians, and straight men express a simple lack of interest (except for the almost inevitable anecdote about the straight man who unknowingly tried to pick up a male femaler). The women who assert their ability to read the male femaler usually mention a specific body part:

"just look at the hands"; "you would never see hips like that on a woman"; "it's the Adam's apple." Of course, this is easily refuted by reference to men with small hands, women with narrow hips, and the not insignificant number of men who have no visible Adam's apple. In the case of transsexuals, a variety of modifications are made to reduce readability, including surgically shaving the Adam's apple. My personal assessment is that a number of transsexuals achieve true unreadability, as one might expect, since enormous physiological and behavioral changes are pursued, not to cross-dress but to become the sex represented by the gender of the dress.

Gay drag queens are a different case. Even those who come closest to passing produce the illusion through highly feminized cover-up, heavy makeup, tight short dresses, high heels, etc. Thus they become readable in the many situations where almost no woman would appear that way. It is interesting that people such as Raymond are so opposed to such objectified sexuality, because often it is the very element that makes maleness so clear. While it objectifies femaleness, it also separates the drag queens from the representation of "real women." This seems perfectly appropriate, as potential readability is always at least a part of the drag queen's appearance. *Bodies That Matter* provides an extensive analysis of the goal of "realness" in *Paris Is Burning*. The very term "realness" requires some category of unrealness. If the simulacrum is absolutely identical to the original, then it is not "realness," it is simply real. So even if a drag queen is not at all readable, her readability is an essential (I use that loaded word intentionally) part of her drag queen-ness. This is especially true of the gay male who does not perceive himself as transsexual. The darting glances of the transsexual are often looking in fear of being read, but for the gay drag queen, to achieve the status of being unreadable would be to embody the female in a counterproductive way.

But what is the sexual component of such appearance? Ekins provides the specific category of the "erotic femaler," but arguably all "male femalers" have to some degree an erotic intention. Fetishism, in a quite strict psychoanalytic sense, has been emphasized by many theorists of transvestitism in its various forms. If the most important aspect of the drag queen is the "real" male within this object, then presumably the drag queen embodies the phallic woman. If phallic displacement to the fetish is the explanation for all non-human objects of sexual desire, then it clearly applies here. According to Marjorie Garber's extensive exploration in *Vested Interests,* "The history of the fetish in representation . . . indicates that the fetish *is* the phallus, the phallus *is* the fetish."[15] If the goal of the cross-dresser, particularly the heterosexual one, is an erectile response to the sexualized synecdoches of female garb this would be an appropriate interpretation. However, in a broader view of sexualization, there are other possibilities.

The sexualized space is not found only through the fetish, or at least the fetish as usually constituted. Many women have rejected the idea of a simple equation of phallus and sexual drive. In *Space, Time and Perversion* Grosz provides a very complex argument about lesbian fetishism:

> the masculine woman takes an external love-object—another woman—and through this love-object is able to function as if she *has*, rather than *is*, the phallus. As with the fetishist, this implies a splitting of the ego: it is this which inclines her to feminism itself, insofar as feminism, like any oppositional political movement, involves a disavowal of social reality so that change becomes conceivable and possible. . . . The categories that Freud proposed as universally relevant—the function of the phallus, the Oedipus complex, the ubiquity of the castration threat, and women's status as passive—surely need to be contested in order that social relations themselves can be transformed.[16]

Although others have so argued, drag is not in itself a political statement, an attempt at a broader transformation of social relations. However, it can be seen as falling in the psychoanalytic category of disavowal and, to follow Grosz, as a disavowal which goes beyond simple questions of the phallus and the role of castration. Perhaps in the present context it would be better to describe sexual desire as a multiplex space. Butler provides an alternative with, instead of one phallus, many: "If what comes to signify under the sign of the phallus are a number of body parts, discursive performatives, alternative fetishes, to name a few, then the symbolic position of 'having' has been dislodged from the penis as its privileged anatomical (or non-anatomical) occasion."[17]

Here Butler seems to go beyond the many-lipped sexualities of various French feminists, but the symbolism remains rather genital. In *Volatile Bodies* Grosz presents the alternative of the "Body without Organs" of Deleuze and Guattari, but finally rejects the BwO on feminist grounds.[18] Many have said that its numerous contradictions (e.g., "The BwO is not a scene, a place, or even a support upon which something comes to pass," "the BwO is all of that: necessarily a Place, necessarily a Plane . . ."[19]) make the BwO simply a vapor. One element, however, approximates one view of the drag queen: "The BwO is not opposed to the organs; rather the BwO and its 'true organs,' which must be composed and positioned, are opposed to the organism, the organic organization of the organs."[20] Thus as the drag queen seems to deny the organic, in employing the clothing which does not suit the natural man, so drag reinstates the organs by making this outer place of the displaced body into the manifestation of desire. And as Deleuze and Guattari suggest, it is most definitely not an erasure: "Dismantling the organism has never meant killing yourself, but rather opening the body to connections that presuppose an entire assemblage, circuits, conjunctions, levels and thresholds, passages and distributions of intensity, and territories and deterritorializations measured with the craft of a surveyor."[21]

QUEEN OVER ALL HE SURVEYS

However, as Grosz notes, the attractions of Deleuze and Guattari are in the end amorphous. The very impetus of male femaling would seem in some sense to require "organs," and its desires are more specific than those many plateaus of the BwO. The various subjects give various explanations, from the transsexual assertion that the self knows herself to be female to the transvestite's simple observation that it "feels good." The mind responds to a drive within: the male desires an experience which in some sense is denied to his gender and *apparently* to his sex. In the case of the drag queen, it is rather a body which, while with organs, requires redefinition, re-placement.

Butler observes that Monique Wittig offers a "model of a more diffuse and antigenital sexuality."[22] Butler suggests that this can be taken to a level which could be called "postgenital." If such a term can be applied to the drag queen, it provides an interesting contradiction to both the view of drag as fetish, the pursuit of the false genital, and the view of the transsexual, for whom the genital is usually a goal, whether or not achieved. For this drag queen, the whole "thing" is sexualized; it is not just a series of associations. It has become a commonplace in sexual therapy to explore beyond the genital. Judging sexuality by some technical device which gauges the engorgement of the penis is far too simplistic. Perhaps psychoanalysis might make the same move. If the body represents all the body, everything at once connected to and divorced from the mind, then it is more than the phallus. It moves slightly toward what might be the ultimate phenomenology: the Body as Organ. A balance of self and not-self as object within the self can be represented through a more expansive sexual geography, such as this "place of love," the drag queen. The fetish tends to be seen very much as an object. It can be an object in action, such as the whip, but it is first an object. However, gender performativity offers many more possibilities to the motion of the object. In its various spaces, the active embodiment of female sexuality becomes the goal, regardless of the sex of the body embodying.

One important contradiction is the place of drag in the gay community. While it is generally esteemed as performance, its performativity is often derided. Drag hookers do well, but most define their customers as heterosexual (although obviously heterosexual with a bit of a kink). One gay friend of mine who has never done drag said rather cynically that he always believed gay men did drag to avoid sex. I have never felt that myself but I can see the argument, especially in that as a come-on to the homosexual, male drag seems to have little success. The explanation is usually the obvious one: "If I wanted a female I would get a real one." The extent of this feeling, or perhaps it would better be called a prejudice, is shown in that many drag queens, long after they have come out of the closet as gay, keep their female clothing very much behind a closed door. But perhaps this confusion should not be so surprising; given that sociobiologists are always telling us that we present ourselves sexually in order to attract our target, the choice to appear in drag seems contradictory. Narcissism seems a reasonable explanation of this process. Drag is a way of inhabiting desirability, regardless of whether the desired object responds. It offers the "sexy feeling" so often asserted in advertisements for commodities which convey female sexuality.

I have often questioned gay men about their response to the female sex object. It has always surprised me that so many claim to have no interest whatsoever. Those who admit a glance or two explain it in a few different ways. One explanation places the gay male at some point on the transsexual continuum, and therefore in some sense a feminized gaze narcissistically interested in depictions of female sexuality. Another sees the sexualized female as an aesthetic object and therefore fitting the gay fascination with art. A third sees female sexuality as performance and thus fitting another stereotype, the gay male as theatrical. I would expect the gay male to be interested for another reason, however; the objectification of sexuality as a specifically female thing. This might seem a strange proposition, especially in a gay context. Magazines such as *Details* and *Gentleman's Quarterly* exist on the assumption that men want to present themselves sexually. It is difficult to see why all those tight zippered tops exist if men are not sex objects. But contemporary Western society has evolved to the point where this is very much a minority culture. We seem to have gone quite a distance from the human peacocks of the Renaissance courts.

The first reason for drag is the obvious one given above; that the body is the female body and therefore the sexualized body is female sexuality. Wittig goes so far as to say in "The Point of View: Universal or Particular": "There is only one: the feminine, the 'masculine' not being a gender. For the masculine is not the masculine, but the general."[23] To return to the comment about the effeminate homosexual, drag could be the search for a gender which the not-masculine homosexual lacks. But the specifics of drag's sexuality present something else, once again in opposition to the phallus. In *Bodies That Matter* Butler considers the philosophical tradition which emphasizes the materiality of the female. If this is the case, does female garb make the male body more materially sexual? It becomes less the confusing general power of the phallus-which-is-not-the-penis and instead the specifically sexual power of the tight dress and displayed cleavage.

There are many other possible reasons. One would seem to be the route which has been followed by the hegemony of male heterosexual power. While the possibility of a female subject position has developed, society has strongly asserted that the norm, the default option, is the male heterosexual. Thus it is only logical that the primary object should be the female heterosexual. Perhaps as a corollary, it has been assumed that if the heterosexual female is the subject she does not respond to the male object in the same way. The logical example is *Playgirl,* which many claim is of more interest to the homosexual male than to the heterosexual female. (I should note here the many observers who have claimed that women appreciate the visual representation of sexuality much more than this suggests. Regardless of the accuracy of the assumption of the lack in the female gaze, it has been a guiding philosophy in the commercial representation of sexuality.)

The primary male sex objects of the cinema are seldom hypermasculinized, male versions of Mae West. Considering a couple of exceptions, Arnold Schwarzenegger and Sylvester Stallone, it is interesting to see how recent they are and how often ironized. Others, such as Montgomery Clift, James Dean, Clark Gable, and Brad Pitt, have different sexualities to offer, but the male Marilyn Monroe is not among them. This suggests that in our contemporary society, while male sexual performance is a constant subject of discussion, especially since the advent of Viagra, the performativity of male sexuality is nebulous, at times obscure, and often rather skewed. Discussing a Wall Street lawyer in a Hugo Boss suit as a sex object overlooks the dividing line between power and sexuality, a dividing line that still exists, however fine. If there is a performativity of male sexuality in the mainstream culture which is separate from economic power, it is very difficult to define. Attempts to represent the male stud-muffin seem plagued with difficult definitions. A recent radio program asserted the United Parcel Service deliveryman as sex object. This is not Stanley Kowalski, but what it is I am not at all sure. According to the program the appeal has something to do with those nondescript brown uniforms.[24]

But what of the body within? I have suggested that the male body is an important element of the drag queen, regardless of the many possible interpretations of that body. And despite my comments about Mae West and Marilyn Monroe, there is a frisson to the male within that creates much of the energy without. To offer just one experience, I once went in drag to an academic banquet. The response was ongoing, including appreciative laughter from many heterosexual women and scornful stares from many heterosexual men. My subjectivity enjoyed both sides of this reaction. And in this small, over-educated crowd, it led to an evening of discussion of gender, well beyond the usual topic of whether drag demeans women. For example, when I applied lipstick while sitting at the table, the straight man next to me stated that it was tacky to apply lipstick in public. I presume he would not have said this if I were a real woman. The result was a lengthy discussion of what private/public means in terms of gender, particularly in light of various beauty regimens and regimes.

But I again seem to have slipped away from the body per se. I think I have good company in this in that two of the most prominent body theorists, Butler and Grosz, often do the same. At one level it is difficult to see how this is to be avoided. Grosz provides the best analysis of the mind/body split I have encountered, particularly in her assessment of the concept of the body image:

> The body image does not map a biological body onto a psychosocial domain, providing a kind of translation of material into conceptual terms; rather, it attests to the necessary interconsistency of each for the other, the radical inseparability of biological from psychical elements, the mutual dependence of the psychical and the biological, and thus the intimate connection between the question of sexual specificity (biological sexual differences) and psychical identity.[25]

Grosz is arguing that there is no such thing as an appropriate or inappropriate psychic description of the body and that therefore all possible "body images" are both of and separate from the body and mind, not accurate or inaccurate but multiplicitous, not the body or mind but the bodymind. As the jacket blurb by Butler states, *Volatile Bodies* sets "a high critical standard for feminist dialogues on the status of the body." And yet does Grosz's focus actually move the body from raw substance to focus? Is she not caught within the mind of the body? And is the mind of the body ever the body? The usual response to this binary is the claim that one cannot separate the mind from the body. In this case, the even more troublesome game is the attempt to split the body from the mind. Grosz is denying the ephemeral view of the body image (as in statements such as "overweight people just have a bad body image") but what is the alternative? The end result of this argument in the present context is that the link and discontinuity between the male body and the "body image" of the male body in female clothing are meaningful, but do not necessarily constitute the meaning assumed by the mind of either the observer or the wearer. There is a triangulated mind-body-body image which gives this scene resonances well beyond the myriad interpretations made by the wearing minds or the observing minds.

Regardless of my emphasis on surface and clothing here, the packaging of the drag queen reconfigures the male body to *look like* the female body. Butler notes that one reason the female body is traditionally the gendered and material body is in opposition to the mind, which is assumed to be male. Grosz polemically asserts, "corporeality must no longer be associated with one sex (or race) which then takes on the burden of the other's corporeality for it. Women can no longer take on the function of being *the* body for men while men are left free to soar to the heights of theoretical reflection and cultural production."[26] In dressing in female clothes that create the figure of the female body, the drag queen at once impersonates this corporeality, this position as *the* body, and yet, through the fact that this is now a male body, asserts how immaterial this material is. To return to Grosz's claim about body image, the drag queen at once shows the absurdity of the assumption that the image of female sexuality is intrinsically a part of the female body, calls into question assumptions that the female body image denies that soaring male mind, and also denies that the male body is of no consequence in this series of gendered associations.

So while it is the male body within the female covering, is it in some sense *the body?* Here I think I am truly limited to my personal experience. Many cross-dressers have asserted the sensuality of nylons, the joyful constriction of corsets, etc. All I can say is that this has not been my experience. Rather, my subjectivity, and I think I can say very much my mind, responds to the appearance of my male body in female clothing. Thus for me this is almost a defining element of the mind/body dichotomy. While it is important to me that it is my body within, the experience is very much scopophilia: it is looking at my body within the dress which appeals to me. It is seeing my body within. Even when there is no mirror around I enjoy the sense of being seen, the Bishop Berkeleys around me who I perceive perceiving. And the sense of being scene. The female attire is very much the Derridean supplement, the thing written on top which is both obviously superfluous and also absolutely intrinsic. The drag queen is thus a graphological experience. Its text is a palimpsest but always a text, a thing which has been written and which continually manifests a process of writing.

As, perhaps, is male feminism. In part, I choose to blend these two simply because two things that give me a kick are wearing dresses and studying feminist theory. I also feel, however, that something more links the two than my idea of fun. In the conclusion to a 1983 essay on male feminism, Elaine Showalter engaged in a *jeu d'esprit* which she might wish to temper now but which nevertheless gives a good introduction to my point here. Showalter offered her "dream of the feminist literary conference of the future": "The diacritical woman rises to speak, but she has no head. Holding out the empty sleeves of her fashionable jacket, she beckons to the third panelist. He rises swiftly and commands the podium. He is forceful; he is articulate; he is talking about Heidegger or Derrida or Lévi-Strauss or Brecht. He is wearing a dress."[27] The sensibility here was not at all uncommon at the time and still remains in many quarters. The anger underlying it can be seen in the title of Suzanne Moore's 1988 article "Getting a Bit of the Other: The Pimps of Postmodernism."[28]

At one level, this might seem but another version of Grosz's attack on the female as body. Feminism is presumably an assertion that the female is not just body, but is quite capable of theoretically soaring. But what constitutes the specifics of that soaring? If all that is required in feminism is the attributes of the female, then why not the woman without a head or the man in a dress? The problem is not just the tendencies of postmodernism, which seem the specific targets here, but also the division between the attributes and the self, or between the mind and the body. There seems to be a belief that a discussion of the outer, the corporeal female, must be linked to the inner, the female mind. In this article Showalter fears a disruption of that link that might be produced by perversions of gender.

A central focus of the attack in these articles is on the view of the feminine presented by various French theorists, some, but by no means all, male. Grosz's rejection of Deleuze and Guattari's BwO, discussed above, is an example. The sense of the argument is well-captured by Jane Gallop in her confrontation of Jean Baudrillard. I shall quote at some length to establish the principles involved in what is rather like a dialectic:

> He does not consider it an insult to say that woman is only appearance. Baudrillard is writing against the history of writing against appearances. He is for appearances, and against profundity, so that when he says that "woman is only appearance" it should be taken as a compliment.
>
> Nonetheless, when I read this passage, as a woman, I feel insulted. Baudrillard would have it that my feeling of offense is a great error which stems from my inscription within the sort of masculinistic essentialist thinking which condemns appearances as misleading mediations of essences, realities, and truths.
>
> Yet, in considering the passage carefully, I decide that it is not what he says about "woman" that offends me so much as what he says about "women": "Women would do well," he advises, "to let themselves be seduced by this truth." It is the phrase "would do well" (*feraient bien de*) that irks me. Although he puts "insulting" in quotation marks [to call woman as appearance an "insulting formula"] he uses the word "truth" (*verité*) straight. He knows the truth—the profound or hidden truth, I might add—about women, and women "would do well to let themselves be seduced" by the truth he utters.[29]

All of us who are somewhere on what might be called the "queer axis" realize the impossibility of using the word "truth" straight. No matter how often the truth is let out of the closet it never becomes straight. But we also know the multiple powers of seduction. And any drag queen knows the importance of appearance.

At the end of her piece, Gallop does a more extended turn on Baudrillard's belief in seduction as opposed to feminism. She offers the alternative of being seduced by feminism but she doesn't explain what she means by feminism in this context. If, as I assume, feminism is some direct assertion of power by women, it is difficult to see this as seductive. The most prominent definitions of "seduce" in the *Oxford English Dictionary* are based on some version of "to lead astray" or "to tempt, entice, or beguile to do something wrong, foolish or unintended." It seems to me that Baudrillard has it right in the implication of seduction leading to something at least apparently untoward; I doubt that the empowering of women fits.

Instead I would like to try to slip between Gallop and Baudrillard, to allow the seduction but not be tempted toward that straight truth. One answer is to follow the suggestions of Butler and play with the seductions of gender performance and gender performativity. Thus the problem becomes not women as depicted by Gallop, a social fact. Instead it becomes an opportunity, the possibility of "woman." Like the drag queen, the male feminist takes on a supplement. One of the obvious difficulties is that it is more than possible that for the person living as a woman this supplement can be instead a denial. This is invariably the argument of those opposed to drag queens but it often works as well for those opposed to male feminism. The drag queen and the male feminist use attributes associated with women, female sexuality and philosophical and theoretical responses to women in society, often in directions which discomfort those same women.

I realize there are many obvious difficulties in this. Does either the female clothing or male feminism suggest that to be a woman is to be Showalter's figure without a head? Does it produce a position with no substance, only surface? That might be the spirit behind Grosz's claim that the transsexual cannot experience life as a woman. But if I might be permitted to deny the question of essence, to simply set aside the question of whether there is something intrinsic to being sexed as a female, the distinction between living as and representing as seems to me possibly viable. In this article I trace only a minute few of the surfaces associated with the feminine and the feminist. But I would argue that establishing some of these as important but also not substantive, at the level of Baudrillard's appearances, can enable a separation between the appearance of gender and many of the experiences lived by women.

Jane Gallop seems to me a particularly interesting example for this discussion. Her recent *Feminist Accused of Sexual Harassment*[30] attempts to trace a feminism which offends many women's view of feminism. She has been attacked for trying to embrace two contradictory positions: the overt one being feminist and the covert one being a powerful academic who uses that power in sexually harassing students. But she questions the possibility of a female being in this second position. She instead reflects on the "classic case" of sexual harassment which is a male superior harassing a female inferior. She seems unable to accept the possibility that a female professor can take on the supplement of male power and be transformed. She does not accept the variant dangers of the seduction of the female. But the indeterminacy of gender is not a free space. It has limitations and constraints, some of which can be specific to the sex of the person within the gender and some of which are dependent on that sex. I am not claiming that the female professor is the obverse of the drag queen, but at the same time if there is a gender to institutional power it is presumably male, and dichotomies must be recognized in order to be survived. The drag queen who denies the male within is a figure of pathos. The male feminist who denies his male privilege is adding to rather than defeating sexism. The female professor who denies her institutional power is doing much the same.

As Grosz most clearly has pointed out, the simple binary of sex and gender has resolutely failed. There is something almost intrinsic to sex; "almost intrinsic" is my oxymoron, not hers, but it seems a good fit for the problem. It is why Prosser is so assertive about the indeterminacy of gender and yet is himself transsexual. The sex cannot be denied, no matter how much a gender theorist might wish to deny it. So the drag queen and male feminist move into genders that have specific resonances because of the apparently variant sex behind the gender. Perhaps the only way a born female can inhabit those genders that way is to somehow move out into the male sex as gender before taking on the female gender. As I look back at that sentence I realize how mind-boggling such a possibility seems. Yet I have at least a glimmer of that process in Mae West. And perhaps this is at least a preliminary description of Jane Gallop's trajectory, although hers might arguably end with a map of infinite detours.

This might seem like just so much dancing, whether by a drag queen or a male feminist. In *Sexual Subversions: Three French Feminists,* Grosz encapsulates this problem of the isolation of whatever constitutes the feminine:

> the masculine domination of the right to speak on behalf of the feminine is an effect of its capacity to achieve a certain distance from its objects of analysis. The masculine is able to speak of and for women because it has emptied itself of any relation to the male body, thus creating a space of reflection, of specul(aris)ation in which it claims to look at itself and at femininity from outside. This presumed "outsideness" is equated with objectivity.[31]

I hope I have not attempted to deny the male body in this discussion of supplements for it. Similarly, I trust I shall not be accused of claiming objectivity.

And yet, I certainly accept "outsideness." But I would argue that such outsideness, when aligned with a number of the values which might be associated with insideness, might allow for productive separations, not simply the deformed errors feared by Showalter. There still might be the need for the strategic essentialism to which Diana Fuss[32] refers, in which women act as though Woman, but there is a value to a separation between women as sociological space and the individuals who inhabit that space, and woman as performance and as performativity. The sociological woman is thus the position and experience of those who live that gender, whether born women or transsexual. Foregrounding aspects of gender representation or theorizing about the figure of Woman in our culture necessarily shapes that position, but does not define it and should not be used to deny it. Those who are women in that sense have been economically disadvantaged, legally restricted, and medically oppressed. Such processes as affirmative action in the workplace and reproductive rights are necessary responses to such oppression.

But there are other parts to the possibility of woman. A group which at times seems highly disadvantaged in such discussions is heterosexual women. A number of recent commentators have been trying to find a way in which the heterosexual woman can overcome the "anatomy is destiny" arguments of Andrea Dworkin and Catharine MacKinnon and produce the female who has sexual relations with the male penis as a viable feminist and, even more, an individual. Camille Paglia's paeans to Madonna are but the most public example of this. The separation of the highly gendered—sexuality and theory—from the sociological category, can be liberating in exactly this way. The issue need not just be that a man, Baudrillard, inflicts "straight truth" on women in the name of seduction. No one should be allowed to do that. Instead, the multiplicity of appearance that Baudrillard labels as woman is a gender production which can be theoretically liberating for anyone. If I allow myself to be drawn to the theories of Derrida this does not preclude me fighting for the appointment of a woman in my department. I remember many years ago when in discussion Derrida used the word "invagination" in a specifically literary way. Asked about the implications for women of such a usage he said that it had nothing to do with women, it was just a word. I cannot agree that this is the case, but perhaps it should be. Woman as appearance is a product of the gender traditions of our culture. Woman as seductress is the same. To inhabit the theoretical slipperiness of the endlessly polysemantic is an opportunity for both male and female. To inhabit the sexuality of stockings and a garter belt is also. To extend Butler's argument about the denaturalization of gender, the stockings and garter belt show that the female sexuality which is the figure for substantiality is just a figure and a signifier in motion.

I must develop here, on closing, my comment at the outset that this is very much a personal essay, even more than usual a product of my own subjectivity. While I cannot subscribe to the claims of abnegation in Leo Bersani's "Is the Rectum a Grave?", I share his belief that one's own position in sexuality has a significant effect on understanding.[33] A famous gay theorist once said to me that after many years of being a top his first experience as a bottom made him understand what it means to be gay. As someone who has always been, as the books say, "anal passive," perhaps I am not the best drag queen to consider the possibility of the phallic woman. As I said to one of my classes, "I get fucked, therefore I am."

This does not, of course, mean I am a woman. My last photograph offers little obvious drag except the eyes (Figure 8). The deer caught in the headlights? The doe caught in the headlights? What does s/he want? If not the phallic woman, I remain, as the line goes in *Priscilla, Queen of the Desert,* "a cock in a frock on a rock." I am a man who at times inhabits the space of female sexuality. I would say the same about my ventures into feminist

Courtesy of Pamela Lewis

FIGURE 8.

theory. And I always remain responsive to those more experienced, in whatever sense that word might be taken, with *écriture féminine,* or with lip gloss and eyeliner.

NOTES

1. The first photograph is by Beatrix Thomasi, of Hannover, Germany and the other three are by Pamela Lewis, a Canadian who lives in Brisbane, Australia.

2. Richard Ekins, *Male Femaling: A Grounded Theory Approach to Cross-Dressing and Sex-Changing* (New York: Routledge, 1997).

3. Janice Raymond, *The Transsexual Empire: The Making of the She-Male,* 2nd ed. (New York: Teachers College Press, 1994); Judith Butler, *Bodies That Matter: On the Discursive Limits of "Sex"* (New York: Routledge, 1993), 126. Lest some think Raymond's position exceptional, a very similar case, that the primary effect of male-to-female surgery is to demean women, is made by Germaine Greer in *The Whole Woman* (New York: Doubleday, 1999).

4. Jay Prosser, *Second Skins: The Body Narratives of Transsexuality* (New York: Columbia University Press, 1998).

5. Butler, *Bodies That Matter,* 130.

6. Prosser, *Second Skins,* 50.

7. Elizabeth Grosz, *Volatile Bodies: Toward a Corporeal Feminism* (Bloomington: Indiana University Press, 1994), 207.

8. Prosser, *Second Skins,* 176.

9. André J. Gide, *Si le grain ne meurt* (Paris: Éditions de la Nouvelle revue française, 1924).

10. Butler, *Bodies That Matter,* 127.

11. Judith Butler, "Critically Queer," *Gay and Lesbian Quarterly* 1 (1993): 24.

12. Butler, *Bodies That Matter,* 13.

13. Judith Butler, *Gender Trouble: Feminism and the Subversion of Identity* (New York: Routledge, 1990), 137.

14. Grosz, *Volatile Bodies,* 120.

15. Marjorie Garber, *Vested Interests: Cross-Dressing and Cultural Anxiety* (New York: Harper Collins, 1992), 121.

16. Elizabeth Grosz, *Space, Time and Perversion: Essays on the Politics of Bodies* (New York: Routledge, 1995), 153–154.

17. Butler, *Bodies That Matter,* 89.

18. Grosz, *Volatile Bodies,* 167–174.

19. Gilles Deleuze and Félix Guattari, *A Thousand Plateaus: Capitalism and Schizophrenia,* trans. Brian Massumi (Minneapolis: University of Minnesota Press, 1987), 153, 161.

20. Ibid., 158.

21. Ibid., 160.

22. Butler, *Gender Trouble,* 27.

23. Monique Wittig, "The Point of View: Universal or Particular," *Feminist Issues* 5, no. 2 (1983): 64.

24. In an email to me, Kerryn Goldsworthy suggested this might be simply the tradition of the sexual irresponsibility of the deliveryman, from Chaucer through O'Neill's *The Iceman Cometh* to the pizza boy of so many porn movies. This is possible but I think the UPS man represents something else.

25. Grosz, *Volatile Bodies,* 85.

26. Ibid., 22.

27. Elaine Showalter, "Critical Cross-Dressing: Male Feminists and the Woman of the Year," in *Men in Feminism,* ed. Alice Jardine and Paul Smith (New York: Methuen, 1987), 116.

28. Suzanne Moore, "Getting a Bit of the Other: The Pimps of Postmodernism," in *Male Order: Unwrapping Masculinity,* ed. Jonathan Rutherford and Rowena Chapman (London: Lawrence & Wishart, 1988).

29. Jane Gallop, "French Theory and the Seduction of Feminism," in *Men in Feminism,* ed. Alice Jardine and Paul Smith (New York: Methuen, 1987), 113–114.

30. Jane Gallop, *Feminist Accused of Sexual Harassment* (Durham, N.C.: Duke University Press, 1997).

31. Elizabeth Grosz, *Sexual Subversions: Three French Feminists* (Sydney: Allen & Unwin, 1989): 128.

32. Diana Fuss, *Essentially Speaking* (New York: Routledge, 1989).

33. Leo Bersani, "Is the Rectum a Grave?" in *AIDS: Cultural Analysis, Cultural Activism,* ed. Douglas Crimp (Cambridge, Mass.: MIT Press, 1988), 197–222.

Chapter 7

A Man

ALPHONSO LINGIS

> To subordinate ourselves to the possible is to let ourselves be banished from the sovereign world of the stars, the winds, the volcanoes.
>
> God subordinates himself to the possible, setting aside the aleatory, abandons the game of exceeding the limits. A star exceeds the divine intelligence. A tiger has the silent and lost grandeur which God lacks.
>
> To remain virile in the light requires the audacity of a mad ignorance: to let oneself be embraced, crying with joy. It is to await death—in response to an unknown, unknowable presence. It is to oneself become love and blind light, to attain the perfect unintelligence of the sun.
>
> —Georges Bataille[1]

The distinctive male traits—penis and penetrator in copulation, greater size (20 percent on average) than females, and different pattern of, and on average greater, muscularity than females—materialize sexual and social behaviors. These traits co-determined the original division of labor in societies. Male identity and pride can issue in practices of dominance and brutality. Masculinity is seated in "secondary" differentiating characteristics of the male body—the angularity of the male body, the specific hirsuteness, the deeper tonality of the voice. Masculinity denotes appearance and also demeanor and behavior, and is elaborated in distinctive speech, gestures, postures, and garb, and in courtship, teasing, and games: the domain of seduction.

We are indeed impressed by someone superlatively male. One prizes one's own superlative maleness. Who is not awed by the splendor of a bull, a buck antelope, a ram, or a male silverback gorilla? And—noblesse oblige—one expects the guy with such balls to be enterprising and forceful in actions. We are captivated by the glamorous masculinity of medieval knights and samurai, nineteenth-century cavalry and naval officers, banditos decked out in black and silver, and high-society conmen suave and charming. Knights, bullfighters, skydivers compound male splendor with masculine glamour.

But what we especially care about is being a man, a real man.[2] Virility is what we look for, not in our foreman, manager, commander, nor in our protector, but in our buddy, our companion.

Virility is not simply an ethical trait, produced by character management and determination. It requires the chance of a body that is sexually excitable, that has the physical power to be courageous, the strength to impose justice.

The sense of oneself—confirmed by the recognition of others—one acquires by male traits and behaviors, and the sense of oneself one acquires by masculine handsomeness and seduction are destabilized by the dark and painful craving for exposedness to the naked body of a stranger. One perceives that virility is bent on some florid and mortal explosion. Virility is affirmed in sexual arousal—and chance. Chance arousal, chance in general.

The virility of a bus driver, a window washer, or a junior executive asserts itself in sexual arousal before a woman who denudes herself before him deliberately and provocatively, or a naked woman caught sight of by looking down upon a bedroom or shower room window. It affirms itself in sexual arousal before a naked male deliberately flaunting himself or unknowingly being watched. In his *White Book,* Jean Cocteau drew a picture of a penis in erection and labeled it: "The part of a man that never lies."[3] When he is no longer compulsively aroused by a chance body contact in the subway, a chance view into an apartment window in the next building, a man recognizes the loss of his virility. The moment of virility comes when one finds oneself aroused by nakedness, but a nakedness that exposes chance, hope, and terror.

Someone undresses before our eyes and under our embrace. In denuding her and himself, she and he take off the uniform, the categories, the endurance, the reasons, and the functions. As our bodies become orgasmic, the posture held oriented for tasks collapses, the diagrams for manipulations and operations with utensils, tools, and machines dissolve from our legs and hands, which roll about dismembered, exposed to the touch and tongue of another, moved by another. Our lips loosen, soften, glisten with saliva, lose the train of sentences; our throats issue babble, giggling, moans, and sighs. Our sense of ourselves, our self-respect, shaped in fulfilling a function in the mechanical and social environment, our dignity maintained in multiple confrontations, collaborations, and demands, dissolve; the ego loses its focus as center of evaluations, decisions, and initiatives. Our impulses, our passions, are returned to animal irresponsibility. The sighs and moans of another that pulse through our nervous excitability, the spasms of pleasure and torment in contact with the non-prehensile surfaces of our bodies—our cheeks, our bellies, our thighs—irradiate across the substance of our sensitive and vulnerable nakedness. Our muscular and vertebrate bodies transubstantiate into ooze, slime, mammalian sweat, and reptilian secretions, and releases of hot, moist breath nourishing the floating microorganisms of the night air. The extreme pleasure of orgasm, the most intense pleasure we can know, is borne by an anguished abandon to cadaveresque decomposition.

The surge of virility is the feeling of nakedness in oneself, the nakedness of one's glands, one's penis, the compacted coursing of blood and passion. It is the compulsion to trespass over the lines which one's own clothing, one's uniforms, one's categories, one's responsibilities fix. Denuding before a stranger is the transgression of interdictions. It is the compulsion to give oneself over passionately to a destiny marked out by chance events and apparitions.

The physical radiance which one did not fabricate, nor did one's parents, destines one for what lies beyond usefulness and serviceability. How often we have seen in the brightness of a factory worker in Oklahoma, the flair of a dockworker in Haiti, the dash of a rickshaw puller in Pakistan, physical splendor so extraneous, so irrelevant to this job and this subordination! How we have felt the constriction, the degradation, the oppression that these jobs are on them!

What chagrin to see someone recognizing his beauty, flair, and style, and setting out to use them! We do not see virility in the fashion model or personal trainer whose body is the product he sells or rents out.

One can find virile existence only inasmuch as one is seduced. The perhaps otherwise integrally servile individual, the soldier, the factory worker, the computer programmer, who feels the surge of virility before a naked body feels the provocation of hope, the incitement to despair and terror. He awakens to a destiny he sees outlined in the figure of that nakedness.

One who knows the surge of virility in himself is attached to it, but not as a goal or an achievement. He laughs over it, laughs over his hard-on, his obsessed nights. His laughter recognizes that his manliness does not point him to what the corporals or corporations recognize as an objective, nor to what his own intentions and ambitions recognize as good for himself, nor even what would be good for the denuded stranger he has caught sight of. His laughter assents to all bad as well as good luck; his laughter celebrates festivity, license, and puerile pleasure, lubricity, and wickedness. The decision of one who plays with chance must be risked, in ignorance of the game being played by others.

The sense of virility is opposed to functional servility. In making oneself useful, in character planning, in getting trained, in disciplining one's body and one's mind, in reprogramming one's movements, one's forces, one's circadian rhythms to functional diagrams and operations, one subordinates oneself to a functional system; one escapes a nature essentially indifferent to our intentions and desires; one lets oneself be banished from the sovereign world of the stars, the winds, the volcanoes. One subordinates one's forces, one's body, one's perceptions, one's mind to the layout, equipment, and operation of a factory, an office, a corporation. An assembly-line worker, a supervisor, a security guard, an electrician, a computer programmer, a junior executive are divested of virility. Any female, properly trained, can serve as well. In doing so, she does not become virile. The perception that the modern corporate workplace has no place for virility, nor womanhood, is expressed in today's zero-tolerance policies for any kind of sexual image or words, policies readily adopted by giant multinational corporations. Maleness may well serve the lean-and-mean corporation; virility defines outlaws.

The office worker goes off, for the time the company allows him once a year, to the wilderness to find his virility. He goes not with fellow-workers, whose varied competencies reconstitute a team in the wilderness camp, but with his adolescent son, in order to find again the incompetencies and risks of his own adolescence.

Virility gives itself over to the omens and coincidences that signal the path of a destiny; it involves a specific strength of the body. Virility requires courage. Fitness and expertise insert the body into a productive system; the courageous body is a body attuned to chance, to hope, and to terror.

The simple deployment of massive male size and musculature without adventure and risk brutalizes others but also brutalizes oneself. The self-indulgent intellectual, whose skin not exposed to the sun is pale and dry, who has the sagging stomach of men who indulge in nocturnal cogitation inscribing words over their visceral sensations—to speak of courage in such a one is ridiculous. Courage is not involved in the professionalized shaping of the body in training and discipline. It is absent from commercial body culture, exalted in celebrities and advertising, and from the fitness that a yuppie maintains as part of his image.

The highest strength is not the mobilization of the musculature of the body by an industrial, military, or athletic program. Courage is the trance into which a body is cast by the chance vision of a great hope and great risk. Musculature reaches its highest degree of versatility and endurance in ecstatic trance.

Despite Socrates and his slogan "An unexamined life is not worth living," despite Kierkegaard replacing love with the unending examination of the intentions involved and motives for love, we do not admire and do not trust actions that issue as the conclusions of reasoning from principles and intentions rationally justified. It is not virtue we admire, but natures, people with sound instincts. We do not trust our children, or even her own, to a mother who pursues an interminable psychoanalysis of her conscious and unconscious motives. It is that woman with the big heart, the farm woman beaming over calves, piglets, chicks, the aging prostitute longing for nothing more than to give tenderness and love, the woman in the old folks' home watching the children play in the park across the street and caring for her old cat, that we trust.

"It was the head tracker's marvelous swift response that captured my admiration at first," John Hersey wrote, "his split second solicitousness when he heard a cry of pain, his finding in mid-air, as it were, the only way to save the injured boy. But there was more to it than that. His action, which could not have been mulled over in his mind, showed a deep instinctive love of life, a compassion, an optimism, which made me feel very good."[4] In virile courage we do not see virtue programmed by the reasoning mind but a body entranced and ecstatic. Nothing is more flagrant than courage, which we do not see in front of us but feel pulling at our heart. So transparent is courage that we do not see courage in another without feeling the pounding of that very courage in us. Our trust then is not an assured dependency on his courage, but a surge of courage in ourselves.

The courage that mobilizes the body is shadowed by its simulacrum—muscular power entranced not by chance but by certainty—by a political or religious doctrine that gives itself out as truth. In the measure that, in the determination of storm troopers for an ideology, certainty drives out chance, coercion replaces courage.

Virility is lost by giving up. By arranging for alibis. And by selling out.

One sees them everywhere—greasy, ill-dressed, self-indulgent slobs, guys you could not imagine stirring the juices of any passerby. They are blokes who by the age of forty have given up. Who still have half their lives to live, but who have decided they will never be attractive to other humans. Nobody will ever want to pull them into the sack. The only reason they go to the bar really is just to drink martinis or beer. Yet, how they are addicted to the spectacle of sports!

Giving up begins by giving in, it begins in comfort. It begins each time comfort enters as a factor in any decision. It begins when one does not go down the Grand Canyon because the trail is hot and dusty and the mule the guide is offering lurches; when one does not even go to Italy and France because of the hassles of not understanding the language and not digesting the food; when one did not set out to escape Czarist Russia by hiding in a haywagon by night. Unmanliness is seen in a soft, flaccid, gluttonous body.

For how many men the press of family and professional responsibilities, economic necessities, the importance of a long-term job function as alibis! Alibis for not being compulsively aroused by chance nakedness, alibis for not ecstatically opening one's eyes to the fierce bird of hope and risk soaring in the skies of chance. He took on this summer job lest a buddy would roar by on a wreck of a motorcycle and shout, "Let's travel the hemisphere!" He hastily married and sired a child in case his buddies would rush off to break out a revolution. How many family and professional responsibilities were first taken on in order to function one day as an alibi for not taking chances, not plunging into passion, not fighting for justice!

One loses one's manhood by selling out. One exchanges the hot passions of youth for eroticism, ecstasy, and justice for the cold passions of age for wealth, power, and fame. How much cowardice is there in the greed for wealth, power, and fame! Indeed, everything one despises in oneself turns out to be some cowardice.

If parliamentary democracy seems so alien to virility, it is because in a mass electoral system, to stay in power is an essential concern of every politician. And to stay in power inevitably means compromising with the financial resources of special interests.

Their father is now infirm and incontinent, she told me—and egoistic, demanding, and cantankerous. Unable to afford the costs of a nursing home, he has been moved into the home of her brother. Their whole childhood, she remembered, their father never stopped picking on this brother, beating him up, ridiculing him. She herself cannot forget it, but her brother is now visibly not asserting any kind of dominance, not taking his revenge. She herself has enough of the bilious and querulous behavior of the father now and has to get away from him within an hour. She can hardly believe how her brother takes no account of it. In fact, she realized, for her brother growing up and being a man now means taking care of family members in need or in decline.

Manliness—that is to not take anybody's shit. It is also not to shit on others, and not to let anybody shit on others.

Injustice—the use of one's strength and brightness, flair, and dash to acquire the goods of which the needy and the talented are thereby deprived—makes one lose one's virility in greed, self-indulgence, and brutalization. Nature does not distribute its goods according to need or merit. Virility, the force at grips with chance, strives against the injustice of bad luck. Virility is maintained only in the passion for justice.

Anger is a virile emotion. Not the violence unleashed in frustration, that is, in weakness, or the bluster of unoccupied and peevish brutality. Anger is the force of inner vigilance against comfort, alibis, and corruption. Virile anger concerns the unjust, the inadmissible, the intolerable. The emotion casts itself from the first beyond the perception of what can reasonably be expected or demanded. It exercises a refusal, a resistance, an intractable vigilance. It marks a demand put on the lucid perception of what is possible and what is doable.

You were nicknamed by your comrades *el Gallo*—the rooster, the cock. Once, while at dinner at your grandmother's house, you went into the kitchen, and, with the door open, suddenly turned and held the maid and made love with her. Your friends saw how lusty you were, but you were always hermetic about sexual encounters, even in your diaries. They never were "conquests." Your first steady was beautiful and intelligent but rich. You came to dinners at her family mansion in the unwashed shirt you had worn playing rugby all week. You married a Peruvian half-breed when she became pregnant. When your child was born, you left for combat. During the years of combat, to protect women who had come to fight from being sexually used, you enforced separate quarters for them. One night one of those women could not sleep and went out for a walk. You drove by in a jeep, and stopped. "What are you doing here?" "I couldn't sleep." "I am going to attack Cabaiguán," you said. "Do you want to come?" "Sure," she said and climbed into the jeep. "From then on," she recalled years later, with a playful smile, "I never again left him or let him out of my sight." You married her and four years later left her for combat again. The only trust fund you would leave them would be a world in which a little more injustice would have been fought against. On another continent a woman turned up, unable to forget you from a chance meeting in Eastern Europe, and stayed with you in the struggle against all odds which was to end in disaster.

Long into maturity, you had that adolescent body. You had those fiery black eyes, voracious and malicious, under high arched eyebrows. Your forehead was sculptured with overhanging brow, your nose was fine and sensitive, your lips full and supple, framed by a thin-arced mustache. Your curly reddish beard had sprouted when you were well into manhood. Women spoke of the beauty of your intense gaze, a smile so tranquil that it overturned one's heart. They spoke of your quick movements, your sprinting gestures; yet your body was not high-strung but calm. Barely surviving an infantile pneumonia, you fell victim to an asthma so severe you had to be taken to a resort town in the mountains. You were too sick to go to school; your mother tutored you. You excelled in rugby. You climbed the highest mountains in Peru and in Mexico. You would sleep only a few hours. The strongest fighting men saw your adolescent-looking body, choking with asthma, outlasting them in endurance. All your life the asthma attacks threw you into the panicky convulsions of a drowning man.

But it was not your own state of bad health but the weeks you cared for your dying grandmother that had motivated you to change from engineering studies to medicine. You were a doctor who never had an office and not once wrote a bill for services rendered. Wherever you happened upon someone afflicted by a harsh blow of chance, you stopped to clean and disinfect and bandage. After every battle, your first priority was to bind the wounds of your fallen enemies. You befriended despised animals, stray dogs, mules, you kept a white rat with you and played with it between raids and battles.

In the Andes, in Algeria, in Egypt, in Ghana, in India, in Japan your flashing spirit spotted the most curious things and greedily feasted on them. You wrote that you would serve the new state for five years. You held a key administrative post, but fed your family on the common rations. Your associates told of a long meeting about urgent matters that lasted the heat of the day; you never opened the thermos of coffee someone had set beside you. When asked why, you muttered, "There wasn't enough for all." You spent the weekends working fourteen hours a day without pay on the docks or in the cane fields. Those who are working alongside of you steal glances at you from time to time, seeing in your unself-conscious brightness and unadorned style a blessing that chance cast in their lives of deprivation and desperation.

You were in exile from earliest manhood. You quickly relinquished the position of authority to go to other continents to offer your forces and your life wherever men and women suffered oppression. We have not seen anyone like you since, so annealed by the rage against injustice. You once said to a woman who thought you might be related that if she felt indignation over injustice anywhere on the planet, she was your sister. You said that every real man must feel on his own cheek a blow that strikes the cheek of anyone. For you to see injustice was to go fight it, leave everything and go yourself, gun in hand.

You were already reading Rimbaud and Freud at the age of thirteen. You were a man of exceptional intelligence rising out of experience in combat, in social administration, in diplomacy, in a diversity of cultures. You were a man of exceptional insight and theoretical power and you left writings that will long be studied. But you have been, in the last half of the twentieth century, the single most admired man in all the lands whose injustice you found marked out with your anger. Your image will continue to be found on the walls of huts in slums all over Latin America and Africa and Europe, and we will continue, from time to time, to put in words some of the things you mean to us.

October 9, 1967, La Higuera, Bolivia. 1:10 P.M. The subofficer, Mario Terán, volunteered to carry out the order to shoot the prisoner. But when he is about to enter the building, he is trembling with fear. The prisoner is seated on the floor, shoulders against the wall. His leg wound has stopped bleeding. He sees his executioner trembling, and says, "Shoot, coward, you are only going to kill a man." Terán steps back, shuts his eyes and fires. Then with eyes shut, he fires again wildly. Another soldier comes in to fire, finally, the shot that put an end to the life of the prisoner.

"Che"—scholars say an originally Guaraní word equivalent to "buddy" or "mate," alive in Argentinean popular usage after the Guaraní Indians had been exterminated. Also used as "Hey!" "Wow!" "Can't be!"

Our Che, our buddy, our comrade.

NOTES

1. Georges Bataille, *Œuvres complètes,* vol. 5 (Paris: Gallimard, 1973), 207, 256.

2. "She was no longer a girl—she showed herself a woman." "She is a real woman." What qualities, deeper than cultural, broader than biological, are being recognized? There are those unfeminine women in Faulkner, shying away from none of the work their men do, but who, at decisive moments, show themselves to be women. There are crisp, cool-headed, successful business executives who, at some moment of crisis in their own lives or in the lives of people dependent on them, proved to be women. There are nurses in wartime and in refugee camps; there are nuns, who at some decisive and revealing moments show themselves to be women. To become a woman is not simply being biologically female and maturing, and it is not a program, construction, or performance, like making oneself feminine.

Does not the project of deconstructing the social construction of virility involve the judgment that virility—just like womanhood, and the figures of outlaw, desperado, punk, streetsmart adolescent, drag queen, queer—is an evaluative category constructed for its perceived social benefits? But before any ethical or social judgment, we must first understand the passionate force that cares about being virile and having a real man for a buddy—or about being a real woman, a queer, a drag queen . . .

We further have to understand how passion communicates. It is not the category, implanted in the language and practices of a culture, that propagates virility. It is virility that communicates virility to others, it is heroism that ignites heroism, it is carnavalesque high-spiritedness that spreads carnavalesque high-spiritedness.

3. Jean Cocteau, *The White Book* (San Francisco: City Lights, 1989).

4. John Hersey, *A Single Pebble* (New York: Knopf, 1956), 100–101.

Chapter 8

Turnabout

*Gay Drag Queens and the Masculine
Embodiment of the Feminine*

STEVEN P. SCHACHT

With an effervescent tone in her voice, the co-mistress of ceremonies, Jack-E (Empress V, X, XV of Reno, Nevada), reads from Eunice's cue card:

> Shane and Zenith, I would like to congratulate you both on a great year
> . . . [for] the personal problems you both have had to endure, I commend
> both of you. Shane, thank you for learning how to sew. I wish you all the
> best in California, and remember, your mother is just a phone call away.
> Shane, I love you very much. Zenith, girl, hasn't this been a fanfare. My
> applause to you for sticking with it, and keep on going. Raymond is here. I
> am also a phone call away. I love you. . . . Ladies and gentlemen, please
> welcome my co-emcee, and one of the best emcees on the circuit, Her Most
> Imperial Majesty, Empress Sixteen, the fabulous Eunice Kennady Smith.

Her introduction delivered, the focused light from a single spotlight appears on two large, side-by-side doors in an otherwise dimly lit ballroom. This prompts Eunice's entrance and the beginning of her Emcee Performance/Ball Chair Presentation dedicated to the Snow Leopard Emperor XIX, Shane Kennady Smith, and Empress XXIII, Zenith Rockafeller, who are stepping down this evening from their reign.

While a steady parade of people will be honored during tonight's event, "Coronation '95, An Evening in the Ice Palace: A Tribute to the Great Musicals of All Time," none is more venerated, powerful, or held in higher regard in this setting than Eunice. Not only is she Empress XVI of the Imperial Sovereign Court of Spokane (ISCS), but she is also the founding Queen Mother and the one and only Empress of the Imperial Sovereign Court of the State of Montana. Moreover, Eunice organizes almost every important event sponsored by the ISCS and many of the shows staged by the Montana court, and serves as a quite entertaining emcee for court happenings throughout the region. Further illustrating her ubiquitous influence, she has over 120 children, grandchildren, and great-grandchildren (predominantly other past and present empresses, emperors, princesses, and princes) residing all over the West Coast and inland Northwest. To be a member of Eunice's esteemed family, denoted by the Kennady Smith last name, is both a tribute to and an indication of one's standing in the regional court community.

And yet, Eunice is not really the biological matriarch of a long lineage of royal family members. She is a gay man and a female impersonator who, within a socially disparaged community, has created her own kindred dynasty of sorts.[1] Eunice's lofty station, like that of other drag queens in this setting, is predicated upon her successful presentation and promotion of idealized images of traditional feminine beauty—seemingly being the operational "other"—in such a relational manner that it situationally affords her masculine power and authority.

The dominant culture most typically views the feminine, especially its extreme manifestations, as the stigmatized other, a burden, a handicap, harmful, and providing the basis for discrimination and a subordinate status.[2] In direct contrast, gay men within this drag community commandeer many of these same cultural notions of feminine embodiment and use them as the basis of personal prestige and power. In fact, as this chapter demonstrates, drag queens within this context who most successfully present traditional images of the hyper-feminine come to embody a dominant status in the group. Conversely, that which is most symbolically associated with masculine appearance is rendered subordinate to the seeming omnipotence of those most convincingly doing the feminine; masculine-appearing men and lesbians (those most embodying traditional images of masculinity), instead of women, are the relational signifiers of those holding power in this hyper-gendered setting.[3]

This essay considers my ethnographic experiences in a drag community. Instead of viewing female impersonators as stigmatized, peripheral individuals in our society or the gay community, as some previous researchers have, this study examines a locale where such individuals are the most esteemed and sovereign.[4] While still locating the transgendered at the cultural margins, other gender theorists and writers have argued that since drag queens demonstrate "female" and "male" to be nothing more than imitative performances and states of being, they contest present gender regimes by example.[5] My analysis demonstrates, however, that at least in this drag setting, once female impersonators' motivations for donning women's attire—to embody positions of authority in relation to gendered others—are more comprehensively examined, an only partially emancipative image emerges which in application is more a mutated reflection of preexisting inequalities.

In the section that follows, the court's explicit and implicit goals, how it functions as a status-conferring conduit for typically marginalized individuals, and the demographics of the court's membership are explored in terms of how they provide a context in which drag queens can embody positions of authority and dominance within the group. I also discuss my involvement in the group's activities. The third section of the essay describes my one-time experience of being a drag queen at an annual event called "Turnabout," and my experience of how the masculine embodiment of the feminine confers power and status on those undertaking such presentations of self. The essay concludes with a discussion of the promise and limits of drag queens who situationally parlay an otherwise stigmatized state of being into a relationally "superior" status.

LOCATING THE MASCULINE IN THE VICISSITUDES OF A DRAG COMMUNITY

The Court

Over the last six years, I have participated in several different drag communities. Of all these settings, I have been most actively involved (from fall 1994 to fall 1998) with the ISCS, eventually becoming a core member of the group. The stated purpose of the ISCS, as written in its detailed and rather extensive bylaws, is to function as a "non-profit charitable organization . . . for the common good and general welfare of the Gay community, friends and residents of Spokane and the Inland Northwest, and the United States of America." Accordingly, shows sponsored by the group during fiscal year 1995/96 raised over $35,000 for various local AIDS-related community groups, such as Children With AIDS, the Spokane AIDS Network, and the Inland Northwest AIDS Coalition. Most of the events staged by the court also have the implicit purpose of increasing awareness about the risks of unprotected sex. The court also maintains a disaster fund from which members can draw limited monies ($100) for medical or personal emergencies. Reflecting the ISCS's charitable commitment to the larger community, the group annually raises money (over $2,000 in the fall of 1997) for and personally distributes Thanksgiving and Christmas baskets of food to low-income people in Spokane. It also awards three to four $500 to $750 scholarships to individuals in need, which are presented at the yearly coronation ball. Members of the court, the larger gay community, and residents of Spokane are all eligible to receive food baskets and scholarships.

While the court's contributions to the gay and larger straight community are significant, the charitable emphasis of the group may provide an even more important service to its members. In a society that often tries to oppressively deny the existence of gay and lesbian individuals,[6] the ISCS serves as a structural arrangement that bestows upon its members, especially female impersonators, a level of respectability, affirmation, and in some cases, interpersonal power otherwise often largely unavailable to them. One of the fifty-eight similar court systems located throughout North

America originally founded by gay activist José Sarria, the ISCS has existed for over twenty-five years, and is reported to be the second-oldest group of its type in the Pacific/inland Northwest, and the first gay, lesbian, or transgendered organization in Spokane.[7] In all, the court provides its almost exclusively gay and lesbian members an established, formal venue of affiliation and acceptance on the local, regional, and national levels.

Gay Drag Queens

Almost all of the ISCS's core participants and leaders are gay men who appear as female impersonators. In many ways, the drag queens are the court's icons; while more numerous in past years, they now account for only about one-third of the active membership due to several deaths from AIDS. Drag queens are strong proponents of and adherents to quite conservative images of traditional feminine beauty. An elegant "woman" removes all visible body hair, does a face with noticeably but tastefully applied makeup, wears the latest, most glamorous fashions and accoutrements (high heels, big hair, long fake finger nails, and conspicuous jewelry) befitting this image, and always carries herself in a ladylike manner (small steps, head held high, sashaying hips, and sipping her drink with a straw). The image they are most typically attempting to present would perhaps best be described as a cross between a Las Vegas showgirl and a movie star (i.e., Heather Locklear, Barbra Streisand, or Elizabeth Taylor, depending on age).

Like proud parents vicariously living through the actions of their child, gay drag queens affectionately refer to their manufactured female personae in third person. Using terms of the "other" both in and out of drag, female impersonators will make comments such as, "Misty was flawless last week," "I still need to lay Caress out for next weekend's show," or "I'm not sure if Paige will run for empress this year, but if she does, she'll kick Kelsey's ass." And while drag queens in this setting hold their constructed female identity in the highest regard, it is important to note that none aspires to be a transsexual or wears women's attire for expressed erotic purposes (like transvestites, who often are straight men).[8] Moreover, the only time they wear women's clothing is during court functions; otherwise, their lived identity and corresponding appearance is entirely male.[9] Quite simply, the drag queens of the court are gay men who don women's clothing to play an esteemed role in this context; actually aspiring to live any sort of concrete feminine identity (as transsexuals do) is seen as undesirable. As one of the more prominent queens of the court put it during a discussion we were having about preoperative transsexuals: "That's taking it too far. When I go home after a show, I like to rip my breasts out and make love like a man."

Thus, gay drag queens in this setting present traditional images of the hyper-feminine but have no desire to actually subsume such a status. Their drag personae are viewed as the real estate—an object—upon which they aspire to exercise power and authority. Their subjective sense of being is not that of a woman, nor is such a state of being desired. Albeit veiled in multiple layers of feminine imagery and mannerisms when in drag, the female impersonators of the court still think of themselves as entirely men. What results is the masculine embodiment of the feminine. This becomes more apparent when considering their role in relation to gendered others in the context.

Gay Drag Kings

Another one-third of the court is comprised of gay men who play the role of what I have previously termed "gay drag kings."[10] The image they aspire to present typically falls somewhere between the macho men of the Village People, Garth Brooks, and the male emcee for a Las Vegas show. These men, typically sporting good thick mustaches and bedecked in expensive-looking tuxedos, tight-fitting leather pants, or jeans, cowboy hats and boots, in appearance present themselves as the masculine, often hyper-antithesis to the feminine. They also carry themselves in a stereotypical masculine manner: sitting with their legs spread apart, taking long strides when walking, and drinking their favorite beer out of a long-neck bottle. Both in appearance and mannerism they are without question men.

Yet, the role they relationally embody is that of signifier of the importance and power of the drag queen in this context. Situationally, this involves them playing the behind-the-scenes roles of beading and sewing outfits for their favorite drag queen(s), serving as "dressers" for various drag queens by helping them change outfits between sets at shows, working as runway attendants, and setting up and taking down stages for larger shows. They are also expected to serve as escorts to the drag queens at shows, especially when they are tipping[11] other performers, and to be back-up dancers in larger production numbers sometimes organized by drag queens. Further designating gay drag kings' relational role in the court, during some of their performances (lip-synching songs), they will dedicate a number to a favorite female impersonator who is present. Finally, the male personae of the court are also strong supporters of traditional gender images in application to both themselves and those whom they deem worthy of their support—the most hyper-feminine-appearing queens.

Thus, although gay drag kings are quite masculine in appearance, they are subordinate to the gay drag queens. Their presence, in a direct inversion of gender relations in the dominant society, literally props up and testifies to the opulent power of the female impersonator. Through their obsequious but often inconspicuous actions they are the "good men" behind every successful drag queen. In fact, one can often judge how popular and powerful a given queen is by the size of her entourage of drag king attendants. Moreover, which drag queen a given drag king is associated with often is a direct function of how much individual status he holds in the court. The role the king most embodies is minion to the queen.

Lesbian Drag Kings and Queens

The remaining participants of the court are lesbians (one-third of the active group membership), largely found in one of two basic gendered roles: butch and femme, or, as I have previously conceptualized them, "lesbian drag kings" and "lesbian drag queens."[12] Lesbian drag kings account for close to 80 percent of the female membership and embody a position quite similar to the gay drag kings.

Accordingly, lesbian drag kings have adopted a very masculine presentation of self, most typically with quite short hair and male attire (largely the same as that worn by gay drag kings), some taping their breasts, and in general, presenting themselves with a corresponding demeanor of stiffness and being "cocky." The uninitiated might mistake many of these individuals for real men, because of their convincing appearance and gesture. Lesbian drag kings have frequently served as emperors (six of the twenty reigning emperors have been lesbians) and held the appointed title of Imperial Crown Prince on several occasions. With only one empress and two princesses in the history of the court having been women, lesbian drag queens are a minority as title holders and in numbers. I would speculate that the reason lesbian drag queens are such a rarity is that their presence potentially throws into question the apparent necessity of drag queens in the context, and who is to be considered "fairest" in the land.

While some are popular performers, in general lesbians are like gay drag kings: for the most part they are valued for the important supportive, often behind-the-scenes, roles they play (i.e., good tippers and hard workers), and almost entirely relegated to auxiliary positions in the court. As such, the status they too embody is one of subordination to the gay drag queens. And although sometimes treated as the equals of gay drag kings, they are definitely the followers, not the leaders, of the court.

Myself

As for my participation in the court, over the past seven years I have emceed a show, performed in close to twenty-five shows as a male, and attended close to a hundred different shows and ten monthly court meetings. My involvement in the court was further deepened when my spouse at the time, Anna Papageorge, and I became close friends with several core ISCS members—holding and attending numerous parties, eating meals out at restaurants, and watching movies. For over a year, members of the court were almost my sole source of non-professional social interaction and, in many ways, my primary reference group.[13] This resulted in my spending anywhere from ten to forty hours a week with court members, either attending organized court functions or in smaller, less formal friendship groups.

Notwithstanding Turnabout (described in detail in the following section), the participatory/experiential location I embodied in undertaking this ethnography (specifically during court events) was the subordinate role of drag king. For instance, on a couple of occasions, performing as a man, I dedicated my song to a favorite drag queen present, and frequently served as a dresser and escort for tipping other entertainers. I also modeled clothes during a court-sponsored fashion show and walked with the court in male attire at several out-of-town shows. I was also asked to serve as an appointed prince, a masculine position within the group, and, although external circumstances prevented me from doing so, this demonstrates that I was considered a male persona by the group. While being a drag king taught me a great deal about what drag queens symbolically represent to the group, it was through my participation in an annual court-sponsored event called "Turnabout" that I was able to experientially appreciate what being a gay drag queen in this context means.

TURNABOUT: EMBODYING A PRIVILEGED DESTINATION

What's Up[14]

25 years of my life and still
I'm trying to get up that great big hill
of hope
for a destination
I realized quickly when I knew I should
that the world was made up of this
brotherhood of man
for whatever that means
so I cry sometimes when I'm lying in bed
to get it all out what's in my head
then I start feeling a little peculiar
so I wake in the morning and step
outside I take a deep breath
I get real high
then I scream from the top of my lungs
what's goin' on.
            —4 Non Blondes (1991)

With the exception of the yearly coronation, Turnabout is perhaps the most anxiously awaited and talked about event staged by the ISCS. This annual competition allows the drag queens of the court to appear as "men," and more importantly, the "boys" to be "girls." Much of the excitement surrounding Turnabout is in the intrigue of trying to figure out the "real" male identities of the ephemeral drag queens and, relatedly, the expressed rivalry of the participants competing to present the most compelling feminine image. For those who want to do female drag but cannot for various reasons, it is also both an excuse and an opportunity to be treated like a "queen" and feel the "joys" of the transformation involved, if but for one night, like Cinderella.[15] Based on my participation in this event, I will first share the intimacies of being a drag queen for an evening. This radical transformation of myself in terms of appearance and mannerism, and others' responses to such self-presentation, enabled me to fully understand drag queens' masculine embodiment of the feminine.

My rather extensive preparation for becoming a drag queen began the night before the event with Anna and I going over to Cher and Eunice's[16] home to watch movies and for me to try on possible dresses. I picked one of their older, looser-fitting silver and black designer gowns to wear that did not, at my request, require my penis being tucked.[17] Cher selected matching hair (a blond wig) and the body hair on my upper shoulders and chest was shaved. I was briefly instructed how best to walk in the pair of black three-inch-high heels that they also loaned me. Learning to walk in this type of shoe, although it made my calf muscles feel strange and was somewhat painful to my toes, seemed to come far too easily to me. Having previously viewed high heels—at least on me—as something alien to my gender identity, perhaps I thought something so different would also be very difficult to master; this would also be indicative of some of my own sexist assumptions about wearing women's clothing. Truthfully, high heels felt much like the hockey skates I wore when I was younger—painfully tight but necessarily so for support—and were not nearly as prohibitive of walking as I had envisioned them to be.

The following evening, after shaving my face as closely as possible just before leaving home, we returned to their house at 6:30 so that Cher could do my makeup. Cher, who was out of drag, began by putting my mid-back-length hair up into a very tight, feminine-looking bun on the top of my head. Next, he melted putty on a spoon with a cigarette lighter and painfully applied it to cover, I was told, my too-bushy, masculine-looking eyebrows. Over this, a dull skin-color base was thickly painted to conceal the putty. The rest of my face and neck were then liberally smeared with a different type of base that was gently blended into that covering my eyebrows. Rouge was lightly daubed on my lower cheeks with a powder puff to highlight and raise my cheekbones. Next, very thin but quite noticeable black eyebrows were penciled on just slightly above my concealed ones. Black, blue, and reddish eyeliners were then painted on and accented with lavish mid-length false eyelashes and thickly applied black mascara. What I was told was normally an easy task, doing eye makeup, was made extremely difficult by my uncontrollable blinking, which resulted in me painfully getting eyeliner and mascara in my teary eyes (having never worn glasses or contacts, whenever anything comes near my eyes, I seemingly automatically close them). Once my eye makeup was finally and successfully completed, I noted that it restricted my view and felt as though I had tunnel vision. At nearly 8:00 P.M., we stopped for dinner.

After eating, my metamorphosis continued, with bright red lipstick being applied as well as a slightly lighter shade around the edges of my lips. Thereafter, I was forced to drink out of a straw so as to not mess up my lip makeup. My blond back-combed wig was then secured to my own hair with barrettes and further sculpted with a pick and copious amounts of aerosol hair spray to better flatter the contours of my face. Stripped to my underwear, I next put on a pair of opaque Danskins, two pairs of nylons (several layers of leg coverings were required so that I did not have to shave my legs), a rather tight-fitting dance belt that flattened my pelvic area (which was further accentuated by carefully pushing my genitals between my legs), and a girdle-like brassiere with prosthetic breasts (as these are rather small, two sets were required for me to appear to have reasonably large breasts). With assistance, I put on my dress feet-first so as not to mess up my hair and makeup. This was followed by bright red fake fingernails being glued to my own nails and a large single earring being clamped to my right ear (my ears are not pierced, but my left ear was covered by my styled hair). I slipped on my heels and then was given a small black purse in which to carry my lipstick, a compact with powder puff, a hand-held battery operated fan (not only was it quite hot in all this clothing and makeup, but this was a warm August evening), and other personal articles such as my keys and checkbook.

All told, my transformation from Steve to Jacqueline St. Eve (my deceased mother's first name with a variant of my real first name) took almost three hours. Walking around their home in full drag before Eunice drove me down to the show, I directly learned the sources of several hyperfeminine gestures and movements undertaken by drag queens. Because of my fake nails, delicate hand movements became a necessity. Thus, whenever my wig tickled my face, I had to ever so carefully brush wisps of it back with my fully extended fingers, and then gently apply fresh powder to my face to alleviate the strong urge to scratch my face. Otherwise I would have messed up my makeup—not to mention my concern that I might put one of my sharp fake nails in my already hurting eyes.[18] In my rather restrictive attire as well as the high heels, I felt my legs being distended, which forced my buttocks and chest to protrude in opposite directions to maintain my balance, and found myself limited to taking smaller, almost tipsy, lady-like steps. What I had previously seen as exaggerated feminine mannerisms took on a far more practical meaning to me.

During the whole process of my makeover I took great pleasure in frequently viewing myself in mirrors and posing for pictures. I truly felt that I was undertaking a transformation in being. Upon completion of my metamorphosis, the prior me was no longer visible (as everyone who saw me that night noted, as well as everyone who has since seen pictures of me in drag). It was replaced with a glamorous new me (especially considering that normal attire for me is tank tops and shorts in the summer or jeans and T-shirts during colder months). And although I felt some discomfort wearing all the unaccustomed clothing and accoutrements selected in the creation of Jacqueline, I did not feel effeminate or lesser because of my appearance. To the contrary, I felt special and very confident, something I attempted to present in my mannerisms as I practiced my new look. Once I mastered a look I felt appropriate to my new persona, with lots of advice from Cher and Eunice, I was ready to step out for the evening and make my debut as a man embodying the created image of Jacqueline St. Eve.

Upon our arrival at the bar, I quickly discovered that seven other Turn-about queens and I would be the focal point of the night's activities, and I subsequently became quite aware of the "rewards" given in this context for my efforts to radically transform my gendered appearance. Everyone was circulating, trying to ascertain the "true" identities of the drag queens on parade. Much to my delight, everyone Eunice introduced me to made gushing comments about how beautiful I was, and no one could figure out who I was until either he (Eunice was out of drag) told them or they heard me speak. Most were quite surprised to learn my "true" identity. Further concern for and deference to me in drag was expressed in the form of free drinks for the night (as a contestant), people continually offering to light my cigarettes or asking me to pose for pictures, gentle reminders of how best to carry myself, and ongoing comments, even after my identity was revealed, about how pleasing I looked (e.g., "Doesn't she look like Sable Lake [an admired out-of-town queen] in Everett?" "You should think about doing drag again/at coronation.").

When it came time for me to perform, Tina (the reigning empress, who was out of drag and emcee for the night's activities) announced me in a spirited and affirming manner as "a living example of what the court is all about . . . community outreach . . . a straight man who has shaved his back and part of his chest . . . a wonderful supporter of all the court's activities . . . Jacqueline St. Eve." Although I had always been met with strong ap-proval in the form of applause when previously performing as a "man," the audience seemed even more appreciative and louder than usual. More-over, I was given over $25 in one-dollar tips (far more than I had ever received before), which I was allowed to keep since this was a non-fundraiser event. While some of the positive response to my lip-synching "What's Up" (the song quoted at the beginning of this section) may have been the result of my previously noted personal circumstances, I still felt very genuine and sincere appreciation for my performance. And while I was secretly disappointed that I did not win the title of "Miss Turnabout 1996," even though several individuals thought I should, people still make congratulatory note of the debut of Jacqueline St. Eve and ask when she will make her next appearance.

The contest at the bar ended about 1:00 A.M. Since my swollen feet were throbbing by then, I removed my shoes and, still in drag, drove Anna and me back to Eunice and Cher's. Since I still had my nails on, I learned to shift the manual transmission using an extremely loose grip. Using baby oil, it took me nearly half an hour to remove all my makeup, and some of it, such as my eyeliner and the base on my ears, did not wash completely off until I showered the following day. Removing my restrictive, sweaty garments and accessories and changing into loose shorts and a T-shirt truly felt like an act of emancipation (I can only speculate as a male how oppressive it must be for the many women in our society who, to varying degrees, undertake such painstaking, time-consuming rituals on a daily basis). And yet, the whole ordeal was not only an exciting learning experience but something that was quite fun to do and to now say I have done (I keep a blown-up picture of myself in drag in my office at school and enjoy the responses I receive from students and faculty). Quite simply, I felt a sense of accomplishment at convincingly presenting myself as a woman and seemingly mastering, at least in appearance and demeanor, the embodiment of this contextually superior state of being.[19]

My one-time experience of doing drag gave me several other crucial insights about the meaning and value attached to the large amount of energy spent on transforming one's exterior appearance and seeming gender embodiment. In a largely gay male context, where almost everyone present of key importance "has" the phallic in the traditional Lacanian sense—i.e., they are "real" men—a tension arises over who will serve as its signifier and "be" the phallic.[20] Prior to participating in Turnabout, I initially thought "being" the phallic was a role embodied by female impersonators. That is, like women in society, drag queens appeared to be the appropriate and supportive contrast to those who seemingly "have" the phallic in this already hyper-masculine setting. Their presence, at least in image, merely seemed indicative of the phallic's omni-importance in this subcultural realm of masculinity.

After doing drag, however, just the opposite seemed true. Men who undertake radical transformations in their appearance, such as I did, differentiate themselves from everyone else present sufficiently that they come to embody a "rare" and "special" status in an environment where there is already an overabundance of those seemingly "having" the phallic. Gay men who successfully present themselves as hyper-feminine in appearance and demeanor are rewarded with prestige, power, and authority for their significant endeavors. Embodying the role of "drag king" prior to Turnabout, I continually had to pay homage and defer to the female impersonators present, but in drag I was treated in this manner and very much appreciated it. Instead of playing a secondary, subordinate role, for this evening at least, I temporarily embodied a position of esteem and authority. Perhaps this explains why several important "men" in the context would do drag more frequently if their partners would allow them, and every "man's" anxious anticipation of this yearly event. They, too, want to "have" and wear the glass slipper, the phallic, if only for one night out of the year. These hierarchies, inverse in mere appearance as played out in the court when compared to the dominant culture, demonstrate the fluid, transitory, and situational basis of fulfilling and embodying the seemingly predestined gendered states of men and women.

THE MASCULINE EMBODIMENT OF THE FEMININE

> Being Jem Jender allows me to do and say things I wouldn't otherwise say or do as a man. It's an entirely different person. I cherish Jem Jender. . . . She represents a kind of freedom that I don't have as James O'Connor-Taylor. . . . I'm really just a shy boy from New Hampshire with a ballet background, but when I put on a blond wig and strap myself into a corset with an eighteen-inch waist and size-twelve Vivienne Westwood heels, I become a different person. It's a treat and I wish everyone could do it![21]

In the dichotomous gendered reality that surrounds us, the only way a person can truly appreciate and understand her or his assigned gender is through interaction with its converse, whether it be present or imagined.[22] What it means to be a male or a female is entirely relational in meaning and neither concept can exist without an appropriate contrast or interaction denoting its reality.[23] Thus, being a woman or a man in our culture is equally defined in prescribed terms of what one is supposedly not.[24] Moreover, in this binary outlook the state of being masculine, and all that is associated with its embodiment, is viewed as inherently superior to what is seen as a lesser, stigmatized, feminine identity. Not surprisingly, perhaps, this explains why the worst insult one man can direct at another is to somehow ascribe some feminine characteristic to the targeted party, and why most men often go to extreme measures trying to escape any such associations.[25]

Yet within the hegemony of this dichotomous view of gender, how is it that the drag queens of the court are able to embody what is otherwise seen as an inferior identity, the feminine, and transform it into a dominant state of being? I believe this is accomplished through the masculine embodiment of the feminine. These female impersonators, who have no subjective knowledge of being a woman nor desire to experience the world as a woman, utilize a very masculine (objective) view of hyper-feminine appearance and mannerisms. As my own experience of being a drag queen taught me, successfully appearing as a woman in this setting is simply a skill to be mastered for the purposes of garnering esteem and power in relation to others. The more compellingly real one appears as a vision of female beauty, albeit a vision defined through the eyes of men, the greater the rewards. Feminine appearance merely becomes a vehicle—the real estate— with which these men pursue and often embody a dominant status within this context. After all, everyone in the setting knows that the drag queens are really men (outsiders are the only ones to become confused about this underlying assumption) but this reality is momentarily suspended and re- placed with idealized images of the feminine.

Drag queens' embodiment of the feminine is not, however, about some sort of true appreciation of or admiration for women in our society. To the contrary, not only have I frequently heard both gay drag queens and kings make quite misogynist statements about "real girls" and lesbians, but in this and many similar settings I have been involved in the drag queens commonly make such statements as "We make better women than women do," and "Female impersonators could teach women a great deal about how to be better/real women." What the participants of this setting are really paying homage to is male superiority, however men might chose to express it, including the masculine embodiment of the feminine. Like fa- mous male athletes or actors, drag queens use the body as both a canvas and a tool with which they come to embody superior states of being in relation to others. Through such an objective lens—strictly one of appear- ance and mannerism—men are seemingly better than women at every- thing, including being a woman.[26]

Doing drag does allow these men a "freedom" to temporarily become something different than they otherwise are, gay men, and a venue to re- place this stigmatized identity with something seen as "absolutely" "fabu- lous" and "flawless" (three terms frequently used in this context to describe drag queens). It affords them opportunities to do and be things most would never dream of as simply a gay man—embody positions of authority and superiority. And given the very real oppression that many members of this context experience outside of it, the status-conferring focus of the court is an escape and affirming shelter from these outside realities. All of these are things I appreciate and respect about the group.[27]

However, having constructed this safe haven from the outside world with the very binary gender worldview that the dominant culture uses to oppress them, the sub-cultural space that drag queens embody is anything but seditious.[28] While the transgendered text of the court and drag queens in general may perhaps be correctly read by the outsider as somehow sub- versive and potentially destabilizing of present gender regimes, this is nei- ther the intent of drag queens nor an actual outcome in the setting itself. Yet drag does demonstrate gender to be nothing more than a form of imitation and fabrication, which, as I have written elsewhere, does point to emancipatory possibilities.[29] But having so convincingly impersonated dichotomized gender relations, although with an inverse appearance, dominance and subordination is still an inevitable outcome. For those of us who search for truly egalitarian ways of relating to others, new, more radical forms of embodiment will have to be explored.[30]

NOTES

This essay was originally presented as a paper at the annual meetings of the American Sociological Association, August 1999, in Chicago. I thank Jill Bystydzienski, R. W. Connell, Doris Ewing, John Ruark, Beth Schneider, John Stoltenberg, Lisa Underwood, and the editors of this anthology for their helpful comments and suggestions on earlier versions.

1. Since participants of the setting refer to drag queens as she, her, mother, sister, and so forth, and they are addressed by their female performance names (in drag and sometimes out), I have employed this same usage in this essay.

Some previous researchers have found it useful to distinguish between the terms "female impersonators" and "drag queens," most notably Holly Brubach and Michael James O'Brien, *Girlfriend: Men, Women, and Drag* (New York: Random House, 1999); Vern L. Bullough and Bonnie Bullough, *Cross Dressing, Sex, and Gender* (Philadelphia: University of Pennsylvania Press, 1993), 240; Julian Fleisher, *The Drag Queens of New York: An Illustrated Field Guide* (New York: Riverhead Books, 1996), 14; Marjorie Garber, *Vested Interests: Cross-Dressing and Cultural Anxiety* (New York: Routledge, 1992), 132. Given that the participants of this setting use them interchangeably, I have adopted a corresponding approach here.

2. Susan Bordo, *Unbearable Weight: Feminism, Western Culture, and the Body* (Berkeley: University of California Press, 1993); Susan Brownmiller, *Femininity* (New York: Linden Press, 1984); Naomi Wolf, *The Beauty Myth: How Images of Beauty Are Used against Women* (New York: Anchor Books, 1991); Iris Marion Young, "Throwing Like a Girl: A Phenomenology of Feminine Body Comportment, Motility and Spatiality," *Human Studies* 3 (1980): 137–156; Iris Marion Young, *Justice and the Politics of Difference* (Princeton, N.J.: Princeton University Press, 1990).

3. For more detailed analyses of the hyper-gendered and male basis of this setting see Steven P. Schacht, "The Multiple Genders of the Court: Issues of Identity and Performance in a Drag Setting," in *Feminism and Men: Reconstructing Gender Relations,* ed. Steven P. Schacht and Doris Ewing (New York: New York University Press, 1998), 202–224; Steven P. Schacht, "Gay Masculinities in a Drag Community: Female Impersonators and the Social Construction of 'Other,' " in *Gay Masculinities,* ed. Peter Nardi (Newbury Park, Calif.: Sage, 2000), 247–248.

4. See Roger Baker, *Drag: A History of Female Impersonators in the Performing Arts* (New York: New York University Press, 1994); Richard Ekins and Dave King, eds., *Blending Genders: Social Aspects of Cross-Dressing and Sex-Changing* (New York: Routledge, 1996); Ester Newton, *Mother Camp: Female Impersonators in America* (Chicago: University of Chicago Press, 1979); Roberta Perkins, "The Drag Queen Scene: Transsexuals in King Cross," in *Blending Genders: Social Aspects of Cross-Dressing and Sex-Changing,* ed. Richard Ekins and David King (New York: Routledge, 1996).

5. Judith Butler, *Gender Trouble: Feminism and the Subversion of Identity* (New York: Routledge, 1990); Judith Butler, "Imitation and Gender Insubordination," in *inside/out: Lesbian Theories, Gay Theories,* ed. Diana Fuss (New York: Routledge, 1991), 13–31; Garber, *Vested Interests*; Catherine Chermayeff, Jonathan David, and Nan

Richardson, *Drag Diaries* (San Francisco: Chronicle Books, 1995); Fleisher, *The Drag Queens of New York*.

6. Iris Marion Young, "Five Faces of Oppression," *The Philosophical Forum* 19 (1988): 270–290.

7. For an excellent account of the court system's beginnings and its founder, see Michael R. Gorman, *The Empress Is a Man: Stories from the Life of José Sarria* (Binghamton, N.Y.: Harrington Park Press, 1998).

8. For more detailed discussions of transsexuals and transvestites, see Bullough and Bullough, *Cross Dressing, Sex, and Gender*; Ekins and King, eds., *Blending Genders*; Deborah Heller Fienbloom, *Transvestites and Transsexuals: Mixed Views* (Delacorte Press/Seymour Lawrence, 1976); Magnus Hirschfeld, *Transvestites: The Erotic Drive to Cross Dress*, trans. Michael A. Lombardie-Nash (New York: Prometheus Books, 1991); Annie Woodhouse, *Fantastic Women: Sex, Gender and Transvestism* (New Brunswick, N.J.: Rutgers University Press, 1989).

9. Ironically, when out of drag most of the queens present themselves as fairly masculine and easily pass in public as straight whereas many of the gay drag kings (discussed next), who are the masculine antithesis to female impersonators, often act quite effeminate outside of the court setting, as if trying to embody some stereotypical image of the "limp-wristed" gay man.

10. For more detailed discussion of specific gay drag kings see Schacht, "Multiple Genders of the Court."

11. At shows, most money is raised from members of the audience, who approach the stage during individual performances and give money to—tip—the performers in appreciation. Typically the tip is a single dollar bill. Sometimes popular performers, especially at large, well-attended events, will be given several dollar bills or a larger denomination bill.

12. Schacht, "Multiple Genders."

13. Most of the observations and experiences reported in this essay date from the period October 1995 to October 1996, or between Coronation 1995 and 1996, when I was most involved in the group's activities. During this time, I took several hundred pages of field notes, was generously given over thirty hours of videotape from several important shows, took nearly three hundred photographs of participants, and collected dozens of written documents (e.g., flyers and programs from shows, court bylaws, and the minutes and treasurer's reports distributed at monthly meetings). The arguments put forth in this essay are also indirectly informed by attending numerous shows put on by professional female impersonators in nine cities throughout North America, attending Wigstock in 1998, and being invited to and attending the 1996 Miss Continental Pageant, perhaps the most prominent female impersonator beauty pageant in North America, in Chicago, Illinois.

14. In lip-synching this song, since I was thirty-five at the time, I interjected the words and used my fingers to represent "thirty-five" in the first verse of the song, instead of "twenty-five." Moreover, since I had just become unemployed and was going through a separation from my spouse that subsequently led to divorce, and since most of the court members were sympathetically aware of my personal problems, my performing this song seemed to carry added significance for all the participants. A few court members had previously lip-synched a more upbeat, disco version of this song.

15. Some of the male personae—gay drag kings—would like to do female drag, but are involved with partners who do not want them to. Since all active members of the court are expected to participate in Turnabout, especially gay drag kings, these individuals have a yearly occasion to do drag without any negative sanctions.

16. This is the same Eunice described at the beginning of this essay. Cher, her

drag queen partner, is a former empress and also an esteemed and powerful court member. Given their combined over twenty years' experience of doing drag, I was obviously in very capable hands.

17. This involves pushing one's penis back towards the anus, pushing one's testicles into their sockets, and then taping over one's genitals, rendering this pelvic area flat.

18. Later, I discovered that going to the bathroom without running my nylons or injuring myself was quite a production. I had to gingerly insert my thumbs under my nylons and gently push them down. Once done, equal care had to be taken in pushing my genitals back into place and pulling my nylons up.

19. Still, I have no desire to undertake such a masquerade again in the future. Given that I very much try to embody a feminist state of being, I believe there are real limitations to such hyper-feminine presentations of self.

20. For an excellent outline of Jacques Lacan's relational approach to symbolic sexual differentiation and the role the phallic plays in the construction of gender hierarchy, see Butler, *Gender Trouble*, 44–47.

21. Interview with Jem Jender in Chermayeff, David, and Richardson, *Drag Diaries*, 34.

22. Steven P. Schacht, "Misogyny on and off the 'Pitch': The Gendered World of Male Rugby Players," *Gender & Society* 10 (1996): 550–565.

23. R. W. Connell, *Masculinities* (Berkeley: University of California Press, 1995); Judith Lorber, *Paradoxes of Gender* (New Haven, Conn.: Yale University Press, 1994); John Stoltenberg, "How Power Makes Men: The Grammar of Identity" (unpublished manuscript, 1998); Candace West and Don H. Zimmerman, "Doing Gender," *Gender & Society* 1 (1987): 125–151.

24. Doris W. Ewing and Steven P. Schacht, "Introduction," in *Feminism and Men: Reconstructing Gender Relations* (New York: New York University Press, 1998), 1–17.

25. John Stoltenberg, *End of Manhood: A Book for Men of Conscience* (New York: Dutton, 1993); Connell, *Masculinities*.

26. And I am strangely forced to admit that some of the most attractive "women" I have met in my lifetime, at least in terms of societal notions of female beauty, have been drag queens, especially preoperative transsexuals.

27. There are many more things that I equally appreciate about this community, perhaps the foremost being the many friendships I have made participating in it and, as a result, being forced to deal with my own homophobia. Because of my very personal affiliation with the group and many of its members, writing this and previous accounts of the court and taking such a critical stance toward their activities has been very difficult for me.

28. I thank John Stoltenberg for this insightful observation.

29. Schacht, "Multiple Genders"; Steven P. Schacht, "*Paris Is Burning:* How Society's Stratification Systems Makes Drag Queens of Us All," *Race, Gender & Class* 7 (2000): 147–166.

30. For a suggestive sampling of what some of these relational models might look like, see Steven P. Schacht and Doris W. Ewing, eds., *Feminism and Men: Reconstructing Gender Relations* (New York: New York University Press, 1998).

Part 3. Constructing Male Space

Chapter 9

The Body of White Space

Beyond Stiff Voices, Flaccid Feelings, and Silent Cells

JIM PERKINSON

"So, we have had more than thirty contact hours of discussion about race, class, and gender, in this course. Now I want to know what *you* think. Do you guys think we still have a problem with racism today?" The mocha-skinned woman's challenge was as much a matter of eyes punctuating the bob of her head as of tongue forming syllables. The two other women in class sat eager to the question, eyes on alert, listening through every pore. Every one of the four White men addressed by their fellow student's "throw-down" squirmed his response. Not one could speak to it; all four spoke away from it, discharging their nervousness in long dissembling rambles about not-quite-related subjects. As "subjects of speech," their speaking exceeded their own subjectivity. The dis-ease was almost literal, an affliction of a dis-articulate body, unable to find a voice, performing its awkwardness with all the eloquence of an infection. The classroom suddenly became clinic for a virus[1] that is ubiquitous in this country. More than mere surface appearance gestured here like a symptom. White male embodiment spoke its speechless code like a fever.

The structure and meaning of that restlessness is the subject of this writing in a multiple sense. This classroom scene is emblematic of something as broad as the society that gives rise to its gendered, Black question and as intimate as the hand that is trying to write toward its answer. I will argue in what follows that there is such a thing as "the White male body"—as surely as Rodney King's body on the concrete was made to be "black and bestial"[2]—that is simultaneously (only) social construct and (yet also) lived experience. I will not speak about male embodiment in general, nor middle-class male embodiment everywhere all the time, but only White middle-class male embodiment in its partial constitution and practice as normatively "White." And in elaborating plausible textures and technologies of that particular form of *habitus*,[3] I will not escape my own inquiry. For I also remain the subject of this subject, however much I, too, "speak away from it" in focusing on other White males as my surrogates, my substitutes, my saviors-in-drag.

What follows is an attempt to think through something that does not readily appear in mainstream North American society, because it is the ground from which that social space is typically envisioned and practiced. The White middle-class male body remains the presupposition of gaze, the norm of ontology, the artifact of institutional discipline, the criterion of ethical interrogation, despite its increasing displacement from the presumption of control. I will not seek to investigate exhaustively its reservoir of phenomenality nor its law of constitution. The work here is more a matter of heurism, of occasioning a moment of recognition, displaying a possible genealogy, underwriting the projection of an ethical correction. Its method will be resolutely "double," seeking to gain purchase on "Whiteness" by continual reference to "Blackness," seeking to bring into examined contradiction what more normally is simply presumed contradictory, and raising in the space of that contradiction the possibility of agency. In sum, and by way of anticipation, I will seek to demystify White male embodiment as a privilege of givenness and rework its ethical "placement" as a lifelong practical demand.

WHITE MIDDLE-CLASS MALENESS AS INVISIBLE NORM

The hypothesis already limned in the introductory story is that White middle-class male forms of embodiment in this country are largely unconscious and inarticulate. They tend to encode technologies of normativity that do not require the work of conscious performance. They constitute an unproblematic physicality in the body politic. They navigate social space—both public and private—unobstructed, un(re)marked. The policing of such a body is an accomplished fact of middle-class pedagogy which rarely calls for external reinforcement. It is this body that stands as the hegemonic body *par excellence*. Its particular constellation of meanings—its Whiteness, maleness, middle-classness, and heterosexuality—are produced and reproduced in discourses that are not simply verbal. Indeed, I will claim that a large part of this body's social inscription is accomplished in and by its production and occupation of certain spaces in a normative "realization" of quite particular protocols.[4] That such is the case only begins to come to consciousness for most White males in the challenge of other forms of embodiment that have enough power in a given confrontation to resist those protocols and either explicitly or implicitly interrogate their normativity. Paramount among such moments of challenge, as prototypical of the particular history of this country from its very inception, is the encounter with Black male performances of the body.

African-American innovations of public "Blackness"—as embodied forms of social commentary and contestation—realize the quintessential counter-hegemonic possibility of what it means to be a human being in North America. They do so in various modes of gender inscription and sexual orientation. And they do so in no small measure because Blackness historically has been made to appear (in the discourses of White supremacy and White racism) as the mutually exclusive opposite of Whiteness, as a quality of humanity that was essentially fixed and irreducibly different from the Whiteness it licensed as its "other" pole of meaning. Whatever the actual negotiation of White normativity overall, whether the individuals in question otherwise challenge the social order of domination or largely reinforce its requirements, it is Black cultural elaborations of the body that give sharpest relief to the arbitrariness of social norms of embodiment. Black occupations of public space regularly and continually challenge the limits of allowable deviance in gestural style, sartorial statement, physical posture, and verbal volatility.[5]

In such everyday public improvisations of Black embodiment as a cultural semantics of domination and resistance, Whiteness is forced onto the surface of the social body and into question. In the actual moment of such a conjuration, I will argue, Black urban male forms of embodiment most profoundly unmask "invisible Whiteness" as itself a gendered, heterosexual, class formation. That this writing began with an instance of Black female confrontation of White males does not gainsay that claim, but only points to the complexity of the way race engenders body language and vice versa. It is also important to note here that White middle-class females, as indeed White working-class females and males, and White participants in gay and lesbian lifestyles, also stand as partial "challenges" to the taken-for-grantedness of the dominant forms of White male embodiment. Just as importantly, other ethnic identities and cultural heritages likewise pose implicit critiques of the way Whiteness, maleness, and normative power tend to be conflated in the dominant culture of this country. How such a conflation is made to cohere, and what the theoretical stakes are in recognizing it, requires layered analysis.

FRAMING THE QUESTION OF THE WHITE MALE BODY

Again, the basic presupposition here is that the White male body is not innocent of social history or ethical content. Whiteness and maleness and middle-classness intersect in a form of embodiment that populates certain social spaces with a living norm of ontological power. In a sense, what I am attempting to reveal here is a male body that is not so much a "person" or "subject" as an "archetype" or "hieroglyph," an embodied enactment that is pre-scripted so well, it could be said to stand as the quintessential postmodern form of possession.[6]

The analogue here would be possession-cult enactments like those found worldwide in the ritual practices of indigenous religions, in which initiates regularly give their somatic powers over to energies or scripts that manifest one or another coherent personage for their local communities.[7] In the practices of Haitian Vodun or Cuban Santeria for instance (both of which gain increasing relevance here as they are finding more widespread expression in the urban centers of North America in recent years[8]), "possession" is understood to be a normal and central part of communal life. Indeed, in these particular West African–derived rituals, the moments of possession dramatically realize embodied archetypes in the presence of the gathered community. Each of these archetypal personae (known in their own traditions as *loa* or *santos,* respectively) is recognizable in the theatricality of the ritual performances by virtue of a thickly textured set of bodily enactments, articulated in terms of a highly specific drum beat, preferred food and drink, select clothing style, manifest set of behaviors, characteristic disposition, likely discourse, well-known likes and dislikes, etc. Although pre-scripted in some measure, these "spirit-personae" actually serve as the basis for a highly improvisational time of interaction between the possessed person (or "medium") being "ridden" by a particular spirit-persona and the rest of the "spectating" community, around issues of power and meaning that are current in the community's life outside of the ritual time and space. These alternative identities, unconsciously embodied by otherwise "normal-behaving" community members for the space of the ritual, are recognized and embraced as the immediate manifestations of mythologized forces and figures (Shango, Yemaya, Eshu-Elegba, Erzulie, Guede, etc.) whose presence has gained practical valence in the community as dramatically enacted models of different ways of being human. Here, the multiplicity of the figures embodied in any given ritual celebration gives dramatic currency to the value and experience of plurality. And while specific to each of their historical communities (i.e., indigenous or immigrant Haitian or Cuban groups), these encoded bodily performances are to some degree recognizable across differences of national origin and language throughout the West African diaspora in terms of their rhythmic stylistics and gestural economies.

In some ways, the White middle-class male body enacts a similar "possession," likewise recognizable across national boundaries in the dominant North Atlantic cultures (nuanced, obviously, by cultural differences of comportment and gesture). But as part of the hegemonic formation of these cultures, that embodiment serves to underwrite notions of homogeneity more than plurality. And while the White middle-class male body certainly differs from the possession figures outlined above in its ambient consciousness, at another level (as already hypothesized in the introductory remarks) it could be thought of as not yet having awakened from its possession. Only under pressure from sustained encounters with other forms of embodiment does a rudimentary awakening even become possible.

The classroom scenario described in opening this work depicts one such moment. The discomfort of the White males was not just "mental"; it was a moment of physical dis-ease, of becoming aware of an ignorance in the body, of embodying an uncertainty, an inarticulateness, a supplementarity that was (apparently) evident and "speaking" to others without license or intentionality, but had not yet been wrestled into speech and knowledge in and for itself. On the other hand, an asymmetry of knowing also seemed to become apparent: the Black women knew something corporeally that was more than just skin-color. Their Blackness in that moment of confrontation was an embodied knowledge, a challenge that was "thicker" than the face-value of either their words or their body-surface. It spoke in their eyes, their posture, their silent movements, their command of the floor in that moment. It represented what Michel Foucault would call "subjugated knowledge" in a moment of insurrectionary display, a "local knowledge" rupturing a dominant discourse.[9] In part this writing represents an attempt to become articulate about the precise nature of that moment of confrontation, of what the Black women knew in and as a form of embodiment that the White men did not know in and as their own form of embodiment.

Having said as much in relation to the opening scenario, I want to repeat that I think Black male forms of embodiment represent the deepest moment of challenge to the White middle-class male body. While the Black male body emerges in the imagination of the dominant culture under different stereotypic figures of speech in different moments of history (e.g., in the nineteenth century, as "Uncle" if older and "mellowed" or "Zip Coon" if younger and "dandified"; in the 1960s, as "militant" if defiant and black-leather-jacketed; in the 1990s, as "gangbanger" if young, verbal, and demonstrative, etc.) and (only) as more or less "frightening" depending upon its relative darkness of skin, size, build, age, hair-length, etc., that body remains a regularly revisited "touchstone of terror" in the culture at large. Its attributed terror is constructed out of the gendered significance of its racialization.

The racialization of the Black male body is part of a long history of conceptualization structured (in part) by the more than two-thousand-year-old notion of the "Great Chain of Being," inherited by Europe from ancient Greece, elaborated and intensified by Christian theological convictions during the Middle Ages, that became part of the modern articulation of "race" after 1492. In early modernity, the Great Chain schema organized observable reality into a hierarchy that positioned Africans underneath other human types (ascending from that "African" baseline in a developmental order through "Native Americans" and "Asians" to the "European" top of the line), immediately next to or even still within the category of animality. While constantly revised under "scientific" input, the schema has remained residually operative in the dominant cultural imaginary of modernity such that even in today's multicultural *melange* of "different forms of difference" in North America, Blackness continues to mark the greatest distance from a dominant and dominating

Whiteness (which congeals its own normativity and conceals its power, "un-marked").[10]

In the contemporary effects of such a schema, the social field of vision is regularly (forcibly) opened to historically shifting perceptions of ethnic and cultural difference that are presumed to attach to various types and colors of bodies (e.g., the meanings that attend categories like "Latino," "Pacific Islander," "Asian American," etc.). But in most places in the United States, Blackness remains a virtually inassimilable otherness that establishes a kind of "absolute" difference from Whiteness, in proportion to the degree it is made to bear public meanings of vital potency, virulent hostility, and uncontrollable sexual desire. And while this eroticized imagi-nation of Blackness attaches to both male and female bodies of apparent African heritage, the desire it encodes is heterosexually male in its orienta-tion. The White male domination constellated out of eroticized Blackness is most violently disturbed, and made visible, when the body it faces most clearly challenges its own dominating desire. A body "apparently" potent, hypersexed, wild, strong, uncontained (i.e., "Black") and *male,* raises im-mediate issue with the certainty/power of the maleness codified as "White." But clarifying how such a threat is at one and the same moment *constituted* and *coerced* into a public recertification of White middle-class male (pre)dominance requires careful examination of the machinations of public meaning-making.

One such moment that could easily occupy an entire book of analysis was the 1991 beating of Rodney King. The bringing to bear of baton on body in a social location that simultaneously established that body as "Black," "deviant," "criminal," "bestial," "violent," and "threatening" also silently reestablished another body, not immediately present on that scene, as not any of those things predicated of King's body.[11] That absent body made its presence felt, and reinforced the particularity of its mean-ings, through the institution of policing that particular social space. King was the wrong kind of body in the wrong place with the wrong timing. The disciplinary[12] subduing of his body "clarified" that space as already inhabited by this other body.

On the other hand, Damian Williams' moment of going upside Regi-nald Denny's head with a brick in South Central after the acquittal of King's assailants represented a kind of return of the repressed, a clarifica-tion that some spaces in the urban center are not so easily claimed by the norm of White middle-class maleness. Centrally significant in that South Central theater of contestation was Williams' dance of glee afterwards. The moment was not gratuitous violence; it was ritual theater with profound communal significance. It staged a retaliation, a brief disclosure of the logic of urban space-wars. Just prior to that televised "horror," at the same corner, police had beaten and arrested another Williams family member and two neighbors.[13]

Whatever we might think of the individual morality attending any of these re/actions, what is apparent is that the meeting of these bodies in space and time was not primarily an individual matter. The encounters were profoundly social, complexly racial, densely gendered, thick with negotiations of desire and fantasy and repulsion. None of the figures was merely him- or herself (one of the officers who initially stopped King was female). Rodney King was made to figure young Black maleness in all of its polyvalent terror and fascination for White male authority. Reginald Denny (in spite of his working-class appearance) was made to stand in for the White male middle-class privilege that had secured its prerogatives one more time in the Simi Valley courtroom at the expense of Black male humanity. Violence was the nexus between the two forms of male embodiment, differentially entering into the constitution of both. But the violence that appeared in those two moments is "normally" expressed in a much denser history involving bodily negotiations of place that are not so apparently directed against each other. How that nexus is generally mediated in this society is a function of both time and space, both history and geography. Perhaps the best way into analyzing that mediation is through consideration of a little-known aspect of the Rodney King beating that may have occasioned much of its virulence.

THE SPACE OF RACE

According to the officer who first halted King, California Patrolwoman Melanie Singer, in her testimony against the LAPD officers, King was acting a little silly, laughing and doing a little dance when he got out of his inexpensive Hyundai.[14] Stacey Koon's defense attorney offered a slightly thicker description from Koon's deposition for the Simi Valley trial. He repeated Koon's testimony that King was "on something"; "I saw him look through me," and when Singer told King to take his hands away from his butt, "he shook it at her . . . he shook it at her."[15] In retrospect, then, an unanswerable but unavoidable question emerges. How much of the Blackness King was made to bear in his beating issued from a vague experience, on the part of the White males present, of "impotence"—the paradox of armed authority uncertain before an unintelligible performance apparently directed to a White female in their presence? Seemingly, White male identity was face-to-face here with a threatening "something" that it could sense, but neither interpret nor tolerate. In effect, it interpreted its own violent uncertainty onto that body, made it bear White authority's own brutality in a moment of radical displacement and projection.

The tangled density of signifiers crowding that fraught moment on the pavement between King and the LAPD harbored a long history. Unpacking the overdeterminations would require explorations of the institution and continuing effects of numerous historical practices: slave plantation techniques of producing/managing desire through the controlled breeding of slaves,[16] the violent preservation of the cult of White female virginity and the violent rape of Black women/emasculation of Black men by White masters; the eroticizing of White fears of slave revolts like those in Saint Domingue (Haiti) or, closer to home, Nat Turner's in Virginia; nineteenth-century White working-class traditions of a pornographic form of "blacking up" on the minstrel stage before going out and beating up, sexually mutilating and/or killing actual Black persons;[17] the ritualized lynchings in the Jim Crow South in which castration constituted an essential element of the violence; the way miscegenation fears entered into real estate, mortgage lending, and insurance practices, giving rise to northern ghettos; corporate management of the simultaneously titillating and terrifying cross-over power of Black musics like blues, jazz, R & B, and gospel, eventually producing Elvis Presley and the phenomenon of rock and roll; the more recent frenzy of consumption of modern-day "gladiator"[18] sports figures like Michael Jordan as fetishized primitives in national rituals of surrogate masculinity, etc.

Likewise attention would have to be focused on accounting for the broad cultural ideology of scientific racism underwriting the above. This ever-shifting yet seemingly (given the popularity of books like Richard Herrnstein and Charles Murray's *The Bell Curve*) ever-reproduced ideology absolutizing Black difference from Whiteness was originally constituted in an eighteenth-century amalgam of Anglo visceral horror for things Black,[19] Calvinist theological evaluation of dark skin as indicative of a heart recalcitrant towards God and (thus) predestined to perdition,[20] Enlightenment taxonomic classification of persons of color and cultures of contrast (to northern Europe's own) as lower on the scale of human development, and renascent Greek aesthetic ideals denigrating swarthiness, large lips, flared nostrils, prominent chins, protruding buttocks, etc.[21] Tracing the (per)mutations of this Anglo-Calvinist-Greco-Enlightenment social formation, in and through the proliferation of historical practices sampled above, would only begin to adumbrate the density of the interaction on California Highway 210.

Whatever may have been King's actual intention in his little dance (we were never given his own words about the entire event in any of the news coverage), Black and White male negotiations of embodiment in that moment could not *but* have been overcharged with meaning and energy. Many historical discourses, many cultural norms, many institutional disciplines, many social presumptions, even many family pedagogies suddenly confronted each other on the California concrete in March 1991, outside their usual venues of mediation. While it is beyond the scope of this writing to do more than simply recognize the overdetermination of that encounter, it is worth giving a rough outline of the stereotypical organization of its drama.

Rodney-King-meets-LAPD-on-California-tarmac enacted that urban space

in terms of its racialized gender coding. It was street theater minus its pro-
ducer-director. The space itself supplied much of the apology. Presumably
among other unseen actors on the stage that day was the long history of
White male fear of the Black male body briefly summarized above. A White
woman's "integrity" was seemingly violated by innuendo and suggestion,
in a space that constituted the domain of White male prerogative. The
challenge of King's little dance was arguably perceived as addressed not so
much to the police as police, but to White men in general, more specifically to front-line White male protectors of the more well-heeled White
male organizers and planners "contained" further inside that White space.
Two technologies of male embodiment were thus suddenly on display. The
Black male body was forced to deal with its motions and meanings absent
material technology or legal symbolism. It had to perform its tactic in the
key of improvisation, against the odds, in the face of terror, with only its
own corporeality for a tool. The White male body, on the other hand, was
split: its light-blue-suited enactor had hands on the implements of coercion
and sleeves full of visible license, while its dark-blue-suited possessor was
cloistered in the towers of transaction and labyrinths of power at the heart
of this suddenly compromised White space. The types here are obviously
stereotypes. Yet for all that, they continue to code the spaces and encode
the bodies. The work of culture critic Stephen Haymes, labor historian
Michael Davis, and social historian Thomas Dumm help us further explain
the relationship between space and embodiment contributing to this
urban "theater of the absurd."

In his book, *Race, Culture, and the City: A Pedagogy for Black Urban Struggle*,
Haymes has developed an analysis of the contemporary city as a spatializa-
tion of the meaning and values of race. Not only individual persons and
collective groupings, but social spaces themselves are organized on the
basis of racialization.[22] The replacement of Black, low-income "settlements"
with White, gentrified neighborhoods, for instance, materially reconstructs
the city in terms of an urban mythology in which "White places" are
deemed to be civilized, rational, and orderly and "Black places" to be un-
civilized, irrational, and disorderly. Within this cognitive mapping of public
space, Blackness represents the dangers and disorder of the id and Whiteness the civilizing consciousness of the superego. The White supremacist
thinking undergirding such mythologies mandates "spatial regulation and
control." By means of discriminatory housing practices and redlining, the
city is made to realize a form of urban apartheid: racial ideology actualized
in the material landscape. In relation to our Los Angeles example, it is
important to recognize that Highway 210 is a major linkage between what
could be called "White spaces." King's Black body was interdicted as a
foreign substance polluting the purity of place, and the LAPD officers constituted an ad hoc assemblage of antibodies, attacking the infection on
sight and reasserting the compromised code.

Davis and Dumm deepen our appreciation of the stakes. Davis has writ-

ten various works on postindustrial Los Angeles as an example of the racialized city, in which business assets and voter power have fled to surrounding
suburbs or "edge cities," leaving behind urban communities of impoverished unemployment, "black market" drug traffic, deteriorating housing
(granting tax write-offs to many absent owners), and policing practices that
border on those of postcolonial "war" situations (like Belfast during the
Troubles or the West Bank during the Intifada). In post-uprising Los
Angeles, however, Davis has witnessed a new wrinkle in the management
of urban realities. Recent meetings of geographers, urban planners, traffic
engineers, and developers have generated excitement about the imminent
advent of geographical information systems (GIS). Under this regime,
complex urban systems—traffic flows, zoning, etc.—will be managed via
the linkage of Landsat satellites to GIS software.[23] Image-resolution capabilities of commercial satellite systems are now already approaching the
threshold of distinguishing individual automobiles, and soon may be able
to distinguish people and their pets. The ramifications have not been lost
on GIS experts: one remarked to Davis that "this will quickly revolutionize
the policing of inner-city areas."[24] Here, we confront the frightening possibility that Michel Foucault's metaphor of the panopticon could become all
too material in the urban reality of the near future.

According to Dumm, however, the growing technical possibility of this
"all-seeing eye of surveillance" is only half of the picture. The other new
technological watchword is "monitoring." Its security task is more modest.
Unlike surveillance techniques, monitoring is not concerned with keeping
tabs on individuals; it is rather about the control of spaces. Monitoring
tracks movement through space by way of cameras and/or security guards
concerned not so much with individual identities as with body types in
their range of departure from a putative male norm that is White, heterosexual, and middle-class. Its analogue is the "enclosed community"—a
homogeneous environment constituted through consumption and normalized across a range of behaviors, styles, and appearances.[25] Simi Valley
marks its model. In keeping with postmodern notions of a fractured and
multiple subjectivity, these sites of monitored sameness do allow for some
measure of deviance. The personal fashion statements continuously
pushed forward for consumption by corporate America are allowed for—
but only within a carefully established range of tolerance. "Outside," more
menacing forms of difference are kept at bay through closely monitored
points of entry and exit.

Articulated with this new mode of monitoring is a refurbished ideology of law enforcement tending toward the "somatotyping" (or "body-
typing") of conservative criminologist James Q. Wilson (respected enough
to be named president of the American Political Science Association in
1992). According to Dumm, Wilson's approach to criminality has developed "anatomical correlates of crime," predicting the probability of partic-

ular kinds of behavior.²⁶ Physical traits such as broad chest, low waist, relatively large arms, prominent muscle relief, etc., and of course "color [*sic*]" all point to the possibility of a criminal predisposition. (Under these rubrics, for instance, Rodney King's body "could be said to have informed on him to the police."²⁷) While no one trait is definitive, the more such characteristics cohabit any given body, the more likely that body is to commit crime. A slim, light-skinned African American would thus be slightly less predisposed to criminality than a stockier, darker one—or so goes the theory. But whether such nuances of body-morphology-*cum*-skin-color actually translate into less, or less violent, arrests is anybody's guess (I'm guessing not). In any case, as indicating only a statistical "probability," such traits are not held to erase personal responsibility. The individuals so typed paradoxically remain accountable and thus punishable.

In net effect, then, technology and ideology are once again combining to produce new forms of differential geographies. On the one hand, enclosed communities monitor their borders with ever more sophisticated devices. (Or do monitors devise their communities through ever more sophisticated enclosures?) The result is a citadel of sameness laboring under the straight-up normativities of White, suburban, middle-class, heterosexual law-abidingness. The enclosures embrace various "others," but only so long as they do not deviate too far from the acceptable norm. On the other hand, those who are structured out of these enclosed communities are consigned to the "deviance management" of the judicial apparatuses (e.g., according to 1995 Justice Department data, 30 percent of Black men between the ages of eighteen and thirty were in prison, paroled, or on probation). Their lot is surveillance on their own turf, and monitoring if they attempt to circulate into the new enclosures.

But this tale of two cities also gives rise to a tale of two bodies. If Blackness is in some sense corporeally constituted in surveillance, Whiteness emerges as the bodily schema corresponding to monitoring. Again, these statements are stereotypic and misleading at one level. But as characterizing a set of experiences typical of certain spaces, as emblematic of normative expectations that inform certain practices, they open up a perspective on White and Black male forms of embodiment.

BLACK AND WHITE NEGOTIATIONS OF EMBODIMENT

While once again space limitations on this writing do not permit in-depth exploration, it is important to emphasize that W. E. B. Du Bois, at the turn of the century, had already formulated a thematics of Black embodiment that underscored its constitution under an invasive gaze or surveillance. In his first published writing, Du Bois underscored the power of the eye to constrain the body. His first paradigmatic experience of the meaning of racial difference took place when a grade school classmate interrupted the classroom exchange of greeting cards by refusing his offering "peremptorily, with a glance."[28] That glance, by itself, contained the entire meaning of race for Du Bois. It dropped a veil, shattered a paradise, cleaved his cosmos into two unbridgeable worlds. It is not surprising that Du Bois's later theorizing of race continued to privilege the disciplines of sight. In his most famous paraphrase of Black distinctiveness in *The Souls of Black Folk*, Black identity emerges as a peculiar "consciousness of one's twoness" in which one is ever "looking at oneself through the eyes of the other." It is a gaze with physical effect. It results in the sensation of "two souls" or "ideals" warring with one another in "one dark body whose dogged strength alone keeps it from being torn asunder."[29] Said another way, for Du Bois, Black self-consciousness has ever been the discovery that one's own time and space is already populated with other bodies, other powers, other eyes with peremptory intentions *that cannot be kept entirely outside of one's own flesh*. Blackness (in the United States, at least) *is* the body under surveillance.

More formally I would argue that Du Bois' double-consciousness is a statement not only about Black consciousness within the individual Black body, but about the spatiality of Blackness in general in this country. It foregrounds the fact that Black "room-to-be" has constantly been under the threat of invasion, a threat based not only in Black imagination of White intention, but in the historical reality of White violence. Black preoccupation with "the eyes of the other" is rooted in the concrete memory of *having actually been* invaded and *made* to deal with the other on the inside— not only inside one's head, but inside one's body (in the form of the whip or penis or baton), inside one's house (whether in Africa or on the plantation or in the ghetto), inside one's community (in the form of the overseer or social worker or police officer), inside one's culture (in the form of religious doctrine, musical instrumentation, pedagogical instruction, artisanal tools, domestic artifacts, clothes), etc. That, today, surveillance should be technologized to the point where an entire urban environment can be made to function like an outdoor prison, invaded by a constant supervisory gaze, is, at one level, nothing new or different for Black experience in North America.

In the face of such an invaded circumstance, Black survival could be understood, in part, to have been a constant struggle to combat the effects of such an intrusion, to develop tactics for living under and around such a surveillance. Whatever forms it took, the antidote would obviously have to be capable of countermanding that invasive force "in kind." Against the hard eye of a watching White culture, Black response for over three hundred years now could be said to have taken collective shape (in part) as a harder eye[30] of communal support and surreptitiousness. Anthropologist Thomas Kochman is helpful in grasping, from a comparative White point of view, some of the distinctiveness of that response.[31] As a counterforce to

oppressive White voyeurism, Black culture developed a performative countercompetency.[32] In the forums of barber shops and beauty parlors, in street
rituals of "capping" and porch rituals of "specifying," in call and response
from the pew and "you can't touch this" antiphonies on the dance floor, in
a hundred different tiny gestures of everyday life, Black cultural protocols
demanded and reinforced an oppositional facility.[33] They inculcated dramatic expressivity and elaborated a contrastive sensibility capable of de-
flecting the power of a controlling gaze by communally proliferating the
gazes before which the body-on-display negotiated its meanings. The contradictions of race were relativized in a percussive "multiplication" of the
body, elaborating hidden living space in plain view under the surface-
significance of the incarcerating category (of "Blackness"). Again and
again, culture critics and race theorists have remarked on the difference
between White and Black enculturation in this country in terms of a different set of expectations regarding public expression and physical ex-
hibition. Black culture expects social time and space to be aggressively
negotiated and contested in forms of communication that are physically
and emotionally demonstrative.[34] Its own pedagogical forms rework the
body as what Stuart Hall calls a "canvas of representation."[35]

But if Black forms of embodiment can, indeed, be understood as (in
part) the cultural products of ongoing attempts to deal with various kinds
of surveillance, White habituation in the body is also partially glossed in
the correlative notion of contemporary monitoring. White embodiment in
the public spaces of this country, historically, has been more about the
meeting of norms, quietly fitting in,[36] not causing a spectacle.[37] It has been
constituted in a gaze that solicits conformity, not subversive stylizations of
individuality.[38] It has been disciplined not so much in intense forms of
local community that act as a confirming chorus[39] and supply a range of
innovatory[40] models and improvisational motives, but rather in a more plastic mode of spatiality, governed by more generic ideals. In its genesis as an
"empty negation,"[41] a largely vacuous assertion "that whatever else I may
be, at least I am not Black," Whiteness has not been generative of a White
community per se; there has been no positive White cultural production
coming into being in a serious struggle against invasive powers. Where
"White" identities have indeed forged profound expressions of culture, it
has been under the impress of other necessities, other exigencies of survival. American versions of Irish blarney, German industry, English understatement, Italian humor, Jewish spunk, Dutch Reformed discipline, East
Coast sophistication, West Coast trendiness, Midwestern practicality, Bryn
Mawr taste, Southern hospitality, etc.—all find their conditions of creation
in something other than "White struggle." White desire (as "White") has
simply not been that contested or threatened. Whiteness, as such, has had
no daunting historical enemy. It has faced no hard eye of opposition (until,
perhaps, the emergence of the Black Power movement of the 1960s).[42] It

has more simply been either fascinated or frightened and acted accordingly, usually with impunity. Its only formative condition has been the Blackness it projects and punishes. But there, in fact, we can identify the one operation that gives Whiteness a certain common character.

BLACK AND WHITE EMBODIMENT IN FORMATION

If Blackness is invasive for Blacks, an imposition of meanings that has produced a range of somatic modalities of resistance, Whiteness is evasive for Whites, a cloak of presumed attributes that grants an invisible "surround," requiring only the maintenance of distance (from Blackness). In political economic terms, Whiteness is perhaps the ultimate mystification; it is the (cultural) surplus value realized from subjugating a people inside the category of Blackness.[43] Unlike the effect Blackness has in the body that is made to bear its meanings, Whiteness makes no demands of its bearer other than assent to belonging. Whereas surviving Black skin in the United States requires constant active response to one's own bodily schema—a constant exorcism of invading powers, a continuous "tricking" of syntagmatic meaning by way of creating meaning in the paradigmatic register,[44] deepening the pejorative surface significance of darkness into a polyphonic density of signification, a promulgation of pride, a codification of savvy, a stylization of sophistication—being White is more nearly passive, a gratuitous inheritance. Surveillance makes of the (Black) body surface a site of conflict, a point of aggression, soliciting counterforce. It results in an excavation of depths, away from the eye, a violent demand to create a zone of difference inside the body, between the signifying surface and the safer depths. In the struggle with such a gaze, Black agency makes the body itself a construct of difference. Monitoring, on the other hand, does not solicit bodily negotiation and self-knowing with the same kind of relentless intrusion. It rather fosters a one-to-one correspondence between a surface that matches its space of movement (and thus moves largely uncontested) and the deeper recesses of one's experience, such that the surface, in effect, dis-appears.

White embodiment oscillates "plastically" between fantasy and fear. Where White experience of everyday life takes shape as a form of fascination,[45] moving unimpeded through the consumer spaces of the culture, the reflex in the White body is simply naiveté, presumption. (And here something of the class-coding implicit in the normative formation of "Whiteness" shows up.) White identity in its ideal mode of embodiment is today a creature especially of the suburban enclave (even if such is carved out of urban geography by way of walls and policing and security mechanisms). Middle-class social space (the mall, the suburban street, the office, etc.) is space that appears immediately transparent to the White body (especially if male, as we shall see below). Or said the other way around, the White body is the physical form that most experiences that space as unobstructed, as open to the gaze, vulnerable to the grasp, intelligible to the question (and to the degree that even light-skinned bodies do not experience that space as hospitable because of certain differences of class or orientation, like clothing or gesture, they are then not fully constituted as normatively White). The body that invests such a space, that absorbs and reproduces its presumptions, that receives its inscription, is what is most nearly constituted, in the "common sense" or "political unconscious" of the dominant culture, as "Whiteness." It is a form of embodiment that is not a problem to itself; indeed, it does not appear to itself.

But where White desire perceives a "Black" threat, and draws a line of exclusion demarcating imagined danger, the reflex-effect has been that of an interior distancing. The retreat away from the contestation of contact, the refusal to engage in the negotiation of surface signs, effects a fixation of meanings and certainty. The projection of "otherness" outside, on the Black-appearing body, condenses a sense of self-sameness on the inside, in the safety of an assumed transparency. The payoff of this forcible halting of the vulnerability of exchange is an attempted auto-exorcism of the terrifying ambivalence of desire/disgust.[46] The physical body is closed off in its correlation with its imagined spatiality, reduced to an isomorphic surface, uninitiated in the contradictory depths of either the social or the psychic body. The subjectivity so installed is something less than its imagined space of interiority: the historical obsession with purity translates into a profound social investment in "staying in place," cloistered away from the grotesquerie of polluting surfaces.[47]

We could perhaps then generalize that whereas the racialization of Black bodies involves an unwanted experience of the body surface as a site of conflict and a dialectical mobilization of the deep structures of the body as (potentially) an agentive resource for knowing and refiguring, the racialization of White bodies constitutes an abandonment of agency to an already decided topography of (presumed) transparency in the relationship between body surface, body depths, and social space. The result is a White illiteracy in reading/writing texts of the body.

WHITE AND BLACK MALE EMBODIMENT

While the above characterization is offered as a partial apology for the ways race insinuates itself in the constitution of bodily schemas by means of subtle transactions of gaze, negotiations of space, displacements of propriety, etc., gender is not outside the equation. White middle-class male bodies establish the normative modes of power in middle-class space. Taught early to refrain from touching (other males) off the football field or basketball court, schooled in "macho" affective protocols that dictate hiding or not even feeling the more tender emotions, bombarded relentlessly with Madison Avenue imagery of male potency, rewarded incongruously for conformity to the ideals of dress, gesture, cadence of speech, etc. dictated or managed by the corporate world, White middle-class males all too often fall into forms of embodiment that are largely imitative. By internalizing the subtle cues for bodily performance the culture of bourgeois patriarchy puts forward, such a body is offered social space as a gendered receptacle of bodily being. Space is unproblematic and penetrable, ripe for conquest. It is not encountered as resistive force, demanding counterresistance, risk of violation, performative displacement. It is simply traversed, unthought. The body is not educated as a tactic of negotiation: it has not been forced to deal with itself as dominated from without by disciplines (classroom protocols, police batons, prison bars, troubling glances, etc.) that reduce it to something less than itself or other than its habitual way of being in public. It has thus also not had to do the work of elaborating its own communicative capacities—in concert with other, similarly troubled bodies—into surreptitious codes of countermeaning. It has never had to wrestle with its own opacity, its lack of "fit" in a given space, communicated by suspicious eyes, backed by procedures of pain. It has more normally experienced its space as (erotically) available, its imagined reflection in other eyes as desirable, its rhythm as on time. The White female body has provided some degree of resistance to White male physicality, but most often been violently constituted in thrall to that body's cathecting gaze as its desired object. The Black female body historically has either been dismissed as unattractive or likewise cathected as sexual object. Only the Black male body (and to some extent, the gay body, whatever its color) has regularly offered the kind of contrapuntal coding of time and impenetrable blockage of space that forces the White male body into a confrontation with its own surface, its gendered finitude in time and space, its own peculiar locality and contingency.

Black male otherness again and again has become the target for (White) aggressions that irreducibly owe some of their virulence to socially mediated displacements of emotional conflict in the struggle of male children to come into gendered subjectivity. The genealogical filiation of this violence is profound and polymorphic. The Black male adult body emerges before White male awareness[48] as something not only aberrant and fearful—a "darkness" bearing a penis[49]—but also as prolific in its creativity and expressivity. Its threat as sexual competitor does not derive merely from its unintelligibility. It is also a function of its *competence* as a body.

Of course, all of this is tacit; not many White middle-class males would admit to such cognitions at a conscious level. But the dominant culture in our time does. Commodified urban attitude as cipher for male virility— again, the ritualistic core of the national fetishization of sports—clearly finds its icon of choice in the Black male body at the peak of its performative powers. As a commodity form, this kind of Black maleness is ironically increasingly assimilated in our day as an appendage to White male middle-classness.[50] Very few White middle-class high school basketballers would not affirm a teammate's good play with a high five or make a move on an attractive girl at a school party without a certain kind of rhythmic dance step (ultimately traceable to Black innovations through a long line of White imitation beginning, obviously, with Elvis). And to the degree gentrification represents the postindustrial form of a renascent male quest to return to the "pioneer spirit" of this country,[51] Black male cultural productivity stands before that spirit as the equivalent of "noble savagery." Yuppie enclaves carved out of former working-class or ghetto neighborhoods offer the prospect of appropriating and enjoying urban edginess: the danger of the city is ritually celebrated in dance venues and blues clubs where Black creativity can be assimilated minus its downside costs or its context of desperation. At the same time, the prison-industrial complex grows apace as the second armature of White male middle-class embodiment, structuring actual Black lower-class males as far away from White male life-worlds and from White women as is conceivable in our increasingly crowded social habitats.

In net effect then, White male middle-class embodiment is in part predicated on Black male lower-class embodiment—and vice versa. The (unconscious?) White male fear of raising a daughter (or retaining a wife?) in proximity to a "free" Black penis is profoundly part of the social structure of the suburb or edge city, played out in a long history and a dense layer of materiality. The management of that penis in a range of institutional disciplines can be tracked from the slave plantation, through the postbellum convict-lease system, Jim Crow ritualizations of terror in the South, ghettoization and criminalization of Blackness in the North, continuing redlining and housing discrimination, resistance to school desegregation, the more recent gutting of affirmative action reparations giving Blacks access to historically White schools, and the constitution of enclosed communities of affluence around the male norm of White middle-class heterosexuality whose borders are monitored for conformity to the norm (allowing some dark-skinned males the possibility of partial access as long as the other requisite lifestyle signs of "normalcy" like clothes, cars, quality of commodities, etc. are carefully maintained). The effect of those institutional structures of racialized management is to create spaces that regulate their allowable bodies, which in turn reproduce the norms of the space.

Black lower-class maleness, on the other hand, is confined to "other" spaces in a complex operation of ideology, policing, drug-trafficking, shadow-banking, withdrawal of services, flight of meaningful jobs, stereotyping, and bureaucratic social welfare depersonalization. Without question, the hegemony reigning in such spaces conforms its own inhabitants to varying degrees of complicity in the destruction. But simply learning to survive such spaces also creates a profound encounter with the contingency of embodied life that does not cease to reproduce the Black body as a cultural artifact of no mean accomplishment. That rap music and hip-hop culture find their greatest market among young males in White suburbs and define one of two operative youth subcultures in a country like contemporary Russia, as well as pervasively influencing ethnic musics and youth styles worldwide, suggests something attractively vital is perceptible in Black male work with the body as a site of creative resistance (notwithstanding hip-hop's obvious and justifiably criticized misogyny and sexist violence). In a certain sense, Black lower-class maleness is forced to face the underside of modernity as a surrogate of sorts, to undergo its terrors and treachery as a kind of prophylactic for those "on top." It works out, in its stylizations of the body and syncopations of expression, the new meaning of masculinity as a heroic struggle with danger and death,[52] before being forced to yield those creations to the process of commodification, making those reincarnations of male virility available to the broader culture of White maleness.

On the other hand, the very economic wherewithal that is part of the definition of White middle-class maleness (cf. Cheryl Harris' legal definition of Whiteness as "property") exempts the White middle-class from the worst consequences of late-capitalist consumerism, the ongoing and ever-shifting dynamic that de-develops certain spaces (urban cores, ethnic enclaves, Third World countrysides, etc.) for the sake of overdeveloping other spaces (luxury estates, elite neighborhoods, First World metropoles, etc.). But those entropic spaces become important sites for the production of existential symbols of a refetishized wildness that cannot be produced with the same potency in the leisure spaces of security and comfort.[53] As with the innovations of athletic prowess in the gladiator arenas of spectator sports, so with the innovations of existential attitude in the gladiator arenas of everyday life: the inner city here becomes a site of both danger and desire, the young Black male body a cipher of both violent bestiality and vigorous masculinity. The 'hood becomes a laboratory for the system whose Viagra-like product is for sale far away from the processing plant.

THE ETHICS OF WHITE MALE EMBODIMENT

To the degree White middle-class maleness is not simply, or even primarily, a matter of an individual coagulation of cells given gestural efficacy and communicative competency by an autonomous rationality sitting in the boardroom of the head, the body marks the site of a necessarily (im)moral assessment. In the products it consumes, in the spaces it assumes, in the postures it incarnates, in the gestures it assimilates, in the powers it learns and the structures it confirms, the body is a moral substance.[54] It both marks an ethical placement and means an ethical predisposition. It is innocent of neither its history nor its destiny. Quite apart from its own intentionality, it is already the presupposition of a politics, the metabolism of an economics, the status of a social mobility. The body does not just carry these things; in an important sense, it *is* them. The language of ontology is necessary to get at the depths of the consequentiality, but the choice of words is tactical. The metaphysics proposed here is not finally essentialist: it is an ontology that is partially subject to ethical agency in historical struggle. And the question that emerges with a kind of subtle vengeance is this: What would it mean for a White male middle-class body to begin to live its embodiment in a way that challenged those silent inscriptions and rendered them socially articulate and culturally specific?[55] Given that this body is the presupposition/product of "the system," is a *de facto* norm of a now globalizing culture, how can it be made to signify a different possibility of being human than simply its own reproduction? Even imagining this question as politically relevant is made profoundly difficult by the economic prerogatives today of being able to buy identity in the form of style.

Postindustrial capital has become extremely proficient at mobilizing the least human gesture, the subtlest syncopation of space, the tiniest movement toward innovation, into a new product line. Why bother with a question of the body? To the degree one is successful in partially escaping social inscription and the reproduction of one's position, that very exercise of freedom itself will only be recaptured and made to serve the regnant hegemony. The destiny of freedom as "incorporation" is patent in late capitalism.

And yet, it is equally true that freedom is also always—however epiphanic and fleeting—embodied. Freedom that is not realized (at least) at the level of everyday living, of bodily gesture and local space, is just more ideology. For those whose subjectivity already encodes dominance and normativity at the level of the body, physical displacement becomes a prerequisite for critical thinking and ethical struggle. bell hooks' challenge to White feminist "colleagues" to meet the oppressed not at the center, but in the margins, on their own turf, is doubly apropos of White male "allies."[56]

The insinuation of macrostructure at the level of microstructural codes of the body would seem to imply that one of the preconditions for political struggle and ethical judgment is a bodily *habitus* that embodies the contradictions giving rise to struggle and demanding theoretical attention. Putting the White male body "out of its place"[57] by subjecting it in and to other spaces, other protocols, other codes, indeed, other forms of embodiment, is part of the process of "thought." Thought is always a function of a physicality. The testament of the likes of Frantz Fanon, W. E. B. Du Bois, and bell hooks is that critical thought, creative thought, radical vision, motivated struggle, and ethical precision, are in part a matter of trying to close a gap in one's own experience of embodiment, seeking to give political texture to the social violence felt within one's own bodily schema.[58] This is not to wish violence on anyone; it is rather to suggest that an ethical approach to the violence that is already structured into a sociality is somehow to comprehend that violence in one's own physicality, to become partially vulnerable to its power to rearrange, in a way that affects one's profoundest sense of deportment and renders consciously agentive attempts to resist such structures. Saying such is not to ask for masochism; it is to ask for conscious embrace of a vulnerability that is already mutual and concrete incarnation of a reciprocal give-and-take.

Part and parcel of the argument offered here is a belief that relationship is the very core of ethical assertion and indeed the very essence of human being, that interdependence is the presupposition of value, that "individual morality" is, in fact, an (ideologically not innocent) oxymoron.[59] It is the very meaning of such an ethical perception to insist that overt violence in one social geography, rupturing and determining bodily experience there, is necessarily simultaneously disruptive of the geography and physicality it seems to serve, no matter how inchoate or unconscious the effects of that disruption might prove to be. White male forms of "neutral" and "innocent" embodiment would then necessarily be constituted in a deformation of fear at some subtle social level in inverse proportion to Black forms of contestatory embodiment. Only if the violence predicated of Rodney King's body is traced back *both* to the hand wielding the baton that produced that violence *and* to the seemingly cleaner hands that underwrite and profit from it, will it be possible to bring Whiteness under ethical interrogation. But only if that latter form of White maleness is itself also publicly *revealed* as problematically male in its erotic surveillance, middle-class in its "normal" aspiration, pervasive in its discursive predominance, and specifically limited in its enculturation, will something else become possible. That something else will at least involve White males actively renegotiating their meanings and positions and forms of embodiment in relationship to Blacks (and "Latinos" and "Asians," and gay and lesbian styles, and women of all ethnic backgrounds, etc.). Anything less will leave the hegemonic body scripted in a normative form of ignorance secured by structural domination. White men can learn to speak. They can also learn to jump.

NOTES

1. Michelle Fine, Linda C. Powell, Lois Weis, and L. Mun Wong, "Preface," in *Off White: Readings on Race, Power, and Society,* ed. Michelle Fine, Linda C. Powell, Lois Weis, and L. Mun Wong (New York: Routledge, 1997), x.

2. Patricia J. Williams, "The Rules of the Game," *Reading Rodney King, Reading Urban Uprising,* ed. R. Gooding-Williams (New York: Routledge, 1993), 51–55.

3. As constructed by Pierre Bourdieu, "habitus" designates the taken-for-granted patterns of perception and calculations of response to one's cultural environment and social others. These patterns normally operate almost outside of con-

sciousness, but can be brought to the forefront of intentionality if put under pressure by sudden change (Bourdieu, *Outline of a Theory of Practice,* trans. R. Nice [Cambridge: Cambridge University Press, 1977], 17).

4. Richard Dyer, "White," *Screen* 29, no. 4 (1988): 44–64.

5. Cornel West, "Black Culture and Postmodernism," in *Remaking History,* ed. B. Kruger and P. Mariani (Seattle: Bay Press, 1989), 93.

6. Arthur Kroker, *The Possessed Individual: Technology and the French Postmodern* (New York: St. Martin's Press, 1992).

7. Many cultures have some form of possession cult; while distinctive and constantly undergoing change in their historical contexts, they resemble each other in some ways. See Sheila Walker, *Ceremonial Spirit Possession in Africa and Afro-America: Forms, Meanings, and Functional Significance for Individuals and Social Groups* (Leiden, Netherlands: E. J. Brill, 1972).

8. This is due both to growing numbers of immigrants from Haiti and Cuba and to increasing interest and adherence among already "naturalized" Americans of various cultural and ethnic backgrounds, including those thought of as "White." See Karen McCarthy Brown, *Mama Lola: A Vodou Priestess in Brooklyn* (Berkeley: University of California Press, 1991).

9. Michel Foucault, *Power/Knowledge: Selected Interviews & Other Writings, 1972–1977,* ed. C. Gordon (New York: Pantheon Books, 1972), 81–84.

10. For instance, recent statistics indicate a marked increase in "interracial" dating in the United States, except for the coupling of "Whites" and "Blacks." Statistics regarding residential mobility continue to indicate African Americans as the least mobile segment of the population (Michael Davis, *The War against the Cities,* 1993, 33–34).

11. Judith Butler, "Endangered/Endangering: Schematic Racism and White Paranoia," in *Reading Rodney King, Reading Urban Uprising,* ed. R. Gooding-Williams (New York: Routledge, 1993), 15–22.

12. Michel Foucault, *Discipline and Punish: The Birth of the Prison,* trans. A. Sheridan (New York: Vintage, 1979).

13. Michael Davis, "Los Angeles Was Just the Beginning." in *Open Fire,* ed. G. Ruggiero and S. Sahulka (Los Angeles: Open Pamphlet Series, 1993), 220–243.

14. Houston Baker, "Scene . . . Not Heard," in *Reading Rodney King, Reading Urban Uprising,* ed. R. Gooding-Williams (New York: Routledge, 1993), 38–50; Ruth Gilmore, "Terror Austerity Race Gender Excess Theater," in *Reading Rodney King, Reading Urban Uprising,* ed. R. Gooding-Williams (New York: Routledge, 1993), 23–37.

15. Gilmore, "Terror Austerity," 29.

16. Hortense Spillars, "Mama's Baby, Papa's Maybe: An American Grammar Book," *Diacritics* (Summer 1987): 65–81.

17. David Roediger notes that this phenomenon occurred immediately after city leaders outlawed White participation in Black-led public celebrations like Independence Day in the 1830s. The implication is that it may reflect, among other things, a kind of warped nostalgia for what had been a vitalizing form of control (Roediger, *The Wages of Whiteness: Race and the Making of the American Working Class* [London; New York: Verso, 1991], 106).

18. Robert D. Kaplan, "Was Democracy Just a Moment?" *Atlantic Monthly,* December 1997, 55–80.

19. Winthrop Jordan, *White over Black: American Attitudes toward the Negro, 1550–1812* (New York: W. W. Norton & Co., 1968), 7–8.

20. Roger Bastide, "Color, Racism, and Christianity," in *White Racism: Its History, Pathology and Practice,* ed. B. N. Schwartz and R. Disch (New York: Dell Publishing Co., 1970), 270–285.

21. Cornel West, *Prophesy Deliverance! An African-American Revolutionary Christianity* (Philadelphia: Westminster Press, 1982), 47–65.

22. Stephen N. Haymes, *Race, Culture, and the City: A Pedagogy for Black Urban Struggle* (Albany: State University of New York Press, 1995), 4, 21–22.

23. Michael Davis, "Uprising and Repression in L.A.: An Interview with Mike Davis by the *Covert Action Information Bulletin*," *Reading Rodney King, Reading Urban Uprising*, ed. R. Gooding-Williams (New York: Routledge, 1993), 142–156.

24. Ibid., 149.

25. Thomas Dumm, "The New Enclosures: Racism in the Normalized Community," *Reading Rodney King, Reading Urban Uprising*, ed. R. Gooding-Williams (New York: Routledge, 1993), 178–195.

26. Ibid., 183.

27. Ibid.

28. W. E. B. Du Bois, *The Souls of Black Folk* (New York: Fawcett Publications, 1961), 17.

29. Ibid., 17.

30. Robert Ferris Thompson, *Flash of the Spirit: African and Afro-American Art and Philosophy* (New York: Vintage Books, 1983), 5–9. West African traditions of *ashe*-eyed elders, communicating potency and power through the quality of their gaze, are intensified in the experience of slavery and racism, reinforcing that form of communication as a survival tactic.

31. Thomas Kochman, *Black and White Styles in Conflict* (Chicago: University of Chicago Press, 1981). Kochman argues, for instance (on page 110), that both oppressive social conditions and the need for status among peers, on the one hand, and a distinctive aesthetic sensibility, on the other, contribute to the "spectacular exhibitionism," "intensity," "aggressivity," and "vital expressivity" of Black cultural protocols. "Doing your thing" is a matter of asserting oneself *within* the group, "playing off against others—competitively and cooperatively at the same time"—so that all benefit from the power demonstrated.

32. Ibid., 110, 131. This countercompetency is encoded even into everyday behaviors, such as the rhythmic style of walking called "bopping" or the hand-to-hand exchange called "giving skin," to ignite a sense of spiritual connection and invite and even demand reciprocity. Kochman notes that Black performative style has been particularly admired by the larger society in the performing arts (such as music, dance, theater, and sports) while generating mixed responses at the everyday level of attire, or of ways of walking, standing, talking, greeting, etc., and encountering out-and-out rejection in the schoolroom and workplace.

33. Ibid., 18–19. For instance, Kochman differentiates the classroom style of Blacks from that of Whites by emphasizing that because the former "consider debate to be as much a contest between individuals as a test of opposing ideas . . . attention is also paid to performance" (24). Winning, here, "requires that one outperform one's opponents: outthink, outtalk, and outstyle them. It means being concerned with art as well as argument" (24). "Individuals develop and demonstrate their degree of togetherness by respectively developing and demonstrating their ability to contend. Black performers do so when they heat up the environment while . . . proclaiming their own cool" (127).

Kochman analyzes the interlocking and synergistic "revitalization of energy through emotional and spiritual release" characteristic of Black cultural activities under a three-fold *call and response* pattern: "(1.) a sufficiently powerful agent-stimulus to activate the emotional (spiritual) forces that the body has imprisoned, (2.) a structure like song, dance, or drum that allows for the unrestricted expression of those forces that the agent-stimulus has aroused, and (3.) a manner of participation that gives full value to the power of the agent-stimulus and to the individual's ability to receive and manipulate it" (108). The latter "manner of participation" "entails a mind/body involvement of considerable depth, what blacks call *getting down into* the mode through which emotional release and spiritual rejuvenation are effected" (108). What then appears to Whites as a loss of emotional control is actually a ritualized expression of greater control in which Blacks "transferred a measure of control from themselves to the feeling mode (sorrow, exultation, spirit possession) and to the cultural form (song, dance, greeting exchange, call and response) through which the emotions are released and within which they are also contained" (115).

34. Indeed, Kochman asserts, "The requirement to behave calmly, rationally, unemotionally, and logically when negotiating is looked upon by blacks as a political requirement—and to accede to it in advance is considered as a political defeat" (ibid., 40).

35. Stuart Hall, "What Is This 'Black' in Black Popular Culture?" in *Black Popular Culture,* ed. Michele Wallace and Gina Dent (Seattle: Bay Press, 1992), 21–33 (esp. 27–29). Hall has remarked that the distinctiveness of Black diasporic traditions is reflected especially in the uses these cultures have made of the body, along with a focus on style as the primary subject, rather than merely accidental accretion, of cultural production, and on music rather than writing (or its deconstruction). As the depth-structure of cultural life, bodily performance pinpoints one of the major places of contrast between diasporic and dominant cultures. Hall offers that Black cultures worked on the body as a "canvas of representation" because it was often "the only cultural capital [they] had available" (27). In arguing this, Hall asserts that the repertoires of Black popular culture "were overdetermined from at least two directions" (28): by their inheritances and by the diasporic conditions in which those connections with heritage were forged. "Selective appropriation, incorporation, and rearticulation of European ideologies, cultures, and institutions, alongside an African heritage," Hall says (while citing Cornel West), "led to linguistic innovations in rhetorical stylizations of the body, forms of occupying an alien social space, heightened expressions, hairstyles, ways of walking, standing, and talking, and a means of constituting and sustaining camaraderie and community" (28).

The importance of such a recognition, according to Hall, is that Black diasporic cultures exhibit "no pure forms at all" (28). Rather, these forms are always "the product of partial synchronization, of engagement across cultural boundaries, of the confluence of more than one cultural tradition, of the negotiations of dominant and subordinate positions, of the subterranean strategies of recoding and transcoding, of critical signification, of signifying" (28). Black popular culture produces vernacular forms that are marked by hybridity on the *inside,* that thus appear as contradictory by definition. The signifier "Black" carries the weight not of an essential differentiation of diasporic from dominant culture—a self-sufficient "their tradition versus ours"—but rather of a dialogic strategy of adaptation, "molded to the mixed, contradictory, hybrid spaces of popular culture" (28). It is an aesthetic strategy of difference that rewrites the binary opposition Black-White in terms of an "and" in the place of the usual "or" (e.g., Black *and* British rather than Black or British) (29). But Hall is also insistent that such a claim not be read as simply another form of binarism. As with his colleague Paul Gilroy's way of thinking about "double-consciousness," Hall argues that such a strategy is rather a way of dislocating or moving outside of the oppositionality altogether. Identity is not exhausted in the "and" any more than it was clarified in the "or." Hybridity, here, simply encodes one particular historical struggle in which identity is sometimes caught and out of which it is forged. There are other struggles that give rise to other forms of identification in the same life.

36. Kochman, *Black and White Styles*, 30. In describing White self-assertion, for instance, Kochman says it "occurs as a social entitlement" that, even when granted, must be "low-keyed . . . showing detachment, modesty, understatement."

37. Steven Pile, *The Body and the City: Psychoanalysis, Space and Subjectivity* (New York: Routledge, 1996), 230.

38. Kochman, *Black and White Styles*, 114, 155. Kochman cites a communications study in which the observed performances of "white and well-to-do black first graders reflected the cultural norms of the dominant society" in being literal, obedient, modest and uniform, with "little to distinguish one child's performance from that of another" (154). On the other hand, "the poor black children" who were part of the experiment "were literally performing, emphasizing both individuality and vitality . . . greater verbal creativity and more dynamic oral presentation" (155) for which they would have received failing marks had the experiment been an actual test in school. Kochman says, "White culture values the ability of individuals to rein in their impulses. White cultural events do not allow for individually initiated self-assertion or the spontaneous expression of feeling" (30). "[C]lothes should be drab and inconspicuous, colors of low intensity, sounds quiet, smells nonexistent, words emotionless" (114).

39. Ibid., 107. In noting the group quality of Black performance, its emphasis upon call and response, Kochman says "the black performer's role is not just to demonstrate but also to instigate," to vitalize the energies and images "from which the performer and the audience together draw spiritual sustenance" (134). In comparison, the undemonstrative behavior more typical of Whites is pejoratively labeled "gray" by Blacks, and failure by a Black person to come up with sufficient intensity of response in a Black-on-Black interaction may be criticized as "acting White."

40. Kochman notes that "the emphasis on developing one's own style also helps to explain why one does not see in the black community the kind of public imitation of star performers that one finds in the white community . . . To do so would signify to other blacks a lack of individual resourcefulness, imagination, and pride" (ibid., 135).

41. Dyer, "White," 44.

42. Howard Winant, "Behind Blue Eyes: Whiteness and Contemporary U.S. Racial Politics," in *Off White: Readings on Race, Power, and Society*, ed. Michelle Fine, Linda C. Powell, Lois Weis, and L. Mun Wong (New York: Routledge, 1997), 41–53.

43. Cheryl Harris, "Whiteness as Property," *Harvard Law Review* 106, no. 8 (1993): 1709–1791.

44. Henry Louis Gates, Jr., *The Signifying Monkey: A Theory of Afro-American Literary Criticism* (New York: Oxford University Press, 1988), 49.

45. Charles Long, *Significations: Signs, Symbols, and Images in the Interpretation of Religion* (Philadelphia: Fortress Press, 1986), 137.

46. Pile, *Body and the City*, 207.

47. Ibid., 250–256.

48. Ibid.

49. Playing off of Freud's problematic epigram of adult woman's sexuality as a "dark continent." Sigmund Freud, "The Question of Lay-analysis: Conversations with an Impartial Person," in S. Freud, *Two Short Accounts of Psycho-analysis* (Hammondsworth: Pelican, 1962), 91–170.

50. Haymes, *Race, Culture, and the City*, 50.

51. Ibid., 106.

52. George Hegel, *Phenomenology of Spirit*, trans. A. V. Miller, analysis and foreword by J. N. Findley (Oxford: Clarendon Press, 1977), 117–119.

53. P. Stallybrass and A. White, *The Politics and Poetics of Transgression* (London: Methuen, 1986), 5.

54. Robert Bellah, *Habits of the Heart: Individualism and Commitment in American Life* (Berkeley: University of California Press, 1985), 71–81.

55. Gloria Albrecht, *The Character of Our Communities: Toward an Ethic of Liberation for the Church* (Nashville: Abingdon Press, 1995), 98.

56. bell hooks, *Yearning: Race, Gender and Cultural Politics* (Boston: South End Press, 1990), 151–152.

57. In the sense in which Michel de Certeau has differentiated "place" and "space." Place is the provenance of strategies of domination; in its operation, dominating forms of power constellate, secure, and attempt to valorize a particular location. On the other hand, the tactics of resistance are more opportunistic; subordinate powers seize spaces in momentary takeovers that must usually be quickly abandoned (de Certeau, *The Practice of Everyday Life,* trans. S. F. Rendall [Berkeley: University of California Press, 1984]).

58. bell hooks, "Black Women Intellectuals," in bell hooks and C. West, *Breaking Bread: Insurgent Black Intellectual Life* (Boston: South End Press, 1991): 148–150; Frantz Fanon, *Black Skin, White Masks,* trans. C. L. Markmann (New York: Grove Weidenfeld, 1991), 109–114; Du Bois, *Souls of Black Folk,* 17.

59. Bellah, *Habits of the Heart,* 76–78, 84.

Chapter 10

Brothers/*Others*

Gonna Paint the White House Black . . .

CRAIG WILKINS

This essay concerns itself primarily with the intersection of Black male identity and space. In this analysis, I will use the Million Man March as the *beau idéal* in which to contextualize and illustrate the construction of Black male identity in spatial terms. In revisiting this event, my purpose is not to directly address all the arguments repeated for or against the March and its organizers in and out of the Black community, but rather to highlight a less critically investigated possibility of the March itself. My tenacious reading of that event requires a theoretical reflection on identity and space, which, in mapping that terrain, will invariably cut across issues of sex, race, gender, and class. While each of (post)modernity's big four figure prominently in my thinking about the M3 event, I will not heed every analytical stop sign at every intersection, as a *thorough* critique of *each* issue in its relation to space and identity is beyond the scope of this essay. I will, however, render this reading from "locations of experience"[1]—which bell hooks argues return one from the process of theorizing to concrete practice—that emerge along the crossing *roots* of space and identity. It is useful to think of the M3 event in this manner—experience as theory and practice—primarily because when experience is a valid location from which to theorize, the participants of the March become "public intellectuals" of a kind; from the experience—the theoretical work—of these million-plus public intellectuals emerges a practice of spatial appropriation and creation that is exchanged as a strategy for creating and securing Black male identity. Having said that, let us begin our journey . . .

I. THE SPACES OF POWER . . .

I am a pebble, the world is the pond I have been dropped into. I am at the center of a system of concentric circles that become fainter as they spread. The first circle immediately around me is strong, and each successive circle is weaker. My duties are exactly like the concentric circles around the pebble: strongest at the center and rapidly diminishing toward the periphery. My primary duties are to those immediately around me, my secondary duties are

to those next nearest, my tertiary duties to those next, and so
on. Plainly, any duties to those on the far periphery are going to
diminish to nothing, and given the limited resources available to
any ordinary person, her positive duties will barely reach beyond
a second or third circle.

—Henry Shue[2]

If this passage is—as intended—an illustration of American cultural and
social relations, then in American society Shue's first circle can be understood as being singularly occupied by the Euro-American man. Predicated
upon a particular notion of history, the White male has emerged, justifiably
or not, front and center in the theater of American identity formation. Not
only has his brotherhood assigned itself top billing, it also has assumed the
playwright's authority to define the subject positions of the remaining
actors as it sees fit—and how it sees fit is always to its own advantage. Satisfied with the apparent spatial impermeability that reinforces their power
and authority, White males have unilaterally secured their central position
on the American stage by a variety of ideological means, whereby a singular
notion of "male" simultaneously embraces and protects their own guild
and excludes *other* actors from leading roles.

Further observation reveals Shue's second circle occupied by the Euro-
American female. The overtly and covertly disseminated ideology of the
White woman as the ultimate paradigm of female subjectivity in American
culture exists despite the White male's failure to resolve her assigned dichotomous subject positions as both worshipped and worshiper, queen and
worker bee.[3] Awash with patriarchal and paternalistic platitudes, the image,
position, and power of the White woman has been—comparatively speaking[4]—just to the right and slightly behind the White male, fitting for one
who will bear and nurture heirs to the power and authority inherent in this
construction of national color.

An equally distorted image of the African American woman can be
found in the third circle.[5] It is clear that the bodies of Black women have
always been a benign, somewhat controlled—and controlling—fetish of
White men and women alike. Conflicting images of the African American
female as surrogate child-rearers, confidantes, welfare mothers, (un)will-
ing mistresses, and sisters in the struggle for economic, social, political,
and spatial equality constitute past and present notions of Black female
subjectivity[6] essentially as "Black Back-Ups."[7] Stuart Hall has suggested that
the partnership between past and present is an imaginary construction and
clearly, such fossilized views of the Black female are principally products of
a (D. W.) Griffithized ideological imaging of the past, produced through a
lens leveled at the Black female body that has never quite been in focus.[8]

Relegated to the fourth circle in this hierarchy we find the African
American male. The naturalized image of the brutal, base, highly sexualized, aggressive, animalistic, angry male is constantly broadcast through

airwaves—and hairwaves—to an all-too-receptive public.[9] Resisting being situated in the fourth circle—the visually transparent and peripheral spaces of society—Black men have historically attempted to make a separate, different circle in Shue's pond, a deeper, more reaffirming impression in the cultural sea. From public auction to Public Enemy, from Reverend King to Rodney King, from H. Rap Brown to gangsta rap sound, every attempt by Black men to make the transparent visible has met with various and often violent forms of resistance outside and inside their community. This resistance was manifested most recently on October 16, 1995, in the contemporary form of immovable subject of power versus irresistible spatial force.

II. THE IMMOVABLE SUBJECT OF POWER . . .

Space intervenes in the historical dialogue concerning social relations, and American nationalist culture has positioned males—read White males—as its principal spatial conquering heroes. The power of American nationalist culture is embodied in a spatial organization that determines who will live where and why, and in physical manifestations that decide what particular architectural forms will symbolize and why. These seemingly "natural" decisions are constructed on, and legitimized by, the spatial foundations initially conceived by René Descartes and later further developed by John Locke. Locke's concepts of space were created and employed at a moment in American history when it was necessary to legally define and conjoin space, place, and property (think Manifest Destiny), and his theories have fundamentally, materially, and substantively shaped Western civilization— especially in the area of spatial understanding. But, as I will explain below, the notion of space put forth by Locke is also uniquely and fundamentally invested in something equally important and less visible. Legal scholar Cheryl Harris has identified this particular element as " 'whiteness'—a characteristic that only white people have,"[10] and it has become a transparent and readily accepted requirement for desirable spatial construction in our society. Before moving further, as this is critical to this essay's premise, I will take a moment to bring a little "color" (pun intended) to this transparency by shedding a little (sun)light on the Whiteness of Lockean space.

John Locke posited that space preexists our knowledge of it, that in a particular way, space is essentialized, visible only by the position of bodies within it.[11] For him, our ability to know and fix the limits of space is defined by the relationship of bodies to each other. It is through these relationships that spatial boundaries become visible. The point where these bodies are at rest, determined by the relative positions of two or more bodies, is what Locke calls place.[12] These concepts are illustrated in Figure 9:

Lockean notions of space and place are definitive, discernible on a mathematical scale. Because space can be mathematically determined (this

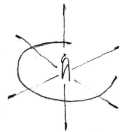

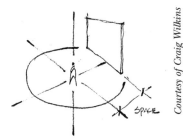

SPACE PRE·EXISTS.

SPACE IS INTERRUPTED BY
OBJECTS. THE LOCATION
OF THE OBJECT IS CALLED
"PLACE".

WE EMPLOY SIGHT OR TOUCH TO
GAIN KNOWLEDGE OF SPACE.

SPACE CAN BE PERCEIVED THRU
THE RELATION OF A MINIMUM
OF TWO POINTS OR PLACES.

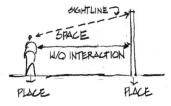

PLACE

PLACE

PLACE

FIGURE 9.

piece is this distance from that piece and is this long, this wide, etc.), land can be apportioned, and the concept of entitlements—rights—over the apportioned land is established. Thus a fundamental principle of property is established: the rights (entitlements) to or over a thing, in addition to the thing itself.[13] These rights included "not only external objects and people's relationships to them, but also all of those human rights, liberties, powers, and immunities that are important for human well-being, including: freedom of expression, freedom of conscience, freedom from bodily harm, and free and equal opportunities to use personal faculties."[14] Property can be secured only by exercising these rights. Rights not exercised are thus forfeit, and in the case of land, are considered wasted and render the land subject to resettlement.[15] Lockean notions of space do not recognize a cultural right to land.

This notion of property—the exercising of rights and entitlements *over* a thing—can be seen in the relationship between Blacks and Whites in eighteenth-century America. African Americans were legally defined as property primarily—if not solely—because they were *Black,* while Whites were *not* property because they were *White.* Blacks were *objects* (property), while Whites were *subjects,* part of the civil society, and therefore had access to property. As Locke asserts, "there is another sort of servants, which by a peculiar name we call them slaves, who being captives taken in a just war, are by right of nature absolute dominion and arbitrary power of their masters . . . and being in the state of slavery, not capable of any property; cannot be in that state be considered as any part of civil society; the chief end whereof is the preservation of property."[16] The knowledge of being "not-Black" and therefore not subject to becoming property, and the consequent expectation that one's rights—one's very identity—will be recognized and protected, permeate the foundation of a Lockean idea of space in the form of *Whiteness*. As Harris puts it, "Because the system of slavery was contingent on and conflated with racial identity, it became crucial to be white; to be identified with white to have the property of being white. Whiteness was the characteristic, the attribute, the property of free human beings."[17] The relationship between Black and White bodies is no longer defined explicitly by a master/slave perspective. But, and this is crucial, this does not mean (a) that this relational (and therefore spatial) concept is dead, nor (b) that some new form of relational (and therefore spatial) hierarchy has not taken its "place."[18]

A critical analysis of Locke's understanding of space reveals a theory in which bodies *define* knowable space. They are essentially where the ability to know Locke's space *ends*. As something that preexists and is "disrupted" by bodies, space is primarily empty, symbolic, establishing objects only for its own definition. Locke's theory fossilizes spatially defining symbols as static and still: improvable, but immovable.[19] As a result of immovable symbols defining space, *Whiteness* becomes embedded in the foundation of, and critical to, the determination of desirable space. It is inarguable that in this nationalist culture, the power of *White*[20]—the body of *White*—maintains a place on the American stage as its most important, historic and immovable actor. This is most clearly demonstrated in the capital city, where the essentialized *end* of space is distinctly visible in the grand and noble gestures to the principles owed to the *White* cities of Athens and Rome, whence the symbols of our national architecture have been appropriated: the *white* marble on the *white* Capitol; the *white* temple *White* House; the tall *white* Freudian gesture to the center of *White* male patriarchal power, its origins carefully *white*washed. In a city where homelessness and poverty is hardly new(s), the appropriation of land and space for the purposes of doing nothing should be understood in its proper context. In a city that is predominately Black, the power and purity of *White* reigns supreme.

III. THE IRRESISTIBLE SPATIAL FORCE . . .

Into this empty, fossilized, symbolic space, a call was issued, and in true diasporian fashion, a million-plus men responded to the waves of a pebble in a spatial sea. At a moment when the focus on the Black male body as an object of fascination, pleasure, and fear is raised to the level of obsession,[21] they came. Over loud and sometimes volatile objections, they came. From points as near as southeast D.C. and as far as South East Africa, they came. Under the intense, unrelenting scrutiny of *other*—predominately White—men, they came still. They came to (re)create a ritual of recognition and validation. In this moment of reflection, this crossing of routes and roots, they came to celebrate existence. Under threat—both overt and covert—from men of authority and power, they came strong to attend a gathering on the Mall. To the capital; to center stage, they came. To a place where the "scale of the structures reminds the mass[es] . . . that they enter the precincts of power as clients or as supplicants . . . subject to remote authorities they only dimly know or understand,"[22] something (real) wicked this way came. Black men came to reject the spatial imposition of separation strategies based on color*less*—not color*blind*—definitions of maleness. They came because Black men and women have historically been required to employ material culture in transformative spatial strategies of survival, so much so that it is in "the context of 'place making,' [that] blacks form their individual and collective identities."[23] By gathering around the transformative strategies of atonement and abstinence for ethical, moral, and political purposes, Black men came to demonstrate the importance of space to their identity project. They came to (re)make their place in American culture. The descendants of Memphis, Congo Square, and Afrolantica[24] gathered "in a new and alien place [to] unify themselves and create sacred space."[25]

IV. THE FEAR OF (BLACK MALE) SPACE . . .

Why was this claiming of space so frightening to other (fe)males? Was it the notion of atonement? No. For decades, men—African American men in particular—have been called on to atone for patriarchy, sexism, paternalism, and a variety of other "isms." Any gesture in this direction should have only been seen as a positive and progressive move on the part of men. So, no, the country's objection wasn't to the notion of atonement.[26]

Was it the notion of abstinence? I think not. Our society typically reifies abstinence with the secular and the sacred: sex and religion. Sex has always been intimately, insidiously, and ideologically intertwined with the representation of the Black male.[27] Demonized as lecherous and lascivious, the natural and inevitable site of deadbeat dads, dangerous denizens, debauchery and disease, any and all discussions that keep this essentialized position clearly in the public view justify the enormous effort to curtail and control this "natural predilection," and is surely worth any violation made—for their own and the public good—to the Black male body. That is a long way of saying essentially, no, the problem here was not the notion of sex. OK, so might it have been the religious aspect? Again, I would have to find fault with this supposition. We hold our right to religious expression so tightly in our sometimes intolerant little fingers that even the most ardent Western perspective recognizes the commonality of abstinence with its most disagreeable Eastern counterparts. Of course, they won't make the mistake of equating abstinence with spirituality, nor would I. I merely raise this issue to demonstrate that it was not this aspect of abstinence that was troubling others.

Well, could it have been the more basic elemental notion of men themselves? Nah. Men have gathered in the heart of America for years. Actually, for better or worse, they have been posited as *the* heart of America: in war, in business, in relationships, in culture. As Soul Brother #1 has loudly proclaimed, "This is a man's world" and the exercise of men's privileged position of authority is symbolized in the very organization of the gathering space chosen by the fraternity of the fourth circle. The symbolic representation of (the) authority in this society—the wide-open, empty space of the lawn of the Washington, D.C., Mall—is an undeniable reminder of the appropriation of space to support, celebrate, and further the aims of power. The power of America. And who is America but her men? And who are her men? White men. No, the objection wasn't to the idea of *men* per se.

What *was* objectionable was the employment of a collective agency that wanted to define Black male identity *against* this White spatial backdrop —in spite of the very visible signs of what—and where—America's males should be. Historically, men have always gathered space in the creation of identity: at the office, in the bar, on the ball field. But for Black men, "self-representations of black masculinity in the United States are historically structured by and against dominant (and dominating) discourses of masculinity and race, specifically (whiteness)."[28] Herbert Muschamp, architectural critic of the *New York Times,* has noted, "Since cultural values tend to coax up their opposites, a space dedicated to harmony and independence can easily become a battlefield,"[29] and his observation suggests the origin of the fear. If power reflects and refines the spatial relations of its inhabitants, then it stands to reason that it was the fraternity of the fourth circle—their emergence in, and their use of, America's front yard—that became objectionable. It was just all too real.

The gathering spaces of Black men are habitually known to America through proxies and substitutes, where Black bodies are "centralized in [a] faceless space, peripheral [even] at the social center."[30] Black male space, residing "somewhere between the too visible and the not visible enough,"[31] is known and fossilized by America through film, TV, the census tracks, crime statistics, newspapers, and magazines[32]—media which displace White male aggression; recent episodes in Arkansas, Oklahoma, and Colorado are *problems to be solved* while similar events in Chicago, New York,

and South Central are *pathologies to be endured*.[33] The Martiniquean psychoanalyst and revolutionary theorist Frantz Fanon observed that "not only
must the black man be black; he must be black in relation to the white
man,"[34] making clear not only the operation of Locke's space/place relationship in creating and situating identity (*your [Black] place is always in
relation to my [White] place*) but also the importance of "knowing your place"
to the construction of that identity (*my [White] space is the standard by which
your [Black] place is judged*). The Mall simply could not be a Black male
space, for that would require drastic reconfiguration of the space/place
relationship dynamic (*your [Black] space is the standard by which my [White]
place is judged; pathologies become problems*), and where, exactly, would this
relegate White men? What then, would be their *place?* As Muschamp noted,
the Mall—both a real and symbolic *space* of harmony primarily because
Locke's spatial dynamic is firmly established (*everybody knows their place*)—
has now become a battlefield for identity—and the stakes are quite high.

V. WHERE (WHITE MALE) SPACE ENDS . . .

Lockean space is a space of no motion, no resistance; it is a dead space.
Locke's space, by positioning the body as solid, impenetrable, the place
where space *ends,* represents space as the between, the leftover, the undisturbed. As Locke himself puts it, "Solidity is so inseparable for the Idea of
the Body . . . [and] Space is not Body."[35] Lockean space is anti-body. Bodies
never occupy space, but become definitive markers of *what* and *where* space
is. Lockean space dichotomizes and polarizes the predominant understanding of space by legitimizing its inherent Whiteness as *the* desirable
defining factor—and the implied non-Whiteness of space as undesirable.
Any *other* space created in this system is inevitably measured against its original, White paradigm and will always be found wanting.[36] This process remains largely unexamined in spatial terms, but its effect is inarguable:
African Americans rarely enjoy the benefit of space, as they are historically
and routinely rendered "visually transparent, peripheral, part of the landscape, ready to be moved, cleared and discarded for spatial use and improvement."[37] When the relational foundation of Lockean space has to
navigate between aspects of identity and rights, or put another way, when
space is defined by a White body and a Black body, typically the White
body, while recognizing the Black body because it is necessary to the definition of (Lockean) space, at the same time does not recognize the Black
body's right to access space.[38] Regarding Black bodies in nationalist—read
White—space, bell hooks has eloquently concluded, "Our very presence is
a disruption."[39]

Locke's space is incompatible with the project of Black identity construction, as its very tenets—the fixed, the *end,* the disruption—all work to

deny African American access to space. Those three precious little words—
learned at an early age to be employed for primarily selfish reasons in the
dominant culture—"that Black man" have historically sufficed to make
this point about the disruption of, and access to, space painfully clear. They
are enough to make the seemingly permanent unequivocally temporary,
for both Black and White. Enough to strip away the illusion of spatial empowerment and to render visible the temporality of Black access to Locke's
space. Enough to completely dichotomize space again, again, and again.
Enough to keep the Black body in its *place,* and keep (White) *space* safe.
Whether they are heard under the colonizer's multi*colored* but not multi*cultural* flag, or from the lips of the Scottsboro accusers, Charles Stuart, Susan
Smith, or in any of the hundred other Ellisonian[40] moments that fill the
day of every member of the fourth circle fraternity, the utterance "that
Black man" is enough to immediately and immeasurably diminish Black
space to nothingness. It removes the aegis of space and renders naked
the Black male body. In this paradigm, Black (access to) space is always
temporary, exposed, and objectified. It is a space where everybody knows
their *place,* and that *place* is based on an absolute, undisturbed, and unques-
tioned relationship to Whiteness.

VI. WHERE (BLACK MALE) SPACE BEGINS . . .

It was within this most unreceptive space, one that suggests, if not demands, ideological subjugation, that the project of Black male identity reconstruction was undertaken. It would have been so much easier for Black
men to have begun this project in seclusion in the woods with author Robert Bly's "hairy men,"[41] but they chose not to reinforce animalistic perceptions of the Black male. No, their work would originate at the symbolic and
material heart of the objection, in the face of their opposition, within view
of all the fossilized images of Black male subjectivity. For the fraternity
of the fourth circle, the backwoods, bayous, and over- and underground
railroads had outlived their usefulness as shields and escape routes from
domination. Realizing Boley's long-ago whispered promise of a space
"where your supreme thoughts can be put into action without any fear or
hesitancy,"[42] Black men were unhesitantly, even joyously, calling out those
three precious little words, "that Black man," in an expression of a truly
forbidden love: the love of the humanity *of* Black males *between* Black males.
They were calling to themselves and to the world, creating a space without
fear of hesitancy. While on the surface this appropriation of the Mall seems
to do little more than repeat the spatial organization so aptly described
by George Clinton's "Chocolate City/Vanilla Suburbs" analogy, or (more
recently) the power relations of the professional athletic theater, where
Black bodies appear on the sports stage for the visual pleasure of a predom-

inately White (male) owner and audience, further examination will show something quite different.

From a nationalist spatial perspective, bodies end space. They define boundaries as a termination of something. A particularly bleak way of perceiving bodies, this is in fact not typical of what the body actually does. The *end* that is so embedded in Locke's space is an extremely static—if not malignant—notion of the body. These end bodies can only be realized in the ideal, where they can truly end—thus the "deadness" of Lockean space. In reality, in lieu of a body which will not cooperate, symbolic spatial substitutes become idealized: from the gridded organization of the colonial city of the past, through the signature structures of the corporate city of the present, to the delusionary and manufactured nostalgia of the Celebration city of the future, these are the *White ends* of space that saturate and define most of the physical environment. But, as Muschamp pointed out, those same boundaries "coax up their opposites," as they simultaneously mark the *initiation* of something. In this manner, bodies can be alternatively understood as where space begins. It is this notion of space—this respect for the body—that is theorized and demonstrated by the spatial practices of the fourth circle public intellectuals. This is a continuation and transference of the diasporian tactical[43] struggle to rescue the Black subject from the Negro object,[44] particularly in spaces that represent an erasure of their identity and, concomitantly, the presence of repressive White male power. What begins here is the *active creation of space* and a *challenging of place* that is fixed, leftover or undisturbed. This challenge of space and place is fueled by the realization of both as not static or dead, but in reality *actualized* by bodies that interact in the manner theorized by the neo-Marxist French theorist Henri Lefebvre. Lefebvre posits that space is a social construct, that "spaces are produced" and are experienced, or lived, by bodies in motion that constantly intersect and engage (see Figure 10).[45]

A simple example of Lefebvre's theory is a typical classroom. How does one *know* it is a classroom? Is the space in question deemed to be a classroom because there was a class held in the space last week, or last month? This would allude to Michel de Certeau's notion that space has a history. But is this enough? What if there is no immediate access to history? What about the design, you ask? Maybe. It may certainly help recall the history or indicate a use, but for Lefebvre, the knowledge that one is in a classroom emerges primarily because there is a teacher/student dynamic—even if the subject positions "teacher" and "student" are constantly blurred and trespassed. If, in the same space, a dance troupe were practicing, then the space would be a practice space—not a classroom. If there were a film being shown, then it would be a theater—probably a poorly designed one, but a theater nonetheless. This is the interaction that Lefebvre speaks about. It is both "work" (the interaction) and "product" (what is created by the interaction),[46] and must be understood as the social activities that

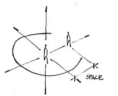

SPACE DOES NOT "PRE-EXIST."

IT MUST BE PRODUCED OR CREATED BY INTERACTIONS OR "PEFORMACES" W/ PEOPLE.

WE EMPLOY "INTERACTIONS" W/ OTHERS TO GAIN KNOWLEDGE OF SPACE.

SPACE CREATES & IS CREATED BY INTERACTIONS W/OTHERS.

KNOWLEDGE & HISTORY OF SPACE IS CREATED THROUGH ITS USERS & ITS USE.

NO INTERACTION
NO SPACE

INTERACTION
SPACE

FIGURE 10.

Courtesy of Craig Wilkins

occur in a particular time and place that constitute—and are *specific* to— the establishment of a distinct form of social communication. These social activities—referred to by Lefebvre as the group's "spatial practices"— facilitate the production and reproduction of both the place and the characteristics of the spatial relationships of any defined group of people.

Emerging from a location of experience, Lefebvre's space is antithetical to the anti-body, dead space that Locke theorizes. Lefebvrean space resists Lockean hegemony and exposes as questionable his proclamation that "Space is not Body." This is precisely the space of the fourth circle. It is a space that is not fixed by dead bodies; it is alive; it is mobile. It moves when its creators move, sways when its creators sway, and leaves traces on whatever it touches. It is a space in motion, a space which is transformative, transferable, woven. The space of the fourth circle is a *suture*,[47] a space:

> produced in the slippage, or gap, between sign and referent, event and meaning, and gathered into performed forms and tactile reminders. Picture the wild proliferations of a cultural space in all the restless coming and going, all the dismembering and *re-membering* of things, people's eccentricities amassed over the years, the automatic scanning for *signs*, the continuous imagining of the "real" through the mediations of stories of things that happen.[48]

But in what manner did Black men create a space of their own? What strategies did they employ? What "restless comings and goings" were demonstrated? What remembering took place? What are the stories that were told?

VII. CONSTRUCTION OF A (BLACK MALE) SPACE . . .

It has been argued that "[a]ll forms of procession—military review, presidential motorcade, celebratory parade, civilian protest—consist of power moving through space."[49] The "comings and goings" of the fourth circle, their movement through—and subsequent appropriation of—America's front yard, draw on and demonstrate the reworking of power for their homologous identity (re)construction processes. Employing Lefebvre's notion of space, the identity strategies that were employed by African American males are specific to a time, place, and social formation, but are also historical—they have a memory, a past, albeit a sometimes forgotten past: "identity is fleetingly experienced in the most intensive ways and sometimes socially reproduced by means of neglected modes of signifying practices like mimesis, gestures, kinesis, and costume."[50] A. J. has argued that the "culture that's going to survive in the future is the culture that you carry around in your head,"[51] the physical location, in the last instance, of remembering. It was therefore not a little *gesture* of remembering when the members of the fourth circle fraternity, as part of their induction ritual demonstrated by the procession of members through space, as part of their reshaping and redefining of the nationalist culture, turned their collective backs and minds on the Lincoln memorial and faced the Capitol or *capus mondi,* signifying "the head of the world." Quite deliberately, the fourth circle turned their backs and minds on the incomplete promises of the past to look ahead by "using the resources of history, language and culture in the process of becoming rather than being: not 'who we are' or 'where we came from,' so much as what we might become, how we have been represented and how that bears on how we might represent ourselves."[52]

Employing the Mall in their identity project required the fourth circle to transform that space's traditional uses of leisure, passive looking, and adulation of power, position, and status for their own purposes of responsibility, active participation, and resistance to vassalage. Black men were required to essentially *unknow* their place. At the moment the fraternity of the fourth circle gathered in that space recreated and enhanced in this country's infancy by the hand of a Black man—Benjamin Banneker—they began the process of transforming the icons of power that have been historically wielded against this very project of Black male identity, this *process of becoming* a Black male. In a decidedly anti-nationalist move, the Mall became a space of resistance. This space, this theater of White male power and authority so hostile to the body of Black men, the illogical spatial and political marginalization that places Black men in the panoptic space of Foucault by an overdetermined exercise of power that monitors their Ellisonian existence, was profoundly transformed into what Goldberg calls "a place of peace, of shelter from care, doubt and division, a geography of relative self determination and sanctity."[53] This "place of peace" called into question the authority and ideology of a definitive, fixed use of space[54] and the notion of an essentialized identity that is shorn of any liberating symbolic, linguistic, or historical dialectic with the subject: what spaces that emerge from a Lockean paradigm represent for African American males. Space becomes a place where differences are not fossilized, but actively negotiated, similar to Foucault's heterotopias.[55] It creates a "space for imagining the inevitable failures of representation, [without which] new claims of textual solutions to the political problems of the subject and object, meaning, difference, and cause take on the gray tint of a new positivism."[56] In essence, fourth circle space becomes a kind of celebratory heterotopia.[57]

The brotherhood was essentially telling a *new story,* a story read through the dialectical spatial practices of African American males that enacted an entirely different pedestrian speech act, creating a space—a safe *place*—other than is presently known through spatial proxies. This performance opposed any "proper" use of space and, as bell hooks argues, is a "documentation of a cultural genealogy of resistance . . . that highlights the cultural practices which transform ways of looking and being in a manner that resists reinscription by prevailing structures of domination. [A] [s]ubversive historiography [that] connects oppositional practices from the past with forms of resistance in the present, thus creating spaces of possibility where the future can be imagined differently."[58] Directly engaging hooks' thesis, the fourth circle "reinscripted" the Mall into a "space of possibility" by rejecting the hegemonic spatial manipulations of the dominant culture that continue to impose historically unacceptable and oppressive spaces through the systematic devaluation and erasure of Africentric subjectivity and history. The appropriation of this space for the specific purpose of reaffirming Black male identity construction was made legible by the ensemble and interaction of people and elements engaged in the *story* (who we are) and *performance* (how we might represent ourselves) of everyday life. "Black identity is not simply a social or political category . . . it is lived as a coherent (if not always stable) experiential sense of self. Though it is often felt to be natural or spontaneous, it remains the outcome of practical activity: language, gesture, bodily significations, desires."[59] These "practical activities," or performances, situate the performer in the world in a specialized way and provide a collective link with others through the telling of a recognizable story—a truth that *embodies* values rather than *representing* them.

In this instance, the spatial performance of Black men tells a specific story about a way of living. Within that performance, a fundamental diasporian spatial practice that has survived the Middle Passage, its *palimpsestic* nature and intent become legible. African American spatial practices are palimpsestic in that they engage in an erasure of dominant spatial understandings of "proper" and its hegemonic physical manifestations, while simultaneously constructing a specific spatial consciousness in the same location through a diasporian use of history, language, culture, gesture, bodily significations, desires, etc. These spatial practices are *a way of life*—a manner of perceiving and being in the world; they are not *representation*, they are *reality*. In that very real, material sense, the Mall became the fourth circle fraternal house. And unlike the fraternal houses of the past, the workings of this house were open to the public,[60] no hazing was allowed, and *place* was determined by a new relationship, one that was created between Black male bodies in a very (in)different relationship to White.

This project of the fourth circle Brotherhood had as its oppositional teleology the reappropriation of urban space and the liberating redistribution of bodies within it. In this site where Whiteness has become *the* predominant signifier of desirable space, the fourth circle membership situated the "affirmation of Black cultural differences as . . . a starting point for self development."[61] Black men journeyed to the Mall—to the "head of the world"—to claim space, to challenge place, and to name themselves in the head of America—and in their own heads. At that moment of spatial appropriation, the essentialized elements employed by America for the construction of Black male identity erupted in a host of dichotomies: Black men exhaled and imploded, standing in their publicly created private space as the men who they are and are thought to be, for all the world to see their non-existence. This public exposure was a consciously chosen sacrifice of their private space for political capital. Any sense—much less retention—of the private in the omnipresent panoptic surveillance of Black men should be considered, in the present capitalist society, a *resource* to be treasured and defended. It is tantamount to wealth: constitutional capital of the rarest kind, which is typically protected and hoarded in a capitalist society. But their willing exposure, their sharing of that private space, presents a challenge to that mode of securing and amassing resources. As bell hooks has argued, "The sharing of the personal is also about sharing power,"[62] and in claiming the (symbolic) space of American power as their fraternal home through their sharing of experience, the public intellectuals of the fourth circle engaged in an eloquent act of spatial resistance unavailable in Lockean space.

On this day, "[a]s the contradiction among the features creates the harmony of the face,"[63] Black men held an open enrollment for membership and the fraternity of the fourth circle was open to all types of Black male subjects. "Lines between self and other are blurred and special forms of pleasure are created as a result of the meetings and conversations that are established between one fractured, incomplete, and unfinished racial self and others."[64] In "coming to terms with our routes,"[65] the members of the fourth circle came from all over and in many guises. One million strong, they came, rewriting space and carrying membership applications from those unable to make the journey home. No particular social class, no particular political position, no particular economic status. Its members were Christian, Muslim, Hindu, and atheist. It included gay males, fathers abandoned and fathers who abandoned, teenage fathers and elder sons. The abled, disabled, and enabled. Mixing "the mortar of the age of brotherhood out of the dust of the idols,"[66] this fraternity offered an alternative for the construction of Black male identity, that "process of becoming" which had been dropped by the institution that formerly facilitated it—the churches—and been picked up by the new institution for the construction of maleness in the Black community—the gangs.

VIII. WHAT THIS (BLACK MALE) SPACE HAS WROUGHT . . .

Clearly, the fraternity of the fourth circle is a cause for concern to *others* primarily because the construction and recognition of this fraternity is not advantageous to what is currently offered as (White) male identity. White men are understood in our nationalist culture as the naturally dominant, while Black men are reciprocally positioned as the natural enemy. While it is obvious that both groups of men share common traits and even goals and aspirations, surprise and concern is raised when Black men attempt to mobilize theirs. Such measures seem to "underline [the Black man's] difference from . . . white [men] by presupposing his natural aggression."[67]

Fanon said, "Since the other hesitated to recognize me, there remained only one solution: to make myself known,"[68] and it was in that spirit that the spatial practices employed by Black men at the moment of the Mall aimed at removing the peripheral from their space and making visible the transparent. This meeting then, wasn't about atonement to anyone *other* than Black men for letting their fraternal/societal memberships lapse, and all that has subsequently ethically, morally, and politically entailed. Their atonement was ethical in the sense that on that day, through this ritual of movement and recognition, "men were incorporated into a brotherhood dedicated to ethical instruction."[69] One million public intellectuals were, through shared experience, theorizing and adopting new requirements for this brotherhood and recruiting new theorists based on these requirements. The space created between bodies gave Black men the possibility of a space that would allow them to break free from their all too long-standing—and too limiting—battles over the ownership of corners, blocks, and neighborhoods. Their space—created by brothers combining the coasts of Cali and New York, by brothers theorizing the integration of the long-ago separated Chicago and Clarksville—reaches beyond the notion of neighborhood or even city into a *safe space* that can be carried from the Mall over time and distance, becoming a shared space that extends over

states and nations. Their atonement was moral in the sense that to popu-
late these extended spaces, Black men ostensibly had to become (re)dedi-
cated to certain responsibilities to themselves, their relationships, and their
community: eliminating drug dependency, excessive alcohol consumption,[70] and the pathological cycle of family irresponsibility, violence, and
so-called paternalistic government dependency[71] within their brotherhood.
And finally, their atonement was political in the sense that, in an extended
space that was dedicated to the development of the African American community, Black men were laying claim to a history/tradition as political capital, not at any fixed moment, nor in any definitive manner, but as a source
to be shaped and employed; not as a rationalization to go back, but as a
motivation and a method to move forward.

What is of critical and lasting importance here is that the moment on
the Mall required the brothers and the *others* to *see* a different, long-forgot-
ten manner in which to employ space: toward the empowerment of Black
bodies. Black bodies can be employed in strategies that create spaces that
are transferable and transportable; spaces that affirm the identity of their
users, that are, in fact, dependent on those identities. Theirs is not the
space that is determined by the deconstructive symbols of power that surround many urban environments—the symbols of neglect that scream,
"See ya, wouldn't wanna be ya"—revealing the ultimate homage to Locke:
leftover spaces filled with leftover (Black) bodies that stay forever in their
place. The moment on the Mall reminded the fraternity that there is an
alternative to which they have considerable historical and cultural access,
one that requires not just the inert body but the active spatial practices of
the Black male for its very existence. The spatial practices of Black males
palimpsestically transform—literally give an*other* meaning—to the symbols
of Locke's space. The notion that Black is no longer fossilized as a body
that *ends,* but as one that *begins,* exposes the lie to fourth circle public
intellectuals that their environment is unseemly, wholly without merit, con-
tumacious, and of course, inevitable; that they are destined to live where
the physical, emotional, and intellectual remnants of this nationalist culture's civil disturbances coalesce to convince them that their lives are envi-
ronmentally predetermined; and that they are required to live their lives
based on these false realities. The space created by the fourth circle fraternity revealed that space and community are not immutable and, with that
realization, urban communities immediately become *spaces of possibility,* not
predetermined holding pens for the urban unfortunate. That moment on
the Mall has provided fraternal members with a blueprint for an*other,* re-
covered kind of spatial construction. If we understand this fraternal space
to be a space that is created by social interactions that challenge rather
than accept structural domination, and that takes its cue from spatial practices of diasporian origins, we have a radically different view of space, par-

ticularly urban spaces, from that currently being employed in the built environment, and one that holds enticingly open the possibility—if not the necessity—of Black female participation.

In a system where spatial and cultural dichotomies manifest themselves in a particularly callous disregard for the powerless in the built environment, in a city where the spatial dichotomy starkly highlights the gulf between the ideals, representations, and realities of living in America, in the space that at its creation was the embodiment of an authoritarian hegemonic power that defined Black male subjectivity in *fractions* of Whiteness, the public intellectuals of the fourth circle acknowledged their membership and renewed ancient ties to the brotherhood, but more importantly, to humanity. Black men came to add the final two-fifths to the Constitution and left with a blueprint for individual and communal spatial transformation. And maybe, that's the space where Black men—and women—should have started all along. Fear? That's (an) *others* pathology.

NOTES

1. Tanya McKinnon, "bell hooks Interview," *Signs: Journal of Women in Culture and Society* (Summer 1996): 818.

2. Henry Shue, "Mediating Duties," *Ethics* 98 (July 1988): 687, as quoted by David Theo Goldberg in *Racist Culture: Philosophy and the Politics of Meaning* (Cambridge: Blackwell, 1993), 198.

3. "[W]hite women were, quite literally, the repository of white civilization. White men tended to place them protectively upon a pedestal and then run off to gratify their passions elsewhere" (Winthrop D. Jordan, *White over Black: American Attitudes toward the Negro, 1550–1812* [New York: W. W. Norton & Company, 1977], 148).

4. This important distinction is powerfully argued by bell hooks, Doreen Massey, Gloria Steinem, Rosalyn Deutsche, Judith Butler, Barbra Friedman, Janet Scott, et al.

5. I am hesitant to get into, nor is this piece the forum for, a debate on who is more at risk in the Black community: males or females. In many instances, I believe this is a false dichotomy that keeps the Black community internally at odds. I also note that it assumes a particular type of male and female, exclusive of gays, lesbians, transsexuals, and transgendered people. And although I do realize that by accepting and employing a hierarchy of circles I open myself up to a particular kind of criticism from, at the very least, Black feminists, as I mentioned earlier, this piece is theorized from the location of experience, which requires me to spend a rather substantial portion of my time pursuing the "at risk" issues embedded in space that are particular to Black men. I trust that my concern will be understood as not exclusive, but specific.

A prominent reason for my placing Black males in this fourth circle undoubtedly has to do with my position as a Black male, but equally influential, I think, is my position as an architect, urbanist, and scholar. From these vantage points, I have observed both in theory and in practice the pervasiveness of an insidiously ubiquitous surveillance that is leveled on the body of the Black male—in no small measure due to the growth of the prison complex industry—that places Black men in a particularly troublesome and dangerous position in space. According to the Washington-based Sentencing Project, nearly one in three Black men in their twenties is behind bars or elsewhere in the court/prison/probation system. Other reports have over two in three Black males between sixteen and thirty-five years old under some kind of judicial observation, be it probation, juvenile supervision, prison, halfway houses, or work release programs. Because Black men are—for a variety of reasons both internal and external to the Black male fully documented elsewhere—typically underemployed or economically disadvantaged, the specter of a new form of slavery and disenfranchisement, with private corporations and government selling human capital, is raised.

While questions about the state's role in citizenry punishment and corrections abound, questions of a new form of slavery, with private corporations and government selling human capital, questions of propriety—ethical, moral, legal—have seemed to take precedence. Is it proper for imprisonment to be administered by anyone other than government and its employees, who should have no financial engagement with the incarceration—and the length of that incarceration—of fellow citizens? Is the "profit motive" incompatible with justice? Even as society begins to struggle with these questions, as one of the fastest growing industries in the country, the housing of prisoners by private corporations has become big business.

Prior to the current move to privation of prison facilities, there was a hue and cry about prison overcrowding and the need for early release. As stated by Scott Vath in an article entitled "Prison Privatization Proves A Profitable Tool For Locking Up Prisoners" (*American City and County*, March 1993, V.108, N.3), 32D:

> New prison construction and available cells have fallen far behind the drastically growing prison population. According to the U.S. Department of Justice, the number of sentenced American prisoners under the Bureau of Prisons from 1970 to 1990 increased from 336,000 to 774,375, while the figure for jail cells—332,309—has remained virtually unchanged since 1970"

But currently there is a shift in the prison discourse that moves to posit that there are not enough prisoners. As Daniel Seligman argues:

> We need more prisoners. How many more? Levitt's article does not squarely address this question, but his calculations indicate that we could raise the prison population to 1,350,000 before we would be putting away people whose crimes cost less than their incarceration. The figure implies that we need a 23% boost in prisoner totals
> (Daniel Seligman, "A Prisoner Shortage," *Fortune*, 11 November 1996, 60).

The rise in the move to privatization is analogous to another form of enslavement, as previously stated:

> From 1980 to 1993, the number of inmates in federal and state prisons nationwide almost tripled, rising to a record 948,881 people . . . To keep criminals working—and out of trouble—there's a push for prisons to do more business with private companies

(Paula Moore, "Prison Work Programs Unlock Profits for CPSI," *Denver Business Journal*, 17 June 1994, 1A) In a moment that is reminiscent to the discussions that contributed to regional and finally national conflict and the end of one form of enslavement, it is the labor issue has been the most contentious. Eileen Courter:

Complaints from private sportswear manufacturers and retailers have prompted state officials to review operations at Michigan State Industries, a prison-based operation. The bulk of MST's $25 million annual sales comes from the state itself . . . Under state law, MSI can only sell to federal, state and local governments and to private nonprofit organizations. But that includes school districts, prime targets for prison products such as baseball jackets, sweatshirts and other athletic wear.

(Eileen Courter, "Prison labor problems, U. S. style; Vendors slam sportswear made in Michigan jail," *Daily News Record*, 4). In addition, the *American Metal Market* reports:

The recent decision by Congress to keep federal prison shops under the banner of the Federal Prison Industries (FPI) from selling their products to the general public is being hailed by office furniture manufactures around the country, who cannot compete with FPI's furniture on a cost basis.

("Prison products decision hailed," *American Metal Market*, 25 December 1995, 4) There has been hardly any mention of the individual prisoners—who are disproportionately Black males—in the opposition's cry as their activities become more criminalized and their sentences become more disparate and their access to legal advice becomes more limited.

Within bell hooks's assertion that *"Black women must work harder than any other group in this society to value our bodies, our selves and our lives,"* (bell hooks, "When Brothers Are Batterers," *Essence*, September, 1994), 148, there are remnants of the effects that such surveillance has on the psyche of the brothers and sisters that interact with each other daily, which in no way excuses flagrant acts of violence by the brothers against both women and men (bell hooks, "When Brothers Are Batterers," *Essence*, September 1994, 148). The added fact that the prison project has turned its profiteering eye toward African American women (who, for reasons that fluctuate between survival and self-esteem, have adopted many of the physical practices and ideological characterizations of their increasingly criminalized—but not criminal—brethren), and the woefully poor health care access for women of color, just to mention a few currently conflating elements, make a strong argument for their location in the fourth circle also. Because the prison population is constantly under surveillance—as in the previous days of human chattel—severely limited in exercising individual rights and choices through the attacks on the legal aid system, and forced into labor production for private capitalist means with little or no compensation, the move to privatization affects Black males and females alike in and out of the surveillance system. And while the number of Black women in prison has nearly doubled in the last six years, Black men still outnumber Black women in the system by a six to one ratio. Further, the author John Edgar Wideman has argued that Black men are increasingly at risk as more and more of the street culture that they have created as a means of survival has become criminalized—and commercialized ("The Politics of Prisons: Doing Time, Marking Race," *The Nation*, 30 October 1995). African Americans in general, but males in particular, do not view this spatial surveillance.

It is these, possibly arguable, reasons that have led me to situate Black males in the unenviable position of the fourth circle for this piece. However, in many instances and in the long run the positions of third and fourth are permeable, and the effects of spatial apartheid forms are equally ruinous for all African Americans regardless of their sex.

6. Linda L. Ammons, "Mules, Madonnas, Babies, Bathwater: Racial Imagery

and Stereotypes," in *Critical White Studies,* ed. Richard Delgado and Jean Stefancic (Philadelphia: Temple University Press, 1997). Ammons describes these images thus:

> Scientists exploring stereotypes about African Americans repeatedly find that blacks consistently receive the most unfavorable attributions. Among those that were created to keep black women marginalized were Mammy, the asexual nursemaid of white children; Aunt Jemima, the mammy-cook with a name; and Jezebel, the black seductive temptress. Modern caricatures include Sapphire, an emasculating, hateful, stubborn woman; the matriarch, the strong, single mother with no needs; and the welfare queen, the over-breeding, lazy, cheating, single black mother. These representations are so powerful that the sight of a woman of African decent can trigger responses of violence, disdain, fear or invisibility. (277)

7. Kate Rushin, *Black Back-Ups: Poetry by Kate Rushin* (Ithaca: Firebrand Books, 1980):

> This is dedicated to all of the Black women riding on buses and subways back and forth to the Main Line, Haddonfield, Cherry Hill and Chevy Chase. This is for the women who spend their summers in Rockport, Newport, Cape Cod and Camden, Maine. This is for the women who open those bundles of dirty laundry sent home from those ivy-covered campuses. . . . At school in Ohio, I swear to Gawd there was always somebody telling me that there the only person in their whole house who listened and understood them despite the money and the lessons was the housekeeper. And I knew it was true but what was I supposed to say. . . . This is for the Black Back-Ups. (18–19)

8. Reference here is to filmmaker D. W. Griffith and his fictional, apologetic film propaganda, *The Birth of a Nation.*

9. See Farai Chideya, "Who's Making What News," *Don't Believe the Hype* (New York: Plume/Penguin Group, 1995), 241–252, for statistics. John Edgar Wideman points out, "Today, young black men are perceived as the primary agents of social pathology and instability" ("Politics of Prisons," 505).

Toni Morrison's *Sula* (New York: Plume/Penguin Books, 1982) places the present observations of Wideman and the statistics of Chideya in a historical context:

> Sula was smiling. "I don't know what all the fuss is about. I mean everything in the world loves you. White men love you. They spend so much time worrying about your penis they forget their own. The only thing they want to do is to cut off a nigger's privates. And if that ain't love and respect, I don't know what is. And white women? They chase you all to every corner of the earth, feel for you under every bed. I knew a white woman wouldn't leave the house after 6 o'clock for fear one of you would snatch her. Now ain't that love? They think rape soon's they see you, and if they don't get the rape they looking for, they scream it anyway just so the search won't be in vain. Colored women worry themselves into bad health just trying to hang on to your cuffs." (103)

10. Cheryl I. Harris, "Whiteness as Property," *Harvard Law Review* 106, no. 8 (1993): 1727.

11. "I shall begin with the *simple idea of Space.* I have shewed above, that we get the *Idea* of Space, both by our Sight and Touch; which, I think, is so evident, that it would be as needless, to go to prove, that Men perceive, by their Sight, a distance between Bodies of different Colours, or between the parts of the same Body; as that they see Colours themselves; Nor is it less obvious, that they can do so in the Dark

by Feeling and Touch . . . This Space considered barely in length between any two Beings, without considering any thing else between them" (John Locke, *An Essay Concerning Human Understanding* [New York: E. P. Dutton and Co., 1910], 167).

12. "Another Idea coming under this Head, and belonging to this Tribe is that we call *Place*. As in simple Space, we consider the relation of Distance between any two Bodies, or Points; so in our *Idea* of *Place*, we consider the relation and Distance betwixt any thing, and any two or more Points, which are considered, as keeping the same distance one with another and so considered as at rest . . . That our Idea of Place, is nothing else, but such a relative Position of any thing" (ibid., 169–171).

13. Harris quotes Jeremy Bentham's *Theory of Legislation:* "Property is thus said to be a right, not a thing, characterized as metaphysical, not physical." She also quotes James Madison: "[Property] embraces everything to which a man may attach a value and have a right" (Harris, "Whiteness as Property," 1725–1726).

14. Ibid., 1726.

15. The notion of creating value is also central to the Lockean spatial/property theory. I will not go into it here as it is somewhat tangential to the main argument, but it is important to acknowledge, for as Harris states, "Although the Indians were the first occupants and possessors of land in the New World [and] the land had benefit in its natural state, untilled and unmarked by human hands, it was waste and therefore, the appropriate object of settlement and appropriation [by Europeans in America]" (ibid., 1721). The ability to create value—as proof of usage, as an indication of a right—is central to this concept of identity, is fully indebted to the notion of "Whiteness" and is difficult to locate, as this idea of usage, or labor, securing land to create value from the property obscures it. This ability to create value is central to the notion of identity in a Lockean perspective.

16. John Locke, *The Works of John Locke,* vol. 5 (London: Thomas Davidson, Whitefriars, 1823), 386–387.

17. Harris, "Whiteness as Property," 1728.

18. Frantz Fanon and Toni Morrison have articulated the continued existence of always-already residual master/slave dynamics. "The elements that I used had been provided for me not by 'residual sensations and perceptions primarily of tactile, vestibular, kinesthetic, and visual character,' but by the other, the white man, who had woven me out of a thousand details, anecdotes, stories . . . some identified me with ancestors of mine who had been enslaved or lynched . . . I was the grandson of slaves in exactly the same way in which President Lebtum was the grandson of tax-paying, hardworking peasants" (Fanon, *Black Skin, White Masks* [New York: Grove Press, 1967], 111–113).

"These speculations have led me to wonder whether the major and championed characteristics [of national identity]—individualism, masculinity, social engagement versus historical isolation; acute and ambiguous moral problematics; the thematics of innocence coupled with an obsession with figurations of death and hell—are not in fact responses to a dark, abiding signing [Black] presence" (Morrison, *Playing in the Dark* [New York: Vintage Books, 1992], 4). Also see Jordan, *White over Black.*

19. "The parts of pure *Space*, are immovable, which follows from their inseparability . . . Thus the determined *Idea* of *Space* distinguishes it plainly and sufficiently from *Body;* since its parts are inseparable, immovable, and without resistance to the Motion of Body" (Locke, *Essay Concerning Human Understanding,* 173).

20. See various texts on "White" and its (spatial) implications such as: Harris, "Whiteness as Property"; Steve Pile, *The Body and the City: Psychoanalysis, Space and Subjectivity* (New York: Routledge, 1996); Michelle Fine, Linda C. Powell, Lois Weis, and L. Mun Wong, eds., *Off White: Readings on Race, Power, and Society* (New York:

Routledge, 1997); Marshall Berman, *All That's Solid Melts into Air* (New York: Simon & Schuster, 1988); Peter Hall, *Cities of Tomorrow* (Oxford: Blackwell Publishers, 1994), chapters 2, 3 and 11; Peter Kivisto, "Changes in Public Housing Policies and Their Impact on Minorities," in *Race, Ethnicity and Minority Housing in the United States,* ed. Jamshid A. Momeni (New York: Greenwood Press, 1986); Kenneth Jackson, "The Spatial Dimensions of Social Control: Race, Ethnicity, and Government Housing Policy in the U.S. 1918–1968," *Journal of Urban History* 6, no. 4 (1980): 419–452; John Mollenkopf, *The Contested City* (Princeton: Princeton University Press, 1983); Dell Upton, *America's Architectural Roots: Ethnic Groups That Built America* (Washington, D.C.: Preservation Press, 1986); Richard K. Dozier, "Tuskegee: Booker T. Washington's Contribution to the Education of Black Architects" (Ph.D. dissertation, University of Michigan; Ann Arbor: University Microfilms International, 1992); Susan Deyner, *African Traditional Architecture* (New York: Africana Publishing Company, 1978); Suzanne Preston Blier, *The Anatomy of Architecture: Ontology and Metaphor in Batammaliba Architectural Expression* (Chicago: University of Chicago Press, 1994); Le Corbusier, *The Radiant City* (New York: Orion Press, 1967); among others.

21. "This figure of black masculinity consistently appears in the popular imagination as the logical and legitimate object of surveillance and policing, containment and punishment. Discursively, this black male body brings together the dominant institutions of (white) masculine power and authority—criminal justice system, the police and the news media—to protect (white) America from harm" (Herman Gray, "Black Masculinity and Visual Culture," in *Black Male: Representations of Masculinity in Contemporary American Art,* ed. Thelma Golden [New York: Whitney Museum of American Art, 1994], 177).

"There are many in this society who have developed ways to profit from the image of the 'dangerous black man.' Black 'gangsta' images appear in the marketing of products such as malt liquor, compact disks, clothing, soft drinks, television programs, feature films, and home security systems. In addition to its use in enhancing the sale of commercial products, there is also the social marketing of the image of the 'dangerous black man,' in which the 'products' marketed are social ideas. The ideas promoted through social marketing are social issues. The most consistent source of portrayals of African American men as dangerous, and the source generally perceived by the public as being most credible, is television news" (Randolph G. Potts, "The Social Construction and Social Marketing of the Dangerous Black Man," *Journal of African American Men* 2, no. 4 [1997]: 12).

"The American complex about race is geared chiefly to suppressing black males" (Jan Nederveen Pieterse, *White on Black: Images of Africa and Blacks in Western Popular Culture* [New Haven: Yale University Press, 1992], 178).

22. Murray Edleman, "Space and Social Order," *Journal of Architectural Education* (November 1978): 3.

23. Stephen Nathan Haymes, *Race, Culture and the City: A Pedagogy for Black Urban Struggle* (Albany: State University of New York Press, 1995), 72.

24. Reference here is to the chapter "The Afrolantica Awakening" by Derrick Bell in his book *Faces at the Bottom of the Well: The Permanence of Racism* (New York: Basic Books/HarperCollins, 1992).

25. Quoted from an interview with poet and oral historian Brenda Marie Osbey in the 1997 documentary film *Claiming Open Spaces* (Urban Garden Productions, Cleveland, Ohio).

26. Many Black women have decried the meeting of the fourth circle. I am of the opinion that the very visible presence and primary position of the Nation of Islam had much to do with the image of an exclusivity that was culturally and histor-

ically permanent rather than temporally specific. That aside, many concerns can be summarized by Mary Ann Clawson when she argues that by "addressing only men and recognizing men alone as moral actors [fraternity] ritual defined masculine identity through a discourse that effaced women and home," and Angela Davis when she argues even more stridently that "No march, movement or agenda that defines manhood in the narrowest of terms and seeks to make women lesser partners in this quest for equality can be considered a positive step" (Clawson, *Theatre of the Fraternity, 1896–1929* [Minneapolis: Fredrick R. Weisma, 1996], 68; Davis quoted in Marlene Cimons, " 'Unity' March Exclusion Divides Women," *Washington Times,* 17 October 1995, A14). I shall argue against these views in this particular article, regarding this most unusual fraternity, as both perspectives are rather narrow readings of the M3 event.

There has rarely—if ever—been a time when Black women have not played a significant part in defining masculinity in the African American community. From their time as (un)willing immigrants attempting to adapt to new roles in an alien social structure, raising the male children of others while attempting to (re)construct gender identity for their own, to the significant effort that some single mothers exert competing with the newly powerful male fraternities of blue (Crips) and red (Bloods) to impart gender identities to their oftentimes fatherless sons, Black women have played a vital role in the formation of Black male subjectivity. The members of the fourth circle were the fathers, brothers, and sons that they help to shape, who were now taking some responsibility for their beings. As such, this was a moment created and shared with Black women. One should be careful not to confuse physical absence with no presence.

bell hooks has stated that "what is dividing Black men and women right now is that so many more Black women are concerned with well-being, self-discovery and healing than Black men" (quoted in Lisa Jones, "Sister Knowledge," *Essence,* May 1995, 188). The M3 event gave Black men the opportunity to begin the journey down their own road to self-discovery and healing, not in the historically (un)observable spaces (the street corner, the back alley, etc., places where women are visually and physically excluded or included on limited and oftimes degrading terms) but in full view of their sisters, mothers, daughters, wives, lovers, and friends. Black men had to initiate this journey for themselves, by themselves, with themselves, but they chose to do it in plain view, making a commitment not only to each other, but also to Black women, in such a way that they can—and must—be held accountable for failure to finish the journey. The question becomes, Would the physical presence of Black women have produced a substantially different outcome? I don't know the answer to that, and I don't think anyone does.

27. The connection between sexual politics, racial politics, repression, and power dates back to the formation of this society. Jan Pieterse writes: "The ambivalence referred to earlier—the sexualization and tabooization of the Other—here took the form aimed specifically at controlling the sexuality of the black man. . . . For white males, this situation meant a sexual gain, because it gave them access to white women as well as black. . . . The sexualization of black men may also have its roots in the guilty conscience of whites. . . . [T]hey also transferred their own lusts and their anxieties of black male retaliation to their fear of black men as sexual threats to white women" (Pieterse, *White on Black,* 174–175). And Ronald Segal notes: "Certainly, color prejudice was not limited to the South, but nowhere else in the hemisphere was marriage between whites and persons of color, slave or free, outlawed. . . . There were instances recorded, and inevitably more that went unrecorded, of sexual relations between white women and black men. But this was a practice beyond mere condemnation. It revealed the possibility of a sexually driven

white womanhood in the starkest of contrasts to the delicate, decorous vision that floated at the summit of Southern manners. It confronted a patriarchal culture which regarded the act of sex as the use of the female by the male. *It roused that sexual jealousy and fear which racism, in its very emphasis on the animal prowess of the black male, promoted*" (Ronald Segal, *The Black Diaspora: Five Centuries of the Black Experience Outside of Africa* [New York: Noonday Press/Faber & Faber, 1995], 59; emphasis mine).

28. Gray, "Black Masculinity and Visual Culture," 175.

29. Herbert Muschamp, "Looking at the Lawn, and below the Surface," *New York Times*, 5 July 1998, section 2, 32.

30. Goldberg, *Racist Culture*, 198.

31. Homi K. Bhabha, "Culture's In-Between," in *Questions of Cultural Identity*, ed. Stuart Hall and Paul Du Gay (London: Sage Publications, 1997), 56.

32. Cameron McCarthy, Alicia Rodriguez, Shuaib Meecham, Steven David, Carrie Wilson-Brown, Heriberto Godina, K. E. Supryia, and Ed Buendia, "Race, Suburban Resentment, and the Representation of the Inner City in Contemporary Film and Television," in *Off White: Readings on Race, Power and Society*, ed. Michelle Fine, Linda C. Powell, Lois Weis, and L. Mun Wong (New York: Routledge, 1997), 232.

33. Goldberg, *Racist Culture*, 197. He positions the pathology in much more succinct terms of crime and space (emphasis mine): "So certain types of activity are criminalized—hence conceived as pathological or deviant—due to their geographical location in the city. Because of statistical variations in location, 'other kinds of crime are either not important, not widespread, or not harmful, and thus not really crimes at all.' This location of crime serves a double end: *It magnifies the image of racialized criminality and it confines the overwhelming proportion of crimes involving the racially marginalized to racially marginalized space*. . . . [Crime becomes] something 'they' [Blacks] do."

34. Fanon, *Black Skin, White Masks*, 110. Frantz Fanon, a Black intellectual in a whitened world, joined the Algerian National Movement during its initial war for independence from France. He elaborated on the ways in which the colonizer/ colonized relationship is normalized as psychology in such seminal tomes as *The Wretched of the Earth* and *Dying Colonialism*. Fanon is considered one of this century's most important theorists of the African struggle for independence from colonial oppression.

35. Locke, *Essay Concerning Human Understanding*, 172.

36. This determination of "desirable space" can be seen in the current manifestations of the city: White flight from city neighborhoods—and the concomitant effect of middle-income people of color's desire for the same; negative reinvestment in predominately Black neighborhoods; the past phenomenon and current repercussions of urban renewal; and boundaries both physically real—the Cabrini Green and Robert Taylor homes in Chicago—and mentally real—the eight-mile thoroughfare in Detroit; Back Bay, Boston; Bensonhurst, New York; Southeast Washington, D.C. One only has to look at the map of the Los Angeles metro area to determine the predominately Black and Latino areas and see these manifestations clearly delineated.

The practice of Locke's theories—and their inherent "Whiteness"—can also be traced in historical material constructions. Kenneth Jackson explains the Emergency Relief Act that authorized the Home Owners Loan Corporation (HOLC) and the Federal Housing Administration (FHA) in 1934 by the federal government:

Four categories of quality—imaginatively entitled First, Second, Third, and Fourth, with corresponding code letters of *A, B, C,* and *D,* and colors of green, blue, yellow, and red—were established. The First grade (also *A* and green) areas were described as new, homogeneous, and "in demand as residential locations in good times and bad." Homogeneous meant "American business and professional men . . ." The Second security grade (blue) went to "still desirable" areas that had "reached their peak" but were expected to remain stable for many years. The Third grade (yellow) or "*C*" neighborhoods were usually described as "definitely declining," while the Fourth grade (red) or "*D*" neighborhoods were defined as areas "in which the things taking place in *C* areas have already happened."

The HOLC's assumption about urban neighborhoods were based on both an ecological conception of change and a socioeconomic one. Adopting a dynamic view of the city and assuming that change was inevitable, its appraisers accepted as given the proposition that the natural tendency of any area was to decline—in part because of the increasing age and obsolescence of the physical structures and in part because of the filtering down of the housing stock to families of lower income and different ethnicity. Thus physical deterioration was both a cause and effect of population change, and HOLC officials made no real attempt to sort them out. They were part of the same process. Thus, [African American] neighborhoods were invariably rated as Fourth grade, but so were any areas characterized by poor maintenance or vandalism. Similarly, those "definitely declining" sections that were marked Third grade or yellow received such a low rating in part because of age and in part because they were "within such a low price or rent range as to attract an undesirable element. (Jackson, "Spatial Dimensions of Social Control," 423)

Fearing, unjustifiably, the loss of investment if racial separation was not reinforced, the *Underwriting Manual*, the handbook on proper appraisal procedures issued by the FHA to its appraisers, openly recommended "enforcing zoning, subdivision regulations and suitable restrictive covenants" (ibid., 436). The FHA would not loan to African Americans who wished to live in predominately *non-African American* neighborhoods, because due to its subjective and highly questionable risk-rating system, the FHA desired to keep sites segregated. The FHA would not lend to African Americans who wished to live in predominately *African American* neighborhoods because those areas were "*C*" or "*D*" areas (because of the existing African American presence) and not a good risk. In another example of the temporality of Black access to Lockean space, in this scenario, African Americans are *both cause and effect* of neighborhood deterioration, according to the FHA criteria.

37. Goldberg, *Racist Culture*, 188.

38. Fanon, *Black Skin, White Masks*, 119–120: "As the other put it, when I was present, it was not, when it was there, I was no longer."

39. bell hooks, *Yearning: Race, Gender, and Cultural Politics* (Boston: South End Press, 1990), 148.

40. The reference here is to Ralph Ellison's seminal work, *Invisible Man* (New York: Random House, 1980).

41. Robert Bly, poet, author and editor of the poetry magazine *The Fifties* (later renamed, as decades went by, *The Sixties* and *The Seventies*), has written several essays that explore maleness, such as the influential "Iron John." Bly has led many retreats for men trying to help them understand their male natures. At many of his literary readings, Bly performs chants and dons primitive masks and thongs to explore and express the nature of masculinity—which has been referred to as his "hairy man."

42. Scott Malcomson, "Having Their Say," *The New Yorker*, 29 April 1996, 138.

This article discusses the small town of Boley, Oklahoma, established in 1907, which began as—and essentially remains—an all-Black town.

43. I am using the term "tactic" here as defined by Michel de Certeau as a "calculus which cannot count on a 'proper' (a spatial or institutional location), nor thus on a borderline distinguishing the other as a visible totality. . . . It has at its disposal no base where it can capitalize on its advantages, prepare its expansions, and secure its independence with respect to circumstances. . . . it is always on the watch for opportunities that must be seized 'on the wing.' . . . It must constantly manipulate events in order to turn them into 'opportunities' " (de Certeau, *The Practice of Everyday Life* [Berkeley: University of California Press, 1984], xix). While the tactics of diasporian struggles for identity emerge in this manner, they are engaged in deconstructing each of the conditions that hold this understanding of "tactic" in place.

44. The author/poet David Muria has argued that the nationalist culture creates a veil of ignorance about the condition of marginalized cultures. The ideology of the nationalist culture allows only atomized bits of marginalized cultures' histories to be heard. This ideological process works not only to keep marginal histories dispersed but frames an acceptance of hegemony, as the marginalized choose fragments of their culture and history that will facilitate advancement/acceptance within the nationalist cultural program. This "fragmentation" is much worse in the case of African Americans simply because, unlike many marginalized cultures here in America, there has been a continued ideological negation of any cultural *origin*—a critical location of historical memory—for African Americans. In this passage from *Color and Democracy: Colonies and Peace* (New York: Harcourt, Brace and Company, 1945), W. E. B. Du Bois illustrates two aspects of the nationalist culture's negation of African American bodies that is embedded in our understanding of space:

> [I]n the Immigration and Naturalization Service of the United States Department of Justice passengers arriving on aircraft are to be labeled according to "race," and are determined by the stock from which aliens spring and the language they speak, and to some degree nationality. But "Negroes" apparently can belong to no nation: "Cuban," for instance, refers to Cuban people "but not to Cubans who are Negroes"; "West Indians" refers to the people of the West Indies "except Cubans or Negroes"; "Spanish American" refers to peoples of Central and South America and of Spanish descent; but "Negro" refers to the "black African whether from Cuba, the West Indies, North or South America, Europe or Africa" and moreover "any alien with a mixture of blood of the African (black) should be classified under this [Negro] heading."

Du Bois points not only to the negation of Africa(n) by replacing it with the all-encompassing term "Negro"—neither a nation nor a place, but an *object* or *thing*—but also to the erasure of the cultural specificity of each of the diasporian identities now collected under the inadequate term "Negro." Illustrating the fragmentation that Muria outlines and that Homi Bhabha describes as "partial cultures" (*The Location of Culture* [New York: Routledge, 1995]), "Negroes" now belong to "no-place," having been removed from their original location, stripped of their subjectivity, and relocated as objects according to a set of strategic hegemonic rules defined by the dominant culture that effectively eliminate any historical claim to space. I am using the term "strategic" here as defined by Michel de Certeau in *The Practice of Everyday Life* as "the calculus of force-relationships which becomes possible when a subject of will and power [in this case, diverse cultures] can be isolated from an 'environment' " (xix).

45. Henri Lefebvre, *The Production of Space* (Oxford: Blackwell Publishers, 1995), 84. Michel de Certeau might describe these bodies in motion as "pedestrian speech acts" that in fact "secretly structure the determining conditions of social life" (*Practice of Everyday Life*, 96).

46. Lefebvre, *Production of Space*, 102.

47. Stuart Hall, "Introduction: Who Needs Identity?" *Questions of Cultural Identity*, ed. Stuart Hall and Paul Du Gay (London: Sage Publications, 1997), 5: "I use 'identity' to refer to the meeting point, the point of suture. . . ."

48. Kathleen Steward, *A Space on the Side of the Road* (Princeton: Princeton University Press, 1997), 26–27.

49. Lawrence Vale, *Architecture, Power and National Identity* (New Haven: Yale University Press, 1992), 9.

50. Paul Gilroy, *The Black Atlantic: Modernity and Double Consciousness* (Cambridge, Mass.: Harvard University Press, 1993), 78.

51. Arthur Jafa, "69," in *Black Popular Culture*, ed. Michele Wallace and Gina Dent (Seattle: Bay Press, 1992), 252.

52. Hall, "Introduction," 4.

53. Goldberg, *Racist Culture*, 205.

54. Lefebvre, *Production of Space*, 84: "Surely, it is the supreme illusion to defer to architects, urbanists and planners as being experts or ultimate authorities in matters relating to space."

55. Foucault posits that there are sites constructed by society that are made specifically for the purpose of linking irreducible sites. These sites are spaces of performed interactive communication that Foucault introduces as "heterotopias." In these links—these heterotopias—all of the sites of the society come together: "There are also, in every culture, in every civilization, real places—places that do exist and that are formed in the very founding of society—which are something like counter-sites, a kind of effectively enacted utopia in which the real sites, all the other real sites that can be found within the culture, are simultaneously represented, contested, and inverted. Places of this kind are outside of all places, even though it may be possible to indicate their location in reality . . . I shall call them, by way of contrast to utopias, heterotopias" (Michel Foucault, "Of Other Spaces," *Diacritics* 16, no. 1 (1986): 24).

56. Steward, *Space on the Side*, 24.

57. As theorized by Foucault, heterotopias are classified into two types—crisis and deviant. The crisis heterotopias are described as "forbidden places, reserved for individuals who are, in relation to society and to the human environment in which they live, in a state of crisis: adolescents, menstruating women, pregnant women, the elderly, etc." Crisis heterotopias can, then, be described as "temporary" sites, temporal in nature. Deviant heterotopias, on the other hand, are described as places where "individuals whose behavior is deviant in relation to the required mean or norm are placed. Cases of this are rest homes, psychiatric hospitals, and of course prisons"; they are more spatial in nature (Foucault, "Of Other Spaces," 24–25).

I argue in another essay (Craig L. Wilkins, "The Space *In-Between* Sight and Touch," *Dichotomy: The Journal of the University of Detroit Mercy School of Architecture* 13 [Spring 2000]) that there is another type of heterotopian link that can be theorized, one that is particularly urban, observable in the spatial practices of urban material culture and not limited to the elements fossilized by Foucault, that I call "celebratory heterotopias." Celebratory heterotopias are created by spatial practices that challenge the very limitations and boundaries of crisis/deviant definitions. The relations that construct the celebratory contest, work, and constantly rework the authority of these particular categorizations, in the process appropriating and palimpsestically altering dominant spatial understandings. The performed communication of the celebratory challenges the dominant spatial paradigm's essentializing ideology and questions its appropriateness as a "universal" aesthetic by demonstrating that alternative relations can be created. As such, it follows that alternative spaces—and heterotopias—can also be created.

Also, unlike crisis/deviant heterotopias, participation in celebratory heterotopias is a decision made by the participants themselves, for themselves. Participants consciously choose celebratory heterotopias as part of an overall strategy of challenge, change, and spatial evolution. While this choice is partly a reaction to social marginality and the threat of being placed in the restrictive crisis/deviant heterotopias, it remains an exercise in self-determination—even if it is only seen as a mode of survival. The authority—to assign to another heterotopia, to spatially marginalize, to name—is challenged and defied, a demonstration of agency in its most basic form. In this space, agency is a prerequisite and the relationships that construct the space are entered into freely and are influenced collectively. The celebratory is a place where the challenge to cultural—and consequent spatial—alienation produces a euphoric, empowered subject as opposed to the melancholic subjects sentenced to crisis/deviant spaces. These celebratory heterotopias do more than celebrate, they cultivate, and from these spaces emerges a subject that has constructed an advantageous (counter)identity, heretofore unavailable within Foucault's spaces.

58. bell hooks, *Art on My Mind* (New York: New Press, 1995), 151.

59. Gilroy, *Black Atlantic,* 102. Also see Steven M. Friedson, *Dancing Prophets: Musical Experience in Tumbuka Healing* (Chicago: University of Chicago Press, 1996) and Howard Morphy, *Ancestral Connections: Art and an Aboriginal System of Knowledge* (Chicago: University of Chicago Press, 1991). Friedson and Morphy present similar frameworks for identity construction and meaning that are anchored in the notion of performance: the meaning of rituals and ceremonies lies in experiencing them, and that experience provides the context for acquiring knowledge—which must be performed to be known. Meaning and identity are therefore located in both performance and story.

60. "In one sense, the ritual, *a secret performance,* was the means by which the order expressed moral authority over its members and asserted their oneness" (Mary Ann Lawson, "Spectatorship and Masculinity in the Scottish Rite," *Theater of the Fraternity* [Minneapolis: Weisman Art Museum, 1996], 53. Emphasis mine).

61. Greg Tate, "Preface to One-Hundred-and-Eighty Volume Patricide," in *Black Popular Culture,* ed. Michele Wallace and Gina Dent (Seattle: Bay Press, 1992), 245.

62. McKinnon, "bell hooks Interview," 823.

63. Fanon, *Black Skin, White Masks,* 136.

64. Gilroy, *Black Atlantic,* 79.

65. Hall, "Introduction," 4.

66. Fanon, *Black Skin, White Masks,* 136.

67. Jordan, *White over Black,* 115.

68. Fanon, *Black Skin, White Masks,* 117.

69. Lawson, "Spectatorship and Masculinity," 53.

70. The degree to which liquor affects the Black community is staggering. As Thomas D. Watts and Roosevelt Wright, Jr. document in their book *Black Alcoholism: Towards a Comprehensive Understanding* (Springfield: Charles C. Thomas, 1983), 5: "Within the black community 'alcoholism ranks almost certainly as the number one mental health problem if not the most significant health problem' (Boure, 1973: 211). Harper, a noted expert on alcohol and blacks, takes the position that

'alcohol abuse is the number one social problem in Black America' (Harper, 1976: 1). Larkins (1965) refers to alcohol abuse among blacks as an explosive and ignored social problem. Next to the problem of racism, alcohol abuse can be characterized as black America's primary health and social problem." Clearly, the references that Watts and Wright use are over twenty years old, but while AIDS and homicide are the fastest-rising causes of death, and heart disease is still the leading cause of mortality, alcohol and its related illnesses—to which a healthy percentage of the previously mentioned conditions could be attributed—rank as one of the most consistent killers in the Black community.

Watts and Wright go on to cite a rather essentialized hypothesis on the causes of such alcohol abuse: "Sterne and Pittman have formulated a conceptual framework that identifies two etiological motives for differential patterns of drinking among blacks: (1) the use of alcohol for its utilitarian value (utilitarian drinking); here alcohol is used as a means for coping with the many hardships and problems of personal adjustment and (2) the use of alcohol for conviviality value (convivial drinking); here it is presumed that alcohol use facilitates smoothness (Sterne and Pittman, 1972)" (13). They also cite a study that found that many "blacks choose to drink because . . . liquor stores and liquor dealers are readily accessible" (ibid.). If these citations are to be accepted, then—as in any homicide investigation— opportunity, motive, and means have been identified and contribute to one essentialized version of the Black male. In other words, had not the outside factors of rampant accessibility, overdetermined identity, and cheaply distilled and acquired product been present, "he or she might have been financially successful; instead the person lives modestly, sometimes in debt, because his or her alcoholism has interfered with educational attainment, establishment of a successful marriage, and other factors that would have increased the likelihood of success. This simplistic vignette suggests that the effects of alcoholism on income operate via indirect avenues" (John Mullanhy and Jody Sindelar, "Alcoholism and Income: The Role of Indirect Effects," *Milbank Quarterly* [Summer 1994]: 359).

It would seem logical then to attempt to curtail the opportunity, motive, and means for alcohol consumption in the Black community. As reported in *Time* magazine, "The emotional ground swell against the advertising of vices is fueled by a powerful combination of health consciousness, consumer activism and community pride. In New York City, Chicago and Dallas local residents have been whitewashing inner-city billboards to obliterate the images of such products as cigarettes and Cognac" (Janice Castro, "Volunteer Vice Squad," *Time*, 23 April 1990, 60). In all these instances, the charge has been led in the Black communities of these cities and headed by the institution that at one time was the primary location for Black male identity formation and the foil for other locations—the Black church.

The Black community is aware of the environmental racism practiced by city planning and zoning agencies that allow a disproportional number of liquor stores in predominately Black communities in the inner—and outer—city, and the hypocritical attempts at legitimization of distillers by sponsorship of Black college scholarships, design awards, sporting and cultural events, and "Think when you Drink" campaigns even as they target particularly high-alcoholic-content beverages specifically at Black customers. However, it is an uphill battle to limit opportunity, means, and motive when "while sales decline in volume . . . high margins will enable revenues to grow by 2–4% a year for liquor, 2–7% for wine and 1–3% for beer," and given that the majority of Black drinkers tend to drink the harder liquors ("premiums" in industry parlance), and premiums "carry the industry—not on volumetric items, but because they have better profit margins . . . the stabilization or growth of premiums helps offset declines in other segments" (Susan Karlin,

"Liquor, Wine, and Beer: Forecasters Anticipate Continued Declines in Consumption of Alcoholic Beverages," *Adweek's Marketing Week* 30, no. 37 [1989]: S112).

71. Some of the conservative movement's central themes are family values, work ethic, and individual and sexual responsibility. Their thinly veiled attacks on the welfare system and other social support systems are the manifestations of these themes. Typically, these attacks are in language that connotes African American abuses of these programs. For example, a *Wall Street Journal* editorial stated, "The emergence of a growing and self-perpetuating 'urban underclass' that makes our cities close to uninhabited is a demonstrable consequence of the present, liberal-inspired welfare system" (Irving Kristol, "A Conservative Welfare State," *Wall Street Journal,* 14 June 1993, A12). Clearly, this is a coded indictment of the pathologies of the urban (read Black) community and the current social program structure. In truth though, on the issue of sexual responsibility: "Recent studies refute the idea that African-Americans are 'sexually irresponsible' and indicate that in many areas, African-Americans are more responsible that Americans as a whole. Although there are more black out-of-wedlock births, this discrepancy may in part be due to African-Americans having less access to abortion and birth control. . . . A 1993 report on the sexual behavior of young men found that both black and white men had intercourse an average of once a week. . . . [Black men] were also more likely to use condoms." And further, on the issue of government dependency, the facts are that "39% of families receiving welfare are black; 38% are non-Hispanic white; 17% are Hispanic, and 3% are Asian. . . . In strict racial breakdown, the majority of welfare recipients are white" (Chideya, "Who's Making What News," 30, 37).

Part 4. Ethical Significance of Male Bodies

Chapter 11
The Tall and the Short of It
Male Sports Bodies

DON IHDE

The challenge to produce this essay comes from Susan Bordo, who in her essay "Reading the Male Body" complains that males themselves have written little about the male experience of their bodies—"Men have rarely interrogated themselves as men . . . for they generally have not appeared to themselves as men, but rather as the generic 'Man', norm and form of humanity . . . When men problematize themselves as men, a fundamental and divisive sexual ontology is thus disturbed."[1]—I am responding to this challenge. A second inspiration for this article comes from Iris Young, most particularly from her "Throwing Like a Girl," an early essay to which she has also responded retrospectively by noting the experience of her teenaged daughter's somewhat changed situation.[2] As a reader of much feminist literature, beginning with feminist critiques of science and technology—my usual focal interest—but also regarding "bodies," which often enter into phenomenological contexts, I find a set of issues which revolve around how one experiences embodiment.

Within a phenomenological history, the issue falls between two contrasting godfathers, Maurice Merleau-Ponty on one side, and Michel Foucault on the other.[3] One might characterize the Merleau-Pontean perspective as a form of "phenomenological materialism" insofar as his concept of the "lived body" (*corps vécu*) holds that the active, perceptual being of incarnate embodiment is the opening to the world that allows us to have "worlds" in any sense. At bottom, the anonymity of the active, perceiving bodily being he seeks to elicit could be said to be both "preconceptual" and "precultural"; without this sense of body, there is no experience at all. As well, this sense of the body is developed and described from a first-person perspective. In contrast, Foucault's "body" is thoroughly a "cultural body," often described and analyzed from a third-person perspective. The body objectified by the medical gaze in the clinic, the body of the condemned in the regicide, and the subjection of bodies within all forms of discipline are culturally constructed bodies. Insofar as there is "experience," it is experience suffered or wrought upon human bodies.

I have previously used the terms "body one" to refer to the bodily experience which Merleau-Ponty elicits, particularly in *Phenomenology of Perception* (hereafter *PP*),[4] and "body two" for the culturally constructed body which has parallels with a Foucaultean framework. However, what I term "body two" is the cultural-body-as-experienced body.[5] The problem, as it often takes shape in feminist literature, is the combination or non-combination of these perspectives within the *experience* of the writer. Young is particularly good at combining: the sense of both acting, but also of being seen, in the ambiguous transcendence of throwing like a girl; the self-pleasure of, but also social construction of, breasted being; and the obviously unique self/other experience of pregnant embodiment, all combine these themes and announce the ambiguities which keep any clear line of demarcation between "body one" and "body two" from being drawn. Young thus combines, with at least partial success, the notions of lived and culturally experienced body.

Young also indirectly led me to understand, within *PP*, something that I had not previously seen. There, Merleau-Ponty sets up a dialectic between what could be called a "normative" body experience, and the pathological experience which is only indirectly noted in his famous Schneider (who is a brain-damaged aphasic). Young, in the critique included in "Throwing Like a Girl," basically shows that Merleau-Ponty's body experience is abstracted from gendered bodies, and thus implicitly may be describing the focally "masculine," since he does not capture the ambiguous transcendence of female embodiment. That point is granted—but what is the masculine body experience which is inherent in the *corps vécu?* I now argue that the emphasis upon perception within actional situations, the transparency of the "normal" body, the sense of "I can" which occurs in *PP*, *is open to being secretly a "normative" sports body*. This slide from a normative, active, and externally focused body to the athletic body allows certain "body two" aspects to come into play. This healthy, implicitly athletic embodiment contrasts with the debilities of Schneider—but also by extension with virtually any other form of unhealthy, or even less than well-conditioned, sense of body, as well as any ambiguously transcendent female embodiment. The normative body implied is certainly not the feminine one which Young describes, nor an arthritic, aging body, nor even a clumsy unathletic body.

I. GROWING UP MALE: A RETROSPECTIVE

This leads me to something quite unremarked upon in much body literature, which relates to male embodiment and which in its own way may reopen the issues of "body one" and "body two" in ways which find resonance with gender differences and the socialization of how one lives one's embodiment. It will be precisely in a parallel with Young's earliest article, and her subsequent retrospective via her daughter, that I shall make my attempt to "reveal male bodies." I shall begin with the retrospective observations:

I am a "recycled" father in the sense that I now have a young son with my second wife; he was born in my mid-middle age. Hearing of his experiences in elementary school revived the long-ignored memories of growing up male that occasion this retrospective. Initially, I thought that perhaps his experiences would be very different from mine, precisely because his circumstances are so very different. I grew up in a small, largely Scando-Germanic farming community in Kansas and went to a one-room school and a small high school before finally leaving home to attend university. Mark is growing up in a densely populated suburban community on Long Island; he attends an intensive "intellectually gifted" (IG) program in a school system permeated by the values of the university, the Brookhaven National Laboratory, and the high-tech industries of this region. These largely science-dominated values are evidenced in the fact that the local high school produced the single largest number of Westinghouse semifinalists in the nation in 1999. These differences had led me to believe that Mark would not have to experience anything like what I experienced as a boy.

But I was wrong! And, as I shall try to show, part of the reason relates directly to the way masculine embodiment is (still) socially embedded. This social embeddedness is very long-lasting, historically, and is expressed similarly across radically different social contexts. Mark is usually the youngest boy in his class and he still occupies the lower end of the sixth-grade height spectrum, not yet having begun adolescent growth spurts. His peer group does contain some quite large boys, but I must admit that when teams are formed at recess, the boys from the IG classes are usually well outgunned by the boys from the regular classes. The bumper stickers which proclaim "My child is an honors student at ——— School" are countered by "My child beat up your honors student" on other bumper stickers. There had been such "wars" between the IG classes and the regular classes in years before Mark entered this program, but these have been ameliorated under a new principal.

The parents of Mark's IG classmates are mostly professionals (doctors, lawyers, professors, scientists, administrators), together with a goodly number of graduate student families, including a significant number of Asians. (I should note in passing that much of what goes on in boys' culture regarding being "macho" and the like is explicitly disliked and discouraged by their parents.) In the contemporary student terminology, this means that there are basically only "nerds" and "geeks" in his class—certainly no "dirtballs"—but there is also a sub-group which is included in his class, i.e., "jocks." Again, I had (wrongly) assumed that this special group selectivity would modify the pain of growing up male which I had experienced.

Those who are parents will easily recognize the next dimension: cliques or gangs. Within the class there are "first," "second," and "third stringers" (the terminology comes from actual conversations), and these obtain for both boys and girls, separately at this stage, of course. Being aware of this, Mark seeks the prestige of being associated with the first stringers. This aim is difficult to attain for two simple reasons: size and athletic prowess. He manages, but sometimes with difficulty, and often by what I would call "alternative skills." His musicianship is well recognized, and the IG classes dominate the orchestra and, to a lesser extent, the band. He skis, swims, and sails better than most, but these are the wrong sports for most of the school year: soccer, baseball, and football dominate the recesses. He has honed the skills of comedy such that he plays a recognized socially positive role.

Now a time warp, back to my experiences in Kansas during my boyhood: I begin with size—I was the "shrimp" even within my family. My father was 6'2", my younger brother is 6'3", and even my older grown son is also 6'3"—I am only 5'11". But as a younger boy, not only was I shorter than most of my classmates, but a lightweight and skinny (those who know me from much later post-Ph.D. times will probably find this amusing!). When it came time for choosing players for baseball, or even worse, for football or basketball, I always felt the pain of being one of the last boys chosen by the always larger and older jock captains. High school was even worse. I was simply too light to be of much use in football and while I had grown a bit taller, never made it past the second team in basketball. In the end, I chose an alternative means of recognition—many Midwesterners will recognize this—music, and became the drum major of the marching band. That was sufficient to keep me at the edges of the first string, but barely. All of this was painfully *conscious* within adolescent experience.

This suggests enough similarities between boyhood in the late forties and early fifties, and the differently contexted nineties of my son's experience. In both our childhoods, there is a rather direct connection between height and athletic prowess, read quite directly off the body. (There are nuanced exceptions to even this connection, in that there can be tall boys lacking athletic prowess, and short ones who have it and thus can to some degree compensate within the jock domain by sheer aggressiveness.) From here, I will begin to focus upon embodiment in these two frames. It is obviously the "tall" of the "sports body," combined with athletic prowess, which plays a crucial role. To set the stage, I now enter some phenomenological variations actually experienced in later life. The experience of life among basically tall people in the Scando-Germanic setting of Kansas gets repeated today as I often travel to both Germany and Scandinavia—and only there do I find myself average, or even slightly shorter than average. A subtle shock occurred when I moved in early career to Long Island and Stony Brook—I suddenly found myself to be taller than average. The population genetically determining height here is more dominantly Eastern and

Southern Euro-American, plus today a very large Asian-American population. When I first visited South America, I became a virtual "giant" compared to the averages there. To look up or to look down in relation to the other is an experienced bodily comportment which carries many subtle significations—including gender relations, given the dimorphism of the human species. And while the reading-perception of relative height (and prowess) is much less direct in adulthood than in childhood, it remains one variable within inter-body perceptual situations.

Here, I can turn to another set of variations which complicate the situation even more: one of my admired professors in graduate school was Paul Tillich. I took three courses with him and in each case the location was a vast lecture hall at Harvard—usually with three to four hundred persons in attendance. He was something of a cult figure in the intellectual climate of the time. I finally met him face-to-face when asked by a colleague to serve him a glass of sherry at a cocktail party after a lecture at MIT. I gladly did, and was amazed to find that I was looking down upon someone whom I had always thought something of a giant from the perspective of an audience member looking up to him behind a stand-up lectern. I have since had similar experiences with several other notable persons. Social "size" may differ from bodily size within these variations. The aura of size which does not correspond to physical size is clearly a social-psychological phenomenon. The complementary phenomenon—a "Napoleon complex"—may also be noted; short persons deliberately establishing power, not through size but through styles of assertion, are familiar (beware short administrators!). All of these variables are obviously contingent since, as Sartre has so often pointed out, one chooses the style with which one lives one's circumstances—one can live size aggressively, meekly, etc. I am not arguing body determinism, only persistent social patterns which include bodies.

Implicitly I am pointing out that in male socialization, particularly in childhood, the role of body size and prowess is poignantly important. Much is read directly off bodily size and skill. Is this different from female experience? (I do not pretend to speak for female experience, except referencing what I read in the literature.) It is probably the case that boys are rarely concerned deeply with body parts. Here, the external focus echoing Merleau-Ponty seems to hold. Boys do not have to worry about breast size (although that occurs for females in adolescence and thus outside the frame I have selected); not even penis size, for the most part, plays any important role. In my own youth, I can remember only one occasion in which any size comparison was actually made. Bordo has pointed out the hiddenness of the penis in dress, display, and other social situations (now modified slightly with the ascendance of beefcake phenomena and the nude or near-nude "hunk"): "The penis remains private and protected territory. The woman's body has become increasingly common cultural property . . . the penis has grown more, not less, culturally cloaked over time. Is it possible to imagine a *Newsweek* cover on testicular cancer, illustrated comparably to the cover on breast cancer?"[6] Nor do boys seem to develop the same awareness of "the gaze," the feminine response to which includes crossed legs, motions to cover or hide body parts, etc., as if the gaze were a "penetration" into areas of privacy. At least, for boys, the gaze is relatively muted. Boys do, in adolescence, learn the "cool" gendered gestures of sitting—not with crossed legs, but laying back with spread legs. (A colleague has pointed out one of Norman Rockwell's pictures, which depicts a skinny youth aggressively handling a pair of "Indian clubs" in front of a mirror. A magazine lies open on the floor to a Charles Atlas advertising cartoon of the movement from the ninety-pound weakling to the muscular athletic body of the post-Atlas course. Rockwell could hardly be termed a Lacanian!) Does this imply a gaze of some sort within male socialization? The male response, if not one of protective hiding, is nevertheless a felt cultural norm.

But there is another equivalence to female experience which, in some ways, is possibly worse. If the implicit sports body which can connect to the Merleau-Pontean tradition holds, it is largely what is exterior and actionally outward-directed which counts: how far I can throw the baseball is more important than the size of my biceps; how fast I can run the dash is more important than the appearance of my calves; how well I can execute the jackknife is more important than how my buttocks look. At a high school reunion some decades after graduating, my former coach had one memory of me—the second stringer who, once, just before the bell, lofted the basketball for a goal from the center court—then we lost anyway. It was my only "moment of glory," according to him. Of course, my memory of him was not so kind either: I remembered him as the person who deprived me of a good foundation in geometry and algebra, since his teaching method was to assign problems to the class and then gather the first team around his desk to plot strategy for the next game. By late secondary school I had learned to dislike the whole jock culture of the times.

But, if the external performance remains short of the ideal expectation—if I can't throw or run or dive well—is not the sense of failure or "falling short" a similar, deeper social phenomenon—indeed, one which affects the whole sense of who I (bodily) am? It is not some part which is deficient, it is the whole (bodily) self. Such experiences lead to multiple strategies: withdrawal into total geekhood (some of Mark's companions accept this role, including one very large but unathletic boy); excelling in recognizable, acceptable alternatives—here Mark has an advantage since music, computership (now a big social factor among boys), and, at least in the IG program, intellectual brilliance are possible avenues, compared to music and drama alone for me (the anti-intellectualism of my Kansas context was quite powerful comparatively, so those pursuits were best kept secret); multiple compensation strategies (bravado in storytelling, making macho comic strips, computer games); and the like. These strategies all help create a socially constructed aura which partially—but only partially— compensates for one's "deficient" embodiment. Size combines with performance in this hermeneutic of shortcoming.

There is a developmental aspect to this as well: one hopes that with time, the height differences will diminish—tale after tale of late growth is common among male adolescents—and sometimes sports acuity also comes later, while social maturity lessens the direct reading of size and acumen off bodies. But before this happens, there is the pain of the hybrid body-social construction which occurs in young male culture. Long after my boyhood, it still remains the case that the sixth-graders dominate the lower-graders on the bus, that the bully-boys rule the recess times, and the jocks are first to receive female attentions (this, no doubt, reflects something more general than single gender formation). If one is short and lacks the presumed ideal agility, one suffers through boyhood.

The above, of course, is the stuff from which boyhood coming-of-age stories are made. Only some boys, presumably those at the top of the heap (tall, athletic, strong, and handsome) ever have the ease which too often is attributed to the entire class of males. For most, it is struggle, the discovery of alternatives, even the dream of revenge in some other form, which characterizes boyhood. Boys growing up experience insecurities, tensions between social expectations and bodily realities, and variations upon recognizable gender themes. And while the male experiences display differences from the descriptions females give of similar phenomena, the differences are not so stark as to be unrecognizable as variations within the wider spectrum of human embodiment. My analysis so far reveals a movement of convergence.

II. THE "MAUSS ILLUSION" AND GENDER RECIPROCITIES

In anthropology, a well-known phenomenon is the "Mauss illusion." When one first encounters a new cultural group, given one's concerns and theory biases, what will stand out are the *differences,* often rather than or even selectively enhanced over the similarities, between "them" and "us." (In the extreme, anthropological sensitivity to the Mauss illusion is probably one factor which leads to the accusation that much anthropology ends in "cultural relativism.") In the realm of contemporary gender studies, there is often a gender Mauss illusion which troubles much of the literature, beginning with enhanced differences and escalating to the extremes of universal patriarchy claims. In what follows, I shall partially revert to a kind of parody of the current arguments which revolve around such notions as "the gaze," "the phallus," and more generally, "binary." I am implicitly arguing that much of the current debate seems caught in its own myths, which prevent more subtle recognition of convergences, similarities, and degrees of distinction within the gender wars. The debates often accent divergences rather than convergences. If the result of the movement to democratically pluralize the gender situation were to be the substitution of simply another myth for the previous one concerning the roles of genders, then only the polarities would have shifted.

A. Gazes, Male and Female

One can easily find, within the autobiographical tales above, that the dynamics of idealized normativities may be found both in male and female childhood experiences. If there is some idealized breast size and weight limitation for adolescent girls, this is matched, for young boys, by the Charles Atlas body size. Anorexia on one side is matched by the search for proteins, or worse, steroids, on the other. This dynamic is a reciprocal one, at base similar but taken in the binary directions which also correspond—at least as recognized in much of the current debate.

I have been trying to show that boys, like girls, also have intense insecurities over body image, although more in terms of bodily capacities, even if these insecurities take variant forms. The intellectual danger is to extrapolate or exaggerate these differences. I once read a sociological study (and I would footnote it were I to be able to find it) that polled both women and men with respect to an "ideal" breast size, with the following purported results: the males reported a much wider range of desirable or acceptable "beautiful" breast sizes than did the women, who noted a much more precise and narrow range of what counted as "beautiful." Does this indicate a keener awareness of a male gaze or a more intense intra-feminine sedimentation of such idealizations? Unfortunately, the poll did not reverse the issue and deal with some phenomenon which might be more acute for males. (I have sometimes, in class, reversed the issue by talking about middle-aged male "bellies." In that case, though it is hard to tell whether it is the affected male or his spouse who is more concerned, if middle-age potbellies are negative signs, then this might imply a negative female gaze.) The contemporary passion for exercise, body development, or retention of a youthful body, for everything from jogging to the health club phenomenon, seems to be gender balanced in at least reciprocal ways. Beefcake and male go-go has as its equally still minoritarian counterpart the female versions of Charles Atlas in magazines showing overmuscled women lifting weights. In these cases, the older binary reciprocities converge and gazes may be either male or female.

From whence "the gaze"? Within the phenomenologically related tradition (for the moment ignoring the powerful impact of the neo-Freudian influence of Lacan), a form of the gaze arises with Foucault. In *The Birth of the Clinic,* the medical gaze fixes the patient; in *The Order of Things* the objectivistic mode of sight in the Classical Era is itself the invention of perception; in *Discipline and Punish* there are the penal enactment of punishment on the body of the condemned and the disciplinary gaze of the panopticon.[7] All describe a form of the gaze which simultaneously objectifies and enacts control over the selectively *passive* bodies Foucault has a penchant for depicting. This, as in so much of Foucault, is a virtual binary opposite of the Merleau-Pontean *corps vécu.* Merleau-Ponty's is the *active* body, filled with actional experience, in contrast to the culturally fixed and acted-upon body of Foucault. Even older than Merleau-Ponty or Foucault is the gaze of Jean-Paul Sartre's *Being and Nothingness,* in which the primordial conflict of seeing/being seen by the objectifying/objectified gaze is at the root of all interpersonal social relations.[8] In short, the tradition of interpreting sight as an objectifying gaze was already well established in the midcentury. Yet, all these elevations of the gaze have counterparts in forms of vision which are neither objectifying nor controlling. Martin Buber's *I and Thou* is a relation of mutual recognition and respect of a sacred sight, the objectification of an I-It relation balanced by the non-objectifying I-Thou; Gabriel Marcel's *Being and Having* emphasizes the mutually participatory; and even Merleau-Ponty argues, against Sartre, that conflict is only possible upon the basis of a deeper recognition of similarity and participation (*PP*).[9] In short, even within this family of philosophical traditions, the notion of the objectifying gaze occupies only one side of a debate. Do the gender wars adopt, *post facto,* only the one emphasis?[10]

A deep phenomenology of vision shows that such visual perceptions are necessarily multistable rather than simply objectifying. Only a shallow enculturalization of both a reduction *to* the visual as the dominant epistemological perceptual dimension, and a reduction *of* vision to objectification could support the notions of the gazes which too often dominate the literature presently. There is also a second objection to the reification of the gaze: if vision can be both objectifying and participatory in different stabilities, it is also *doubled* by virtue of being both feminine and masculine in overlappings. The gender "system" includes male and female gazers with the gazes never being singularly one gender. Here again, Young recognizes that such phenomena as pleasure in dressing, makeup, and fashion, and even self-pleasure in one's body[11] are not some simple response to a male gaze. Rather, she includes both presumed male gazes and feminine self-gazes, a doubled glance.

The same applies to males: at the age of eleven, which I have chosen as the target for male coming-of-age with respect to bodies, boys are not yet very, if at all, interested in girls (and vice versa). Preadolescence is largely a time of youthful male bonding and much of the dynamic, even the negative dynamic of lacking a sports body, is an intra-male phenomenon. But not entirely. The Charles Atlas skinny-to-muscled image is intra-male in the sense that it suggests the desire to have bodily power, and yet in the ads it is also aimed at attracting female attention. It is here that the gender system again enters, at least as background. As the transition to late preadolescence occurs, seeking the attentions of the girls in the class intensifies in spite of the dominant awareness of male/female competitiveness and interchange.

First attentions may be ironically negative. In Mark's sixth-grade class, in a phenomenon quite different from anything I remember from the same age, two practices stand out. First, there is anonymous note-passing. One form it takes is the "geek tease" note. Whoever is on the bottom of the geek pole receives notes from girls who claim to "love" him. This is obviously a rather nasty joke which the geek may take seriously, only to have his advisors, who are more savvy, disabuse him (Mark prides himself on this revelatory role since he is not the bottom geek). The second is the directly insulting telephone call, again anonymous. Perhaps not yet knowing about caller ID or return call technocapacities, the caller has sometimes been identified by parents—sometimes it turns out to be precisely the girl who is the object of some initial attention. In one case, the caller was a very popular girl and it turned out she—along with at least one other accomplice—had called many of the boys in the class with similar put-downs. What I am depicting here, of course, is part of the gender system which includes both boys and girls. The girls, as well as the intra-male bonders, help establish the set of relations which usually also reflect the hierarchies of who is favored and who not. The anti-geek tone, and later the pro-jock admiration, repeat precisely the social structures of my experiences fifty years earlier, albeit with differences appropriate to the changed modes of boy-girl communications.

B. The Phallus

Here I must disagree, by way of an inversion, with Susan Bordo. She claims, "The phallus is haunted by the penis, and the penis is most definitely *not one*. . . . Rather than exhibiting constancy of form, it is perhaps the most visibly mutable of bodily parts . . . far from maintaining a steady will and purpose, it is mercurial, temperamental, unpredictable."[12] My disagreement is that it is, rather, the penis which is haunted by the phallus! In the perspective of a Merleau-Pontean, "I am my body," it is the penis which must somehow live up to the phallic cultural expectations. And the insecurities of growing up—but also of aging—rest in this phenomenon.

While I am certain that I have a penis, I cannot remember when I first became aware of the phallus (I suspect it was when I learned something about ancient Greek initiation rituals), and I remain unsure of whether or not I "have" a phallus or what relation I have to the "phallic." The problem here is that the phallus, in its most recent incarnation, seems to be an invention of the gender wars. This version of the phallus seems most usually to entail *power*, particularly of a political-cultural sort, plus a sense of deep association with masculinity (it rarely, today, invokes the sense of *fertility* that it had in ancient cultures). In short, it is taken as another code for generalized patriarchy. Here a subtle aspect of the current gender debate frame appears: it is frequently claimed that the unawareness of the phallic is precisely what is to be expected of the male, because the exercise of phallic power has been thoroughly culturally internalized. Here, again, I disagree by virtue of inversion with Bordo. Although she claims that we appear to ourselves, not as men, but as generic "Man," the painfulness of the childhood experience which rests within the two senses of "body" I have elicited belongs neither to the generic "Man" nor to the mythological "phallus."

Epistemologically, I am disturbed by the forms of unawareness taken over into an unconscious—this because there are so many variants of unconscious knowledge (an oxymoron). In the deepest sense, I may be unaware of how my neurons are firing or what capillaries engorge with blood as I experience the beginnings of an erection. But I am definitely not unaware of what is happening in this movement within my experienced embodiment. However, the physiological unconscious is simply not the same thing as either a psychological or cultural unconscious which is never totally unconscious. Such hybridizations are what I consider to be the deep fallacies of the Freudian-inspired traditions. Physiologically, neurons and capillaries are not experienced precisely because the constitution of such entities is necessarily a constitution of things out there, available only to the observer's perspective, and couched in third-person language. I do not and cannot "see" my brain—nor, for that matter, any of the interiorities of the physiological—except as an "other." One does not experience, or even see, the firings and expansions of one's own neurons or capillaries—unless they are imaged in a "third-person" instrumental situation. The hybrids—which are often inventions of the Freudian traditions—which fill presumably unconscious *experiences,* are not constituted in the same way.

This applies to notions of phallic power. As a long-time experiencer of "power" in academic settings—as a chair, a dean, a program director—I was explicitly aware of the power (and its risks, ambiguities, responsibilities, and contexts) with which I was charged. I was less aware of its phallic nature, except when that, too, became more explicit. Sometimes it did. Once, at a farewell dinner for a provost, the deans (all male) began a crude "penis-waving" contest about how each had been more aggressive and hard-minded than the others in decision-making, and whether the incoming female president would have enough "balls" to carry the day (she did—but this is clearly an indication that the phallus is not simply male). This power which can and does get experienced and which floats in and out of the sign of the phallus is very different from the non-experience of neurons and capillaries. It is a hybrid phenomenon which is presumably both "out there" but lived in first-person experience.

Part of the problem here is oversimplification and overgeneralization: there are styles and varieties of power, not all of them phallic, and there are phallic implications which are not always related to power, and there are female uses of phallic power just as there are male uses. The "hard" woman is, indeed, a cultural icon: Bette Davis movie characters, *Smilla's Sense of Snow,* the genre of female warriors in movies and television including Xena, all complement the already-mentioned female bodybuilders.

The phallus is a mythical construct which, like all myth, does contain a kind of imaginary power, but an ambiguous power which produces multiple cults and offshoots rather than a singular empire. It is a part of the malleable and the reconfigurational which, even if more dominant in certain configurations than others, nevertheless spills over any clear and clean boundaries.

C. Binaries

It should be obvious by now, given the trajectory of this article, that I believe that unqualified binaries are for simpletons. If there are both male and female gazes which also overlap, and if phallic power can be exercised by both males and females, even if these phenomena are often more strongly associated with dominant, rather than recessive, cultural practices, then any overgeneralization becomes suspect. At the very least, a beginning qualification insisting that contrary to "males are hard/females are soft," some males are soft and some females are hard, must be appended to the discussion.

An analogy may be helpful: much traditional philosophical work in aesthetics is done by way of attempting to define or circumscribe what can count as an "object" of art. Yet, as soon as some definition is set forth, no matter how ingeniously or carefully, in the context of modern or postmodern art, the artists—in reaction, which is itself part of the avant-garde tradition—immediately create an art object which does not and cannot fit the definition. This spilling over is part of the art trajectory since modernity. In short, art practice itself overtly revolts against aesthetic proscription as part of the art practice. I am contending that in a similar late modern or postmodern setting the same dynamics can and do often apply to the "gender wars." The parallelism between deconstructive strategies, which first turn everything into a text, and then move from a common-sense notion of texts into an increasing emphasis upon marginalia, notes, postcards, margins, intertexts, etc., also applies to the gender discussions. The postmodern blurring of *all* boundaries and indetermination of texts is equivalent to the indetermination of sexes and genders. One can easily recognize this ambiguation in the current gender discussions which, far from binarism, now contain the range from male/female through the polysemy of queer theory, bisexuality, transsexuality (see Butler), cyborg theory, hybrids (see Donna Haraway), and onward. This is one way of defeating overly simple binarism.

I am not deploring this development; to the contrary, the ambiguation does serve to resituate what can be taken as a problem or set of problems. I will mention two here: first, the current arguments between "essentialists" and "non-essentialists" seem to me to be a dead end. If there is anything essential, i.e., deterministic, about being male in contrast to being female, then any actions which are or can be taken will not threaten that essential difference since it couldn't be exceeded actionally anyway. A hard determinism would be the physiological equivalent to the law of gravity, within or under which all motion occurs. On the other hand, the biotechnological fantasies that imaginatively extend even to "male pregnancy" at one extreme, or to a totally female-virginal mode of reproduction at the other, but which take increasingly ambiguated concreteness in fertility experiments, could presumably make for unthought-of indeterminacies even at the biological level. Thus, if there were some sort of physiological essentialism, in today's biotechnological world—at least as fantasized—even such determinacies potentially dissolve. Ironically, non-essentialism ultimately dissolves binarism as well.

This, in turn, points to the now thoroughly culturalized problem as to why there remains such persistence and apparent resistance to gender model change. How, in spite of radically different contexts, do my son's and my own experiences of growing up male remain so recalcitrantly similar? Whatever "social construction" is, it is not something which appears to be easily made malleable or ambiguous even in the rapidly changing world of technological civilization. In this case essentialism turns out to be cultural persistence, but effective for all that. In other words, there are essentialist and non-essentialist functional equivalents within both the biologically determinable and the socially constructed versions of the discussion. "Conservatives" are those who hold to some persistence of biology, although this essentialism is effectively under attack through biotechnological (and thus through technoscientific-*cum*-cultural) means, while "liberals" who hold that everything is socially constructed come up against the virtually impenetrable persistence of social patterns (whereby boys, denied toy guns by parents determined to redefine juvenile gender patterns, end up inventing their own by turning sticks into weapons, etc.) Functionally, there are both biological and social patterns resistant to change but equally, such resistances reside within larger gestalts whose interlinking parts make piecemeal changes difficult. In short, I am arguing that the essentialist/non-essentialist debate resolves into the same set of functional problems which are complexly both political and developmental.

III. WHERE, THEN, ARE BODIES REVEALED?

After following at least one person's development in the light of gender experience and in the context of embodiment, accompanied by some history of gender debate literature, where do we end up? My line of argument has attempted to reveal something about bodily awareness in a male context. Today, however, that awareness can itself get caught in current gender discussions in such a way that it, too, may undergo a Mauss illusion when male and female experience is taken in a binary way. But, without speaking for either particular or generic feminine experience, what can be said of possible reciprocities of experience? The quasi-autobiographical has the advantage of concreteness and particularity. Susan Bordo has become expert in this voice style. One glimpses, within the philosophical context she holds, so much that is autobiographical and experiential, with a richness of suggestion that the favored anonymous style of much past philosophy has lacked (writers such as Kierkegaard and Nietzsche, for example, are obvious exceptions). This version of gender discourse, of course, veers toward the literary.

And this voice too has problems. "Reading the Male Body" only shows glimpses of the autobiographical. Bordo obviously knows something about actual male penises and sympathetically contrasts them with the mythical solidity of the mythical phallus. But in a much more autobiographical piece, "My Father the Feminist," literariness reveals its weakness. In this paper, Bordo elicits a rich sense of growing up Jewish in a patriarchal family. Her father dominates, plays the male, and for a long time fails to "get it" with respect to his feminist daughter. The contestative but loving relationship between father and daughter conjures up the rich sense of family life in this ethnic tradition. Yet, in the telling, literary devices emerge which seem to possibly belie more mundane actualities: Bordo becomes, as in the Singer tale *Yentl the Yeshiva Boy*, the female replacement for the missing (rejected) boy-scholar. In the arguments which sharpen her wit and intelligence, her father unknowingly begins to provoke the latent feminism which later matures. As in so much good literature, an irony begins to dominate, and by the end of the story, one can wonder—and since I accept the intentional fallacy as fallacy, I cannot speculate about the author's intention—whether the best way to produce a brilliant feminist might not be to be a patriarchal father! Here, a more complex binarism serves an ironic end, but at the same time could be taken as a justification for itself. Thus, if philosophy can produce its own fly bottle, so can autobiography. Similar ironic twists bedevil both the Nietzschean and Kierkegaardian traditions.

How, then, can one combine the richness of autobiographical concreteness with the wider implications of the general patterns, even universality, within the one remaining human species, *homo sapiens sapiens*? My own partial answer is that all structures and patterns—and these exist—display *multistable sets of limited possibilities*. This is clearly a phenomenological notion derived from variational theory, but set in a non-foundationalist context. Gender(s) are multistable. Anthropology surely has taught us this, since even the *National Geographic* has long displayed cultural patterns which vary and invert what is perceived as "masculine" and "feminine" in different groups. Certain African males wear complex makeup, featuring contrasts for eyes and dark lipsticks, and do dances to attract females—and this is considered masculine in that context. Contrastingly, for the over thirty years I have spent summers in Vermont, the lipstick-free, uncut hair, jeans-and-flannel-shirt-styled women, bespeaking a certain "country" air, have remained in place and in contrast to today's black- or black-outlined lip designs of Stony Brook undergraduate women. Yet both can easily be identified as a kind of feminine statement within the multiplicities of American culture. As for contemporary masculine, the outrightly boring universality of the ball-cap, bill forward, backward, sideways, is part of that statement, today accompanied by multiple earrings in one or both ears, the latter body fashion unthinkable in my boyhood.

Late modern multistability is itself part of the pluralizing of cultures—a bricolage of culture fragments adapted easily by both males and females in late industrial culture. One does not know what this will do for "patriarchy," for "feminism," or for the gender discussions, but one can know that the myths of the past today appear quite ambiguated in the light of much actual practice. And all of us are, for better or worse, embedded in these more overtly recognized multistabilities. Yet for all this, the horoscope calendar in the Chinese take-out in our village, which displays two very young children clothed only in underpants, each opening up to do a self-look, expresses the obvious: differences remain.

EPILOGUE

In fairness, I need to bring the readers up to date concerning Mark. This essay was written when Mark was still in sixth grade; he is now in seventh grade in junior high school. While there remain echoes of the elementary-school tensions, much of the earlier situation has been modulated. First, the new school is much larger and more diverse, with new sets of friends and groups, so that only some of the previous set remain core friends. Second, the expected growth has begun and he is now well-situated among the "average"-sized boys. Third, he has exceeded all expectations with respect to his alternative activities. In the last month of elementary school he entered and won a major prize for piano composition which was publicized throughout the region and in the schools. From this, he went on to perform the composition in various university and conference settings within a new group, the small number of prize-winning composers. The result was a kind of confidence which today has spilled over into writing, different styles of composition (electronic plus piano), and continued high-level performance in class. In short, he has partially transcended some of the in-group values expressed above and begun to find his own *metier* (if this sounds too much like a proud father, you will simply have to take that into account).

NOTES

1. Susan Bordo, "Reading the Male Body," *Michigan Quarterly Review* 32, no. 4 (1993): 697.

2. Iris Young, "Throwing Like a Girl," in *Throwing Like a Girl and Other Essays in Feminist Philosophy and Social Theory* (Bloomington: Indiana University Press, 1990). The retrospective, "Throwing Like a Girl: Twenty Years Later," is in *Body and Flesh,* edited by Donn Welton (Oxford: Blackwell, 1998).

3. I count Foucault, despite disclaimers, to belong to the "phenomenological" tradition. Not only was he a student of Merleau-Ponty, but reading Foucault reveals many apparently deliberate inversions of Merleau-Pontean claims and examples, indicating his heritage.

4. Maurice Merleau-Ponty, *Phenomenology of Perception* (New York: Humanities, 1962).

5. See my "Bodies, Virtual Bodies and Technology," in *Body and Flesh,* ed. Donn Welton (Oxford: Blackwell, 1998).

6. Bordo, "Reading the Male Body," 698.

7. Michel Foucault, *Birth of the Clinic* (New York: Random House, 1974); *Discipline and Punish* (New York: Random House, 1994); *The Order of Things* (New York: Random House, 1973).

8. Jean Paul Sartre, *Being and Nothingness* (New York: Philosophical Library, 1956).

9. Martin Buber, *I and Thou* (New York: Charles Scribner's Sons, 1970); Gabriel Marcel, *Being and Having* (New York: Beacon, 1951).

10. I refer to numerous references to "THE male gaze" as if they were one.

11. See "Breasted Being" and "Pregnant Subjectivity" in Iris Young, *Throwing Like a Girl and Other Essays in Feminist Philosophy and Social Theory* (Bloomington: Indiana University Press, 1990).

12. Susan Bordo, "My Father the Feminist," in *Men Doing Feminism,* ed. Tom Digby (New York: Routledge, 1998).

Chapter 12
Revealing the Non-Absent Male Body

*Confessions of an African Bishop
and a Jewish Ghetto Policeman*

BJÖRN KRONDORFER

Confessional writing, it may be argued, is a gendered activity: although women engage in this form of writing, it seems to attract more men because it is a relatively safe way of making public what before was private, of admitting vulnerabilities and personal flaws, and, above all, of acknowledging old sins (wrongdoings, errors of judgment, etc.). The act of confessional writing is safe because no other voice can interrupt the flow of the introspective and retrospective construction and interpretation of the male self.[1] What is shared with the public in a self-revealing manner is the meaning the writer attaches to lived experiences of the past. Those experiences are recounted in order to indicate to the imagined audience that the present narrator is no longer identical with the person he used to be, or with the choices he once made. The distance created between the confessor's present and past selves grants him a certain immunity: by relying on the preemptory operation of subtle or overt self-accusation, the writer avoids public accusations for his past sins; he is thus free to seek some understanding and, perhaps, compassion from the reader. In confessions, the male writer establishes a narrative background of already lived experiences against which he, as present narrator, wishes to be judged and forgiven.[2]

Given the focus on perceiving the male self as capable of asserting a new identity after acknowledging past sins, it is not surprising that confessional writings have been variously praised or criticized as a primarily Christian and Western phenomenon.[3] To assume that men can "turn around" (which is at the heart of the Christian concept of *metanoia*, repentance) and, through a process of introspection, rethink, reassemble, and reconstitute the self in accordance with a newly ascertained set of (moral) standards is to presume a particular relation between an autonomous self and a *telos* in history: the male self, capable of obtaining self-knowledge by abstracting from previous experiences, strives toward acting coherently in history, a history that moves toward the fulfillment of a grand or divine design. The Latin root of "confession" already points to these aspects of self-assertion and transcendence: *confiteri* means "not only to admit sins but to praise God."[4]

Augustine's *Confessions* serve as a perfect example of this literary genre—Northrop Frye even credited Augustine with inventing the "confession form."[5] The African bishop reflected on intimate details of his life not in order to please the audience with profane distractions but to direct their attention to God (which is why the *Confessions* contain, to many modern readers' dismay, lengthy segments of prayer and praise to God). As an "*architexte* of Western autobiography," Augustine's self-revelations exemplify the nondivisible task of *confessio peccati* (confession of sins) and *confessio fidei et laudis* (affirmations of faith and songs of praise).[6] "Let me confess," Augustine writes, "what I know of myself. Let me confess too what I do not know about myself. For what I know of myself I know because you [God] grant me light."[7] God provides an external perspective that enables Augustine to reflect on himself; God is also imagined as Augustine's prime reader.

The recently discovered testament of Calel Perechodnik, *Am I a Murderer? Testament of a Jewish Ghetto Policeman,*[8] seems to have little in common with this literary tradition of confession. In the face of impending death, Perechodnik finished his writing in his hiding place in the gentile part of Warsaw on August 19, 1943. Given this context, it would seem more reasonable to place his work, which Perechodnik himself had entitled "A History of a Jewish Family during German Occupation," among the body of archival and published Holocaust diaries, testimonies, and memoirs rather than in the company of Augustine's *Confessions.* Yet, his writing does not easily fit the style of other personal and "factually insistent"[9] narratives on the Holocaust. Though Perechodnik, like other Jewish writers during and after the Shoah, sees himself as a witness who must recount the horrors so that they will not be forgotten, he is not primarily concerned with chronicling his life or the events around him. Rather, he feels compelled to write because he wants to understand himself. He wants to understand why—after his ordinary life had been ruptured by the Nazi occupation of his Polish town—he had "entered the ranks of the Ghetto Polizei"[10] and thus become an accomplice to the murderous policy of the Germans. "If I believed in God," Perechodnik writes, "I wouldn't have written this [book] at all" (xxi). In contrast to the African bishop Augustine, the Jewish ghetto policeman cannot establish a divine perspective; the imagined prime reader is not God but his wife (who is, when Perechodnik begins his writing, already dead).

I am a reader neither Augustine nor Perechodnik could have foreseen. Augustine pleaded with God and a male Christian audience in the Roman empire; Perechodnik pleaded with his (dead) wife and the "democratic nations" (155) to take revenge on the Germans. The perspectives I bring to their writings are not necessarily those of the ideal reader they imagined. But to a man who was raised Christian and born in Germany after the Holocaust, their confessional writings resonate. Augustine stimulates mostly my intellectual curiosity (maybe against what he as a rhetorician had hoped to accomplish, that is, to affect my "heart" and spiritual choices); Perechodnik affects me emotionally and morally (though he wishes Germans to be destroyed). When I first read *Am I a Murderer?* I felt the immediate urge to respond, first by telling friends and colleagues about the book, later in writing: to express in language the sadness I felt; to write against my tears.

PERECHODNIK'S CONFESSION

Perechodnik variously refers to his manuscript as a memoir, a diary, an eternal monument to his wife, a second child, and, above all, a deathbed confession (xxi, 189, 191, 192, 202).

> This is a confession about my lifetime, a sincere and true confession. Alas, I don't believe in divine absolution, and as far as others are concerned, only my wife could—although she shouldn't—absolve me. However, she is no longer among the living. She was killed as a result of German barbarity, and, to a considerable extent, on account of my recklessness. Please consider this memoir to be my deathbed confession. (xxi)

Perechodnik presents a painfully honest account of what he perceives as his moral failures: his failure to grasp the extent of the German deceit of the Jewish people and of the Nazi will to annihilate them; his failure to have courage and foresight; and, most importantly, his failure to protect his wife and daughter from being transported to Treblinka. "There is nothing quite like this in the history of confessions," writes Frank Fox in the introduction to *Am I a Murderer?* "This is not Saint Augustine troubled by his own salvation or Jean-Jacques Rousseau remembering a childhood peccadillo. This is a twentieth-century man bereft of all beliefs, shorn of all human relationships, who begs to be understood even as he confounds us" (x).

Most confounding are the events on August 19, 1942, the day of the *Aktion,* the German euphemism for the liquidation of the ghetto of Otwock. During the *Aktion,* Perechodnik—as part of the Jewish police force—helps guard the remaining Jewish inhabitants as they await deportation, his wife Anna (Anka) and daughter Athalie (Aluśka) among them. Ironically, they are shipped to their death on Aluśka's second birthday. Exactly a year later, he finishes the last page of his confessional writing: "Today, August 19 [1943], is the day of my wife's Golgotha. . . . These diaries—although I wrote in the preface that they should be considered as a deathbed confession—are basically an account placed before You [Anka] on the anniversary of Your death" (191). During the eighteen months of his job as ghetto policeman prior to the *Aktion,* Calel Perechodnik comes across as lethargic and cynical (in his own words, "naive" and "fatalistic" [14, 191]); after the *Aktion* he is filled with despair, rage, and self-loathing, despite the fact that he sometimes describes himself as being "without feeling about everything" after the loss of his "dearest beings, my wife and daughter" (110).

The events on August 19 offer a key to understanding what drives Perechodnik to write his confessions in his hiding place: guilt, shame, and anger urge him on as much as his despair over having only the most trivial reasons for his choices and behavior as ghetto policeman. "They tell us to load the remaining people into cattle cars," he writes about the last hours of the *Aktion.* "O cursed Germans! How wise you are! How quickly we become the obedient marionettes in your hands! We work briskly; the demon of revolt no longer dominates us, not even a feeling of pity for the remaining Jews" (44). Later, already imprisoned in a labor camp, he asks himself: "Was this the result of a heart turned to stone or a sign of a bad character?" (114).

In contrast to Augustine, who pleads with God (and the reader) for forgiveness of his previous bad judgments and moral failures ("I do not blush, Lord God, to confess your mercies to me and to call upon you. . . . You are present, liberating us from miserable errors" [71, 110]), Perechodnik pleads with his wife for forgiveness, a theme that runs throughout his manuscript. He longs for but feels undeserving of his wife's forgiveness (just as Augustine feels toward God). "Am I a murderer, my wife's executioner?" he asks after the *Aktion* (54); and the concluding sentence of his confession spells it out one last time: "Anetka, have You really forgiven me?" (194).[11]

READING BODY AND GENDER

A question may be legitimately asked at this point: what do the confessions of a fourth-century Christian bishop in Roman Africa have to do with the testament of a twentieth-century Polish Jew who died in the Holocaust? From a strictly historical perspective, very little. But as a contemporary reader, I was immediately struck by common themes that run through the confessional narratives of these two men. Both contain a sense of revelation (with its core meaning of a dramatic disclosure of something previously not realized): Augustine acknowledges his previous errors of judgment in light of his discovery of the power of a transcendental God, whereas Perechodnik realizes his errors of judgment as his life is increasingly confined by the ubiquitous presence of Nazi genocidal anti-Semitism. Within these frames, both men report and reflect in personal terms on issues of choice and control, morality and faith, guilt and forgiveness, hope and despair, human failure and the im/possibility of redemption, and on their relationships to their parents, spouses, children, lovers, friends, enemies, and God.

Augustine's and Perechodnik's responses to the circumstances of their lives that compel them to write are radically different; yet in their dissimilarity, they are, like mirror images, linked to each other. Whereas Augustine's *Confessions* portray a deliberate spiritual search, in which the body is seen as an obstacle to Christian salvation, Perechodnik's "deathbed confession" tells of forced flights and escapes, in which the Jewish body is the prime target of destruction. Whereas the *Confessions,* which "recount Augustine's own salvation history,"[12] are a narrative of (relative) success, in which the self evolves spiritually through the classical stages of death of the old self, conversion, rebirth,[13] the ghetto policeman's testament is a narrative of failure, a modern document of unmaking, of the destruction of the self as "other" (as seen through the eyes of Nazi ideology). In Augustine's case, the voluntary submission to God's will triumphs over his desire for bodily pleasures and creates a spiritually reborn, Christian man; in Perechodnik's case, the political will of the Nazis to annihilate European Jews triumphs over his increasingly desperate attempts to keep a Jewish body alive.

As a contribution to this volume on *Revealing Male Bodies,* I wanted to explore the remarkable parallelism between Perechodnik's testament and Augustine's *Confessions.* I concluded my proposal with the following paragraph: "In general, my contribution will illuminate aspects of the male body as a site of resistance and of male lived experience of power and powerlessness. Issues of identity and spirituality are part of this exploration. The historical and cultural divide between these two narratives will not be rendered invisible. Rather, I hope to make the differences fruitful by occasionally inserting my own voice as a reader with his own embodied history."

Even as I was writing these lines, I was aware of the tension I created between different motivations: to assess cognitively what had touched me deeply (speaking in the voices of husband and father of two young daughters); to venture a comparison between a spiritual autobiography and a Holocaust narrative (speaking in the voices of a religious studies scholar and a Gentile born and raised in Germany); and to problematize the discourse on the male body in men's autobiographical writings (speaking in the voice of a male cultural critic). By inserting fragments of these voices, I wanted to address the danger that academic writing about the male subject can easily become a "device of self-distanc[ing]" rather than "self-touching," as feminist autobiographical criticism has suggested.[14] As I am trying to convey why Augustine's and Perechodnik's self-presentations are relevant to men's experiences today, I want to stay in touch with my roles as man, father, and scholar.

The body plays a key role in Augustine's and Perechodnik's writings (for the former, the issue is desire; for the latter, survival), but both men assume

252 / Björn Krondorfer

a facticity about their body that prevents them from seeing it as gendered. In this sense, the male body is not absent in male confessional writings, but neither is it consciously claimed as a gendered body. Unfortunately, the failure to grasp the gendered condition of the body robs them of the chance to take full advantage of the confessional form. Ideally, confessions could provide men with a safe medium to reflect critically and contextually on, first, their former perceptions of their gendered body (the making); second, on their determination to change their attitudes toward the body (the unmaking; or, in traditional terms, the act of acknowledging past sins); and third, on their envisioned restoration (or dissolution) of the body (the remaking).[15] But the confessional discourse on the male body rarely takes its genderedness into account. Male confessional writings have portrayed male bodies in various ways—a battlefield of opposing desires, a measure to gauge progress from the old self, an object unrelated to the true self, a manifestation of men's difference from women, or a mirror of the mental and spiritual condition—but the body of the heterosexual male confessor is usually not subjected to critical inquiry. Because it has been viewed for so long as the normative body, its dependence on the cultural assumptions that go into the making and unmaking of the male body remains obscured.

In light of such gender obliviousness, I intend to speak of the *non-absence* of the male body (rather than its presence) in confessions by men: although the male body is always *in* the text, it is not *present* in the text as a consciously gendered body. By speaking of the non-absent male body, I wish to introduce an analytical category that will make the male body visible anew in confessional writing. A non-absent male body, I hope to demonstrate in the writings of Augustine and Perechodnik, deflects attention from the male confessor as moral agent and gendered subject. To speak of the non-absent body requires the cultural critic who is interested in the task of "revealing male bodies" to read between and against the intentional revelations of the author. Margaret Miles has articulated the dual obligation of critical reading in her short study on Augustine's *Confessions:* to be both an "obedient reader" who "endeavor[s] to grasp what [the author] worked to communicate" and a "disobedient reader" who "highlights features . . . considered accidental or incidental to his self-revelation."[16]

Augustine's *Confessions* illustrate well the non-absence of the male body. While the body is constantly referred to as the locus of false pleasures that prevent a Christian man from finding true happiness in God, Augustine does not problematize his body and embodied self as a product of gendered desires and expectations. The *Confessions* implicitly assume that the post-lapsarian male body "naturally" expresses certain desires, which are, interestingly, neither culturally nor metaphysically determined. Men's desires are a product of neither culture nor God's original good creation but the result of Adam and Eve's original sin. Because a body in the state of original sin depends on (and hence "desires") what is necessary (hence "natural") for the physical survival of the human race, man left to his own devices is unable to suppress entirely his carnal appetites (for food, sex, power, beauty). The male body "naturally" seeks pleasure in food and sexuality because they are necessary for survival, and seeks power and beauty because they seem essential to (man's) life.[17] Augustine considers these drives not to be part of original creation but inevitable restrictions placed on the freedom of humans after the Fall. Just as humans cannot undo original sin and return to a state of innocence by their own will, a man cannot overcome his carnal desires without God's mercy. What men can do, however, is commit themselves to struggle against desires, thus preparing the grounds for a spiritual rebirth that brings them closer to God. Ultimately, however, salvation is dependent on God's mercy.

Augustine exemplifies humanity's bleak condition by pointing to the problem of nightly emissions—a physical activity that serves as sign and reminder of original sin. Even as a celibate bishop, Augustine admits, he fails to control "sensual images" in his dreams which cause involuntary emissions. He bemoans this dilemma in Book X (the first of what some critics call the "non-autobiographical" books of the *Confessions*).[18] There he no longer writes retrospectively about the sinful self but writes as present narrator about the converted self. "I have now declared to my good Lord what is still my present condition in respect to this kind of evil [i.e., nightly emissions]. . . . I hope that you will perfect in me your mercies to achieve perfect peace" (204). Man can control his body only to a certain extent; it is up to God to change this recalcitrant "evil" of man's postlapsarian, carnal nature.

> By the time my students at a public, liberal arts college reach this passage in the *Confessions* (in a course titled "Ascetics, Saints, and Sinners"), many are already frustrated by Augustine's overly conscientious and zealous self-scrutiny. They read his confessional statement about nocturnal ejaculations as one more sign of a guilt-ridden personality, and they frequently advise him *post mortem* to "get a life."
>
> I, however, find it quite astounding that a man in his position writes so intimately about his body. He could have easily remained silent on this point, for no witnesses could have proven him wrong. Although the spilling of semen is put into the purposeful context of lamenting his lack of control over it, he still makes his bodily fluids part of a public discourse on spirituality, and is in this regard more daring than most modern men, myself included.

An obedient reading can reveal that Augustine's confessional project aims at the ultimate disappearance of the body (just as his *Confessions* in general aim at self-effacement in light of God's power and grace).[19] Augustine would like to see his body vanish, but his body never leaves him. He will have to live with it until the final moment of release from this bondage, the moment of death. But precisely this moment escapes the grasp of all autobiographers. "The total communion with God," Lionnet writes, "can only be achieved at a point and time outside of autobiography, that is, in *death*."[20] Paradoxically, Augustine tries to persuade his audience of the insignificance of the male body/self by revealing in detail selected moments of his embodied self (e.g., the famous stealing-of-pears episode in Book III); by doing so, he writes himself into history and, unbeknownst to him, into the Western canon, thus immortalizing his battles with carnality.

A disobedient reading reveals the non-absent body at places where Augustine does not want us to see it. Feminist criticism, for example, has repeatedly pointed out that Augustine's suppressed male desires reappear, positively, in the form of maternal language about God and, negatively, in the form of a fictive construct of *woman*.[21] "What am I but an infant sucking your milk and feeding on you?" Augustine writes, imagining a nurturing God (52). But women, with the exception of his mother, Monica, cannot be part of his spiritual rebirth; Augustine's female partner and lover of thirteen years (about whom the reader learns little in the *Confessions*) is but one of the victims of a confessional discourse that is not consciously gendered.

Ironically, the male body is non-absent even when its biological maleness appears to be most present. When, for example, Augustine voices his displeasure over the nocturnal spilling of semen, he describes an activity obviously limited to the male body, yet he jumps to abstract theological conclusions—a rhetorical operation which is possible only because he presumes the male body to be normative. Rather than examining nocturnal emission as a specific male issue that may require gender-specific responses, Augustine turns it into a generic human predicament that will lead him to articulate the concept of original sin. Not to reflect on the body as a *male* body privileges the male experience as normative and has social consequences in gender relations. The result of a non-absent male body is that non-male bodies no longer fit the norm. Nothing can be learned about spirituality, for example, from the experiences of his female lover, nothing from the ways women manage and control their bodies and desires. Their experiences are excluded, rendered invisible, or, at best, must accommodate to the norm.

CHOICE AND CONTROL

Bringing the question of gender awareness to Perechodnik's deathbed confession will also reveal a non-absent male body, though in a different way than in Augustine's case. For the African bishop, it is the opulence of carnal desires—that is, the inevitable human tendency after the Fall to covet more than is necessary (food, sex, power, beauty)—which leads him to treat the body as an obstacle to moral improvement and salvation. For the Jewish ghetto policeman, it is the scarcity of choices (food, love, power, safety)—that is, the Nazi policy to take away what is necessary for survival—which leads him to commit immoral acts and which makes irrelevant any thoughts about bodily pleasure. Against his will, Calel Perechodnik is reduced to the most basic needs. "I did not have the energy to take the rudder in my own hand," he writes a few days after the *Aktion*. "A rapid current and a strong wind pushed all Jews into one direction: to Treblinka. . . . For days on end I lay senseless on my bed; at night I went on duty at the police station" (64). The experience of not having enough to live on throbs like a bleeding heart below the surface of the text, and it is difficult to imagine Perechodnik being plagued by "sensual images" in his dreams, like Augustine. From Perechodnik's perspective, to contemplate the theological/anthropological significance of nocturnal emissions is an indulgence, a luxury. Hence, we do not find the same detailed scrutiny of the male embodied self in his deathbed confession as in Augustine's work. Perechodnik's primary concern is his moral failure, not the body, and certainly not a body consciously gendered—in spite of the fact that the physical threat against his Jewish body is an ever-present reality in his life (and for the reader, in the text).

For Augustine and Perechodnik, the relationship between body and morality is enmeshed with two existential concerns: control and choice. How does control over one's bodily needs shape one's moral choices? Augustine responds to this concern by correlating moral freedom with release from bondage to the body: man's ability to make moral choices increases to the extent that carnal desires decrease. The bishop of Hippo writes to persuade his audience that man's voluntary commitment to control the body's insatiable appetites (a source of much anxiety for Augustine) is rewarded with moral and spiritual freedom. "You [God] snapped my chains. . . . What I once feared to lose was now a delight to dismiss" (155). And persuasive he proved to be! From the margins of Roman society, Augustine succeeded in blazing a new trail into the declining hegemony of the Roman empire, opening up the option for an alternative life and identity: the celibate man.

Like Augustine, Perechodnik perceives the issues of choice and control as central to how the body influences morality. Unlike Augustine, his anxiety is not rooted in the oppositional pairing of moral freedom and bodily bondage but, almost inversely, in the interdependence of bodily freedom and moral agency: external restrictions placed on his body result in his loss of moral freedom. Put differently, the more Perechodnik loses control over his physical survival, the more restricted his ability to make good moral choices. From amidst destruction, he writes to curse the "monstrousness of our times" (114), which has only one objective: a dead Jew.

Morality, body, God. Despite the centrality of choice and control in Augustine's and Perechodnik's experiences, they understand the consequences of their activities in strikingly different terms. Whereas Perechodnik perceives the Nazi encroachment on his *Jewish* body as leading him to act immorally, that is, against his family and community, Augustine perceives his voluntary restrictions on his *Christian* body as leading him to act morally and establish an intimate relationship with God. Perechodnik finds himself in a position where he is forced to sever the ties to his wife and daughter in order to save his body from the Nazi onslaught: "[M]y dearest daughter, you are looking at me through the barbed wire. . . . You stretch out your hands to me, but I have no right to take you. If I do that, I will immediately get a bullet in my head" (36). In the process, he loses his faith. "If I believed in God, in heaven or hell, in some reward or punishment after death, I wouldn't have written this at all. . . . I don't know how to pray, and as for faith, I have none" (xxi).[22] Augustine, on the other hand, deliberately decides to break away from his lover of many years and other sexual relations in order to save his soul and be socially and mentally free for God. "Lord, my helper and redeemer, I will now tell the story, and confess to your name, of the way in which you delivered me from the chain of sexual desire, by which I was tightly bound, and from the slavery of worldly affairs" (141). Whereas Augustine volunteers to abandon sexual relations in order to find faith in God, Perechodnik is forced to abandon Anka and Aluśka (the fruit of his sexuality) and loses faith in God. Augustine writes to persuade the reader of the moral gain of separating from one's sexual partner(s); Perechodnik writes out of despair over the loss of morality that contributed to the irreversible separation from his loved ones.

Morality, relationships, kinship. Augustine and Perechodnik respond differently to the choices which they can (or cannot) control. Augustine, for example, tries to keep his composure when sending his nameless partner and lover back to Africa. But the text is suffused with his hurt. "The woman with whom I habitually slept was torn away from my side," he writes, revealingly choosing a passive voice. "My heart which was deeply attached was cut and wounded, and left a trail of blood. She had returned to Africa vowing that she would never go with another man. She left with me the natural son I had by her" (109).[23] This child is introduced three books later as "the boy Adeodatus, my natural son begotten of my sin," who passes away in his teenage years. Augustine, the man of many words, reserves only a few lines for the departure of his female lover and the death of his only child. "Early on you [God] took him away from life on earth. I recall him with no anxiety; there was nothing to fear in his boyhood or adolescence or indeed his manhood" (163–164).[24]

The ghetto policeman, on the other hand, is devastated by the loss of his wife Anka and daughter Aluśka, and openly grieves, curses, and vows revenge. "Anko, Anko, let your beautiful eyes gaze for the last time at the heaven, at the sunset. Send me your last greeting—a benediction or a curse," Perechodnik writes as he imagines her arrival at Treblinka; and, yearning for a faith now broken, he continues, "Anka, Aluśka, Rachel, and you sisters and brothers of mine, how I would like to say from the depths of my afflicted heart the prayer *El Mole Rachamim* for the repose of your souls. . . . We the sons, brothers, husbands of yours still living, we shall avenge you with blood. Amen" (50–51).[25]

> As father of two- and five-year-old daughters, I am deeply affected by Perechodnik's description of his final moments with two-year-old Aluśka. During the *Aktion*, the Germans had deceived the Jewish policemen into believing that their wives and children would be spared. However, when all Jews were loaded into the cattle cars, the Germans started to separate the remaining children: they were not to be released. "Beside myself, I grab Aluśka, blood of my blood, bone of my bone, and I place her to the side. She stands alone, hungry, sleepy, surprised. Maybe she does not understand why the father, always so good to her, leaves her in the dark. She stands and does not cry; only her eyes shine, those eyes, those big eyes" (45).
>
> Stop reading, stop writing! I am fighting tears. Each time I read this passage, I cannot control my grief. I can say to myself: I am not living in the ghetto; I am not Jewish; I live in the rural parts of Maryland where my daughters are relatively safe; I am German; I come from a country and family of bystanders and perpetrators. But these rationalizations don't help. I remain most strongly identified with Perechodnik's confession at this very moment, and I hurt. For me, this is a primal scene, which cuts through time and space, through cultural and religious differences, even through my intellectual reservations about falsely identifying as a German with Jewish victims of the Shoah. But Perechodnik's experience speaks to me, because it speaks to my worst fears: a forced separation/ abandonment of my daughters while I look on helplessly.
>
> How different Augustine's description of his son's death! "I contributed nothing to that boy other than sin," he declares, crediting God, not his lover, for raising the child to become "a fine person," with an "intelligence [that] surpassed that of many serious and well-educated men. . . . Who but you [God] could be the Maker of such wonders?" (164).
>
> I have always wondered whether to believe Augustine's equanimity. Does he really not mourn his son's death, a man whose grief is abundant when he describes the loss of male friends or of his mother, Monica? As bishop of Hippo, he might have chosen to downplay his emotional attachment to Adeodatus, for his son was a reminder of his own sinful past, another obstacle to his spiritual rebirth. Augustine is known for his

employment of rhetorical devices.[26] But an apologetic reading of Augustine may be wishful thinking on my part: as long as I can believe in the possibility of a subtext, I am not left with Augustine's cruel distancing of his child—so different from Perechodnik's lament, "blood of my blood, bone of my bone."

COLLABORATION, RESISTANCE, AND
THE QUESTION OF GENDER

As obedient readers, we may despair with Calel Perechodnik over the loss of his loved ones and the cruel choices he was forced to make, or we might be confounded by his decision to abandon his family in order to save his own body. But we would hesitate to reproach him for his gender blindness. If your survival is at stake, any discourse on the gendered subject and male embodiment seems largely academic. Perechodnik focused on describing and examining his behavior as a *Jew* under the Nazi assault, not as a Jewish *man*. Hence, as modern readers we may be willing to overlook the fact that his confession does not thematize and problematize the male body, and hence renders invisible certain (albeit limited) privileges he had.

We know, for example, that the option to join the ghetto police was open only to men. Perechodnik could have refused to join, as did other men (and thus escape the accusation of not possessing a moral backbone). His wife Anka, on the other hand, never had such a choice and, as a consequence, would not have found herself in the position of assisting in the deportation of her daughter and husband. We would have to imagine Anka's deathbed confession—had she had a chance to write one, or the wish to do so—as significantly different from her husband's. It is in this light that gender, far from being the latest academic fad,[27] must be problematized even in situations of life at the extremities, such as the Shoah.

A disobedient reading of *Am I a Murderer?* needs to take another look at the non-absent male body: rarely the focus of Perechodnik's reflections, and constantly at the brink of disappearing behind his anguish over the loss of moral choices, his body is nevertheless present in the form of the Nazi threat to annihilate it. It is a negative presence, a body in the process of annihilation; or, as Perechodnik remarks, a body to be "utilized as a valuable raw material—for example, as natural fertilizer or as fat" (15). In the context of such unprecedented genocidal violence, we can speak of Perechodnik's body as doubly non-absent: historically, his Jewish body is the target of annihilation, its presence one of gradual destruction; textually, his male body disappears as a gendered body in his own writing.

To theorize a doubly non-absent body in Holocaust narratives written by men would open the door for a careful gender analysis without violating the experience of victims and survivors.[28] Rather than pitching the study of the Holocaust against gender studies, the scholar-critic would always remain aware of the assault on the male body as primarily a *Jewish* body (and thus remain empathetic with the core of Holocaust narratives: the destruction of Jewish people and culture), but also stay alert to the male body as a *male* body, that is, to the genderedness of the writing subject and his experiences.

In Perechodnik's case, the concept of the doubly non-absent body opens the possibility of approaching a central ethical concern posed by *Am I a Murderer?* Is Perechodnik a collaborator, an accomplice, or a repentant sinner? Is his deathbed confession a document of collaboration, opportunism, or resistance? The book invites such questions and tempts quick answers. Jewish ghetto policemen were widely despised by the ghetto population during the war as well as by Jews who survived the Shoah. They stand accused of voluntarily aiding the Nazis in their dirty work for base motives (such as greed, the selfish will to survive, etc.). In the afterword to *Am I a Murderer?*, Paweł Szapiro, the editor of the original Polish publication, writes that "a public confession" of a "perpetrator" can be "read as a display of shamelessness . . . rather than proof of an authentic penitence" (215). Perhaps it is not even prudent to publish such a document, for it may violate "the sanctity of the victims" (215) and cause ignorant or anti-Semitically inclined people to conclude that Jews were helpmates in their own destruction. Given these objections, the publication of the original record of a Jewish ghetto policeman is a breathtaking moment in the historical documentation of the Shoah.[29]

It would be difficult, however, to read Perechodnik's deathbed confession as the document of a corrupt soul. Despite the fact that Perechodnik volunteered for the ghetto police, one would be pressed to argue that he acted out of free will. We can accuse Perechodnik, as he accuses himself, of being deluded and deceived by the Nazis willingly, at least to a certain degree, but he does not exhibit the mind of a perpetrator. "I was, after all, a policeman, one of the most prominent," Perechodnik writes about his position before the *Aktion*. "I was also a personal friend of the Ghetto Polizei commandant . . . and I believed that I could feel completely secure about myself and my family" (22).[30] And later: "It is interesting that every catastrophe in history is foreshadowed; there are always some signs . . . [but] rarely does anyone believe them" (28).

Like other Jews, and especially those employed in the ghetto self-government, Perechodnik held on to the belief that there was some logic behind the apparent randomness of the cruel Nazi occupation policy; the Nazis offered plenty of deceptive evidence to make Jews believe there were some reasons behind the early arrests and deportations, until it was suddenly too late to resist. Only after the *Aktion* does Perechodnik understand the full extent of his delusion. "You see, Anka," he admits in the final pages of his work, "I was terribly afraid of death—not before the Otwock *Aktion* but after it. Before the *Aktion,* I was a fatalist. . . . But I never imagined that You would perish and I would remain alive" (191).

The effort to stay alive, which consumed most of Perechodnik's waking hours after the *Aktion,* can be interpreted as a willful act of resistance to the Nazi intention to annihilate his body. His body was to vanish from this earth, just like any sign of the despised Jewish culture. But Perechodnik, more than just keeping his body alive, started to write his confessions, for whose preservation he made careful arrangements. Against the threat of imminent annihilation, he adds another Jewish sign: a written document. If his body didn't survive, which would make it impossible to personally carry out revenge, his writing might at least be preserved, and persuade others of the necessity of retribution: "Then—on May 7 [1943] to be exact—I decided to write down these events. Maybe they will be preserved and in the future will be handed down to Jews as a faithful reflection of those tragic times and will persuade democratic nations to absolutely destroy all those Germans, to avenge the innocent deaths of millions of small Jewish children and women" (155). Perechodnik harbored few illusions about his physical survival. "I know now that sooner or later I will share the fate of all the Jews in Poland," he writes in the opening paragraphs of his preface. "A day will come when they will take me into a field, command me to dig a grave—for me alone—order me to remove my clothing and lie there on the bottom, and kill me. . . . I have seen so many executions that I can just close my eyes and see my own death in detail" (xxi). Without expecting to be able to protect his body, he nevertheless continues writing, uncertain even about the fate of his manuscript. He writes against the almost certain disappearance of both his body and his words (by contrast, Augustine wants his body to disappear but is confident that his words will survive). Is it possible, then, to suggest that Perechodnik's introspective writing constitutes an act of resistance because it testifies to the author's refutation of his dehumanization and "desubjectification" by the Nazis?[31]

To call his deathbed confession an act of resistance is, however, troubling, for it neglects the question of what Perechodnik did in order to stay alive long enough to write it. Perechodnik himself is aware of this dilemma: his living body is a testament to his im/moral choices, which is why his body is the source of his moral anguish. He is alive in part because he helped the Germans put others to death. To be alive and be able to write betrays his active (though limited) participation in the murder of Polish Jews. Even when he contemplates his own death, as in the passage quoted above, the vivid details (dig a grave, remove my clothing, lie there on the bottom) betray his complicity; he knows all these details because he had witnessed them as policeman.

As readers, we have, in the end, the privilege of knowing more than the author does. In a letter dating from 1950, Genia, Perechodnik's young, short-term lover in their common hiding place, talked about his final hours: weakened by typhus, hunger, and despair, Perechodnik perished during the Warsaw uprising—very likely by using cyanide pills.[32] His document, however, was preserved.

The doubly non-absent body (external threat against Jewish body; textual disappearance of gendered body) expresses the reader's uncertainty of how to judge Perechodnik and his writing, oscillating between the extremes of victim or perpetrator, collaborator or resister.[33] Constantly exposed to an external threat against his body, Perechodnik's anguish, despair, loss of moral choices, and "relentless self-exposure"[34] may sway the reader to empathize with this young husband and father, this hunted and haunted twenty-seven-year-old man, who is plagued by his conscience and who hopes against hope to get another chance—not for another life, but for revenge.

The internal, textual disappearance of his gendered body, however, reveals another side. Here, the non-absent body allows him to render invisible some of the responsibility he carries for his decisions. Perechodnik, we must assume, spoke truthfully; but he may not have told us everything, or, as Szapiro points out, "could have written more" about certain events (like the work of the Jewish police in the Otwock ghetto).[35] In some instances, Perechodnik displays a tendency to blame *all* Jews for failing to act, rather than focusing on himself and the specific role of the Jewish ghetto police. He writes for example: "Then, as now, I ascribed the entire blame for all of our misfortunes equally to German sadism as well as to the Jewish religion and traditions" (151)—a sweeping claim that helps to divert attention from his own actions. Elsewhere he claims that "there was no Jew who loudly cursed his executioners before his death. They were all passive, resigned, without hope for life" (79), contradicting his many accounts of the desperate creativity with which Jewish men and women tried to outmaneuver the Germans. His wife, for example, is upset about Perechodnik's failure to make arrangements for his family's protection, such as obtaining a *Kennkarte,* which might have given them temporary relief. Most women, like his wife, were burdened with taking care of their children and the elders, whereas some men, especially functionaries in the self-government such as Perechodnik, had access to better means of survival (food, information, protection, larger freedom of movement, etc.). Whenever Perechodnik moves to generalizations, he obscures some of his responsibility.

A last harrowing story may shed some light on my suggestion that a non-absent male body deflects attention from the author as moral agent and gendered subject. The night before the execution of Jews caught after the *Aktion,* Perechodnik, guarding the condemned, finds a little girl who resembles his daughter Aluśka (who has already been deported).

> I took her from her mother, . . . sat her on my knee, cuddled her, and thus we passed the night. When I heard that the [German] gendarmes were

arriving, I understood that I had to part with her. My charge, whose name I did not know, cried loudly and did not want to be returned to her mother. She sensed that death awaited her on the other side of the screen. She tightened her arms around my neck, and I had to forcefully tear myself away. When I returned her to her mother, I felt as if I killed the child with my own hands. (74)

In this heartrending scene, Perechodnik comes across as a gentle father figure as well as an accomplice to the execution. Since he blames himself for the latter, he is also the repentant sinner. The story unfolds in a manner that seems fated from the start, offering no alternatives of behavior. It sounds as if he has no choices. We have to remind ourselves, however, that he presents himself in this passage as fully present in his body when he comforts the child. He actively seeks her out and cuddles her. His body, however, disappears the moment he abandons her, and he quickly switches to a passive voice ("I understood that I had to part with her"). As he returns the girl to her mother, he assumes again the duty of a policeman, and leaves his "fatherly" body behind. The failure to act as a protagonist at that very moment produces the guilt-ridden chronicler of this event.

This episode can be read, perhaps, as Perechodnik's missed chance to redeem himself. Having lost his own daughter in similar circumstances, he could have tried to do something for this little girl. But as before, he remains awkwardly inactive, his language hiding some of his culpability. "You stretch out your hands to me," he wrote about Aluśka in a puzzling phrase already quoted above (recalling Augustine's use of the passive voice when describing his lover's lone departure to Africa), "but I have *no right* to take you" (36). Why not? He could have taken her hands and suffered the consequences. He has a right to take her, but it comes with the price of putting his body in harm's way. His phrasing expresses a moral understanding fixated on duty. Certainly, short of a miracle, he could not have saved Aluśka's life, nor that of the little girl. But he could have done what he laments that no Jew did: to take the child by her hands, curse the German gendarmes, throw himself against them, and take a few with them into the grave dug for Jews. His genuine attachment to the little girl, however, lasts only until the moment his own body is at stake.

My judgment is harsh. I may not have acted differently from Perechodnik; and, had I acted like him, I am not sure I would have had the courage to preserve my behavior in writing. I probably would have hoped that all memory of such perverse choices would vanish with my own death. But Perechodnik decides against such forgetfulness: he writes. He writes and makes himself vulnerable to accusations by future readers. "I have decided to write this diary not to justify myself but to give truthful testimony" (75). Without a chance to remake himself—the classical ending of confessional writing—he is left with the awareness of his unmaking, which leaves me, as reader, in the midst of his moral dilemma, without any easy resolution.

In the paragraph that immediately follows the story about the little girl, Perechodnik does what Augustine has mastered to perfection in his *Confessions:* he jumps from recounting a specific life experience to raising large and abstract questions. "I hear her voice till today," he writes. "My own thoughts as well: Is there a God? Is there some higher justice that rules this world? If so, why is it silent?" (74). These are legitimate questions, yet one wonders about their timing and placement. Do they not take the edge off of questions that would challenge him personally? What if he had asked: "Where was my courage? Would there have been, for someone in my position, a way to act justly this morning in Otwock? Why did I not cry out?" As feminist criticism has suggested, the move away from male embodiment to abstract reasoning is a move toward self-distancing, a device we can locate in the confessional texts of both Perechodnik and Augustine. I assume that such rhetorical devices (regardless of whether they are employed intentionally or not) help confessing men to cope with the guilt they are willing to admit retrospectively—though these devices also hide the full extent of their culpability.

Despite all their self-scrutinizing, self-loathing, self-accusation, or even self-effacement, confessing men remain in a position more privileged than the loved ones they write about. Confessional writing requires a subject capable of the act of writing, and provides a good chance of immortalizing the author. Augustine's lover and Perechodnik's wife and daughter, in contrast, all disappeared without their words being preserved.

POWER, ACCOMMODATION, AND RESISTANCE

The privilege of the writing subject does not translate automatically into an experience of power and pleasure. As a matter of fact, both Perechodnik and Augustine experience and perceive themselves as powerless: in Augustine's case, it is man's lack of control over bodily desires and the need to acknowledge a far greater, transcendent power, the presence of God; in Perechodnik's case, it is his lack of control over basic bodily needs due to the overwhelming power of the Nazi presence. The two writers employ various rhetorical devices to communicate this sense of powerlessness to their readers, but sometimes their rhetoric renders their culpability invisible, as we have seen above (e.g., hiding behind generalizations and abstraction; switching to a passive voice). As critical readers, we may suspect that Augustine and Perechodnik accommodate to their environment far more than they are willing to admit. But we cannot forget that different things are at stake for them: Augustine's *Confessions* are about spiritual rebirth and Perechodnik's deathbed confession is about physical survival. Behind the similar rhetorical strategies, we see a Christian bishop who remains the protagonist of his narrative, paradoxically against his wish to make God the protagonist (a dilemma he articulates in his qualms about false pride and vainglory),[36] and a Jewish ghetto policeman who never seems to be the protagonist in the events he chronicles, although he accuses himself, and now stands accused, of being one.

As I mentioned before, I tend to respond emotionally to Perechodnik, intellectually to Augustine. This response, I now believe, is among other reasons linked to the degree of each writer's control of (narrative) power. Perechodnik reveals himself to the point that he denies himself the power to control the reader's judgment. Since, at the end, it is up to the reader to judge his culpability, Perechodnik is left vulnerable to harsh verdicts. His confession remains open-ended. Augustine also reveals his culpability, but in a more skillful and guarded fashion. He remains in control of his confessions. As far as Augustine is concerned, by the end of the book the ideal reader has no choice but to acknowledge the power of God.

I am simultaneously drawn to, and frightened by, the risk that Perechodnik took: he rescinded some of the male confessor's privilege and power of reassembling and reconstituting the self retrospectively. Yes, he remains gender-oblivious, hiding the full weight of his culpability. But far more than Augustine, Perechodnik has given up control in the process of narrating the self. Perhaps, Perechodnik's risk can be a model for men's confessional writing today: confessional writing not as an act of reinscribing power but of desisting it.

Is such resistance possible? Foucault's critique of the Western obsession with producing truth through confessions, thereby establishing and maintaining power through knowledge, questions any such attempt. "The obligation to confess," Foucault writes, "is now relayed through so many different points, is so deeply ingrained in us, that we no longer perceive it as the effects of a power that constrains us."[37] Any confessional act, in this view, already accommodates to power.

The question remains: do male confessional revelations reinscribe social norms or do they offer opportunities to resist norms of conformity? Augustine's and Perechodnik's confessions do not provide unequivocal answers.

Augustine and Perechodnik not only accommodate to but also resist the circumstances of their time; and in both cases their embodied selves, imbued with moral ambiguity, play a central role. Augustine resists societal expectations to seek a career in Roman society. After he had forcefully separated from his lover (at the cost of being left with a "bleeding heart"), there seemed few obstacles to his entering the Roman heartland: the African teacher of rhetoric has successfully established a network of important friends in Milan and is newly betrothed to a young girl of the Milanese upperclass.[38] Just then he renounces all sexual pleasures and, with it, social prestige. "The effect of your [God] converting me to yourself was that I did not now seek a wife and had no ambition for success in this world" (153–154).

Perechodnik resists the genocidal violence directed against him as the ultimate "other" by keeping his Jewish body alive, at the cost of witnessing and participating in the destruction of his loved ones. Cramped into his hiding place, he allows himself sexual pleasure only one more time: he sleeps with eighteen-year-old Genia. On the last page, he confesses his sexual affair with her to his (dead) wife and writes with pride that "the words *I love* have not passed" between Genia and him (194). Despite what he did, he wants to come across as remaining loyal to his wife, but as disobedient readers, we now see Genia being moved to a place of silence and irrelevance that she shares with Augustine's lover.[39]

Returning to Africa as an avowed celibate, back to the margins of Roman society, Augustine succeeds in anchoring the image of a new man in the Western canon—a man of God who works within society; the *Confessions* eventually become a classic Christian model for the internal, spiritual remaking of man. Perechodnik's last days are spent under "demolished houses, in bunkers, and in sewers" (204): no image of a new man can emerge from these dark and putrid places, only Perechodnik's portrayal of modernity's violent unmaking of a Jewish man. Let us hope, then, that his document of unmaking becomes, like Augustine's *Confessions*, part of an enlarged canon, and does not fall into oblivion.

"Then no one will shed even one tear on my nonexistent grave. I don't deserve it" (202).

NOTES

I want to thank Ruth Ost for her perceptive comments on an earlier draft.

1. Cf. Björn Krondorfer. "The Confines of Male Confessions: On Religion, Bodies, and Mirrors," In *Men's Bodies, Men's Gods: Male Identities in a (Post-) Christian Culture,* ed. Björn Krondorfer (New York: New York University Press, 1996), 222; I argue there that confessional writing in particular (rather than autobiography in general) is attractive to men because it enables them to talk about intimate details of the male subject. See also Rachel Feldhay Brenner, who writes that "the perspective in autobiography is mainly retrospective, whereas in diary it is contemporaneous" (*Writing as Resistance: Four Women Confronting the Holocaust* [University Park: Pennsylvania State University Press, 1997], 120). See also Philippe Lejeune, *On Autobiography,* ed. Paul John Eakins, trans. Katherine Leary (Minneapolis: University of Minnesota Press, 1989).

2. Françoise Lionnet speaks of "the dual nature of narrator (the converted

self) and protagonist (the sinning self)'' in *Autobiographical Voices: Race, Gender, Self-Portraiture* (Ithaca: Cornell University Press, 1989), 43.

3. Michel Foucault argues that confessions have taken on a central role in ordering civil and religious power in the West since the Middle Ages (*The History of Sexuality: An Introduction*, vol. 1 [New York: Vintage Books, 1990]). For a strong proponent of autobiography as a uniquely Western form, see Georges Gusdorf, "Conditions and Limits of Autobiography," in *Autobiography: Essays Theoretical and Critical*, ed. James Olney (Princeton: Princeton University Press, 1980); see also Laura Marcus, *Auto/biographical Discourses: Theory, Criticism, Practice* (Manchester: Manchester University Press, 1994), 154–162. For views critical of the Western uniqueness, see Jerome Bruner, "The Autobiographical Process," and Julia Watson, "Toward an Anti-Metaphysics of Autobiography," in *The Culture of Autobiography: Constructions of Self-Representation*, ed. Robert Folkenflik (Stanford: Stanford University Press, 1993), 38–56 and 57–79.

4. Lyell Asher, "The Dangerous Fruit of Augustine's *Confessions*," *Journal of the American Academy of Religion* 66, no. 2 (1998): 230.

5. Northrop Frye, *Anatomy of Criticism* (Princeton: Princeton University Press, 1957), 307.

6. Lionnet, *Autobiographical Voices*, 37, 42. Peter Brown writes, "*Confessio* meant, for Augustine, 'accusation of oneself; praise of God' " (*Augustine of Hippo* [Berkeley: University of California Press, 1969], 175).

7. Saint Augustine, *Confessions*, trans. Henry Chadwick (Oxford: Oxford University Press, 1992), 182. Hereafter citations from this volume will be indicated in the text by page number.

8. Calel Perechodnik, *Am I a Murderer? Testament of a Jewish Ghetto Policeman*, ed. and trans. Frank Fox (Boulder: Westview Press, 1996).

9. James E. Young, *Writing and Rewriting the Holocaust: Narrative and the Consequences of Interpretation* (Bloomington: Indiana University Press, 1988), 15.

10. Perechodnik, *Am I a Murderer?* 9. Hereafter citations from this volume will be indicated in the text by page number.

11. Anetka is another name he uses for his wife.

12. Kim Power, *Veiled Desire: Augustine on Women* (New York: Continuum, 1996), 18.

13. Cf. Lionnet, *Autobiographical Voices*, 50.

14. Elizabeth Grosz, quoted in Marcus, *Auto/biographical Discourses*, 218.

15. The idea that, for men, the act of confessional writing is a safe way to express themselves is further explored in Krondorfer, "Confines of Male Confessions," 205–234.

16. Margaret Miles, *Desire and Delight: A New Reading of Augustine's Confessions* (New York: Crossroad, 1992), 11.

17. Augustine distinguishes between pleasure derived from necessities (food, sexuality) and pleasure dependent on cultural variations (beauty). "We restore the daily decay of the body by eating and drinking. . . . [b]ut at the present time the necessity of food is sweet to me, and against that sweetness I fight" (204). Aesthetic beauty, on the other hand, seems more dependent on "human customs" (46) because variations exist in the "arts and crafts in clothing, shoes, vessels . . . pictures, images" (210) or the "custom of singing" (208)—none of which should "go to excess" because it would "produce mental fatigue" (210). Augustine acknowledges "variations in customs" due to a "mutually agreed convention of a city or nation" (46): but insists on three "chief kinds of wickedness": the lust for domination (power), lust of the eyes (beauty), and lust from sensuality (sexuality, food) (47).

18. Some editions even omitted the last books (X–XIII) of the *Confessions* because they did not match the narrative unity of the first books (I–IX), but Lionnet strongly argues for the autobiographical integrity of the entire work (*Autobiographical Voices,* 37).

19. See Lionnet, *Autobiographical Voices;* Asher, "Dangerous Fruit."

20. Lionnet, *Autobiographical Voices,* 44 (italics in original). See also Robert Folkenflik, "Introduction: The Institution of Autobiography," in *Culture of Autobiography: Constructions of Self-Representation,* ed. Robert Folkenflik (Stanford: Stanford University Press, 1993), 15.

21. Augustine's construct of *woman* is a "projection," Lionnet argues, "on the external world of an inner and scary reality" (*Autobiographical Voices,* 52). See also Miles, *Desire and Delight;* Power, *Veiled Desire;* Maggie Kilgour, *From Communion to Cannibalism: An Anatomy of Metaphors of Incorporation* (Princeton: Princeton University Press, 1990), 46–62.

22. His attitudes toward faith and God are more complex than can be explored here; see also pages 39, 74, 78, 101, 153, 158.

23. See also Brown, *Augustine of Hippo,* 88–89; Power, *Veiled Desire,* 99–101; Miles, *Desire and Delight,* 77–80.

24. See also Power, *Veiled Desire,* 103.

25. The Hebrew, "God full of mercy," is the opening of the mourning prayer, recited after a funeral and on anniversaries of a death.

26. Augustine often describes his attachments "in rhetorical language" (Power, *Veiled Desire,* 97).

27. For a recent vicious and polemic attack on combining Holocaust and gender studies, see Gabriel Schoenfeld, "Auschwitz and the Professors," *Commentary* 105, no. 6 (1998): 42–46. "Between the Scylla of an academicized 'Holocaustology' and the Charybdis of a universalized victimology," the senior editor of *Commentary* writes, "the worst excesses of all on today's campuses are being committed . . . by the voguish hybrid known as gender studies" (44).

28. A gendered reading of Holocaust narratives has been applied to women's writing but not, to my knowledge, to men's writing. See Brenner, *Writing as Resistance;* Dalia Ofer and Lenore J. Weitzman, eds., *Women in the Holocaust* (New Haven: Yale University Press, 1998). Young, *Writing and Rewriting,* addresses with much sensitivity the problematics of violating survivor narratives.

29. For a short history of how the manuscript survived the war, how it subsequently found its way into archives in Warsaw and Jerusalem (where it was read by a few historians), and how it was finally published (first in Polish in 1993, then in English in 1996), see the foreword by Frank Fox and afterword by Paweł Szapiro in Perechodnik, *Am I a Murderer?*

30. About the social makeup of the ghetto police, he writes: "It is worth noting that the Jewish police had in its ranks the same number of lecturers, physicians, and engineers as it did illiterates" (69).

31. Brenner, *Writing as Resistance,* 119. Brenner argues that "self-introspection" can be "a mode of resistance" (5).

32. Reprinted in Perechodnik, *Am I a Murderer?* 203–205. The Warsaw uprising refers here not to the Jewish ghetto revolt but to the Polish uprising in the summer of 1944.

33. Istvan Deak writes in a review that Perechodnik displays "neither heroic not quiet virtues. . . . Who can blame him?" ("Memories of Hell," *The New York Review,* 26 June 1997, 38–43).

34. Sidra DeKoven Ezrahi, *By Words Alone: The Holocaust in Literature* (Chicago: University of Chicago Press, 1980), 64. Ezrahi argues that only in "very few in-

stances" does Holocaust literature engage in "relentless self-exposure." Perechodnik's work, I believe, can be counted among them.

35. "We may assume that *Perechodnik's text comprises the truth,*" Szapiro writes in the afterword (*Am I a Murderer?* 216, italics in original), but Szapiro mentions an example of a documented event that Perechodnik should have known of but does not mention (220).

36. On the problem of Augustine's anxiety over the circularity of his attempts at avoiding pride and vainglory, see Asher, "Dangerous Fruit."

37. Foucault, *History of Sexuality,* 60.

38. See Power, *Veiled Desire,* 91–101; Brown, *Augustine of Hippo,* 88.

39. Genia's portrayal of their relationship is remarkably different, as we know from her letter (203–205).

Chapter 13

A Father's Touch

Caring Embodiment and a Moral Revolution

MAURICE HAMINGTON

> Continued existence of humanity may require that we cease to
> turn "mothering" into an activity filled only by mothers.
> —Virginia Held[1]

My daughter, Rosemary, is learning to read. While I knew that this would
be a natural step in her intellectual development, I never imagined the
degree to which reading involves tactile interaction. Rosemary and I must
be in very close proximity, or "intimate space," to read to one another.
When we read out loud together Rosemary is sitting either next to me
or perched on my lap, or we are lying next to each other in bed. This
close personal aspect of reading makes it a warm experience that reinforces this activity for both of us. While our minds soar through adven-
tures, or struggle with words, our bodies are in quiet communication,
expressing ideas not found on the printed pages we are consciously attending to.

Parties everywhere on the political spectrum in the United States are
calling for fathers to be present and more involved in the lives of their
children. Feminists, religious conservatives, educators, politicians, and civil
rights leaders who are unlikely to agree on many issues do generally agree
that in an era when the definition of the traditional family is being renego-
tiated through the emergence of alternative arrangements, the presence
and active involvement of fathers is positive for the family and society. As
evidence that fathers need to be more involved, those interested in this
issue point to statistics on the percentage of families that lack the presence
of a father or on the relative time fathers spend in the actual child-raising
activities of the family. While quantitative issues of presence and time devoted to child-rearing behaviors are significant, a qualitative dimension of
the issue, a discussion of the potential for an important ethical transformation, is being overlooked. There is the opportunity for a *moral revolution* to
take place below the radar of mainstream social criticism and philosophy.

This revolution is grounded in the idea that morality is more than rules, rights, and consequences but is also found in the caring presence and comportment of the body. There are specific aspects of ethical understanding, such as a caring orientation, that find significant resources in the interactions of bodies, and yet the embodied aspect of morality has been largely ignored. Socialization in Western culture has created a gender bias in this revolution: males in particular stand to gain and contribute the most to this new moral orientation. Men, in their roles as fathers, as well as many other roles in society, have for too long been socialized to focus upon issues of duty and justice and not enough on care. The moral revolution I envision springs from the changing ways men's bodies relate to their children.[2]

The father who is present and involved with his children in a positive and healthy manner has opportunities for numerous tactile interactions that in subtle but definite ways foster and instantiate a caring moral orientation. The hand on the shoulder during a conversation, the arm around the waist during a sad moment, the playful roughhousing that lightens up a situation—all of these interactions have a verbal and visual context that we have learned to attend to, but they also have a subtext of touching that also communicates volumes. These interactions are reciprocal, affecting both the toucher and the one who is touched. The mainstream, middle-class maternal tradition has given and demanded more of these tactile opportunities to and for women, but for men the chance for a real change of heart, a moral revolution, is at hand. Economics and changing family roles have created the initial momentum for this moral revolution, but greater recognition and thematization of father-child caring interaction can contribute further. This paper is offered as one step in that direction.

I wish to make the contentious claim that on the whole, men have traditionally been socialized to be morally deficient.[3] Men's behavior indicates this deficiency. Although women are a slight majority of the population, men are a vast majority of those engaging in harmful and unethical behavior as determined by society's laws and morality. The highly publicized school shootings in American cities are an ominous example of the crisis of morality among males. While analysts and pundits sought explanations in religion, guns, video games, movies, and adolescence, few addressed the obvious issue of gender. Gloria Steinem finds irony in the fact that it is those who have the greatest power in society that are acting in morally deficient ways: "White males—usually intelligent, middle class, and heterosexual, or trying desperately to appear so—also account for virtually all the serial, sexually motivated, sadistic killings, those characterized by stalking, imprisoning, torturing, and 'owning' victims in death."[4] Steinem's claims are supported by statistics. Men comprise 92 percent of all prison inmates in the United States. Men commit more crimes against property and against people. Men are six to seven times more likely to commit violence against an intimate associate than women are.[5] While single-variable causal connections are too simplistic for any complex social issue, the moral development and training of men is just as plausible as an area for concern as any other.[6]

The stresses on individuation and separation in male development combined with cultural images of detached masculinity have contributed to a stunting of men's overall moral maturity. Ironically, men have dominated the field of moral philosophy through the ages, creating elaborate written ethical systems—rights-based ethics, religious-based ethics, utility-based ethics, etc. While these systems are not without significant merit, they generally lack an explicit connection to the fundamental human conditions of embodiment and community. Fathers, by definition, are a part of a community, but the tradition of masculine socialization has created sex roles that often limit male interaction with their children in prescribed ways. The breaking down of traditional hierarchical sex roles within the heterosexual family unit has the potential to unleash a new kind of moral power—the power of mutuality and care. Ultimately, I am hopeful about what masculinity can become. Returning to Steinem's observations: "If anything, ending the massive cultural cover-up of supremacy crimes should make heroes out of boys and men who reject violence, especially those who reject the notion of superiority altogether. Even if one believes in a biogenetic component of male aggression, the very existence of gentle men proves that socialization can override it."[7] The object of this article is to attend to the much overlooked physical aspect of the moral development of children in the family, where through simple acts of kindness a moral orientation of care in the cared-for child and in fathers themselves can be reinforced. While care ethics is often associated with feminist ethics, it is men who have the most to gain from this moral orientation, and a great deal of that learning will come through the body.

My claims concerning this potential moral revolution to be found in the physically involved father are radical and ambitious for a short article. To support my argument I will integrate two constellations of ideas: care ethics as developed by Carol Gilligan, and the phenomenology of the body as described by Maurice Merleau-Ponty. I believe that these seemingly disparate theories can be integrated into a notion of embodied care that is crucial to the transformation of fatherhood.

CARE ETHICS AND EMBODIED CARE

There has not been enough attention given to the relationship between fatherhood and caring. Of course most fathers care about their children, but I want to define a corporeal usage of the term "care." First I will provide a little background. In the 1980s the vocabulary of moral discourse expanded as care ethics emerged in the work of several key feminist theorists including Professors of Education Carol Gilligan of Harvard and Nel

Noddings of Stanford. Subsequently, an explosion of articles and books have alternatively criticized and extended this new approach to morality. Care reorients ethical concern onto issues of relationship and the affective dimensions of moral consideration. The philosophical implications of Gilligan's work include challenging the traditional epistemological bases of detached objectivity in moral theory as well as calling into question universalistic moral claims.

Although it is possible to construct a genealogy of care ethics that traces back to David Hume,[8] it is more common to associate care with the modern work that established the term "care ethics," namely Gilligan's *In a Different Voice: Psychological Theory and Women's Development.*[9] Carol Gilligan was a student of Lawrence Kohlberg, who had developed a renowned hierarchical approach to moral development. Kohlberg viewed moral decision-making as undergoing a series of steps beginning with simple efforts to avoid punishment and potentially rising to levels where individuals made independent ethical choices regardless of social convention. Kohlberg conducted a great deal of his early research on males, and subsequently females scored lower on his moral hierarchy. Gilligan saw these differences as not rooted in the deficiency of female moral development, but grounded in a moral orientation not fully captured by Kohlberg's instruments. Gilligan labeled this approach "care ethics."

Gilligan is widely misinterpreted as making claims about innate gender differences in ethical thinking. While her conclusions were drawn from research on the experience of women and girls, and she does recognize the impact of social construction on gender, Gilligan clearly attempts to characterize an alternative moral voice in opposition to what she described as a Kantian ethic of justice.[10] She grounds care ethics in the psychosocial development of human beings. In particular she focuses on issues of separation and intimacy, because the meaning of these experiences has been constructed differently for men and women in Western culture.[11]

Care ethics is a relational approach to morality that emphasizes the particularities and constituents of any given moral dilemma.[12] Many are uncomfortable with the ambiguity inherent in care ethics, because in a care approach rules of behavior cannot be established independent of the concrete aspects and individuals involved in the situation. Context is crucial because of the web of relationships that make up the fabric of any ethical decision.[13] In a care approach the maintaining of right relationship is valorized over what Gilligan refers to as the justice approach, manifested in universal rules, calculated consequences, or individual rights. Fellow feelings animate action. Care ethics presumes humans to be social creatures who fundamentally seek connection. Gilligan does not attempt to offer a superior moral *theory* to traditional justice approaches, but she believes a significant moral *approach* has been largely ignored and marginalized in Western ethical analysis.

Although care ethicists address the need for grounding morality in intersubjective experience, there is little work elaborating the *corporeal* aspect of care. Here is where I break from the contemporary discussions of care ethics to describe the notion of "embodied care." The full impact of care ethics is better explained through convergence with modern philosophies of embodiment in the tradition of Merleau-Ponty, whose phenomenological approach challenges objectivist epistemologies while also providing insight into the human experience and the moral workings of the flesh. The moral dimension of the father as caretaker makes an excellent subject for applying this embodied approach to care. A moral revolution grounded in the relationship of fathers and children will be both profound in its impact and subtle in its transformative process. Merleau-Ponty's philosophy of the body provides a vehicle for finding deep meaning in the phenomenology of simple bodily interaction and movements.

AN EXPERIENCE OF CARE

To facilitate an understanding of embodied care I will recount a personal example: washing my daughter's hair. My purpose is to demonstrate that, despite its history of philosophical and political underdevelopment, care is an essential moral understanding because of the kind of bodies and flesh that we inhabit. In our society "care" is a complex, abstract mode of intersubjectivity masked by a common expression.[14] Although I am focusing upon fatherhood, care can be exhibited in many forms and in many different relationships; therefore any phenomenological description of care is necessarily partial and perhaps unsatisfying.[15] I believe that much care activity is prenoetic and communicated through physical contact as tacit knowledge of the body. Phenomenological accounts provide significant insight, gesturing toward that which we cannot tell, but of course they can never entirely grasp the depths of care. I offer a simple experience in my relationship with my daughter, Rosemary.[16]

> My daughter is seven years old now. I don't need to attend to her body as much as I did when she was an infant or toddler. She can go to the bathroom for herself. She can feed herself and brush her own teeth. But there are still certain aspects of bodily care that I am involved with that will dissipate as she grows older. For example, I wash Rosemary's hair when she takes a bath. There are certain basic steps in the procedure. While kneeling next to the bathtub I thoroughly wet her hair. I apply shampoo and lather her hair up. I rinse out the shampoo, apply conditioner, and then comb out her thin curly hair, which tends to knot. Finally, I rinse her hair a last time. This process has become routine and few words about the washing pass between us. Rosemary usually plays with bath toys and chats away with little attention to my work. There is a

semi-conscious interaction between us, because she knows when to hold her head up or back depending upon what I am doing. There is also a subtler tactile interaction that conveys what might be termed a disposition, an attitude or feeling. My hands touch her head and neck, protect her eyes, work around her ears, and move about her hair. Rosemary knows that I will not be rough or suddenly hurt her, so she allows me into close proximity without hesitation. My actions are consistent and tender while accomplishing the task. There is a subtext of care that creates an atmosphere of trust. The bath is a womb-like experience. Rosemary is naked and warm in the small enclosure of the bathtub, and the world is a seemingly safe and loving place.

As I wash Rosemary's hair, despite the tactile nature of the work, I am not explicitly aware of my hands separate from the task I am performing, nor am I attentive to my own body. My conscious focus is entirely upon Rosemary's body and cleaning her hair, yet I believe there is more at work here than grooming behavior. To make the case for complex modes of communication I turn to phenomenology. Drawing upon the writing of Merleau-Ponty, Drew Leder describes the conscious focus on the activity rather than the involved body parts as the disappearance or recession of the sense organ from the perceptual field it discloses.[17] While washing Rosemary's hair, my skin receives a myriad of sense data including degrees of wetness, the viscosity of the shampoo and conditioner, and the temperature of the water, air, and Rosemary's skin. All of these constitute elements of my tactile perception, or what Leder refers to as exteroception.[18] In the process of washing my daughter's hair my consciousness is outwardly focused, leaving me unaware of my limbs and their movements.[19] An undercurrent of this activity is my care for Rosemary. This care is integrated at the corporeal level into the hair-washing and contributes to super-attentiveness toward the other. Nel Noddings describes the super-attentiveness of caring as engrossment: "At bottom, all caring involves engrossment. The engrossment need not be intense nor need it be pervasive in the life of the one-caring, but it must occur."[20]

Given Leder's notion of disappearance, engrossment appears to be an extension of the manner in which our bodies thematize the world. The human body is capable of allowing our consciousness to attend to immediate activities, all the while oblivious to the finer motor tasks required. Merleau-Ponty describes this thematization as the figure-background structure of perception or perceptual focus.[21] The perceptual disappearance of the sense organ is significant to Merleau-Ponty because it instantiates the subjectivity of the body. "In so far as it sees or touches the world, my body can therefore be neither seen nor touched. What prevents its ever being an object, ever being 'completely constituted' is that by which there are objects. It is neither tangible nor visible in so far as it is that which sees and touches. The body therefore is not one more among external objects."[22] What then, when we touch another human body? In the process of washing Rosemary's hair I will touch water, metal faucets, the porcelain tub, the plastic shampoo bottle, hair, and skin. My fingers will coordinate with my eyes in the process of making a number of subtle muscular adjustments based on experience in the manipulation of the objects and surfaces in this particular space. I don't grab the shampoo bottle with such force that shampoo squirts into the air. I don't jam my hand into the side of the shower door with the same motion that cuts through the water in the tub. My body also makes adjustments to appropriately touch my daughter's head, neck, and hair. These adjustments are not merely calculated to compensate for malleability and hardness; there appear to be other body dynamics at work. It is difficult to articulate what is unspoken, but a careful phenomenology of the interaction reveals that my body is also subtly communicating to Rosemary that I care for her. The human body appears to be built to care because it can free itself from micromanaging movement, thus allowing concentration on the other in a particular manner.

Certainly a child can have similar tactile experiences with a mother, but I argue that caregiving in this manner on the part of the father adds significantly to the moral education of the child. Many Western social traditions have served to hide the male body and truncate embodied experiences of the father within the family. Knowledge of the father's body does not have to be limited to corporeal punishment, roughhousing, or in an era of male abandonment, an absent mystery. Children can know their father's body and touch as accessible, kind, and caring, just as tradition has allowed this understanding of women's bodies. Acts of corporeal care by the father will break down the exclusive connection between motherhood and care. These experiences of the father's body in caring interaction have the potential to alter the quantity and quality of the child's experiences that lay the foundation for moral development—with revolutionary possibilities.[23] Pragmatically, having more than one caregiver providing these experiences reinforces care by degree. Given the experience of caring fathers, future expectations concerning men's behavior and men's bodies can be changed from their historical constructs.

THE IMPACT ON THE CARING FATHER: A BIDIRECTIONAL REVOLUTION

And how will men ever develop an understanding of the "ethic of care" if they continue to be shielded or kept from that experience of caring for a dependent child?
—Annette Baier[24]

Caring is not a unidirectional experience. The one caring is affected by the acts of caring as well as the one cared for. In *The Visible and the Invisible,*

Merleau-Ponty introduces the enigmatic idea of the flesh as an element of Being.[25] The flesh is marked by reversibility. The flesh is bodily experience as touched and touching, as sensed and sentient, as subject and object, and yet the flesh is not identical to an isolated independent body.[26] This reversibility is unified in its spatial experience, but not in time. My hand can experience both being touched and touching, but this experience is not temporally unified in that I do not perceive touch and touching in the same instant. According to Merleau-Ponty, "it is a reversibility always imminent and never realized in fact."[27] This reversibility creates a reciprocity or "weaving relations between bodies."[28]

Through the flesh humanity is interconnected and intertwined. On this account experience is understood as open-ended. An experience of mine is integrated with previous experiences, giving rise to structures and patterns that are further blended with the experience of others in the ongoing emergence of intersubjective meaning. The interaction of bodies forms a system of relations and communication based on these intersubjective meanings. My experience of caring for Rosemary, even though I may not be attending to it consciously, becomes part of how I understand analogous circumstances. For example, if I were to be involved in a policy decision that impacted family life, my own unarticulated embodied caring experiences might influence me. The experience of the other becomes a "generalized I" of unrealized potential in all of my own experiences.[29] The flesh is a powerful nexus between what it is to be other and what it is to be me. In the words of David Abram, "Humans are tuned for relationship. The eyes, the skin, the tongue, ears, and nostrils—all are gates where our body receives the nourishment of otherness."[30] Yet fathers have often been socialized to suppress their bodies' relational tuning.

If involved, embodied acts of caring become an integral part of the experience of fatherhood, then a new element is introduced into what these fathers bring to encounters with the world. Intersubjective meaning may take on new directions from those found in the recent history of masculinity. Psychologists have long recognized this impact. For example, in *Fathers,* Ross D. Parke writes, "Fathering often helps men clarify their values and to set priorities. . . . Fathers can learn from their children and be matured by them."[31] A caring father is transformed by the experience, and male moral development is in dire need of more opportunities to care and be cared for.

The reciprocity that Merleau-Ponty refers to is not a substitutionist understanding of meaning or compassion. The physical existence of our lived bodies does not allow us to claim the experiences of the other, yet there is an experience of encroachment and exchange that constitutes the flesh. "The factual presence of other bodies could not produce thought or the idea if its seed were not in my own body. Thought is a relationship with oneself and with the world as well as a relationship with the other."[32] In the act of washing Rosemary's hair there is a literal and metaphorical reversibility of touch. Our bodies touch and are touched but even more so, our lives are touched by another reciprocal experience of care. The reversibility and the reciprocity are interrelated. I am capable of caring and being cared for and each disposition enables the other through the shared experience of the flesh. Through our tactile interaction, not only does Rosemary experience what it is to be cared for as instantiated in the body, but I experience what it is to care in a pattern of thought and behavior. An unspoken *habit* is reinforced in the exchange between our bodies that impacts the caregiver as well as the one cared for. According to Merleau-Ponty, the body " 'catches' and 'comprehends' movement."[33]

Noddings' work on care manifests the notion of reversibility in terms of empathy.[34] She describes the one caring as not penetrating the other but receiving the other. Engrossment requires a receptivity that allows the caregiver to see and feel with the other. This ability is always partial and fleeting. The reality of corporeal existence is that one can never inhabit another's body and therefore can never claim the other's experience. Yet through the flesh a tacit knowledge can be shared. There is an "inkling" or "shimmering" of understanding of the other which is not fully owned. In the working notes found at the end of *The Visible and the Invisible,* there is a tantalizing indication that had he not met an untimely death, Merleau-Ponty might have worked further on this issue. He uses the term "telepathy" to describe the visible recognition of meaning in the comportment of another's body: "to feel one's body is also to feel its aspect for the other."[35] Such understanding is at the heart of embodied or somatic empathy: care.

As mentioned earlier, I am treading on difficult ground because I am attempting to articulate what is not commonly put into words. The meaning found in embodied experience is not easily transposed onto explicit forms of communication such as language. A neat correspondence of understanding to sign is not present, because the experience of the flesh is radiated over time in the formation of complex interrelated and shifting meanings, in this case, as part of a continuum of care. In *The First Relationship: Mother and Infant,* Daniel Stern describes how infants have a "looming" response or reflexive aversion to the encroachment of the area near their face.[36] Nevertheless, parents typically violate this space by zooming in to kiss and touch the infant. Stern suggests that such behavior prepares the infant for later social and affiliative behavior and is a necessary part of normal development. Personal space is invested with a great deal of social meaning and varies across cultures. Infants develop a bodily understanding of proximity over time, primarily during a prelinguistic stage. The infant and caregiver express no explicit communication about body distance, yet knowledge is exchanged.[37] This bears a resemblance to what Abram refers to as the body's silent conversation with itself.[38] Beyond, and independent of, our verbal consciousness, our bodies carry on a dialogue with the world around us.

Michael Polanyi contends that there is so much that we cannot tell that, "the transmission of knowledge from one generation to the other must be predominately tacit."[39] In describing the phenomenal structure of tacit knowing, Polanyi refers to attending from a proximal term, or object, to a distal term. We invest meaning in the distal term through bodily "subception" or the tacit acquisition of knowledge through transposing bodily experiences into perception.[40] In the caring touch of my hands washing Rosemary's hair, the bodily perception or subception of the proximal experience is transposed into tacit knowledge of care. I don't announce to Rosemary that I am washing her hair with great care because I love her and hope that she will learn what it is to care for someone, nor do I routinely even think this to myself. Rosemary would not describe the experience of hair-washing in anything but the proximal terms—getting her hair wet and having shampoo lathered in it. Yet something more than the given task passes between us.[41]

While someone can care for another from afar, from the standpoint of embodied care, there is no substitute for what is communicated when bodies are close and interacting with one another. Polanyi further clarifies the notion of tacit knowledge by asserting that understanding comes about through active participation or "indwelling."[42] Through indwelling, proximal terms are integrated and interiorized. Care, empathy, and compassion can be described at length but there remains an element of understanding that is only available through direct embodied experience. Rita Manning claims that praxis is an essential part of care ethics: "We cannot develop and sustain the ability to care unless we do some active caring."[43] The relational aspect of care requires some degree of physical presence and involvement that has not always permeated the role of the father in the family. A long-standing argument on behalf of international exchange programs is that the direct formation of relationships will lead to better understanding between peoples. Personal connection provides a better basis for care, although it is not an absolute necessity. It is one thing to extrapolate personal experiences of hunger, loss, and desperation to try to understand the plight of the homeless, and it is quite another to draw upon the actual interaction of shaking the hand of a homeless person, and forming a relationship with someone whose name, face, and circumstances you can recall.

Applying Polanyi's work, Douglas Adams and Phil Mullins argue that when it comes to moral judgment, explicit reasons cannot shape discernment alone.[44] Reasons only become compelling when they are indwelled. They view Polanyi's work as concretizing and personalizing systemic issues of ethical inquiry. This "situatedness" resonates with the work done by care ethicists such as Noddings, who defines a caring act as "to act with special regard for the particular person in a concrete situation."[45] Care is not an explicit knowledge but implicit, tacit body knowledge grounded and practiced in lived interpersonal experiences.

Returning to the moral revolution of the involved father, the impact of the caring interactions extends to both parties. Each is affected and changed. To care for a child's body, not just occasionally but in an ongoing relationship, maps experiences and knowledge that are not easily compartmentalized onto the caregiver's body and mind. The body stands as a unified nexus of experience. Over twenty years ago Nancy Chodorow claimed that dual parenting would have a profound impact on gender relations.[46] I am advocating an extension of that idea in arguing that the quality of embodied interaction can have profound moral implications. In many ways I am putting a particular spin on the historical slogan of the feminist movement that the personal is political when I contend that a deep-rooted experience of caregiving instantiated in the body greatly affects how people address such social issues as war, social welfare programs, world hunger, homelessness, etc. By naming and thematizing these care experiences, philosophy can make a profound contribution to this moral revolution.

EMBODIED IMAGINATION

Given that care is experienced at the level of the flesh through implicit means, what transforms this experience into a moral orientation that can be applied to domains outside of direct experience? This is a significant question that can't be fully treated here, but one response is to regard moral imagination as the linkage between patterns formed through experience and a disposition that can extend to new situations. The role of imagination in ethical consideration has been largely ignored in the rationalist tradition of moral philosophy, but as notions of rationality are challenged so too are the dynamics of creativity, imagination, and emotion.[47] Rita Manning views care ethics as actualized through the imagination: "An ethic of care is not an appeal to abstract principles but to the use of our moral imaginations, where our attention to the particulars of a situation is infused by our involved concern about the other(s)."[48]

One explanation of the linkage between the self and the other is the ability of fleshed bodies to create equivalent structures of meaning in one region and transfer them to another region.[49] A handshake is structured by a particular set of behaviors, yet it invokes a set of meanings far beyond the act. If we did not have this capacity for moral imagination, an ethics based on care would have little to support it. Without an imaginative capacity, one could only care for that which was directly experienced. Even the application of rule-based or consequence-based morality requires imagination.

In order to extend care into new particularities or new situations, a translation needs to take place. These translations do not map a one-to-one correspondence. I do not contend, for example, that my care in washing Rosemary's hair will directly translate into her caring for the environment or for a puppy. However, one experience as part of a pattern of experiences that creates a continuum of care (or what Catherine Keller refers to as an empathetic continuum[50]) makes domain transformation possible. The experiences of care build upon one another and become part of the familiar. Care can become a habit and a resource to draw upon. However, the imaginative possibilities of care are not entirely unlimited. Our experience and our body's potential bind them. The moral imagination draws from its wealth of tacit body knowledge to make its imaginative leap or extension to caring about the non-experienced or indirectly experienced. In Merleau-Ponty's words, the imaginary "finds in the body analogues of itself that incarnate it."[51]

Mark Johnson's work on moral imagination provides a useful insight into the integration of the body and moral understanding. Johnson cites empirical evidence that indicates, "the embodiment of human meaning and understanding manifests itself over and over, in ways intimately connected to forms of imaginative structuring of experience."[52] Human imagination needs a basis for organizing meaning, and it finds a starting place and structure in the body. The perceptual interactions, spatiality, and motility of our bodies within our specific environments provide that structure through "image schemas." Johnson posits metaphors as the principal cognitive method for extending embodied structures to abstract concepts. Through metaphor our imaginations are capable of transcending domains in the application of meaning. Linguistic metaphors provide a clue to the deeper metaphoric structures of the imagination.

Johnson describes moral development as rooted in the emergence of prototypes within human experience.[53] These prototypes become linked to key moral concepts such as justice and fairness, and develop from experience to concept. Johnson's notion of prototype can be applied to care. Children have direct experiences of care prior to developing the concept of care itself. One cannot teach children an abstract definition of care, because there is too much tacit knowledge tied up with this moral prototype. Johnson also notes that these prototypes are not static: "A central part of our moral development will be the imaginative use of particular prototypes in constructing our lives. Each prototype has a definite structure, yet that structure must undergo gradual imaginative transformation as new situations arise. It thus has a dynamic character, which is what makes possible our moral development and growth."[54] The human capacity for moral imagination allows for the extension and expansion of ethical prototypes. This imagination is not just a product of the intellect but is rooted in the body. While Johnson's prototypes and metaphors emerge out of the body's relation to the world, the imagination he speaks of is still rooted in the mind disconnected from the body. Merleau-Ponty writes of a more intertwined imagination—a bond between the flesh and the idea.[55] In this tradition Abram refers to bodily transcendence: "a capacity of the physiological body itself—its powers of responding to other bodies, of touching, hearing, and seeing things, resonating with things. Perception is the ongoing transcendence, the ecstatic nature of the body."[56] We cannot disassociate the creative capacity of the mind from the body's ability to radiate beyond itself.

Rosemary has professed her feelings for a classmate named Andrew ("I love him more than the whole wide world"). One of the qualities that recur in her description of Andrew is that he is very gentle. I am not privy to the dynamics which have shaped Rosemary's feelings, but it does not seem too far-fetched to suppose that she might be working through a "prototype" of care developed though physical and verbal interactions with her parents, teachers, and classmates. Rosemary's body knows what it is to be gentle and she apparently values it. Her prototype will continue to evolve through her experiences with Andrew and many others.

While this discussion of the working of the moral/corporeal imagination was far too brief to capture the depth of research on this subject, it serves the purpose of closing the phenomenological loop. The flesh is the paradoxical locus of both human individuation and continuity. Corporeal existence comes with specific time and space dimensions that do not allow the sharing of identical experiences; it is impossible to have "perfect" empathy for another's situation. However, corporeal existence provides the basis for intersubjective continuity through the flesh of the world. Bodies have definite limitations and potentialities that are shared by members of the species; however, the complex workings of the embodied imagination enable perceptual extensions of the flesh. Tacit and explicit knowledge can be transformed such that real insight, drawn from the body, exists, allowing people to care for one another.

Finally, a brief note on care and agency. Because of the previous neglect of care ethics in the literature it has been necessary to spend the majority of this article arguing for the body's primary role in caring. However, I don't wish to negate human agency. As Sarah Hoagland observes, "Caring is a choice we make."[57] While the human body may be predisposed to care, we must make a decision to care for someone. Many of these care decisions are easier than others but we always have a choice. More than ever, it is now possible for men to broaden socially accepted boundaries of fatherhood to include direct care as a conscious choice.

POSTSCRIPT

While I have attempted to demonstrate how Merleau-Ponty's phenomenology of the body provides a valuable insight to the importance of a care-moral orientation to the understanding of fatherhood, my non-academic side wishes to express that it simply feels right. There is much work that remains to be done on developing the contours of care, and perhaps a diversity of approaches is inevitable and desirable. Nevertheless, I cannot help but write that there is something fundamentally correct about embodied care. The process, methodology, and empirical studies concerning care may have flaws and lacunae, but the basic notion resonates through my body and my experience. We must take care of each other and we must *show* our children how to care for one another. This is not to indicate that we can ignore power dynamics, political realities, or social constructs, but care is a moral imperative of great consequence and should be attended to. It is a powerful thought that with every caring touch I can enable the possibility for the replication of care.

> Rosemary is still at an age when hugs, kisses and "I love you's" flow freely and spontaneously. Sometimes we ask her, "Will you remember how much we love you when you grow older?" and she replies, "Oh Mom and Dad, I will always love you." Her explicit memory of our cuddling conversations will surely fade. There will be many ups and downs in our relationship. Yet perhaps somewhere deep within her body there will remain an implicit knowledge of what it is to care for another that will be expressed to a friend, lover, stranger, or herself.

NOTES

I would like to thank all those who provided helpful insights into various formulations of this article, including David Abram, Margaret Bayless, Will Cowling, Pam Dane, Stephanie Hamington, Anne McGrail, Greg Johnson, Mark Johnson, Terrance MacMullan, and Nancy Tuana.

1. Virginia Held, "The Obligations of Mothers and Fathers," in *Mothering: Essays in Feminist Theory,* ed. Joyce Trebilcot (Torwa, N.J.: Rowman and Allanheld, 1983), 7.

2. The moral revolution I refer to here is different from and yet has some common characteristics with the moral revolution that Sarah Hoagland addresses in *Lesbian Ethics: Toward New Value* (Palo Alto: Institute of Lesbian Studies, 1988), 1. Hoagland is specifically addressing the lesbian community on how to promote connection, "individual integrity and agency within community" (285). I gesture toward a new fatherhood emerging from social changes, which calls on men to be more involved in directly caring for their children. In both cases, care is valorized despite its history of marginalization.

3. Obviously, this is a sweeping charge that does not do justice to the diversity of men's experience. I am primarily addressing the moral behaviors of twentieth-century U.S. White males, but there is a wide variation of experience even within that category. I am being intentionally provocative to bring attention to an overlooked aspect of gender.

4. Gloria Steinem, "Supremacy Crimes," *Ms.* 9, no. 5 (1999): 45.

5. U.S. Department of Justice, Bureau of Justice Statistics, "Criminal Offenders Statistics," 29 November 2000, http://www.ojp.usdoj.gov/bjs/crimoff.htm#inmates (19 January 2001).

6. While perhaps a bit sensationalistic, a thorough review of the damaging social behavior of men can be found in June Stephenson, *Men Are Not Cost-Effective* (San Francisco: HarperPerennial, 1991).

7. Steinem, "Supremacy Crimes," 46.

8. For example, Annette Baier makes the connection between Hume and modern care ethics in "Hume, the Women's Moral Theorist?" in *Women and Moral Theory,* ed. Eva Feder Kittay and Diana T. Meyers (New York: Rowman & Littlefield, 1987), 37–55.

9. Other foundational works on care ethics include Nel Noddings, *Caring: A Feminine Approach to Ethics and Moral Education* (Berkeley: University of California Press, 1984), and Sara Ruddick, *Maternal Thinking: Toward a Politics of Peace* (Boston: Beacon Press, 1989). The differences among each of these approaches to care ethics will not be addressed in this brief paper.

10. According to Gilligan, "The title of my book was deliberate; it reads, 'in a different voice,' not 'in a *woman's* voice.' In my introduction, I explain that this voice is identified not by gender but by theme" (Gilligan, "Reply to Critics," *Signs: Journal of Women in Culture and Society* 11 [1986]: 325).

11. Carol Gilligan, *In a Different Voice: Psychological Theory and Women's Development* (Cambridge, Mass.: Harvard University Press, 1982), 62–63.

12. In her later work, Gilligan begins to theorize that justice requires relationality as well. She employs the metaphor of the double fugue to describe the intertwining of justice and care in the music of ethical thinking (Carol Gilligan, Annie Rogers, and Lyn Mikel Brown, "Epilogue: Soundings into Development," in *Making Connections: The Relational Worlds of Adolescent Girls at Emma Willard School,* ed. Carol Gilligan, Nona Lyons, and Trudy Hanmer [Cambridge, Mass.: Harvard University Press, 1990], 320–328).

13. For a comprehensive account of the value of context in care ethics see Seyla Benhabib, "The Generalized and the Concrete Other: The Kohlberg-Gilligan Controversy and Moral Theory," in *Women and Moral Theory,* ed. Eva Feder Kittay and Diana T. Meyers (New York: Rowman & Littlefield, 1987): 154–177.

14. In this essay, I focus on the relationships between human beings, but care can be extended to interspecies relationships as well. See for example *Beyond Animal Rights: A Feminist Caring Ethic for the Treatment of Animals,* ed. Joseph Donovan and Carol Adams (New York: Continuum, 1996).

15. One of the criticisms of care ethics is that it privileges dyadic relations and in particular the mother-child relationship. See Joan Tronto, "Women and Caring: What Can Feminists Learn about Morality from Caring?" in *Gender/Body/Knowledge: Feminist Reconstructions of Being and Knowing,* ed. Alison Jaggar and Susan Bordo (New Brunswick, N.J.: Rutgers University Press, 1989), 180–181.

16. This is a conscious attempt to speak from my own experience. The effort is not intended to reify heterosexual parental relations as superior care relations nor is it intended to ignore the abuse that has marked the history of father-daughter relations. See Sarah Hoagland, "Some Thoughts about 'Caring,' " in *Feminist Ethics,* ed. Claudia Card (Lawrence: University Press of Kansas, 1991), 252.

17. Drew Leder, *The Absent Body* (Chicago: University of Chicago Press, 1990), 14.

18. Ibid., 39.

19. Often, because I am kneeling and reaching over the side of the tub, I notice

lower back pain. Leder describes the reorientation of the body in the face of the sensory intensification of pain (ibid., 70–73). My body, which was invisible to my perception, suddenly becomes visible. However, there are different experiences of pain. In this case, I notice the pain much later than I would have had I not been so outwardly attentive to my task and my daughter.

20. Noddings, *Caring,* 17.

21. Maurice Merleau-Ponty, *Phenomenology of Perception,* trans. Colin Smith (London: Routledge, 1989), 13.

22. Ibid., 92.

23. Psychological research has steadfastly reinforced the significance of the quality of the father-child relationship in the development of the child. In a review of recent research, Michael Lamb concludes: "characteristics of individual fathers— such as their masculinity, intellect, and even their warmth—are much less important, formatively speaking, than are the characteristics of the relationships they have established with their children. . . . the amount of time fathers and children spend with each other is less important than what they do with that time" (Lamb, "Paternal Influences on Child Development," in *Changing Fatherhood: An Interdisciplinary Perspective,* ed. Mirjam C. P. van Dongen, Gerard A. B. Frinking, and Menno J. G. Jacobs [Amsterdam: Thesis Publishers, 1995], 153).

24. Annette Baier, "The Need for More Than Justice," *Canadian Journal of Philosophy* 13 (1983): 52.

25. In positing the primacy of the flesh, it can be claimed that Merleau-Ponty is describing the fundamental project of philosophy as ontological: an embodied search for being-in-the-world.

26. Maurice Merleau-Ponty, *The Visible and the Invisible,* ed. Claude Lefort, trans. Alphonso Lingis (Evanston, Ill.: Northwestern University Press, 1968), 147.

27. Ibid.

28. Ibid., 144.

29. Maurice Merleau-Ponty, *The Prose of the World,* ed. Claude Lefort, trans. John O'Neill (Evanston, Ill.: Northwestern University Press, 1973), 138.

30. David Abram, *The Spell of the Sensuous: Perception and Language in a More-Than-Human World* (New York: Vintage Books, 1996), ix.

31. Ross D. Parke, *Fathers* (Cambridge, Mass.: Harvard University Press, 1981), 10–11.

32. Merleau-Ponty, *The Visible and the Invisible,* 145.

33. Merleau-Ponty, *Phenomenology of Perception,* 142.

34. Noddings, *Caring,* 30–31.

35. Merleau-Ponty, *The Visible and the Invisible,* 245.

36. Daniel Stern. *The First Relationship: Mother and Infant* (Cambridge, Mass.: Harvard University Press, 1977), 21.

37. In the context of a discussion of care, tacit knowledge is considered positive and functional, but Iris Young points out that "self conscious racism, sexism, homophobia, ageism, and ableism are fueled by unconscious meanings and reactions" that take place at the level of the body (Young, *Justice and the Politics of Difference* [Princeton, N.J.: Princeton University Press, 1990], 133).

38. Abram, *Spell of the Sensuous,* 52–53.

39. Michael Polanyi, *The Tacit Dimension* (New York: Doubleday, 1967), 61.

40. Ibid., 7 and 14.

41. There is a great deal of empirical evidence that indicates that the communication of empathy (real or perceived) is non-verbal. See, for example, Arnold P. Goldstein and Gerald Y. Michaels, *Empathy: Development, Training and Consequences* (Hillsdale, N.J.: Lawrence Erlbaum Associates, 1985), 139.

42. Polanyi, *Tacit Dimension*, 17.

43. Rita Manning, *Speaking from the Heart: A Feminist Perspective on Ethics* (Lanham, Md.: Rowan and Littlefield, 1992), 69.

44. Douglas Adams and Phil Mullins, "Conscience, Tacit Knowledge, and the Art of Judgment: Implications of Polanyi's Thought for Moral Reflection," *Soundings: An Interdisciplinary Journal* 66, no. 1 (1983): 43.

45. Noddings, *Caring*, 24.

46. Nancy Chodorow, *The Reproduction of Mothering: Psychoanalysis and the Sociology of Gender* (Berkeley: University of California Press, 1978), 215.

47. See, for example, the discussion of imagination in Virginia Held, *Feminist Morality: Transforming Culture, Society and Politics* (Chicago: University of Chicago Press, 1993), 92–95.

48. Manning, *Speaking from the Heart*, 89.

49. Merleau-Ponty, *Phenomenology of Perception*, 111.

50. Catherine Keller, *From a Broken Web* (Boston: Beacon Press, 1986), 149.

51. Merleau-Ponty, *The Visible and the Invisible*, 77.

52. Mark Johnson, *The Body in the Mind: The Bodily Basis of Meaning, Imagination, and Reason* (Chicago: University of Chicago Press, 1987), xiv.

53. Mark Johnson, *Moral Imagination: Implications of Cognitive Science for Ethics* (Chicago: University of Chicago Press, 1993), 190.

54. Ibid., 192.

55. Merleau-Ponty, *The Visible and the Invisible*, 149.

56. David Abram, "Merleau-Ponty and the Voice of the Earth," *Environmental Ethics* 10, no. 2 (1988): 103.

57. Hoagland, *Lesbian Ethics*, 283.

POSTSCRIPT

The Phenomenological Challenge—The One and the Many

MAURICE HAMINGTON AND WILLIAM COWLING

To be powerful is to be unproblematic. The rich have little complaint about the economic system. Military powers have few concerns about world arms sales. Incumbent politicians have little motivation to alter campaign systems. In the same manner, the hegemony and normative function of the White, able-bodied male in Western civilization has rendered such bodies unproblematic to the point of invisibility. Whether the venue is popular culture or philosophy, the opportunities for serious reflection on the significance of the male body are few. Male bodies move through our society with much less concern about personal violence, limited opportunities for advancement, or confrontation than do women's bodies. Even our language assumes the normativity of male embodiment. As the original *Star Trek* preamble proclaimed, it is man who boldly ventures forth into uncharted territory. Despite numerous inroads on traditional constructions, the general condition remains: men and their bodies just are, while women and their bodies are wholly other. The very subject of male embodiment is easily dismissed as inconsequential. Why should we problematize the body made in the image and likeness of God?

The articles in *Revealing Male Bodies* challenge the cultural invisibility of male embodiment and point to the significance of multifaceted corporeal experience while simultaneously highlighting the philosophical tension of considering the one and the many. Although this volume is tied together by the common thread of considering men and the experience of their bodies, the articles reveal that commonality to be precarious. For example, the articles in the first section of this anthology address an important aspect of the myth of male power: the phallus. Men share a biological identification with the phallus through the penis, and yet that sharing is definitely bounded. Susan Bordo points out that size does matter, at least on a psychological level, which leads to significant biological, if not functional, differences in male identification with the myth of the phallus. Richard Schmitt addresses racial differences and exploitation in pursuit of the phallus. John Zuern claims that identification with the phallus is a privileged position. In each case, the universal claim to phallocentric advantage is problematized. Male connections with the phallus are not denied, but neither are they homogenized. Here we confront the challenge of the existential phenomenological approach taken in *Revealing Male Bodies:* balancing the one and the many. The challenge is to validate individual experience without universalizing that experience. Although the potential pitfall is a kind of philosophy by anecdote, the tradition has for too long favored the abstract and avoided grounding philosophical ideas in experiential phenomena.

The challenge of the one and the many characterizes the two directions that the editors believe that the discussion of male embodiment can go from here. *Revealing Male Bodies* was always intended as a conversation starter rather than a definitive work. One direction for the conversation is to expand the sites of analysis. Given the limitations of a single volume, only a few of the socially inscribed male typologies have been explored. For example, the anthology includes several articles about male sports bodies but other traditionally male-identified manifestations such as military bodies, corporate executive bodies, priest bodies, or cowboy bodies would be fruitful alternative sites of investigation. While three of the articles dealt with race, their contribution was from the African American experience, which is only one of a number of diverse voices that could be added to this conversation. Truly honoring diversity in the experience of male embodiment would take volumes, but they need to be written. Given the aforementioned challenge of the one and the many, the implication of broad phenomenological accounts of male experience is not entirely clear. Perhaps that lack of clarity stems from conventional ways of thinking that favor abstract, universalized approaches to messy contextual entanglements (and that have not coincidentally avoided the significance of the male body). As one reads Paul McIlvenny on Al Davison's life and work, or Don Ihde's account of his connection to his son, or Björn Krondorfer's emotive reaction to confessional writing, the value appears certain, at least at a visceral level. The genre of writing found in *Revealing Male Bodies* not only provides explicit opportunities for provocative analysis but also offers implicit opportunities for connection and understanding to the largely hidden inner world of male experience. Greater understanding can only happen if more men are willing to recount their corporeal experiences.

The second avenue of potential further discussion is this very unfamiliar process of describing and analyzing embodied experience. What do we do with a man's experience of his body in women's clothes, his disabled body reflected in his art, or his body's impact on his religious writing? In many ways, this kind of reflection defies many of our traditional categories, and therefore its function is not clearly understood. Furthermore, the mode of this writing is not defined. The articles in *Revealing Male Bodies* are characterized by a number of approaches. Is it important to break down actions into comportment, motility, and spatiality in order to understand the body's essence? How and when do we account for social inscription in a phenomenological inquiry? Can a viable social political philosophy be based on very personal corporeal accounts? When we identified the importance of extending the sites of analysis, we hinted that there may be a moral dimension to such an extension because of the possibility of connection and understanding, but what of the moral dimension to the process itself? Phenomenology calls for a suspension of judgment to allow for the existential to be articulated. There may be serious ethical questions in such a process. For example, none of the papers in *Revealing Male Bodies* deals with domestic violence or child abuse, which, unfortunately, are also associated with male embodiment. Would such an account call for a different kind of reading? Because this lens of analysis is relatively new, the questions outnumber the answers. The authors in this volume have provided a glimpse of some possibilities, but much more remains to be done in developing the phenomenological method and corporeal understanding.

Whatever direction the conversation takes, the existence and actions of men's bodies should no longer be passively assumed in the creation of knowledge, in the creation of morality, or in the creation of society. The world opens up to us through our bodies, and the way those bodies are marked by race, gender, sexuality, or ability impacts the world we perceive and the world we create. We hope you will see this anthology as the beginning of a long and provocative conversation.

FURTHER READING

Abram, David. *The Spell of the Sensuous.* New York: Vintage Books, 1996.

Armstrong, David. *The Political Anatomy of the Body: Medical Knowledge in Britain in the Twentieth Century.* Cambridge: Cambridge University Press, 1983.

Austin, John. "The Ourang-Outang in Domestication: Naked Male Bodies." *Antithesis* 5, no. 1/2 (1992): 52–73.

Barral, Mary Rose. *Merleau-Ponty: The Role of the Body-Subject in Interpersonal Relations.* Pittsburgh: Duquesne University Press, 1965.

Berger, Marice, Brian Wallis, and Simon Watson, eds. *Constructing Masculinity.* New York: Routledge, 1995.

Bernal, Mary Rose. *Merleau-Ponty: The Role of the Body-Subject in Interpersonal Relations.* Pittsburgh: Duquesne University Press, 1965.

Bersani, Leo. *The Freudian Body: Psychoanalysis and Art.* New York: Columbia University Press, 1986.

Bigwood, Carol. "Renaturalizing the Body (with the Help of Merleau-Ponty)." *Hypatia* 6, no. 3 (1991): 54–73.

Bingham, Dennis. "Warren Beatty and the Elusive Male Body in Hollywood Cinema." *Michigan Quarterly Review* 33, no. 1 (1994): 149–168.

Boone, Joseph A., and Michael Cadden, eds. *Engendering Men: The Question of Male Feminist Criticism.* New York: Routledge, 1990.

Bordo, Susan. "The Body and Reproduction of Femininity: A Feminist Appropriation of Foucault." In *Gender/Body/Knowledge: Feminist Reconstructions of Being and Knowing,* edited by Alison M. Jaggar and Susan R. Bordo, 121–137. New Brunswick, N.J.: Rutgers University Press, 1989.

———. "Feminism, Postmodernism, and Gender Skepticism." In *Feminism/Postmodernism,* edited by Linda J. Nicholson, 143–158. New York: Routledge, 1990.

———. *The Male Body: A New Look at Men in Public and Private.* New York: Farrar, Straus, and Giroux, 1999.

———. "Reading the Slender Body." In *Body/Politics: Women and the Discourses of Science,* edited by Mary Jacobus, Evelyn Fox Keller, and Sally Shuttleworth, 117–141. New York: Routledge, 1989.

————. *Unbearable Weight: Feminism, Western Culture, and the Body.* Berkeley: University of California Press, 1993.

Bottomley, Frank. *Attitudes to the Body in Western Christendom.* London: Lepus Books, 1979.

Bourke, Joanna. *Dismembering the Male: Men's Bodies, Britain and the Great War.* Chicago: University of Chicago Press, 1996.

Braidotti, Rosi. *Nomadic Subjects: Embodiment and Sexual Difference in Contemporary Feminist Theory.* New York: Columbia University Press, 1994.

————. "Organs without Bodies." *differences* 1, no. 1 (1989): 147–161.

Brenton, Myron. "New Ways to Manliness." In *The American Male.* New York: Coward, McCann and Geoghegan, 1966.

Broch-Due, Vigdis, Ingrid Rudie, and Tony Bleie, eds. *Carved Flesh/Cast Selves: Gendered Symbols and Social Practices.* Providence, R.I.: Berg, 1993.

Brod, Harry. "Pornography and the Alienation of Male Sexuality." *Social Theory and Practice* 14, no. 3 (1988): 265–277.

————, ed. *The Making of Masculinities: The New Men's Studies.* New York: Allen and Unwin, 1987.

Brod, Harry, and Michael Kaufman, eds. *Theorizing Masculinities.* Thousand Oaks, Calif.: Sage Publications, 1994.

Butler, Judith. *Bodies That Matter: On the Discursive Limits of "Sex."* New York: Routledge, 1993.

Caddick, Alison. "Feminism and the Body." *Arena* 74 (1986): 60–88.

Campbell, Andrew. "The Male Body and Contemporary Art." *Michigan Quarterly Review* 33, no. 1 (1994): 89–101.

Chapman, Laura, and Elizabeth Langland, eds. *Out of Bounds: Male Writers and Gender(ed) Criticism.* Amherst: University of Massachusetts Press, 1990.

Clatterbaugh, Kenneth. *Contemporary Perspectives on Masculinity: Men, Women, and Politics in Modern Society.* Boulder, Colo.: Westview Press, 1990.

Cleaver, Eldrige. "The Allegory of the Black Eunuchs." In *Soul on Ice.* New York: Dell, 1968.

Cornwall, Andrea, and Nancy Lindisfarne, eds. *Dislocating Masculinity: Comparative Ethnographies.* New York: Routledge, 1994.

Cussins, Adrian. "Content, Embodiment, and Objectivity: The Theory of Cognitive Trails." *Mind* 101, no. 404 (1992): 651–666.

Deenen, A. A. "Intimacy and Sexuality in Gay Male Couples." *Archives of Sexual Behavior* 67, no. 7 (1994): 166–178.

D'Emilio, John, and Estelle B. Freedman. *Intimate Matters: A History of Sexuality in America.* New York: Perennial Library, 1988.

————. "The Stuff of History: First Person Accounts of Gay Male Lives." *Journal of the History of Sexuality* 3, no. 2 (1992): 314–339.

Deming, Will. "Mark, Matthew: A First Century Discussion of Male Sexuality." *New Testament Studies* 36, no. 1 (1989): 130–145.

Ekins, Richard. "On Male Femaling: Some Reflections between Sex, Sexuality, and Gender." *Sociological Review* 41, no. 1 (1993): 1–22.

Epstein, Julia, and Kristina Straub. *Body Guards: The Cultural Politics of Gender Ambiguity.* New York: Routledge, 1991.

Export, Valie. "The Real and Its Double: The Body." *Discourse* 11, no. 1 (1988–89): 3–27.

Feldenkrais, M. *Body and Mature Behavior: A Study of Anxiety, Sex, Gravitation, and Learning.* New York: International Universities Press, 1973.

Ferguson, Kath. *The Man in Question: Visions of Subjectivity in Feminist Theory.* Berkeley: University of California Press, 1993.

Fielding, Helen. "Depth of Embodiment: Spatial and Temporal Bodies in Foucault and Merleau-Ponty." *Philosophy Today* 43 (Spring 1999): 73–91.

Fisher, Seymour, and Sidney E. Cleveland. *Body Image and Personality.* New York: Dover, 1968.

Fitting, Peter. "Cyberspace/Cyberbodies/Cyberpunk: Cultures of Technological Embodiment." *Utopian Studies* 8, no. 1 (1997): 163–181.

Flannigan Saint-Aubin, Arthur. " 'Black Gay Male' Discourse: Reading Race and Sexuality between the Lines." *Journal of the History of Sexuality* 3, no. 3 (1993): 292–308.

Fleckenstein, Kristie S. "Writing Bodies: Somatic Mind in Composition Studies." *College English* 61 (January 1999): 57–71.

Foot, John. "Sexual Politics in Wilhelmine Germany: The Male Gender Crisis, Moral Purity, Homophobia." *Journal of the History of Sexuality* 2, no. 3 (1992): 388–407.

Foucault, Michel. *The Care of the Self.* Translated by R. Hurley. Harmondsworth: Penguin, 1986.

———. *Discipline and Punish: The Birth of the Prison.* Translated by A. Sheridan. London: Tavistock, 1977.

———. *The History of Sexuality: An Introduction.* Vol. 1. Translated by R. Hurley. London: Allen Lane, 1979.

———. *Politics, Philosophy, Culture: Interviews and Other Writings 1977–1984.* Edited by Lawrence D. Kritzman. London: Routledge, 1988.

———. "The Subject and Power." In *Michel Foucault: Beyond Structuralism and Hermeneutics,* edited by H. Dreyfus and P. Rabinow, 212–236. Chicago: University of Chicago Press, 1982.

———. *The Use of Pleasure.* Vol. 2 of *The History of Sexuality.* Translated by R. Hurley. Harmondsworth: Penguin, 1985.

Gallop, Jane. *Thinking through the Body.* New York: Columbia University Press, 1988.

Gatens, Moira. "Towards a Feminist Philosophy of the Body." In *(En)Gendering Knowledge: Feminists in Academe,* edited by Joan Hartman and Ellen Messer-Davidow, 59–70. Knoxville: University of Tennessee Press, 1991.

Gilbert, Noel. "A Man's World: A Response to *Fire in the Belly* and *The Con-*

struction of Homosexuality in E. M. Forster's Novels." Style 26, no. 2 (1992): 58–73.

Gilbert, Reid. "The Male Dancer: Bodies, Spectacle, Sexualities." *TDR* 40, no. 4 (1996): 170–183.

Goldenberg, Naomi. *Returning Words to Flesh: Feminism, Psychoanalysis and the Resurrection of the Body.* Boston: Beacon Press, 1990.

Goldstein, Laurence, ed. *The Male Body: Features, Destinies, Exposures.* Ann Arbor: University of Michigan Press, 1994.

Gross, Elizabeth. "Philosophy, Subjectivity and the Body." In *Feminist Challenges: Social and Political Theory,* edited by Carole Pateman and Elizabeth Gross, 125–144. Sydney: Allen and Unwin, 1986.

Grosz, Elizabeth. *Volatile Bodies: Toward a Corporeal Feminism.* Bloomington: Indiana University Press, 1994.

Hall, Kira, and Mary Bucholtz, eds. *Gender Articulated: Language and Socially Constructed Self.* New York: Routledge, 1995.

Harper, Phillip Brian. *Are We Not Men? Masculine Anxiety and the Problem of African-American Identity.* New York: Oxford University Press, 1996.

Hekman, Susan. "The Embodiment of the Subject: Feminism and the Communitarian Critique of Liberalism." *The Journal of Politics* 54, no. 4 (1994): 1098–1123.

Hoberman, John. "The Sportive-Dynamic Body as a Symbol of Productivity." In *Heterotopia: Postmodern Utopia and the Body Politic,* edited by Tobin Siebers, 199–228. Ann Arbor: University of Michigan Press, 1994.

Jaggar, Alison M., and Susan R. Bordo, eds. *Gender/Body/Knowledge: Feminist Reconstructions of Being and Knowing.* New Brunswick, N.J.: Rutgers University Press, 1989.

Johnson, Mark. *The Body in the Mind: The Bodily Basis of Meaning, Imagination, and Reason.* Chicago: University of Chicago Press, 1987.

Kibbey, Ann, Kayann Short, and Abouali Farmanfarmaian, eds. *Sexual Artifice: Persons, Images, Politics.* New York: New York University Press, 1994.

Klein, Edward, and Don Erickson, eds. *About Men: Reflections on the Male Experience.* New York: Poseidon Press, 1987.

Krondorfer, Björn, ed. *Men's Bodies, Men's God's: Male Identities in a (Post-) Christian Culture.* New York: New York University Press, 1996.

Lacan, Jacques. *Écrits: A Selection.* Translated by Alan Sheridan. New York: W. W. Norton and Company, 1977.

Lakoff, George, and Mark Johnson. *Philosophy in the Flesh: The Embodied Mind and Its Challenge to Western Thought.* New York: Basic Books, 1999.

Leder, Drew. *The Absent Body.* Chicago: University of Chicago Press, 1990.

Lehman, Peter. *Running Scared: Masculinity and the Representation of the Male Body.* Philadelphia: Temple University Press, 1992.

Lewis, Alfred Allan. *The Male: His Body, His Sex.* Garden City, N.Y.: Anchor Press, 1978.

Lindegard, Bengt, ed. *Body-Build, Body-Function, and Personality: Medical An-*

thropological Investigations on 320 Swedish 20-Year-Old Healthy Army Men. Lund: C. W. K. Gleerup, 1956.

Lingis, Alphonso. *Foreign Bodies.* New York: Routledge, 1994.

Long, Lisa. "The Corporeity of Heaven: Rehabilitating the Civil War Body in 'The Gates Ajar.'" *American Literature* 69, no. 4 (1997): 781–794.

Lopate, Phillip. "Renewing Sodom and Gomorrah." In *Men Confront Pornography,* edited by Michael Kimmel, 25–33. New York: Meridian, 1990.

Mangan, J. A. "Blond, Strong and Pure: Proto-Fascism, Male Bodies and Political Tradition." *International Journal of the History of Sport* 16, no. 2 (1999): 107–122.

Marianne, Lyra-Wex. *Let's Take Back Our Space: Female and Male Body Language as a Result of Patriarchal Structures.* Translated by Johanna Albert. West Berlin: Frauenliteraturverlag Hermine Fees, 1979.

McDonald, Scott. "Confessions of a Feminist Porn Watcher." In *Men Confront Pornography,* edited by Michael S. Kimmel, 157–188. New York: Meridian, 1990.

Merleau-Ponty, Maurice. *Phenomenology of Perception.* Translated by Colin Smith. London: Routledge and Kegan Paul, 1962.

———. *The Primacy of Perception, and Other Essays.* Edited by James M. Edie. Evanston, Ill.: Northwestern University Press, 1964.

———. *Sense and Non-Sense.* Translated by Hubert Dreyfus and Patricia Allen Dreyfus. Evanston, Ill.: Northwestern University Press, 1964.

———. *Signs.* Translated by Richard C. McCleary. Evanston, Ill.: Northwestern University Press, 1964.

———. *The Visible and the Invisible.* Edited by Claude Lefort. Translated by Alphonso Lingis. Evanston: Northwestern University Press, 1968.

Meyers, Gerald E. "Self and Body Image." In *Phenomenology in America: Studies in the Philosophy of Experience,* edited by James M. Edie. Chicago: Quandrangle Books, 1967.

Morgan, Jennifer L. "Some Could Suckle over Their Shoulder: Male Travelers, Female Bodies, and the Gendering of Racial Ideology, 1500–1770." *The William and Mary Quarterly* 54, no. 1 (1997): 167–183.

Morgan, Thais E. "Male Lesbian Bodies: The Construction of Alternative Masculinities in Courbet, Baudelaire, and Swinburne." *Genders* 15 (1992): 37–49.

Nye, Robert. "Honor, Impotence, and Male Sexuality in 19th Century French Medicine." *French Historical Studies* 16, no. 1 (1989): 48–64.

O'Neill, John. *The Communicative Body: Studies in Communicative Philosophy, Politics, and Sociology.* Evanston, Ill.: Northwestern University Press, 1989.

Oosterhuis, Harry. "The Aesthetics of the Male Body." *Journal of Homosexuality* 22, no. 1/2 (1991): 85–98.

Pronger, Brian. *The Arena of Masculinity: Sports, Homosexuality, and the Meaning of Sex.* New York: St. Martin's Press, 1990.

Rabkin, Eric. "The Male Body in Science Fiction." *Michigan Quarterly Review* 33, no. 1 (1994): 44–56.

Ramazanoglu, Caroline. "What Can You Do with a Man? Feminism and the Critical Appraisal of Masculinity." *Women's Studies International Forum* 15, no. 3 (1992): 339–358.

Ramsay, Burt. *The Male Dancer: Bodies, Spectacle, Sexualities.* New York: Routledge, 1995.

Scher, Lawrence R. *Parts of an Andrology: On Representations of Men's Bodies.* Stanford, Calif.: Stanford University Press, 1997.

Schrag, Calvin. "Hermeneutical Self-Implicature." In *Communicative Praxis and the Space of Subjectivity,* 244–267. Bloomington: Indiana University Press, 1986.

Segal, Lynne. *Slow Motion: Changing Masculinities, Changing Men.* New York: Routledge, 1990.

Seidler, Victor, ed. *Achilles Heel Reader: Men, Sexual Politics, and Socialism.* New York: Routledge, 1991.

———. *Rediscovering Masculinity: Reason, Language, and Sexuality.* New York: Routledge, 1989.

Sethurman, R. "Writing Women's Body: Male Fantasy, Desire and Sexuality." *Literature, Interpretation, Theory* 4, no. 2 (1993): 101–127.

Sewell, Brad. "If I Was You Instead of Me." In *The Male Body: Features Destinies, Exposures,* edited by Laurence Goldstein, 106–118. Ann Arbor: University of Michigan Press, 1994.

Sheets-Johnstone, Maxine. *Giving the Body Its Due.* New York: State University of New York Press, 1992.

Shelly, William. "Cognitive Beliefs about Male Sexuality." *Journal of Rational-Emotive and Cognitive Behaviorism* 8, no. 4 (1990): 249–271.

Shildrick, Margrit. *Leaky Bodies and Boundaries: Feminism, Postmodernism and (Bio)Ethics.* London and New York: Routledge, 1997.

Skinner, Marilyn. "Ego Mulier: The Construction of Male Sexuality in Culture. *Helios* 20, no. 1 (1993): 107–133.

Staples, Robert. *Black Masculinity: The Black Male's Role in American Society.* San Francisco: Black Scholar Press, 1982.

Theweleit, Klaus. *Male Fantasies.* Translated by Stephan Conway in collaboration with Erica Carter and Chris Turner. Minneapolis: University of Minnesota Press, 1987.

Thomas, Calvin. *Male Matters: Masculinity, Anxiety, and the Male Body on the Line.* Urbana: University of Illinois Press, 1996.

Waldby, Cathy. *Aids and the Body Politic: Biomedicine and Sexual Difference.* New York: Routledge, 1996.

Weiss, Gail. *Body Images: Embodiment as Intercorporeality.* New York: Routledge, 1999.

Weiss, Gail, and Honi Fern Haber, eds. *Perspectives on Embodiment: The Intersections of Nature and Culture.* New York: Routledge, 1999.

Winkler, Mary G., and Letha B. Cole, eds. *The Good Body: Asceticism in Contemporary Culture.* New Haven: Yale University Press, 1994.

Yardley, Lucy. "Embodiment and Experience: The Existential Ground of Culture and Experience." *British Journal of Psychology* 88, no. 4 (1997): 709–731.

Young, Iris Marion. *Throwing Like A Girl and Other Essays in Feminist Philosophy and Social Theory.* Bloomington: Indiana University Press, 1990.

Ziarek, Ewa Plonowska. "Toward a Radical Female Imaginary: Temporality and Embodiment in Irigaray's Ethics." *Diacritics: A Review of Contemporary Criticism* 28, no. 1 (1998): 60–87.

CONTRIBUTORS

SUSAN BORDO is Professor of English and Women's Studies and holds the Otis A. Singletary Chair in the Humanities at the University of Kentucky. She is the author of many well-known and widely cited books and articles, including the best-selling *Unbearable Weight: Feminism, Western Culture, and the Body,* the first book to draw attention to the profound role of cultural images in the spread of eating problems across race and class. *Unbearable Weight* was a New York Times Notable Book of 1993 and was nominated for a Pulitzer Prize. Columnist Katha Pollitt named it one of the five best books in women's studies of 1993. Bordo's latest book, *The Male Body: A New Look at Men in Public and in Private,* was published in June 1999 to critical acclaim.

WILLIAM COWLING is a doctoral student in philosophy at the University of Oregon. He is the author (with Nancy Tuana) of "The Presence and Absence of the Feminine in Plato's Philosophy" in *Feminist Interpretations of Plato.* Cowling's research interests include the role of embodied narratives in science practice and the manner in which narrative structures frame the content, context, and status of scientific theories.

TERRY GOLDIE teaches English at York University and has taught in Germany, India, and Australia. He is the author of *Fear and Temptation: The Image of the Indigene in Canadian, Australian and New Zealand Literatures* and *Pink Snow: Gay Studies Approaches to Canadian Fiction,* and co-editor with Daniel David Moses of *An Anthology of Canadian Native Writing in English.* This article is part of a work in progress tentatively titled *Terrying: A Theoretical Sexual Autobiography.*

MAURICE HAMINGTON received a Ph.D. in religion and ethics and a Graduate Certificate in the Study of Men and Women in Society from the University of Southern California, and a Ph.D. in philosophy at the University of

Oregon. He served as a Research Scholar in the Study of Women at the University of California, Los Angeles, and was the founding Director of the Women's Studies Program at Mount St. Mary's College in Los Angeles. He is the author of *Hail Mary? The Struggle for Ultimate Womanhood in Catholicism.* He currently teaches at Lane Community College in Eugene, Oregon.

DON IHDE is Distinguished Professor of Philosophy at the State University of New York at Stony Brook. He is the author of twelve books including the recent *Expanding Hermeneutics: Visualism in Science; Postphenomenology; Technology and the Lifeworld;* and *Instrumental Realism.* He has been interested in the role of the body in scientific knowledge and in relation to technologies of virtual reality. Although philosophy of technoscience has been at the center of his interests in recent years, in the essay here he focuses upon a more autobiographical perspective related to growing up male.

GREG JOHNSON is Assistant Professor of Philosophy at Pacific Lutheran University. His areas of specialty are contemporary Continental philosophy, with special interest in hermeneutics, phenomenology, and critical theory. He also teaches political philosophy, philosophy of religion, and feminist theory.

BJÖRN KRONDORFER is Associate Professor of Religious Studies at St. Mary's College of Maryland. His field of expertise is religion and culture, with an emphasis on gender studies, cultural studies, and Holocaust studies. He is the author of *Remembrance and Reconciliation: Encounters Between Young Jews and Germans,* and editor of *Men's Bodies, Men's Gods: Male Identities in a (Post-) Christian Culture* and *Body and Bible: Interpreting and Experiencing Biblical Narratives.* He has edited, with an afterword, Edward Gasfriend's *My Father's Testament: Memoirs of a Jewish Teenager, 1938–1945.* He is the appointed American Academy of Religion (AAR) series editor of the Cultural Criticism Series of Oxford University Press. He also serves on the editorial board of *Living Text: The Journal of Contemporary Midrash,* and was co-chair for the Men's Studies in Religion Group of the AAR. He enjoys parenting his daughters Tabitha and Zadekia.

ALPHONSO LINGIS is Professor of Philosophy at Pennsylvania State University. His publications include *Excesses: Eros and Culture; Libido: The French Existential Theories; Phenomenological Explanations; Deathbound Subjectivity; The Community of Those Who Have Nothing in Common; Abuses; Foreign Bodies; Sensation: Intelligibility in Sensibility; The Imperative;* and *Dangerous Emotions.*

TERRANCE MACMULLAN is a doctoral student in philosophy at the University of Oregon, where he has worked as a Graduate Teaching Fellow for the

Departments of Religious Studies, Philosophy, and the Humanities. He is currently completing his dissertation, which develops a pragmatist critique of Whiteness in the United States. His other areas of interest include social and political philosophy, the history of nineteenth- and twentieth-century American and Continental philosophy, philosophy of religion, and feminist theory.

PATRICK MCGANN received his Ph.D. in literacy, language, and rhetoric from the University of Illinois at Chicago. He currently teaches introductory and advanced writing courses at George Washington University, and has published in *Radical Teacher* and *Composition Studies*. His recent research focuses on explaining how a profeminist men's studies might serve the field of composition.

PAUL MCILVENNY is Associate Professor in the Department of Languages and Intercultural Studies at the University of Aalborg, Denmark. He has published articles on signed talk and Deaf culture, popular public discourse at Speakers' Corner, stand-up comedy performance, homovestism in the new digital media, heteronormativity in intercultural encounters, and gender, community, and embodiment in graphical virtual worlds. He is currently editing a volume entitled *Talking Gender & Sexuality*.

JIM PERKINSON is a long-time resident of inner-city Detroit, currently teaching courses on world religions, African diaspora philosophy, colonialism and racism, death and dying, and social ethics at a number of area colleges (Marygrove College, University of Detroit, Central Michigan University satellites in the metro area, and Ecumenical Theological Seminary). His Ph.D. is in theology, working out a White theological response to Black theology, and much of his scholarly interest and writing has been on the conflation of religious and racial categories in modernity. In addition to more than a decade of work as an urban activist and his academic career, he is a performance poet.

STEVEN P. SCHACHT is Assistant Professor of Sociology at Plattsburgh State University of New York. His primary areas of research and teaching interest are race, class, gender, and sexuality. He is currently writing a book with Doris Ewing entitled *A Feminist Phallacy: The Failure to Include Men* and editing an anthology with Jill Bystydzienski entitled *Forging Radical Alliances across Difference: Coalition Politics for the New Millennium*.

RICHARD SCHMITT was born a Jew in Germany and arrived in the United States after World War II, scarred by racial persecution. Over the years, while writing about phenomenology and existentialism, about Marxism and feminist theory, he has worked against racism. Above all he has tried to do what Whites must do first of all—learn to understand the realities of racial oppression, its history, and the history and condition of those who suffer under it. "Large Propagators" is one in a series of essays exploring racism. Richard Schmitt teaches philosophy at Brown University.

NANCY TUANA was Professor of Philosophy at the University of Oregon during the period this anthology was being created. She is now the Director of the Rock Ethics Institute and Professor of Philosophy at Pennsylvania State University. She works in the areas of philosophy of science, epistemology, ethics, and feminist science studies. She has published *The Less Noble Sex: Scientific, Religious, and Philosophical Conceptions of Woman's Nature* and *Woman and the History of Philosophy,* and is currently at work on *Philosophy of Science Studies.* She has edited six anthologies including *Feminism and Science, Engendering Rationalities,* and *Feminist Interpretations of Plato.* She is currently co-editor of *Hypatia: A Journal of Feminist Philosophy* and series editor of the Penn State Press series *Re-Reading the Canon.*

CRAIG WILKINS, a registered architect, is presently a doctoral candidate at the University of Minnesota, where he teaches courses in architecture and cultural studies. He is a 1998–99 University of Minnesota Thomas Shevlin Fellow, a 1998–2000 U.S. Department of Housing and Urban Development Fellow, and a former Research Fellow at the University of Minnesota College of Architecture and Landscape Architecture's Design Center for American Urban Landscape, where he worked with neighborhood groups in the area of community design. He received his masters degree at the Columbia University Graduate School of Architecture, Planning and Preservation and his undergraduate degree from the University of Detroit School of Architecture.

JOHN ZUERN is Assistant Professor of Computer-Mediated Communication and Literary Studies in the Department of English, University of Hawai'i at Mānoa. He has published in *Dada/Surrealism, Literary and Linguistic Computing,* and *Computers and Composition.*

INDEX

Abram, David, 276, 277–278, 281, 284n30
"Absent referent," 95, 96
Adams, Carol, 87, 90, 91, 95, 96,
   98nn13,23,30, 99n38
Adams, Douglas, 278
AIDS-related community groups, 157
Allen, Tim, on penis size, 20
Ally McBeal, 22
Althusser, Charles, 68
Althusser, Louis, 57, 64–67, 74, 76, 78n36;
   on castration, 67–70; in French Commu-
   nist Party, 71–72; interpellation model of,
   127; on mastery of one's own body, 70,
   79n50
Althusser, Louis (uncle), 68, 69
Althusser, Lucienne, 68, 69, 70
*Am I a Murderer? Testament of a Jewish Ghetto
   Policeman* (Perechodnik), 14, 248–250,
   258, 259, 266nn8–10, 267n29
Andersson, Malte, 31
Animal biofantasies, 31, 36n2
Anzieu, Didier, 113
Arena Homme Plus, 103
At Play in the Fields of the Lord, 28
Augustine, 248, 251, 253, 254, 255, 256,
   257, 260, 262, 263, 264–265, 266nn4–7

Bacon, John, 44–45, 53n24
Baldwin, James, 39, 52n5
Banneker, Benjamin, 209
Barbie, 29
Bataille, Georges, 146, 154n1
Baudrillard, Jean, 140–141, 143
Being and Having (Marcel), 239
Being and Nothingness (Sartre), 239
Bell Curve, The (Hernstein and Murray), 180

Berenger, Tom, 28
Bersani, Leo, 143
Birth of the Clinic, The (Foucault), 238
Black male identity and space: and the African American male, 199–200, 217n9; and
   the African American woman, 199, 214–
   217nn5–7; Black male space begins, 206–
   208, 223n44; black masculinity and spatial
   force, 202–203, 219n21; Blacks as property, Whites as subjects, 201–202; and fear
   of Black male space, 203–205, 219–
   221nn26–27; and fossilized Black male
   space, 204, 213, 221n32; and fraternity of
   the fourth circle, 211, 212–214; and locations of experience, 198, 214n1; and
   Locke's concept of space, 200–202, 205,
   206, 207, 210, 213, 217–218nn11–12; and
   Million Man March on the Mall, 198, 203,
   204, 205, 206, 209, 210, 211, 212, 213;
   and shared safe space, 210, 212; and
   spaces of power, 198–200; and suture,
   208, 224n47; and the White female in
   American culture, 199, 214nn3–4; and
   the White male in American life, 199;
   White male space ends, 205–206
Black men: and historical castration practice
   with slaves, 48; and "Long Dong Silver,"
   25–26; as overendowed Black beasts, 24,
   36n1; penis equated with, 25; and propaganda about Black rapists, 47–48; and
   White male fear of black body, 181; versus
   Whites with civilized penises, 40
Black Power movement, 185
Blackness, 288; Black and White embodiment and, 183–187; Black and White male
   embodiment and, 187–190; and the Black

penis, 188, 189; "Black places" and "White places" defined by, 181; and Black stereotypic figures of speech through history, 177; Black urban male forms of embodiment and, 174–175; and Great Chain of Being, 177; monitoring and somatotyping of, 182–183; and Rodney-King-meets-LAPD, 178–179, 180–183; and the space of race, 179–183; White historical practices of control of, 180; and White male fear of the Black male body, 181; versus Whiteness, 175–179. *See also* White male body
Blum, Deborah, 28, 32
Bly, Robert, 206, 222*n*41
Bobbitt, John, 23
Bodies That Matter (Butler), 126, 133, 136, 145*n*5
Borch-Jacobsen, Mikkel, 8, 16*n*18
Bordo, Susan, x, xi*n*2, 2, 9–10, 16*n*20, 287; on male sports bodies, 231, 235, 240, 241, 244, 246*nn*1,12; on masculine norms and food, 86, 98*n*8; on racism and domination of women, 19–37
Born on the Fourth of July, 103
Brooks, Garth, 159
Brown, D. E., 29, 30
Brown, H. Rap, 200
Brown, Helen Gurley, 28
Buber, Martin, 239
Butler, Judith, 2, 11; on drag, 126–127, 128–129, 130, 134, 135, 136, 138, 143, 145*n*10; on future of the phallus, 72, 74, 75, 77*n*22, 79*n*55; on masculine norms and food, 90, 93, 96; overcoming gender binarism, 242; performative theory of, 100–101, 102, 120*nn*5–6

Candib, Lucy, 50, 54*n*40
Caring embodiment and moral revolution: and bidirectional experience of caring, 275–279; and care ethics and embodied care, 15, 271–273, 283*nn*12–13; of caring males, 270–271, 282*nn*2–3; and communication of empathy, 277, 278, 284*n*41; and embodied imagination, 279–281; and empathetic continuum, 280, 285*n*50; and experiencing care, 273–275; and exteroception, 274, 283*n*18; impact of on the caring father, 275–279; and power of mutuality and care, 271; and quality of father-child relationships, 275, 284*n*23; redefin-

ing the traditional family through, 269–270
Certeau, Michel de, 207
Channing, Carol, 130
Chippendales, 28
Chodorow, Nancy, 279
Chronic illnesses and masculine norms of food, 83–99
Clift, Montgomery, 137
Clinton, Bill, 24
Clinton, George, 206
Cocteau, Jean, 147
Confessional writing: and male embodiment, 14–15, 247–268, 288; male preference of, 247–248, 267–268*nn*1–2
Confessions (Augustine), 14, 248, 251, 252, 253, 263, 265, 266*nn*4–5,17, 267*n*18
Connell, Robert, 113
Corvalaan, Jamie, 23
Cosmopolitan, 28
Cowling, William, 287–289
Critical theory and liberatory theories, 8

Daishonin, Nichiren, 111–112, 115
Darwin, Charles, 35; on sexual selection and penile display, 27, 28
Davis, Bette, 242
Davis, Lennard, 100, 111, 120*n*3
Davis, Michael, 181–182
Davison, Al, 11, 100, 104, 105, 106–107, 110, 111–115, 118–119, 288
Davison, Frank, 105
Davison, Nellie, 105
Dean, James, 137
Deleuze, Gilles, 134, 135, 140, 145*n*19
Denny, Reginald, 178, 179
Derrida, Jacques, 143
Descartes, René, 200
Details, 136
Diamond, Jared, 32, 35
"Dicking around," 9, 63
Dinnerstein, Dorothy, 106, 123*n*36
Disability, 8, 11
Disabled male body: in ableist culture, 104; characterization and identification of, 105–110, 123*n*35; as culturally abnormal or grotesque, 103, 121*n*18; disability and masculinity, 102–103; and "disabled" label, 117; as failure of masculinity, 116; function and appearance of, 111–115; *imago* of, 113; and men's autobiography and disability, 103–105; and mirror symbolism, 111–113; and performative theory,

100–101, 117, 119, 120*nn*5–6; sexuality/
asexuality of, 115–116; and social model
of disability, 104–105, 122*nn*25–26; and
superhero comics, 110, 123*n*43, 124*n*45;
visual and tactile qualities of, 111–115
Discipline and Punish: The Birth of the Prison
(Foucault), 4, 239
Douglass, Frederick, 48
Drag queen: availability and accessibility of,
131; and the Body as Organ, 135; and
"body femaling," 125; and body within,
137; as the Body without Organs (BwO),
134, 135, 140; context and performativity
of, 130, 145*n*11; at the court, 157–158;
distinction between transsexual and, 127;
as "draggle-tail queen," 125, 127; and
"dressers," 159; and "erotic femaling,"
125, 133; and female impersonators, 156,
168*n*1; and fetishism, 133–134; and gay
drag kings, 159–160; and gay men, 128,
135–136; in hyper-gendered settings, 156,
168*n*3; and lesbian drag kings and queens,
160; and "livedness," 128; makeover process of, 162–164; and makeup, 131–133;
male body re-placed by, 129; male femaling and male feminism and, 125–145;
and masculine embodiment of the feminine, 166–168; and mind/body dichotomy, 139–140; mirrors and, 127–128; as
phallic woman, 133, 143; and the phallus,
136, 165, 166; photographs and, 127–128;
possibility of woman and, 142, 143; on
queer axis, 140; and realness/readability,
133; tipping of, 159, 169*n*11; transgenderist, 128; and transubstantiation, 127;
Turnabout, 161–166, 169*n*15; world of,
11, 12
Du Bois, W. E. B., 13, 38, 52, 52*n*1, 191; on
black double consciousness, 183–184; on
racism, 38, 48
Dumm, Thomas, 181, 182
Dworkin, Andrea, 143

Eco, Umberto, 110, 124*n*45
Écrits: A Selection (Lacan), 7, 16*nn*13–14
Ekins, Richard, 125–126, 133, 144*n*2
Esquire, 23
Ethical significance of male embodiment, 13

Fanon, Frantz, 25, 191, 212; on Black men
in relation to White man, 204, 221*n*34; on
White preoccupation with Black genitals,
39, 52*n*6, 53*n*8

Fathers (Parke), 276
Featherstone, Mike, 105
Female impersonators and drag queens, 156,
168*n*1
Femininity: and food practices in United
States, 86; male performance of, 12; mas-
culine embodiment of, 166–168
Feminism: liberatory theories of, 8–9; mis-
conceptions and myths about, 3, 15*n*2;
and Populist campaign against Black and
White women, 47
Feminist Accused of Sexual Harassment (Gallop),
141
Fiddes, Nick, 91, 98*nn*24,29
Findlay, Heather, 25
First Relationship, The: Mother and Infant
(Stern), 277
Fitzgerald, F. Scott, 20
Food: chronic illnesses and, 90–96; in diabetes and meanings of manhood, 91–94,
96–97; and feminine food practices in
United States, 86; and grilling, 89; and
male body as meat, 90–91; and male-
identified foods, 87–88; material-semiotic
theory of, 84–85, 98*n*3; and power and
appeal of steak, 88–90, 98*n*24; and Real
Man Food Groups, 87; and sexual content
of "meat" and "fruit," 87–88
Football: and male bodies, 90–91; and manly
appetites, 10–11, 86–87
Foucault, Michel, 12; on biopolitical techniques of a society, 4, 16*n*5; and black
male space, 210, 224*n*55, 224–225*n*57;
and bodily inscription, 2; on care of self, 5,
16*n*8; "cultural body" of, 231, 246*n*5; feminist perspectives on, 5, 16*n*10; genealogical method of, 4–5, 16*nn*6–7; and male
sports bodies, 238–239; on panopticism,
4, 15–16*n*4; theory and method overview,
3–5; on truth through confession, 264,
268*n*37; and White male body, 177, 182
4 Non Blondes, 161
Fox, Frank, 249
Frankenstein (Shelley), 107, 108
Frankfurt School, 5
Franz, Dennis, 32
Freud, Sigmund, 61; on distinction between
penis and phallus, 7; and feminist theory
on vaginal orgasm, 30; on penis envy/pe-
nisneid, 8, 16*nn*15,21; on phallic mother,
59, 77*n*12; on phallus and sexual identification, 57, 58

Friedman, Susan, 105
Frye, Northrop, 248
Full Monty, The, 28
Fuss, Diana, 142, 145*n*32
Future Lasts Forever, The (Althusser), 57, 67–68, 69, 70

Gable, Clark, 137
Gallop, Jane, 140–141, 142
Garber, Marjorie, 133, 145*n*15
Gay drag kings, 159–160
Gay drag queens and masculine embodiment of the feminine, 155–170
Gaze: female, 238–240; male, 236, 238–240
Gender Trouble: Feminism and the Subversion of Identity (Butler), 130, 145*n*13
Gentleman's Quarterly, 136
Geographical information systems (GIS) and White space, 182
GI Jane, 32
Gide, André, 128, 145*n*9
Gilligan, Carol, 271, 272
Gilman, Sander, 40, 53*n*10
Girls/women, and female perception of too-fat bodies, 19
Glamour, 26
Goldberg, David Theo, 209–210, 224*n*53
Goldie, Terry, 11, 125–145
Gould, Carol Grant, 25, 27, 28
Gould, James, 25, 27, 28
Green, Tim, 86, 89, 90–91
Grosz, Elizabeth, 2; on drag, 127, 132, 134, 135, 138, 139, 140, 141, 142, 145*nn*7,14,16; on future of the phallus, 56, 60, 61, 72, 76*n*4, 78*n*25
Guattari, Félix, 134, 135, 140, 145*n*19
Guevara, Che, 12, 153
Guillaumin, Colette, 57, 63, 73, 76*nn*6–9

Habermas, Jürgen, 5
Hall, Stuart, 185, 199
Hamington, Maurice, ix, 15, 269–286, 287–289
Haraway, Donna, 85, 98*nn*3,5,6, 242
Harper's, 48
Harris, Cheryl, 190, 200, 202, 217*n*10
Hatch, Orrin, 24–25
Haymes, Stephen, 181
Held, Virginia, 269, 282*n*1
Hernstein, Richard, 180
Hernton, Calvin, 39, 53*n*7
Hersey, George, 31
Hersey, John, 150, 154*n*4

Hevey, David, 111
Hill, Anita, 9, 24–26
History of Sexuality, The (Foucault), 5
Hoagland, Sarah, 281, 285*n*57
hooks, bell, 51, 94, 191, 198, 205, 210, 211, 214*n*1
Hume, David, 272, 283*n*8
Husserl, Edmund, 1, 6
Hustler, 20
Hyam, Ronald, 39, 53*n*7

I and Thou (Buber), 239
Ihde, Don, 13–14, 231–246, 288
In a Different Voice: Psychological Theory and Women's Development (Gilligan), 272, 283*n*9

Jack-E, 155
Jackson, David, 104
Jafa, Arthur, 209, 224*n*51
Jazz, 25
Jock, 20
Johnson, Greg, ix
Johnson, Jack, 25
Johnson, Mark, 280–281, 285*nn*52–54
Jordan, Michael, 180

Kaufman, Michael, 85, 94, 98*n*7
Keller, Catherine, 280
Ken (doll), anatomical accuracy of, 29
Kennady Smith, Eunice, 155–156
Kennady Smith, Shane, 155
Keuls, Eva, 24
Kierkegaard, Søren, 244
King, Martin Luther, Jr., 200
King, Rodney, 173, 178–179, 183, 192, 192*n*2, 200
Klein, Calvin, 28
Kochman, Thomas, 184–185, 194–195*nn*31–34
Kohlberg, Lawrence, 272
Koon, Stacey, 179
Koselleck, Reinhart, 61, 78
Krondorfer, Björn, 14–15, 269–285, 288

Lacan, Jacques, 35, 73, 74; on distinction between penis and phallus, 7; on human desire, 60, 77–78*nn*21–23; and male sports bodies, 238; on mirror image and child's perception thereof, 112–113; on phallic mother, 7, 8, 16*n*14; on phallus as privileged signifier, 57, 58–63, 76*n*10,

77nn11,18; theory and method overview, 3, 7–8

Laqueur, Thomas, 29, 34

Lawrence, Maggie, 102, 112, 115

Leder, Drew, 274, 283n17

Lee, Peter, 20

Lefebvre, Henri, 207–208, 209, 224n45

Legotien, Hélène, 67, 72

Lerner, Gerda, 51

Lesbian drag kings and queens, 160

Liberatory theories, 8–9

Life Its Ownself (Jenkins), 83, 89, 97n1

Lingis, Alphonso, 11–12, 146–154

Lion King, The, 129

Locke, John, 200–202, 205, 206, 207, 210, 213, 217n11, 218n12

Locklear, Heather, 158

MacKinnon, Catharine, 143

MacMullan, Terrance, 1–16

Madonna, 143

Mailer, Norman, 25

Male Body, The: A Physician's Guide to What Every Man Should Know about His Sexual Health (Morgentaler), 26, 27

Male confession: *Am I a Murderer? Testament of a Jewish Ghetto Policeman* (Perechodnik), 248–250, 251, 258, 259, 266nn8–10; by Augustine, 250, 260, 262, 263, 264–265; and choice and control, 254–258; collaboration, resistance, and gender in, 258–263; and confessional writing, 247–248; *Confessions* (Augustine), 14, 248, 251, 252, 253, 254, 263, 265, 266nn4–7,17, 267n18; by moral agent and gendered subject, 261–262; morality, relationships, and kinship in, 256–257; and nocturnal emissions, 254, 255; and "non-absence" of body, 252; power relations and, 263–265; reading body and gender in, 250–254; as safe expression, 252, 266n15; and sexuality, 256, 264–265; writing as resistance, 260, 267n31. *See also* Perechodnik, Aluśka; Perechodnik, Anka; Perechodnik, Calel

Male eating habits and moments of failure, 83–99

Male embodiment: as new area of study and directions, x, 288–289; themes and interconnections of, 9–15; theorists and methods on, 3–9

Male embodiment studies: in Continental European philosophy, 1–2; in feminist studies of embodiment, 2–3; and impact of social power on the body, 2; interdisciplinary discussion of, 1; phenomenological investigations of, 1–2; and role of feminist gaze, 3, 15n2

Male Femaling: A Grounded Approach to Cross-Dressing and Sex-Changing (Ekins), 125–126

Male identity and pride, 146

Male sports bodies: and alternatives to athletic performance, 236–237; and essentialism/non-essentialism debate, 242; and gazes, male and female, 236, 238–240; gender binaries and, 242–243; and growing up male, 232–237; height and athletic prowess of, 234–235; Mauss illusion and gender reciprocities and, 237–244; and the phallus, 240–242; and postmodern bodily awareness, 243–245; and privacy of the penis, 235–236; social size and body size in relation to, 235; and socially embedded masculine embodiment, 233

Male traits, 146

Maleness, described, 146

Manly appetite, and type II diabetes, 10–11, 83–99

Manning, Rita, 278, 279

Marcel, Gabriel, 239

Marx, Karl, 68

Marxism, 8

Masculine norms of food and health, 10–11, 83–99. *See also* Food

Masculinity, described, 146

Material-semiotics, 84–85, 98n3

Mauss illusion, 237, 244

McCarthy, Joseph, 5

McCarthy, Thomas, 5

McGann, Patrick, 10–11, 83–99

McIlvenny, Paul, 11, 100–124, 288

Meat on the Hoof (Shaw), 90

Meggyesy, Dave, 89

Men Can Stop Rape, 95, 96

Men's Health, 103

Merleau-Ponty, Maurice, ix, 1; and bodily experience, 232, 235, 236, 246n4; on embodiment, 271, 273, 274, 275–276, 277, 280, 281–282; on figure-background structure of perception, 274–275, 284n21; and the gaze, 239; and the "lived body," 231; on relationship of body to world, 6–7, 16nn11–12; and temporality, 57, 76n5; theory and method overview, 3, 6–7

Middleton, Peter, 110
Miles, Margaret, 252
Minotaur's Tale (Davison), 106, 120*n*11, 123*n*37
Monroe, Marilyn, 130, 137
Moore, Alan, 115
Moore, Demi, 32
Moore, Suzanne, 139
Morgentaler, Abraham, 26, 27
Morris, Jenny, 116
Movable Feast, A (Hemingway), 20
Mullins, Phil, 278
Murray, Charles, 180
Muschamp, Herbert, 204, 205, 207, 221*n*29
Muscles, cultural meanings of, 31, 36*n*3

National Geographic, 244
Neuman, Shirley, 104, 105–106, 122*n*23
Nietzsche, Friedrich, 4, 16*n*6, 244
Noddings, Nel, 271–272, 274, 277, 279

Order of Things, The (Foucault), 238–239
"Other," 101, 116, 158, 183, 187, 189, 287

Paglia, Camille, 143
Pain, denial of, 90–91, 94–95
Paris Is Burning, 126–127, 133
Parke, Ross D., 276
Patriarchy: and racism, 52; and same-sex marriages, 75
Penis: approximating function of phallus, 61, 78*n*28; distinction between phallus and, 7; proper length of, 26–27; and sense of virility, 148; sexual selection of, 27; size of, 287; and stereotyping the male experience, 13–14; tucking of, 162, 169*n*17; Western cultural ideal of phallus and, 9, 16*n*19; and White society's obsession with Black penises, 10
Penis envy/penisneid, 8, 16*nn*15,21
Penis size: adult male underestimation of, 20; cultural perspectives on matter of, 19–37; descriptions of, 21; historic valuing of, 22; inverse proportion of to intelligence, 24; and Ken (doll), 29; and locker room phobia, 23; men's versus women's interest in, 32; non-Western enhancement of, 23, 29, 30; and penile augmentation, 22–23; range of preferences in and responses to, 30; and "shower syndrome," 23; in want ad specs and stats, 21
People, 26

Perechodnik, Aluśka, 249, 256, 257, 261, 262
Perechodnik, Anka, 249, 256, 257, 258, 259
Perechodnik, Calel, 14, 248–250, 254–265, 266*nn*8–10
Perkinson, Jim, 12, 14, 173–197
Pertschuk, Michael, 35
Phallic economy, 7, 11
Phallic mother, 7, 8, 59, 77*n*12
Phallic woman, 133, 143
Phalloplasty, 9
Phallus: and Althusser's model of interpellation, 57, 64–67, 78*n*36; cultural perspectives on size of, 19–37; distinction between penis and, 7; and drag, 134, 136; female uses of, 242; first awareness of, 240–241; future of the, 55–80; Lacan on human desire and, 60, 77*nn*21,22, 78*n*23; Lacan's privileged signifier model of, 57, 58–63, 76–77*n*10, 77*n*18; and masculine hegemony of sports, 56; and meaningful male bodies, 62, 78*n*30; and myth of male power, 287, 288; as penis's symbolic double, 31, 36*n*4; in phallic economy, 7; privileged position of, 288; racial differences and exploitation in pursuit of, 288; stereotyping the male experience of, 13–14; temporality of, 56–57; as vestibular apparatus, 62–63; Western cultural ideal of penis and, 9, 16*n*19
Phenomenology of Perception (Merleau-Ponty), 6, 16*n*11, 61, 232
Pitt, Brad, 20, 137
Playgirl, 20, 21, 137
Polanyi, Michael, 278
Pollack, William, 33
Pompeii ruins, 22
Postcolonialism and liberatory theories, 8–9
Potency, 50
Pragmatism and liberatory theories, 8
Presley, Elvis, 180, 189
Priscilla, Queen of the Desert, 143
Prosser, Jay, 127, 128, 142, 144*n*4, 145*n*8
Psychology Today, 35
Public Enemy, 200

Quaglieri, Anthony, 35
Queer theory and liberatory theories, 8

Race, Culture, and the City: A Pedagogy for Black Urban Struggle (Haymes), 181
Race theory and liberatory theories, 9
Racism: aesthetic, 33; and castration practice

with slaves, 48; in Great Chain of Being, 177; and history of slavery in North America, 44–45, 53n23; impact of Civil War on, 45, 46; legislated racism, 45–46; and penises of Black men, 38–54; and Populist campaign against Black and White women, 47; and racialization of the Black male body, 177–178; toward Scotsmen, Jews, or Gypsies, 43; sexual racism, 50, 51–52; as sexual/carnal hatred, 38, 52n2; and White–Black sexual relations, 45; and White civilized penises, 40. *See also* Blackness; White male body

Rape, and women as "absent referents," 95, 96

Raymond, Janice, 126, 133, 144n3

Real Men Don't Eat Quiche (Feirstein), 87

Reems, Harry, 20, 21

Reynolds, Burt, 28

Rheinschild, Gary, 23

Roberts, Roxanne, 89

Rockafeller, Zenith, 155

Rose, Jacqueline, 66

Rosenstein, Melvyn, 22

Rowan, Keith, 89

Rushdie, Salman, 109

Sarria, José, 158

Sartre, Jean-Paul, 1, 239

Saussure, Ferdinand de, 59, 77n14

Savalas, Telly, 32

Schacht, Steven P., 12, 155–170

Schehr, Lawrence R., 71

Schmitt, Richard, 10, 288

Schwarzenegger, Arnold, 137

Second Skins: The Body Narratives of Transsexuality (Prosser), 127, 145n8

Segal, Lynne, 103

Sex/gender distinction, ix, x

Sexual racism: and patriarchy, 50; and White men's concept of own sexuality, 38

Sexual Selection: Mate Choice and Courtship in Nature (Gould and Gould), 28

Sexual selection and penile display, 27–28

Sexual Subversions: Three French Feminists (Grosz), 142

Sexual violence, 95–96

Shakespeare, Tom, 119

Shaw, Gary, 86, 88–89, 90

Showalter, Elaine, 139, 140, 141, 142, 145n27

Shue, Henry, 198–199, 200, 214n2

Silverman, Kaja, 66–67

Singer, Melanie, 179

Singin' in the Rain, 110

Slavery: and castration practice, 48; history of in North America, 44–45, 53n23; and White–Black sexual relations, 45. *See also* Racism

Slingblade, 22

Smilla's Sense of Snow, 242

Smith, Sidonie, 102–103, 109, 116–117, 121n15

Social policing of adolescent males, 14

Souls of Black Folk, The (Du Bois), 184

Space, Time and Perversion: Essays on the Politics of Bodies (Grosz), 134, 145n16

Spiral Cage, The (Davison), 100, 101–102, 115–116, 117, 118, 120nn8–11

Sports. *See* Male sports bodies

Stallone, Sylvester, 137

Stallybrass, Peter, 103, 121n16

Stanton, Donna, 34

Star Trek, 287

Steinem, Gloria, 270, 271

Stern, Daniel, 277

Stone, Sharon, 130

Streisand, Barbra, 130, 158

Stryker, Jeff, 20, 21

Sumida, Stephen, 74

Szapiro, Pawel, 259, 261

Taylor, Elizabeth, 158

Themes and interconnections of male embodiment studies, 9–15

Theorists and methods: Foucault, Michel, 3–5; Lacan, Jacques, 3, 7–8; liberatory theories, 8–9; Merleau-Ponty, Maurice, 3, 6–7. *See also specific theorists*

Thomas, Clarence, 9, 24–26

Thrasher, 56

Tiefer, Lenore, 26

To Wong Foo with Love, Julie Newmar, 129

Torso, 20

Transsexual Empire (Raymond), 126

Transsexuals: distinction between drag queen and, 127; mirrors and, 127–128; and transubstantiation, 127. *See also* Drag queen

Tuana, Nancy, ix–xi

Turnabout, 161–166, 169n15

Turner, Bryan, 105

Type II diabetes, 10–11, 83–97, 97–98n2

Unruliness, 97

Vested Interests: Cross-Dressing and Cultural Anxiety (Garber), 133, 145n15
Viagra, 137, 190
Village People, 159
Virility, 11–12; and courage, 149, 150; versus giving up, 150–151; physical radiance of, 148; and virile anger, 151
Visible and the Invisible, The (Merleau-Ponty), 275–276, 277
Vogue, 21
Volatile Bodies (Grosz), 127, 134, 145n7

Wallace, Michelle, 39, 52n4
Weber, Bruce, 28
Wells, Ida B., 48, 51
West, Mae, 130, 137, 142
White, Allon, 103, 121n16
White Book (Cocteau), 147
White male body: Black and White embodiment in formation and, 186–187; Black and White negotiations of embodiment and, 183–186; in "Black places" and "White places," 181; challenged by Black embodiment, 174–175; and ethics of White male embodiment, 190–192; and fear of the Black male body, 181; in Great Chain of Being, 177; *habitus* of, 173, 191, 192n3; monitoring and somatotyping of, 182–183; as possession, 175–176, 193n6;

and racialization of social space, 179–183; White and Black male embodiment and, 187–190; and White embodiment in public places, 185; and White male middle-class embodiment, 189; and White middle-class maleness as invisible norm, 174–175. *See also* Blackness; Racism
White society: obsession of with size of Black penises, 10; privileges of, 12–13
Wilkins, Craig, 13, 198–227
Williams, Damian, 178
Wilson, James Q., 182
Wittig, Monique, 135, 136
Wizard of Oz, The, 109
Women: and perception of too-fat bodies, 19; with physically fit bodies, 31–32; Populist campaign against, 47; racism and domination of, 38–54; unprotected Black women, 49
Wrangham, Richard, 33

Xena, and female phallic power, 242

Yentl the Yeshiva Boy (Singer), 244
Young, Iris, 2, 231, 232, 239, 246n2

Zen Buddhism, 111, 112, 115
Zilbergeld, Bernie, 50, 54nn41–42
Zola, Irving, 104
Zuern, John, 10, 288